Critical Ethics of Care in Social Work

C000077929

This book argues that the concept of care is a political and a moral concept. As such, it enables us to examine moral and political life through a radically different lens. The editors and contributors to the book argue that care has the potential to interrogate relationships of power and to be a tool for radical political analysis for an emerging critical social work that is concerned with human rights and social justice.

The book brings a critical ethics of care into the realm of theory and practice in social work. Informed by critical theory, feminism, intersectionality and post-colonialism, the book interrogates the concept of care in a wide range of social work settings. It examines care in the context of social neglect, interdisciplinary perspectives, the responsibilisation agenda in social work and the ongoing debate about care and justice. It situates care in the settings of mental health, homelessness, elder care, child protection, asylum seekers and humanitarian aid. It further demonstrates what can be learnt about care from the post-colonial margins, Aboriginal societies, LGBTI communities and disability politics. It demonstrates ways of transforming the politics and practices of care through the work of feminist mothers, caring practices by men, meditations on love, rethinking self-care, extending care to the natural environment and the principles informing cross-species care.

The book will be invaluable to social workers, human service practitioners and managers who are involved in the practice of delivering care, and it will assist them to challenge the punitive and hurtful strategies of neoliberal rationalisation. The critical theoretical focus of the book has significance beyond social work, including nursing, psychology, medicine, allied health and criminal justice.

Bob Pease is Honorary Professor in the School of Humanities and Social Science at Deakin University and Adjunct Professor in the Institute for the Study of Social Change at the University of Tasmania. He has published extensively on masculinity politics and critical social work practice, including four books as single author and 12 books as co-editor, as well as numerous book chapters and journal articles.

Anthea Vreugdenhil is Senior Lecturer in Social Work at the University of Tasmania and a Churchill Fellow. Her research program is broadly situated in the area of care, with a focus on aged care and the changing nature of care in social work and society. Anthea has a track record of high-impact publications, underpinned by a strong policy and practice focus.

Sonya Stanford is Head of Social Work at the University of Tasmania. Her research 'speaks back' to risk thinking and risk practices by critically examining how rationalities and practices of risk impact the wellbeing and outcomes of people who use and deliver welfare services. As a risk researcher, Sonya's research has focused on a wide range of risk dilemmas that arise in social and health care including in suicide risk assessments. Her co-edited book *Beyond the Risk Paradigm in Mental Health Policy and Practice* (with Sharland, Heller and Warner) was published by Palgrave in 2017.

Routledge Advances in Social Work

For a full list of titles in this series, please visit www.routledge.com/Routledge-Advances-in-Social-Work/book-series/RASW

Critical Ethics of Care in Social Work

Transforming the Politics and Practices of Caring

Edited by Bob Pease, Anthea Vreugdenhil and Sonya Stanford

Routledge
Taylor & Francis Group

LONDON AND NEW YORK

First published 2018 by Routledge

2 Park Square, Milton Park, Abingdon, Oxfordshire OX14 4RN
52 Vanderbilt Avenue, New York, NY 10017

Routledge is an imprint of the Taylor & Francis Group, an informa business

First issued in paperback 2018

British Library Cataloguing-in-Publication Data
A catalogue record for this book is available from the British Library

Library of Congress Cataloging-in-Publication Data
A catalog record for this book has been requested

ISBN: 978-1-138-22558-9 (hbk)
ISBN: 978-0-367-15216-1 (pbk)

Typeset in Times New Roman
by Apex CoVantage, LLC

Contents

Contributors

Donna Baines teaches anti-oppressive social work theory and practice at the University of Sydney where she holds a Chair in Social Work and Policy Studies. Professor Baines also specialises in labour studies and the highly gendered and increasingly racialised world of paid and unpaid care work. She has published recently in *Competition and Change, Journal of Industrial Relations* and *Critical Social Policy*. She is currently completing the third edition of her best-selling social work edited collection, *Doing Anti-oppressive Practice: Social Justice Social Work* (Fernwood, 2016).

Ann Joselynn Baltra-Ulloa is Lecturer in Social Work at the University of Tasmania. Jos has worked with migrants and people of refugee background in Australia for many years. Her research interests are in refugee re-settlement, decolonised social work practice, whiteness and critical race theory in social work. She utilises participatory research methodologies in all her research activities to not only learn and facilitate community development but to also evaluate social work practices. Funded by the Tasmanian Community Fund, she co-leads YoungMILE, a leadership development and mentorship program for emerging leaders within the refugee-arrived Tasmanian community. Her dream is to one day learn the language of her ancestors, the Mapuche people of South America.

Jennifer Boddy is Senior Lecturer in Social Work at Griffith University, Queensland, Australia, where she is program director for the Master of Social Work. Much of her scholarship is focused around community development, environmental social work and feminism. Jennifer is particularly interested in understanding and addressing the impacts of climate change on disadvantaged populations such as older people, women and those living in poverty. She has spoken at numerous national and international forums on the effects of climate change on marginalised people. She is currently reviewing social work education nationally for content on environmental social work practice, while also working on embedding environmental social work issues into core courses on the socio-political context of social work practice and social work theory.

Anne Coleman has 20 years of experience as a social worker which includes work with homeless people, policy development and research. Her work includes frontline positions in homelessness services; research into housing, homelessness and public space issues; development of the Queensland government's *Response to Homelessness*; and teaching social work students. Her primary research interests and expertise are in the areas of homelessness, housing and social inclusion/exclusion, and in qualitative research methods that add to our understanding of homelessness. Anne's research highlights the lived experience of people who are public space dwellers. Most recently, Anne was a Senior Lecturer in Social Work at the University of Tasmania. Anne is looking forward to spending more time on activism, staying connected to homeless people and writing more on homelessness.

Sarah Epstein lectures in social work at Deakin University. She has extensive work experience with victim/survivors of sexual assault and in providing group consultation and supervision to workers in the women's and youth sector. Sarah's doctorate examined feminist mothers' experiences of raising sons with a specific focus on the potential for feminist maternal practice to inform the repositioning of gendered subjectivities. Her ongoing research interests involve examining the intersection between feminism and masculinity and looking at ways to re-qualify and privilege the knowledge and experience women's maternal practice produces.

Heather Fraser is a social work academic who started her career three decades ago in shelters for women, young people and children fleeing from domestic violence and/or child abuse. In the mid-1990s, Heather started a PhD about the narratives of love and abuse told by women who had experienced some disruption to living with their birth families. Post-doctorally, the work extended to include interviews with 74 Canadian women and four group sessions with Canadian men in Winnipeg, who participated in the *Men, Romance and Love* groups. Feminist intersectional perspectives that include concerns about species are her theoretical orientations, and care work and emotional labour are related interests. She and Nik Taylor (Sociology) are the co-convenors of the *Animals in Society Working Group* at Flinders University.

Sue Green is a Kalari woman of the Wiradyuri nation, a mother and a grandmother. She holds a Bachelor of Social Work (Honours) and a PhD in Social Sciences. Her PhD was titled *The History of Aboriginal People in the Colony of NSW 1788–1856* and examined how welfare was used as a tool of colonisation. The thesis discussed how Aboriginal people became welfarised as a result of colonisation. Welfarisation is not just about dependency but also about the processes that are developed and the discourse around the processes and people. Sue is an Associate Professor of Social Work at the University of New South Wales and her focus is on Indigenous Social Work Education and Aboriginal Social Policy and Welfare and Aboriginal History. She has also recently been involved in research about carers and the provision of care.

Maria Harries worked in mental health and child and family welfare practice for many years prior to and also alongside her more recent lengthy career as a researcher and academic at the University of Western Australia and Curtin University. She has taught and consulted extensively on ethics in both governance and direct practice and has recently co-authored a book, *Ethics and Child Protection*.

Jenny Hay works as a lecturer in the social work program at the University of Tasmania. She has recently graduated with a PhD, and her thesis is titled *Shining a Light on Care in Direct Social Work Practice*. Prior to returning to study in 2010, she was employed as a social worker with the Department of Education, working with adolescents and young adults. Jenny has a keen interest in social work ethics, particularly ethics of care, and will continue to research, write and publish in this area.

Margaret E. Hughes is a grief and loss counsellor at the Royal Hobart Hospital. After graduating in 2001 from the University of Tasmania with a Bachelor of Social Work with first class honours, she commenced social work in a domestic violence crisis service as well as a community palliative care service. In 2009, while working in a private hospital as a social worker in an inpatient palliative care facility, she completed her doctorate titled *The Lived Experience of Compassionate Love at End-of-Life*. In 2016, Margaret finished working as a Lecturer in Social Work at the University of Tasmania. With a lifelong interest in LGBTIQ issues and domestic violence, she has published in the fields of death and dying, and maintains a devotion to matters of death.

Richard Hugman is Professor of Social Work at University of New South Wales, Australia. He has researched and written extensively about professional ethics, with a particular focus on social work. He served for many years on the ethics committee of the International Federation of Social Workers and from 2008–2014 was its chairperson. Richard also teaches, researches and practices in the field of international social work and social development. Since 2004 he has worked with UNICEF to support the development of social work in Vietnam. His most recent book is *Social Development in Social Work* (Routledge, 2016).

Martyn Jones is Associate Professor of Social Work at RMIT University, Melbourne, where he is co-leading a university-wide initiative to advance research, education and training, and partnerships in Social Support and Care. Prior to his appointment at RMIT 12 years ago, Martyn was director of the social work programs at Deakin University. Martyn has been involved in social work education for many years, both in England and Australia. With a professional background in social work, Martyn has maintained an interest in practice issues, including the impact of organisational and policy contexts, and the place and use of research. The second edition of his co-authored book *Social Work Research in Practice: Ethical and Political Contexts* was published by Sage in 2014.

Sharon Moore is Associate Professor of Social Work and Postgraduate Course Coordinator at the Australian College of Applied Psychology. She has worked in the related fields of social work and critical management education and has a background in comparative ageing and care research. She was involved in the establishing the Carers' Movement in Australia and internationally. Her doctoral research on *Women and Caring* (2000) reflects her continuing interest in intersectionality and a critical ethics of care, particularly from a gender perspective. She is also part of an international Critical Theory Research Network in Aged Care.

Christine Morley is Associate Professor of Social Work at the Queensland University of Technology, Australia. Formerly foundation Head of Social Work at the University of the Sunshine Coast, her intellectual passions include exploring the possibilities for critical social work and critical reflection to make a contribution to social work as an emancipatory project. Previously at Deakin University, Christine has published more than 40 papers in national and international refereed journals, conference proceedings and in edited books as an invited author. She is author of *Practising Critical Reflection to Develop Emancipatory Change* (Ashgate, 2014), and co-author (with Selma Macfarlane and Phillip Ablett) of *Engaging with Social Work: A Critical Introduction* (Cambridge, 2014).

Sharlene Nipperess is Lecturer in Social Work at RMIT University, Melbourne, Australia. Her research and teaching interests are diverse and include critical human rights-based practice, social work ethics, critical multicultural practice, and practice with refugees and asylum seekers and people experiencing mental distress. She is also interested in the relationship between sustainability and human rights and its place in the social work curriculum. Sharlene is President of the Australia and New Zealand Social Work and Welfare Education and Research (ANZSWWER) association and is a member of Social Work without Borders.

Bob Pease is Honorary Professor in the School of Humanities and Social Science at Deakin University and Adjunct Professor in the Institute for the Study of Social Change at the University of Tasmania. He has published extensively on masculinity politics and critical social work practice, including four books as single author and 12 books as co-editor, as well as numerous book chapters and journal articles. His most recent books are *Undoing Privilege: Unearned Advantage in a Divided World* (Zed 2010); *Men and Masculinities around the World: Transforming Men's Practices* (co-editor, Palgrave 2011); *Men, Masculinities and Methodologies* (co-editor, Palgrave 2013); *The Politics of Recognition and Social Justice: Transforming Subjectivities and New Forms of Resistance* (co-editor, Routledge 2014); *Doing Critical Social Work: Transformative Practices for Social Justice* (co-editor, Allen and Unwin 2016); and *Men, Masculinities and Disaster* (co-editor, Routledge, 2015).

Michele Raithby is Associate Professor in Social Work at Swansea University, Wales. Her first degree was in anthropology at University College London, and she qualified in social work in 1986 with practice interests in mental health, regulation and inspection of services, and working with older people. Her research interests include sexuality, gender identity and ageing in social care, and social work education.

Anne-Maree Sawyer has been a lecturer in sociology at La Trobe University in Melbourne since 2010. Prior to her teaching appointment, she was the research fellow on an Australian Research Council–funded project that explored the way in which 'risk management' policies and procedures have been taken up and translated into practice by community-based services in the state of Victoria. The project team conducted in-depth interviews with more than 150 stakeholders from disability, mental health and aged-care services. Before entering academia, Anne-Maree worked as a mental health social worker, first in an old-style psychiatric hospital and later in a psychiatric crisis team. Her interest in 'risk' grew out of her first-hand experiences of the tensions and challenges involved in managing risk alongside the provision of person-centred care.

Russell Shuttleworth, a medical anthropologist and social worker by training, is currently Senior Lecturer in Social Work at the School of Health and Social Development, Faculty of Health Sciences, Deakin University. He was a social worker and support worker for disabled people and older adults. His research expertise is in qualitative methods and critical-interpretive theoretical perspectives. He has conducted disability-related research on issues such as sexuality, gender, leadership and access to health care contexts for persons with speech impairment, as well as a process evaluation of several disability programs. He has also conducted research on both psychogeriatric and sexuality issues in aged care. He is currently conducting research on facilitated sex with people with disability in Victoria, and he is also part of an ARC Discovery Project researching the transition to adulthood for young people with impairments.

Sonya Stanford is Lecturer in Social Work at the University of Tasmania. While working in the fields of sexual assault, disability and ageing, Sonya developed a critical interest in how ideas about risk interface with social justice issues in the organisation and provision of welfare services. She examines how rationalities and practices of risk impact the wellbeing and outcomes of people who use and deliver welfare services. So far, Sonya has undertaken analysis of these research themes in direct social work practice, vulnerability policing, racialised supported income policies, and mental health. Her current research projects critically explore how trust issues impact risk dilemmas in suicide risk assessments, and risk and resilience approaches to bushfire disaster in peri-urban areas. Her co-edited book *Beyond the Risk Paradigm in Mental Health Policy and Practice* (with Sharland, Warner and Rovinelli-Heller) was published by Macmillan in 2017.

Nik Taylor is a sociologist who has been researching human-animal relations for over 15 years, after spending years running an animal shelter. Nik has published four books and over 40 journal articles and book chapters on the human-pet bond; treatment of animals and animal welfare; links between human aggression and animal cruelty including those between domestic violence, animal abuse and child abuse; slaughterhouses; meat-eating; and animal shelter work. She has written for diverse audiences including the *Guardian*, the *Drum* and the *Conversation* as well as numerous blogs and websites. Her most recent books include *The Rise of Critical Animal Studies* (ed., with Richard Twine; Routledge, 2014), *Humans, Animals and Society* (Lantern Books, 2013) and *Animals at Work* (with Lindsay Hamilton; Brill Academic, 2013).

Anthea Vreugdenhil is Senior Lecturer in Social Work at the University of Tasmania and a Churchill Fellow. Building on a 20-year career in health and welfare practice, policy and research, Anthea's current research focuses on care provision with a particular interest in aged care, informal carers and the 'caring society'. She has published widely in key international journals including *Australian Social Work, British Journal of Social Work* and the *Scandinavian Journal of Caring Sciences*. Anthea contributes to government policy as a member of the Tasmanian Government's seniors' policy reference group and is a member of the Australian Association of Social Workers' National Research Committee.

Chris Wever is a social worker and narrative therapist, supervisor and teacher with a Master of Social Work Practice from the University of Tasmania and a Master of Narrative Therapy and Community Work from the University of Melbourne and Dulwich Centre, Adelaide. Following an initial five years in the field, Chris began practicing as an independent social worker in 1993, co-founded Hobart's Narrative Centre in 1998, and has worked since then in independent and collaborative narrative practice. Chris is particularly interested in ideas of relational being and the impact of individualist psychological constructs on people's identities and across professional practice. One of Chris's practice intentions has always been to offer a safe, supportive and inspirational external space for workers. She believes that one of the most significant influencing factors upon her own practice is her participation in regular narrative team gatherings where team members reflect upon and celebrate each other's work in a spirit of acknowledgement, encouragement and exploration.

Paul Willis is Senior Lecturer in Social Work in the School for Policy Studies, University of Bristol, England. Paul qualified in social work at the University of Tasmania in 2002 (Australia), and his former practice experience included school social work with children and adolescents (statutory role) and counselling and community work with sexual and gender minority groups (voluntary agency). As a researcher in social care, his research areas and interests include sexuality, care and ageing; gender identity and ageing; and older men's experiences of loneliness, social isolation and marginality.

Simone Zell holds a Bachelor of Social Work (Hons) from University of Queensland and has worked for over 20 years as a practitioner, policy maker and manager in the areas of education and young people's health and wellbeing.

Simone's practice has spanned community and government agencies and includes developing policy, contributing and leading collaborative projects in the Tasmanian youth sector, and managing a state government youth health service. She has a particular interest in the interface between policy/theory and practice, working collaboratively across sectors and using creativity and kindness to engage with others.

Foreword

This book is concerned with multiple stories about care and its relationship with social work. Thus it broadens understandings about what care is, and what and who it is concerned with. It challenges what social work is by examining histories of care and 'care-less' practices. The book engages with an increasingly complicated present and offers some thoughts for the future.

It is my privilege to write the foreword to this book and thus make a small contribution to the stories that are being told within it about social work and its complex and, indeed, often compromised relationship with care. I would like to draw from the writings on hope by Rebecca Solnit, an activist on climate change and inequality (2016, 2017), as part of my contribution to helping us think about this relationship and about how we might all work together for a better future for ourselves, our relationships with each other and our fragile planet.

Rebecca Solnit helps us be aware of the perils of pessimism and optimism and offers a critically engaged understanding of hope:

> It is important to say what hope is not: it is not the belief that everything was, is or will be fine. The evidence is all around us of tremendous suffering and destruction. The hope I am interested in is about broad perspectives with specific possibilities, ones that invite or demand that we act. It is also not a sunny everything-is-getting-better narrative, though it may be a counter to the everything-is-getting-worse one. You could call it an account of complexities and uncertainties, with openings. "Critical thinking without hope is cynicism, but hope without critical thinking is naivety," the Bulgarian writer Maria Popova recently remarked.
>
> (Solnit, 2016)

My observations, as a white privileged academic woman in the global north, are that there are often very polarised perspectives on the relationship between care and social work. These are often adopted because of attacks on the profession, such as when children die. Social workers can adopt, in such circumstances, defensive positions where they can only allow themselves a self-definition as caring, applying 'innocent' knowledge to do good. This is often sustained by adopting a moral identity that admits of no complexity about the differing needs and claims of members of families. It is driven by optimism about social work and its mandate. On the other hand, pessimism can be found especially among social work academics about the possibilities for care-full practices given the contexts of inequality and neoliberalism within which social workers operate.

Solnit cautions against either optimism or pessimism, as she argues both can act to obstruct change. Optimists can believe everything will be all right if everyone just stops attacking them and leave them to get on with the job. Their moral mandate is clear and not to be questioned, whereas pessimists believe change is impossible especially at a micro level.

This book offers important possibilities for destabilising the conditions within which such binaries thrive. Writings within the ethic of care, as highlighted so well in this book, offer a direct challenge in particular to the divisive language and practices that mark out those who need and use services and those who work with them as 'failing', 'weak' and 'ineffective'. As writers emphasise throughout the book, a critical ethics of care is premised upon a relational ontology where trust, mutuality and connectedness challenge the autonomous individualism of neoliberal policies. Relationality and interdependence between people and what sustains us (such as the environment) are key underpinnings of the critical ethics of care. We all need and receive care within wildly varying conditions and contexts to be sure, but the realities of the human condition cannot be willed away in fantasies of omnipotence and self-sufficiency.

Shaming, blaming and 'othering' are central features of life in neoliberal societies with high levels of inequality (Featherstone, White and Morris, 2014). The work by researchers from a wide range of disciplines on the pernicious impacts on health, trust and feelings of cohesion can leave us with little doubt that we inhabit worlds that are marked by high levels of division and distrust. Clearly social workers and those who use services are inextricably implicated in such worlds. Facing up to ways in which our relationships with each other are impacted upon obliges 'speaking truth to power', sometimes in very uncomfortable ways, and challenges some of the claims to moral righteousness social workers can make especially when they are attacked.

In my recent work I have facilitated social workers and mothers talking to each other about the most painful of circumstances: where children have been removed and placed for adoption, which in England means it is likely there will be no face-to-face contact until the child is 18 at the very least. Such dialogue has facilitated the joint recognition of abuses of human rights, as women experiencing domestic abuse, poverty and mental health problems have been left without the resources needed to care safely, and most importantly they have been left feeling judged and shamed. It has also facilitated dialogue around situations involving 'double suffering', where women who have experienced social suffering harm others who are more vulnerable (Frost and Hoggett, 2008). Such dialogue is rare in societies as divided as ours, where the language of risk has eclipsed a language of need and social workers have become captured by a logic that deals only in prediction and the monitoring of and treatment of risky populations. They can, in such circumstances, speak an instrumental language that obscures pain, hurt and inequality and distances them in a profoundly problematic way from the people who need or are compelled to seek their help. Through collaborative practices, we can begin to author new stories, stories that challenge who and what matters, who can and should be heard, whose suffering can be grieved for and who is left out of dominant narratives (Butler, 2006).

A critical ethics of care can act to challenge undue optimism about what social work is or can be and can help face the human rights abuses that social workers can perpetrate, and it also can act as a vital counterpoint to an equally problematic pessimism. The ethic of care emerged from a body of feminist scholarship rooted in rendering visible practices that have historically been naturalised and therefore invisible. It highlighted the myriad practices that went into making lives liveable and loveable. Everyday practices are vital to our survival and flourishing – what we do and how we do it matters enormously to us and to those we live, work and inhabit the planet with. Pessimism is a dangerous luxury when confronted with such understandings.

As Solnit notes, when we are seeking to challenge and change unjust social arrangements, we cannot always know what impact we will have, but

> It is the belief that what we do matters even though how and when it may matter, who and what it may impact, are not things we can know beforehand. We may not, in fact, know them afterwards either, but they matter all the same, and history is full of people whose influence was most powerful after they were gone.
>
> (Solnit, 2017)

The authors of the chapters in this book clearly feel that *what we do matters*, and the editors are to be commended for bringing them together to produce a work that offers so much food for thought and insights for action. Many of the chapters are rooted in the traumatic history of Australia and the painful learning this has obliged about social work's complicity in practices of colonialism, dispossession and family rupture – a history that is not of course unique to Australia and offers a salutary warning about contemporary practices in child protection in many countries. It is also enriched by understandings of the fragility and precariousness of identities, places and communities and speaks most powerfully to me of the need to use 'head, hand and heart' to take care and live care-fully.

Brid Featherstone
University of Huddersfield, England

References

Butler, J. (2006) *Precarious life: The powers of mourning and violence*. London: Verso.

Featherstone, B., White, S. and Morris, K. (2014) *Re-imagining child protection: Towards humane social work with families*. Bristol: Policy Press.

Frost, L. and Hoggett, P. (2008) Human agency and social suffering. *Critical Social Policy*, 28(4), pp. 438–460.

Solnit, R. (2016) Hope is an embrace of the unknown. *Guardian*, July 15th. Available from: www.theguardian.com/books/2016/jul/15/rebecca-solnit-hope-in-the-dark-new-essay-embrace-unknown.

Solnit, R. (2017) Protest and persist: Why giving up hope is not an option. *Guardian*, March 13th. Available from: www.theguardian.com/world/2017/mar/13/protest-persist-hope-trump-activism-anti-nuclear-movement.

Part I
Framing care

1 Towards a critical ethics of care in social work

*Bob Pease, Anthea Vreugdenhil
and Sonya Stanford*

Introduction

It is widely recognised that everyone at some stage in their lives will require care, whether it be in infancy or old age, at the end of life or due to illness or impairment. In these circumstances, to be cared for is a fundamental requirement for our development as human beings (Lynch, Baker and Lyons, 2009). Beyond this life course perspective, care is also required as a result of political conflicts, natural disasters, refugee and asylum seeker movements across the world, terrorism and environmental destruction resulting from climate change.

In recent years, the concept of care has been the subject of research and scholarship in the diverse fields of sociology, social policy, psychology, health studies, politics, epidemiology, philosophy, economics and epidemiology (Phillips, 2007; Lynch et al., 2009; Armstrong and Braedley, 2013; Tronto, 2013; Gonzalez and Iffland, 2014a; Barnes, Brannelly, Ward and Ward, 2015a; Engster and Hamington, 2015a; Robinson, 2015). Issues of care have arisen as a particular concern in critical social policy studies. In this field, how the institutional logic of neoliberalism is invoked to justify the 'contractual care' of citizens (Culpitt, 1999; McDonald, 2006; Ferguson, 2008) is critically examined against humanitarian values of care that are central to critical social science (Wilkinson and Kleinman, 2016) and 'care professions' such as social work (Bauman, 2000). Most often this analysis reveals a clash in ethics that are associated with what it means to provide and receive care. This book illustrates where these clashes occur as they relate to human and non-human care and caring.

The idea for this book grew from conversations among social work academics at the University of Tasmania, Australia, sparked by the appointment of one of the editors, Bob Pease, as the new Professor of Social Work. We were searching for a collective writing project that would further our research interests and also enable us to challenge, albeit in small way, the growing emphasis on individualised research metrics within our university. Across a wide range of research and practice topics, a common theme which threaded through many of those conversations was care and its place and meaning in contemporary social work. While for some care was explicit in their research agendas, for others it was more implicit. From that core group, we reached out to social work academics and practitioners around

Australia and beyond. We invited colleagues to join with us to reinstate care into the vocabulary of social work: not care as we had come to know it through neo-liberal discourse, but a critical, political version of care. Without exception, our approaches were met with enthusiasm and excitement. This was not, however, to be a naïve endeavour and the 'dark' history of care in social work was not lost on any of us.

All contributors to this volume take a critical theory informed approach to care within the disciplinary frame of social work. The majority of the chapter authors are located in Australia, although the experiences of a number of contributors extend beyond their current Australian location. The Australian context, like other Western countries, is in the grip of neoliberalism where the costs of care are shifted from government and public institutions to the private sphere of the home. As in all Western cultures, liberal individualism underpins governmental approaches to care in Australia. The notion of the free-willed autonomous individual embedded in these approaches to care stands in contrast to the relational and interdependent conception of human beings that informs this book (Lawson, 2007; Moschella, 2014; Barnes et al., 2015a; Gouws and van Zly, 2015).

In the book we argue that care is a political and a moral concept (Williams, 2001). As such, it enables us to examine moral and political life from a radically different lens compared to the conservative moral and political ethos of neoliberalism. Tronto (1995a) argues that care has the potential to interrogate relationships of power to reveal how current institutional arrangements support inequality and injustice. Caring is politically progressive because it encourages us to move beyond the pursuit of self-interest to embrace the importance of caring for other people as a critical ethic for a more socially just world (Tronto, 1995b). It fosters a relational notion of interests that is bound up with caring relationships with others in local and global contexts from both the perspective of when we do care and when we experience care. A critical ethics of care is thus premised upon a relational ontology where trust, mutuality and connectedness challenge the autonomous individualism of neoliberal policies (Lawson, 2007; Zembylas, 2010; Daly, 2013; Barnes et al., 2015a). Thus relationality and interdependence between people and what sustains us (such as the environment) are key underpinnings of the critical ethics of care advocated in this book.

Bringing critical care ethics into social work

Care is a value and it is a practice that can involve work and professional standards (Held, 2004). Being cared for implies the need for others to care in pragmatic terms, in moral terms and in political terms, in both intimate relations in the private sphere and professionally in the public sphere. In the latter context, social work is framed as a caring profession (Lloyd, 2006). Caring provides the basis for many of the interventions that guide social work practice. However, in spite of this, the potential of a critical ethics of care to redress inequality in political and practical terms is largely neglected in social work. We argue in this book that a critical ethics of care should be at the heart of social work (Parton, 2003).

A critical ethics of care is also important in the development of critical social work. However, with few exceptions (Banks, 2014; Barnes, Brannelly, Ward and Ward, 2015b; Bozalek, 2016), critical social work writers have not engaged with the wider political debates about care ethics. Banks (2014) has noted that notwithstanding the ethical themes embedded in social justice–based politics, radical and critical social work have not emphasised ethics as part of their practice. Furthermore, radical social work has been more concerned with justice than care. This may reflect a masculinist bias in the development of progressive social work, mirroring the historical and contemporary gender split between justice and care, where justice is seen to be more characteristic of men's ways of thinking, while women's focus is said to be more oriented to care (Held, 1995). This book aims to address this gap and makes the case that a critical ethics of care provides a new politics for critical social work theory and practice in the context of neoliberalism, risk discourses, evidence-based practice and growing social and political inequalities.

The book aims to bring a critical ethics of care into the realm of theory and practice in social work. Just as Held (2004) asks why she should give priority to justice over caring for others, we ask why critical social work should ignore the ethic of care in developing socially transformative practices in social work in relation to other people and other species. We do not regard care and justice as dichotomous, and the critical concept of care we advocate in this book includes justice. We take the view advocated by Robinson (2015), Tronto (1995a), Held (2004) and others that the development of a critical ethics of care can promote social justice. As such, we argue that it is important for the practice of critical social work and we demonstrate through the contributors' chapters what a socially just approach to care and caring will involve.

Banks (2014) has drawn attention to the dangers as well as the possibilities of critical social work embracing care ethics. Such an engagement must move beyond the regulation of the conduct of social workers and service users to embrace the wider politics of solidarity with those who are marginalised by neoliberalism. This means that a critical ethics of care needs to operate as a moral philosophy to guide practice and to be implemented in caring practices in day-to-day work. We acknowledge this is not an easy task amid the harsh mentality of neoliberal welfare. Research consistently indicates that neoliberalism causes suffering for socially vulnerable people, as well as for practitioners whose task it is to implement neoliberal technologies of screening, monitoring and controlling (see, for example, Frost and Hoggett, 2008; Smith et al., 2016).

Gendering care in social work: moving beyond essentialism

Care often occurs in face-to-face relationships between people (Daly, 2013; Barnes et al., 2015a). In the neoliberal policy context, care is arranged to occur in the private sphere of the family and is predominantly reliant upon the unpaid work of women (Lawson, 2007; Daly, 2013) who are 'locked out' of secure paid work (Williams, 2001). In this book, we advocate the relocation of care from an individual and privatised practice to that of collective and communal responsibility.

Our task is also to argue the value of care wherever it occurs – in both personal and professional contexts.

We acknowledge the debt to feminism and argue that in a socially just ethic of care, care work needs to be distributed equally between men and women. We argue against the view that women are natural carers. In embracing a feminist political ethic of care, we distance ourselves from early essentialist framings of care (Chodorow, 1978; Gilligan, 1982) as reflecting biological differences in women's and men's moral reasoning. Accordingly, the critical care ethics advocated by contributors to this book challenge the essentialist association of women and caring that reinforce traditional gender stereotypes about women and men (Ward, 2015). At the same time, we recognise that women spend far more time than men doing care work and that women often feel morally compelled to undertake care-related tasks. This reflects men's power and privilege and their ability to avoid caregiving responsibilities (Hanlon, 2009) through political strategies that perpetuate gender inequality, such as workforce participation rates.

We are mindful of the dangers of a focus on care reinforcing the private-public split, where women are relegated to the private realm of the home while men continue to dominate the public sphere (Held, 2004). However, this is a concern when care is framed within a narrow ethic only pertaining to women and decontextualised from other cultural contexts. While care ethics is historically grounded in women's experiences of care, critical care ethics generally, and feminist care ethics specifically, also acknowledge the importance of men being engaged in care (Engster and Hamington, 2015b). We argue against the premise that women are naturally more compassionate and caring than men. However, we do recognise that women's socialisation and grounded experiences of caring will mean that women are more likely than men to be predisposed towards caring (Porter, 2006). One of the challenges in developing a critical ethics of care is how to encourage men to care more (Kershaw, 2010). From a critical ethics of care perspective, this means a radical change to existing power relations that are embedded in institutional arrangements. It also means a change in everyday relations and practices of power that are a feature of the more intimate domains of our lives.

Feminist and critical theories of care shift the focus from individualist framings of care to wider collectivist and global approaches. As Lynch et al. (2009) illustrate, the affective system of care is located alongside the economic, political and socio-cultural systems as one of the mechanisms in which equality and inequality are produced. As such, it must become one of the domains in which critical social work is promoted.

The intersectionality of care in social work: addressing privilege and power

Care ethics has been criticised for its lack of intersectional perspective (Hankivsky, 2014; Ward, 2015). Given the unequal gendered division of labour in relation to care, it is understandable that gender will have a primary status in relation to care ethics. However, it is important to remember that class, race, nation and sexuality also constitute important dimensions of care work. Care work is unequally distributed along the axes of gender, class, race and caste (Hankivsky, 2014). As Tronto (2010) has noted, care takes place in the context of non-responsiveness and irresponsibility of members of privileged groups. Consequently, in this book, we promote an intersectional analysis of care in social work that considers race, class, ethnicity, sexuality, disability and age, along with gender.

Conceptualisations of care have also been criticised because of their connections to the global north and Western power structures (Hankivsky, 2014). As editors, we are conscious of the colonial context in which our discussion of critical care ethics takes place. Most of our contributors are white and are located in privileged positions within a colonial society. As such, we need to remind ourselves that the form of critical care ethics advocated here needs to be recognised as partial and not universal. We need to be sensitive to how care is enacted in Indigenous societies and how they may contribute to critical and political ethics of care (Weaver, 2016; Boulton and Brannelly, 2015). As an indelibly white profession, social work needs to incorporate the critique of how efforts to care have caused such damage to Aboriginal people. A critical ethics of care therefore requires new ways for hearing the pain of the profession's efforts to care and to learn the potential to care in critically informed ways.

There has been significant criticism of the ethics of care in terms of oppressing those who are marginalised. Some critical disability activists, for example, reject the concept of care because in their view it involves a representation of disabled people as a burden. They associate care with dependency, paternalism and disempowerment (Wood, 1991; Shakespeare, 2006). We are very conscious of the dangers of paternalistic and colonialist forms of care (Narayan, 1995), where those on the receiving end of care are framed as vulnerable and weak. Such care discourses promote what Grey (2008) calls 'benevolent othering'. In such instances, care can become a form of control and domination by privileged and powerful actors. This critique alerts us to the importance of interrogating the power relations involved in care. It also reminds us that relations of care are rarely so linear: we can be both a carer and in need of care ourselves in intimate relationships and in wider social and political relationships.

Caring beyond local contexts and national borders

Another criticism of care ethics is that it is only relevant in local and familial contexts (Lawson, 2007). What does it have to offer in terms of recognising and responding to the needs of those who are distant from us? What can it contribute to asylum seeker movements across the world, global health inequalities, international debt and global climate change, for example? We believe that it is important to frame care beyond the private sphere, as experiences of 'structured suffering' are global, and catastrophic forms of suffering occur predominantly in non-Western countries (Wilkinson and Kleinman, 2016).

We argue that caregiving is ultimately a societal responsibility and should not be solely the responsibility of individuals (Phillips, 2007). Care also involves institutions and societies at the national, global and transnational levels (Tronto, 1995a). It is a premise of this book that a critical ethics of care in social work can impact global level of inequalities as well as inequalities within nation states (Held, 2004). In this wider view of care, solidarity work on international issues involves an extension of the concept of care.

For Porter (2006), the compassion for others across national borders extends the ethics of care into a 'politics of care', where caring is premised upon empathy for shared human suffering. Tronto (2012) argues that if we understand our relational responsibilities towards others from around the world, there is a stronger basis for encouraging those in the wealthy countries of the global north to accept responsibility for the injustices in the global south. Drawing upon Young's (2007) social connection model of responsibility, she outlines the contribution that a critical ethics of care has for caring for others beyond national borders. Care theory has moved a long way from women's caregiving in the family to critical engagements with global and transnational issues (Hankivsky, 2006; Robinson, 2010, 2015; Bozalek, 2016), and this has important ramifications for how we understand contemporary social work.

Overview of the book

We have grouped the chapters into four broad sections: Framing Care, Situating Care, Unsettling Care and Transforming Care. This structure is the result of a collective, political process and reflects one storyline, among many, of a critical ethics of care in social work. There were difficult decisions to be made along the way including if, and how, to group the chapters. In our deliberations, it quickly became apparent that the need for structure was, in itself, a Western construct with the potential to place some authors and their ideas at the centre while shifting others to the periphery. We grappled with this and have grouped the chapters in a way that we hope at least partially addresses these concerns. Nonetheless, we acknowledge that the grouping of chapters into a section titled 'Unsettling Care' and its placement part way through the book could signal the de-centring of these chapters, which challenge Western, white, heterosexual and able-bodied privilege. These chapters are crucial to the book, and we hope that their co-location increases their power rather than diminishes it.

Part I of the book, Framing Care, begins with this introductory chapter where we have outlined the historical and current concerns about the dangers of paternalistic and colonialist forms of care in social work and acknowledged the critique that the contemporary discussions about care reflect a Western bias that ignores Indigenous and inter-cultural framings of care. Drawing from wider interdisciplinary discussions about critical and political forms of care, we outlined key principles for new ways of thinking about and doing care in critical social work.

Donna Baines in Chapter 2 argues that current managerial models undermine a social ethic of care due to the intense conditions of work and the discourses of individualism and competition characteristic of late neoliberalism. She also argues that professionalism, as it is enacted under neoliberalism, is antithetical to an ethic of care. Drawing on data collected in Australia, Canada, New Zealand, the UK and South Africa, the chapter concludes with an exploration of various strategies used to resist 'uncaring', and the innovative practices social workers and social service workers use to sustain a care ethic in the heart of neoliberal social services.

In Chapter 3, Martyn Jones reviews the features of a progressive concept of care, aligned with the premises of critical social work. He explains how a progressive concept of care affords a necessary counter-proposition for the practice of social work in contemporary organisational and policy contexts by crossing customary borders between professions, organisations, systems and discourses. He identifies how this progressive and critically connected care paradigm is informing a specific initiative being undertaken within one metropolitan university in Australia with the aim of building capacity for socially just systems of support and care into the future.

In Chapter 4, Anthea Vreugdenhil identifies how in the context of a highly regulated profession concepts such as 'duty of care' have come to dominate social work practice. This chapter explores the interplay between the increased regulation of the social work profession and the meaning and practice of care in social work. Through the lens of a political ethic of care, she discusses how social work might be transformed through practices that place the value of care at the centre of social work and move beyond individualistic policies and practices to more emancipatory and collectivist approaches.

In Chapter 5, Jenny Hay notes that an ethic of care and an ethic of justice are commonly presented as distinct moral theories, with proponents of each view critiquing the other. In this chapter, she argues that care and justice are logically compatible, interdependent and indispensable to one another. She observes that in recent decades, care has become devalued and undermined as a focus on scientific, evidence-based practice has become dominant. Drawing on interviews with social workers and social work clients, she argues that attention to social justice is not enough and that a focus on caring practice that acknowledges the importance of trust is also required for social work to develop critical ethical practice.

Part II of the book, Situating Care, begins with Chapter 6 by Anne-Maree Sawyer and Sonya Stanford, who critically analyse how person-centred community-based care is interpolated with formal rationalities of risk. Using the concept of 'social suffering', they examine the social misery that is generated, and often disguised, by such risk thinking. Drawing on research with people recovering from mental health issues, they demonstrate that the lived reality of suffering, engendered by risk-focused responses and procedures, both creates and compounds the pain of inequality and injustice. This perspective provides an opportunity to critically consider organisational and practice strategies of care that could address the wounded 'self' of people experiencing mental health problems.

In Chapter 7, Anne Coleman draws on personal experiences of social work and care with a group of people experiencing homelessness (mainly public space dwellers) in an inner city area in Australia. She documents a journey that led her to question her notions of professional care and to seek a way of bringing together social work's concern for social justice with an ethic of care. Using demonstrations of care from practice, she challenges expert and professional discourses of care, focusing on reciprocity and solidarity. She reviews social work as a 'caring' profession and concludes by considering the implications for critical social work practice.

In Chapter 8, Sharon Moore analyses the changing role of the state, family and market in providing care for older people in Australia, as welfare ideals of universalism give way to both marketisation and privatisation of caring and care services. She notes that market-oriented policies construct care users as consumers and care as a commodity to be bought and sold. This political imagery is overshadowed by the consumer who is assumed to be a self-interested individual embedded primarily in economic relationships. Drawing upon critical gender theory, she argues for the reclaiming of a critical agenda based on anti-ageist challenges from the Carers' Movement and disability activists, as well as critical research into the co-creation and co-production of person-centred care.

In Chapter 9, Maria Harries notes that child protection practitioners work in risk-saturated environments where relationships are fractured, care is fragile and sometimes frightening, and value-based practice with a broader focus than the child is particularly difficult. She argues that there is a high intensity of emotional labour demanded of those 'doing care' in such an environment. Given this context she asks how, if at all, a feminist ethic of care with its attendant and complex view of morality and the centrality within it of relationship, can provide better understanding of how the caring professions can work more 'care-fully' in the contested area of practice called child protection?

In Chapter 10, Sharlene Nipperess explores what it means to care in the uncaring context of punitive measures of government responses to people seeking asylum. Focusing on the Australian context, which has some of the harshest policies in the world directed at asylum seekers, the chapter explores what it means for social workers to care in such a context. She argues that caring is not enough, and that for an ethics of care to have value for social work practice with people seeking asylum, it needs to move towards a critical ethics of care. Such an approach pays attention to the principles of human rights and social justice, as well as incorporating an intersectional analysis and a commitment to critically reflective practice.

In Chapter 11, Richard Hugman focuses on social work practice in areas of humanitarian aid in response to disasters and the impact of conflict. He begins with the question of how concepts such as 'aid', 'relief' and 'development' are constructed as forms of 'caring'. Behind this question, he argues, lies the interconnection of a concern for others ('caring about') with actions that provide tangible responses to need ('caring for'). He examines the ways in which one approach to care can perpetuate neo-colonial social relations while at the same time providing necessary assistance. Using political ethics of care models, he advances a more progressive approach to international social work and social development practice in humanitarian aid.

Part III of the book, Unsettling Care, begins with Chapter 12 by Ann Joselynn Baltra-Ulloa, who challenges and reconsiders the dominance of Western epistemology in creating normative ideas about care and caring. In this chapter, she speaks from the 'periphery' to transcend the accepted and ethnocentric understandings of care and caring to a theorising of care as ambiguous and even contradictory at times. The chapter aims to develop a critical post-colonial perspective where the ethic of care becomes about accepting how marginal caring is and how transformative this marginality can be for re-framing care as an act of refusing and resisting oppression.

In Chapter 13, Sue Green identifies how colonisation has disrupted many aspects of roles within Aboriginal communities, one of them being caring. She explores the meaning of caring within Aboriginal communities prior to colonisation through the use of two fundamental concepts that underpin the life of the Wiradyuri people of Western New South Wales, Australia. The concepts, Yindyamarra and Wirimbirragu Ngurambanggu, outline the importance of having a holistic understanding and practice of caring, which incorporates all elements of the environment, including people. The chapter concludes with a discussion about how the social work profession, through its values and principles has a responsibility to ensure that its practice is embedded within Yindyamarra and Wirimbirragu Ngurambanggu.

In Chapter 14, Michele Raithby and Paul Willis discuss the importance of a critical ethics of care framework, alongside recognition of sexual citizenship, for providing more inclusive care to older people of sexually diverse backgrounds. They point out that care for older lesbian, gay and bisexual (LGB) people remains a predominantly heteronormative preserve. In the chapter, they draw on research findings in Wales in the UK on affirmative, dignified care with older LGB people in long-term care settings. They argue that a critical ethics of care framework can enhance further understanding of the sexual lives of LGB people, and that such an approach can promote care provision that both attends and responds to their sexual personhood as a fundamental dimension in providing care.

Russell Shuttleworth notes in Chapter 15 that within disability studies, the care relationship between carer and disabled person has historically been viewed as an asymmetrical relation with power inevitably in the hands of the former. He observes how this critique was an impetus for the development of a consumer and user-directed model of care in the US and UK and now Australia. Drawing from the feminist ethic of care and critical disability studies, he focuses on notions of mutual recognition and accessible care. He argues that the current discourse on the politics of care within critical disability studies can provide critical social work with important perspectives with which to inform their own reflections on politicised and ethical practice with disabled people.

Part IV of the book, Transforming Care, begins with Chapter 16 by Sarah Epstein, who argues that it is possible to conceptualise the care work enacted by mothers as a deliberate and considered political act that can displace dominant and oppressive ideas about motherhood. Drawing on Sara Ruddick's theory of maternal practice, she argues that mothering is an activity undertaken with specific intention and informed by values as a response to the perceived demands made by raising children. The chapter considers how the idea of maternal practice has broad import for social work practitioners working with women in caretaking roles. Supporting women to identify the discourses they engage with in their everyday mothering can work towards a more socially just recognition of the motherhood experience.

In Chapter 17 Bob Pease notes that the concept of care is located within gendered discourses of femininity, whereby women are defined as carers in both their everyday lives as mothers, wives, sisters and daughters and in caring professions and paid care work. He argues that part of the explanation for men's reluctance to undertaking caring responsibilities is their commitment to dominant forms of masculinity and being a man, which are at odds with the intimacy, emotions and relatedness embedded in the doing of care. The chapter explores the implications of men's increased caring roles for whether or not there is emerging a new caring masculinity, whereby men break with hegemonic masculinity. He also considers whether men reframe caring work in ways that reproduce dominant forms of masculinity, and if so what this might mean for transforming men's caring practices.

In Chapter 18, Margaret E. Hughes considers whether an ethic of care to address both the pragmatic and moral responsibilities of caring is enough and asks why we do not aim higher by engaging with the universal notion of love. She argues that love is a powerful and transformative change agent with a capacity to generate kindness, peace, equality and justice. She asks 'where is the love?', specifically in the context of social work. She proposes an argument for the relevance of love in social work, and argues that by asking where is the love, we move beyond the limitations of a traditional ethic of care.

In Chapter 19, Chris Wever and Simone Zell ask how social workers can do ethical, meaningful work and avoid feeling alienated, overwhelmed and burnt out. They critically analyse self-care discourses in social work that are frequently invoked in response to this question. Such discourses, they note, encourage social workers to do better self-care, and they argue that this construction of self-care rests upon and contributes to dominant Western individualist discourses of independence and personal responsibility for the self. In contrast, they explore an alternative ethic of caring for each other that is founded upon constructs of relational being and collective responsibility.

Jennifer Boddy argues in Chapter 20 that current political approaches to tackling climate change that have focused on adhering to global carbon emissions targets and their economic impacts disregard the importance of addressing social and economic inequities brought about by neoliberalism that prioritises economies over people. She draws attention to research that recognises the interdependence of human health and the natural environment. Consequently, she argues that a critical ethics of care, where inequity is no longer tolerated and people and their environments are valued equally, is needed. Such an approach requires governments and societies to work together collectively in compassionate and caring ways that recognise humanity is a part of nature and not in binary opposition to it.

In the last chapter in the volume (Chapter 21), Heather Fraser, Nik Taylor and Christine Morley note that the vast majority of critical scholarship on caring remains focused on aspects of human caregiving. They argue that human-animal forms of caregiving that are important to many of our clients, communities and selves are ignored. In this chapter, they explain why critical social workers should pay attention to care provided by animals to humans and vice versa. Drawing on both the specialty areas of animal assisted social work and veterinary social work and several human-companion animal studies they have conducted, they ask, what can an intersectional approach to studying cross-species care offer critical social work?

All of the contributors to this book bring a critical care ethics to diverse fields of practice, and provide insights for developing a new politics of caring in critical social work. In line with this diversity, the contributors also bring a range of styles of writing to their chapters, from the highly academic through to the deeply personal. We hope that the book encourages a re-evaluation of the value of care in critical social work. We hope also that the contributors provide inspiration to other social work colleagues to develop critical approaches to care that address the social suffering of people as they face the rising forces of neoliberalism and managerialism in social work.

References

Armstrong, P. and Braedley, S. (eds.) (2013) *Troubling care: Critical perspectives on research and practices*. Toronto: Canadian Scholars' Press.

Banks, S. (2014) Reclaiming social work ethics: Challenging the new public management. In: Ferguson, I. and Lavalette, M. (eds.) *Critical and radical debates in social work: Ethics*. Bristol: Policy Press, pp. 1–24.

Barnes, M., Brannelly, T., Ward, L. and Ward, N. (2015a) Introduction. In: Barnes, M., Brannelly, T., Ward, L. and Ward, N. (eds.) *Ethics of care: Critical advances in international perspective*. Bristol: Policy Press, pp. 3–19.

Barnes, M., Brannelly, T., Ward, L. and Ward, N. (eds.) (2015b) *Ethics of care: Critical advances in international perspective*. Bristol: Policy Press.

Bauman, Z. (2000) Special essay: Am I my brother's keeper? *European Journal of Social Work*, 3(1), pp. 5–11.

Boulton, A. and Brannelly, T. (2015) Care ethics and indigenous values: Political, tribal and personal. In: Barnes, M., Brannelly, T., Ward, L. and Ward, N. (eds.) *Ethics of care: Critical advances in international perspective*. Bristol: Policy Press, pp. 69–82.

Bozalek, V. (2016) The political ethics of care and feminist posthuman ethics: Contributions to social work. In: Hugman, R. and Carter, J. (eds.) *Rethinking values and ethics in social work*. London: Palgrave, pp. 80–96.

Chodorow, N. (1978) *The reproduction of mothering: Psychoanalysis and the sociology of gender*. Berkeley: University of California Press.

Culpitt, I. (1999) *Social policy and risk*. London: Sage.

Daly, T. (2013) Imagining an ethos of care within policies, practices and philosophy. In: Armstrong, P. and Braedley, S. (eds.) *Troubling care: Critical perspectives on research and practices*. Toronto: Canadian Scholars' Press, pp. 35–45.

Engster, D. and Hamington, M. (eds.) (2015a) *Care ethics and political theory*. Oxford: Oxford University Press.

Engster, D. and Hamington, M. (2015b) Introduction. In: Engster, D. and Hamington, M. (eds.) *Care ethics and political theory*. Oxford: Oxford University Press, pp. 1–16.

Ferguson, I. (2008) *Reclaiming social work: Challenging neo-liberalism and promoting social justice*. London: Sage.

Frost, L. and Hoggett, P. (2008) Human agency and social suffering. *Critical Social Policy*, 28(4), pp. 438–460.

Gilligan, C. (1982) *In a different voice: Psychological theory and women's development*. London: Harvard University Press.

Gonzalez, A. and Iffland, C. (2014a) Introduction: The challenges of 'care'. In: Gonzalez, A. and Iffland, C. (eds.) *Care, professions and globalization*. New York: Palgrave Macmillan, pp. 1–29.

Gonzalez, A. and Iffland, C. (eds.) (2014b) *Care, professions and globalization*. New York: Palgrave Macmillan.

Gouws, A. and van Zyl, M. (2015) Towards a feminist ethics of ubuntu: Bridging rights and ubuntu. In Engster, D. and Hamington, M. (eds.) *Care ethics and political theory*. Oxford: Oxford University Press, pp. 165–186.

Grey, B. (2008) *Benevolent othering: Displaying and 'celebrating' diversity*. School of Social and Political Enquiry and School of Languages and Linguistics, University of Melbourne.

Hankivsky, O. (2006) Imagining ethical globalization: The contributions of a care ethic. *Journal of Global Ethics*, 2(1), pp. 91–110.

Hankivsky, O. (2014) Rethinking care ethics: On the promise and potential of an intersectional analysis. *American Political Science Review*, 108(2), pp. 252–264.

Hanlon, N. (2009) Caregiving masculinities: An exploratory analysis. In: Lynch, K., Baker, J. and Lyons, M. (eds.) *Affective equality: Love, care and injustice*. New York: Palgrave Macmillan, pp. 180–198.

Held, V. (1995) Introduction. In: Held, V. (ed.) *Justice and care: Essential readings in feminist ethics*. Boulder, CO: Westview Press, pp. 1–3.

Held, V. (2004) Care and justice in the global context. *Ration Juris*, 17(2), pp. 141–155.

Kershaw, P. (2010) The 'private' politics in caregiving: Reflections on Ruth Lister's *Citizenship: Feminist Perspectives*. *Women's Studies Quarterly*, 38(1–2), pp. 302–311.

Lawson, V. (2007) Geographies of care and responsibility. *Annals of the Association of American Geographers*, 97(1), pp. 1–11.

Lloyd, L. (2006) A caring profession? The ethics of care and social work with older people. *British Journal of Social Work*, 36, pp. 1171–1185.

Lynch, K., Baker, J. and Lyons, M. (2009) Introduction. In: Lynch, K., Baker, J. and Lyons, M. (eds.) *Affective equality: Love, care and injustice*. New York: Palgrave Macmillan, pp. 1–11.

McDonald, C. (2006) Institutional transformation: The impact of performance measurement on professional practice in social work. *Social Work and Society*, 4, pp. 25–37.

Moschella, M. (2014) Social contract theory and moral agency: Understanding the roots of an uncaring society. In: Gonzalez, A. and Iffland, C. (eds.) *Care, professions and globalization*. New York: Palgrave Macmillan, pp. 87–115.

Narayan, U. (1995) Colonialism and its others: Considerations on rights and care discourses. *Hypatia*, 10(2), pp. 133–140.

Parton, N. (2003) Rethinking professional practice: The contributions of social constructionism and the feminist 'ethics of care'. *British Journal of Social Work*, 33, pp. 1–16.

Phillips, J. (2007) *Care*. Cambridge: Policy Press.

Porter, E. (2006) Can politics practice compassion? *Hypatia*, 21(4), pp. 97–123.

Robinson, F. (2010) After liberalism in world politics? Towards an international political theory of care. *Ethics and Social Welfare*, 4(2), pp. 130–144.

Robinson, F. (2015) Care, gender and global social justice: Rethinking ethical globalisation. *Journal of Global Ethics*, 2(1), pp. 5–25.

Shakespeare, T. (2006) *Disability, rights and wrongs*. London: Routledge.

Smith, M., Cree, V.E., MacRae, R., Sharp, D., Wallace, E. and O'Halloran, S. (2016) Social suffering: Changing organizational culture in children and families social work through critical reflection groups – Insights from Bourdieu. *British Journal of Social Work* [online]. Available from: https://doi.org/10.1093/bjsw/bcw087 [Accessed 20 December 2016].

Tronto, J. (1995a) Care as a basis for radical political judgements. *Hypatia*, 10(2), 141–149.

Tronto, J. (1995b) Women and caring: What can feminists learn about morality from caring? In: Held, V. (ed.) *Justice and care: Essential readings in feminist ethics*. Boulder, CO: Westview Press, pp. 101–115.

Tronto, J. (2010) Creating caring institutions: Politics, plurality and purpose. *Ethics and Social Welfare*, 4(2), pp. 158–171.

Tronto, J. (2012) Partiality based on relational responsibilities: Another approach to global ethics. *Ethics and Social Welfare*, 6(3), pp. 303–316.

Tronto, J. (2013) *Caring democracy: Markets, equality and justice*. New York: New York University Press.

Ward, N. (2015) Care ethics, intersectionality and poststructuralism. In: Barnes, M., Brannell, T., Ward, L. and Ward, N. (eds.) *Ethics of care: Critical advances in international perspective*. Bristol: Policy Press, pp. 57–68.

Weaver, H. (2016) Ethics and settler societies: Reflections on social work and indigenous peoples. In: Hugman, R. and Carter, J. (eds.) *Rethinking values and ethics in social work*. London: Palgrave, pp. 129–145.

Wilkinson, I. and Kleinman, A. (2016) *A passion for society: How we think about human suffering*. Oakland: University of California Press.

Williams, F. (2001) In and beyond new labour: Towards a new political ethics of care. *Critical Social Policy*, 21, pp. 467–493.

Wood, R. (1991) Care of disabled people. In: Dalley, G. (ed.) *Disability and social policy*. London: Policy Studies Institute, pp. 199–202.

Young, I. (2007) *Responsibility for justice*. New York: Open University Press.

Zembylas, M. (2010) The ethic of care in globalized societies: Implications for citizenship education. *Ethics and Education*, 5(3), pp. 233–245.

2 Social ethics of care in a context of social neglect

A five-country discussion

Donna Baines

Introduction

In July 2016, my research team undertook interviews with social workers and social service workers in Johannesburg, South Africa. In a post-apartheid, 'developing' nation, South African social workers struggle with conditions that most in the 'global north' will rarely encounter.[1] On the other hand, the social policy shaping social services emphasises collectivity, social development and community mobilisation. This shapes social work services in more socially engaged, rather than individually engaged, and deeply humane ways. For example, at one agency we studied, the staff had not been paid for four months but they came to work every day. I asked in awe, why they kept coming to work when no one was paying them? They said it was because they cared about the people they worked with and they wanted to help their communities.

These two factors 'care' and 'help their communities' were consistently paired and centred in the social workers' explanations for why they were drawn to do social work, why they remained in the work and what they hoped for in the future. Care in this case was seamlessly personalised within the relationship between service users and the workers, and collectivised within a model of community development and mobilisation. As such, it represents a social ethic of care (Tronto, 2015), extending beyond individual self-interests, and advancing values and practices aimed at building a more caring, socially just and socially engaged society. The social policies that scaffold this caring create a virtuous environment in which mutual support and solidarity within communities and between individuals is the aspirational norm.

Data from my studies of social workers and social service workers in more affluent countries, including Australia, Canada, the UK and New Zealand, also show a strong commitment to care on the part of social workers, though it is not centred in the same way in everyday work or enshrined within social policy. Care is often delegitimised by notions of 'professional boundaries' and is much more likely to be individualised, mirroring the individualising services provided in most 'first world' social service organisations. It is also less likely that there will be opportunities for social workers to initiate community development, social development or collective mobilisation. In the current context, collectivisation of services users' issues is likely to come from workers undertaking individual and group resistance to existing social policy rather than reflecting government policy. Finally, rather than affirming social responsibility for care, social policy in the global north tends to undermine collectivism and does little to build or sustain social solidarity or equity. Instead, it encourages people to seek solutions to social problems in the private market and marginalises those unable or unwilling to pull themselves up by their own bootstraps.

The context of care in the five countries discussed in this chapter is shaped by late neoliberalism (Peck, 2010; Rossi, 2013) and the episteme of New Public Management (NPM), funding constraint and managerialism (Cunningham, Baines, Shields and Lewchuk, 2016). Late neoliberalism in this chapter is defined as the period after the Global Financial Crisis of 2007 and recovery of capitalism despite widespread economic instability and decline. This period features policies of austerity, a re-valorisation of the private market and a growing polarisation between rich and poor, privileged and oppressed (Peck, 2010; Rossi, 2013). This chapter will argue that current managerial models undermine a social ethic of care due to the conditions of work and the discourses of individualism and competition characteristic of late neoliberalism. Where an ethic of care does exist, it is usually dependent on the commitment, resistance and goodwill of the individual workers enacting more sociable ethics, rather than a system-wide commitment to social justice. The chapter also argues that professionalism, as it is enacted under neoliberalism, is antithetical to an ethic of care. Drawing on data collected in Australia, Canada, New Zealand, the UK and South Africa, the chapter concludes with an exploration of various strategies used to resist 'uncaring', and innovative practices social workers and social service workers use to sustain a care ethic in the heart of neoliberal social services.

Contexts

Gender

Social work, and all care work jobs, are highly gendered terrains in which the majority of workers, service users and volunteers are women and non-women (including transgender and non-binary people) who experience misogyny.[2] Naturalised notions of females' endless and elastic capacity to care for others, regardless of conditions or contexts, has made it difficult to increase the status or pay associated with this kind of work (Baines, 2017). It has meant that social care work is often regarded as something inherent to femaleness rather than a high-level set of skills and knowledge (Lundy, 2011). The literature on women's inequity in social work has noted that men in social work are much more frequently given supervisory and management roles (Pease, 2011), generally seen as more authoritative, and more often associated with justice policy rather than frontline care (Held, 1995). Female-associated inequity is a cultural-symbolic social injustice as well as a distributive one (Fraser, 2010). It is symbolic in that women and non-women who experience misogyny in social work have less access to affirming identities and full participation in all aspects of social and social work life. In addition, they are associated with less powerful, feminised and delegitimised discourses and practices such as 'care'. These same gender inequities are also distributive injustices (Fraser, 2010) in that women receive lower pay, less opportunities, lower authority, diminished credibility and reduced power to use in everyday work and social change efforts.

Intersectionality

Very few women and non-women experiencing misogyny experience gender injustices in complete isolation from other axes of inequity. Women and non-women experiencing misogyny are always racialised, classed, and perceived by others as dis/able bodied, aged and positioned in various ways vis-à-vis gender and sexual identities, Indigeneity, colonialism and so forth. As Andersen and Collins (2015) note, multiple oppressors intersect at various points and in various contexts to co-construct (Hankivsky, 2014) the kinds of power and experience people have of their social worlds. Bannerji (2000) goes further to argue that while social relations of inequity operate in all contexts, their relative strength varies according to the specific context. For example, in the current era, refugees and asylum seekers are denigrated in Australia principally on the basis of their country of origin and the fact that they are seeking a new country of residence. Gender, age, dis/ability and other axes of inequity do little to mitigate the overarching rejection of their claims for humane treatment and refuge, though those from more comfortable class backgrounds may be able to arrive by plane and spend their detention onshore rather than locked in the horrendous offshore detention centres. Though colonialism founded the unstable and violent regimes from which refugees flee, and Australian and other developed countries benefit from colonialism, these axes of oppression are made invisible in the discourse of 'queue jumping' and 'boat people' (Robinson, 2014).

In a similar way, social workers as a highly gendered group, experience varying degrees of legitimacy in the world depending on their race, gender and sexual orientation, (dis)ability and age. Their capacity to centre care within their everyday practice of social work is similarly crisscrossed by multiple lines of identity and the power these identities accord and can access. The power of these social locations is often not deliberately sought out. Rather, it is accorded as a naturalised privilege or disadvantage. For example, those working and living in countries like Canada, Australia and New Zealand are accorded the privileges of living in wealthy societies built on land stolen from Indigenous people (Carniol, Baines, Kennedy and Sinclair, 2017). This privilege and the disadvantage of colonialised people operates as an unseen but taken-for-granted ground floor on which everyday life operates, though few, if any, of those living in these circumstances sought out these oppressive social relations (Carniol et al., 2017).

Intersectionality and privilege/disadvantage operate similarly in gendered terrains such as social work, where a white, able-bodied woman might have access to more affirming identities and the power to challenge uncaring practices in her social services workplace than a similarly motivated but less powerfully socially located social worker who is a racialised immigrant, is transgender or lives with a disability. The operation of these multiple strands of inequity shape and co-construct the possibilities social workers have to pursue social and political ethics of care in their everyday social work practice. These possibilities are further limited in the context of neoliberalism's now, near-global management policy within social services, namely NPM or managerialism.

Armstrong and Armstrong (2004) note, some analyses *slice* to create multiple, complex pictures of various people in particular places (Glucksman, 2000, p. 16), while others *lump* to identify what is common about women and their work (Armstrong and Armstrong, 2004, p. 5). This chapter does both, relying mostly on lumping in order to explore the care ethics and common experience of social workers in the context of late neoliberalism and NPM. Where intersecting differences or slicing are key to the argument, they are identified and analysed.

New Public Management and managerialism

Since the mid-1980s, policies referred to as neoliberalism and New Public Management (NPM) have dismantled the welfare state, reduced or privatised most social programs and services, and in the process bolstered the legitimacy of the private market as the main driver of social progress and development (Cunningham et al., 2016). Social services were transferred from the public/government sector to the for-profit and non-profit sectors, alongside reductions in wages and working conditions; increases in caseload size, pace and intensity of work; and the use of outcome targets to document services and secure ongoing funding contracts (Carniol et al., 2017). Social work employment became less secure, more likely to be contract, part-time and precarious at the same time as communities became more desperate and high-need due to widespread program cuts and reductions.

NPM has also meant that, in an effort to decrease costs and meet outcome targets, social work practices that are harder to quantify have been reduced or removed. These practices include those associated with community development, open-ended assessments, long-term trustful relationship building and maintenance, and policy critique and debate. Many 'best' practices such as assessments and interventions have been standardised using the same logic of cost reduction (Lundy, 2011). Standardisation makes it easier to replace higher skill, higher credentialed workers with lower skill, lower credentialed workers, or even volunteers (Cunningham et al., 2016). This race to the bottom in terms of wages and credentials raises serious questions about real accountability to service users and the taxpayer, rather than the faux accountability currently sustained within the extensive documentation required within the details of government funding contracts (Baines, 2017).

Professionalism

Professionalism has sometimes been referred to as a process of market closure or a way to protect a particular job title by literally removing it from market forces and arguing that it can only be filled by people with a particular knowledge and set of skills (Macdonald, 1985; Abbott, 2014). Though some argue that professionalism protects the public or confers a much-deserved status and legitimacy on social work, others have argued that it divides the field between those with formal credentials and those with years of practice knowledge but few formal credentials, systemically rewarding the former and disadvantaging the latter.

Invoking the discourses of protecting the public and ensuring quality, the registration of social workers continues to be hotly debated in the context of late neoliberalism. Many assert that most social workers are already highly supervised by numerous levels of managers and that registration merely adds an additional, after-the-fact, off-site form of surveillance and discipline (Lundy, 2011; van Heugten, 2011). As part of the neoliberal project, registration also readies social workers for further integration into the private market as entrepreneurs, private practitioners and consultants, thus moving social work one step further from an ethic of social care, political engagement and social solidarity (Baines, 2017).

Emulating high-status professions such as law and medicine, professionalism has also advocated stark boundaries and distance between service users and workers, casting aspersions of unprofessional behaviour on those who use warmth, care and open-ended relationships as the basis for change-directed, social justice–engaged social work. Similarly, professionalism promotes the notion that professionals can and should be objective. Care ethics are the antithesis to this discourse, emphasising the aspects of human interaction that defy quantification and social distance, and embracing social interactions that include emotion, spontaneity, practice knowledge, reciprocity and dialogue.

Ethics of care

Care ethics place care at the centre of questions of how to foster a good society and positive interactions between people. This includes the care we all receive and all provide at various points in our lives, as well as care as a concept that can be used to reflect on social relations of power, inequity and social justice (Tronto, 2015). Care ethics can guide individual social work practices as well as larger social policy and social relations (Weinberg, 2010).

Dovetailing neatly with the gender-equity emphasis undergirding care ethics (Tronto, 2015), virtue ethics argue that social justice–embracing contexts are needed in order to consistently make ethical decisions, as it is easier to be good in good contexts. Interweaving feminist, care and virtue ethics permits a thick interpretation of ethics focusing on ways of building societies in which equitable, ethical, and fair decisions are easy to make (see Gray, 2010; Carey and Green, 2013). In the absence of a fair society, care/virtue ethics interpretations can foster critical thought, resistance and more community-engaged, social solidarity strategies as central components of ethical social work practice, developing ways to address individual suffering while simultaneously recognising the need for societal change (Weinberg, 2010; Baines, 2015). This chapter argues that in the current context of social work practice, feminist, care and virtue ethics are hard to attain though they are essential to more social justice–engaged practice.

Enacting care in the context of neoliberalism and care as resistance: a central ethic of social work

This section of the chapter draws on exemplar quotes highlighting the centrality of care in data I have collected from social workers in Australia, Canada, New Zealand, South Africa and the UK. Though these countries are positioned differently within the global political economy, at the level of the workplace social work practices are distinctly similar and all are shaped by policies of funding constraint and NPM. Laying it out very clearly, a senior worker in disability services observed, "if we didn't care, we wouldn't be here. With the bad wages and the crap conditions, that's the bottom line – we care." Care was also seen as a way to maintain a sense of integrity, as a community support worker noted: "If you haven't got meaning in these jobs, what else have you got?"

Social workers also put in many hours of unpaid overtime, reflecting their care for service users, co-workers and the services they provide: "the wages are terrible here anyway so why not work even more hours for no pay if it means you can keep a program afloat or keep someone from having to put their kids to bed hungry" (child and family social worker). Another worker told us, "I work late for the same reasons as everyone else, we want to help."

Resistance as an ethic of care

Care was also apparent in the ways that social workers not only fulfilled the expectations of their job descriptions: they often went far beyond them to provide service users with dignity, respect and as much support as is possible in the leaned-out social services in the countries studied. This going beyond expectations included bending rules, doing advocacy and working with others on collective solutions (Baines, 2010, 2017). As one young worker put it, "we didn't make the rules and we don't always stick to them because they aren't always in the best interests of service users." One worker explicitly linked uncaring with resistance: "I'm not here to add to the uncaring of the world. I am here to make a difference." Caring was also frequently linked with advocacy: "We can't wait out this period of conservative politics and watch people suffer. We have to try to make things better." In the context of neoliberalism's disparagement of poor and marginalised people, treating service users with care, dignity and respect are small acts of resistance in and of themselves.

Participating in social change and activism is a further example of care ethics inside and outside the workplace. As one long-term social worker noted, "I see social activism as my outlet, my chance to be me and to be the social worker I thought I would be when I started this job years ago." Another social worker added, "It's only natural that we would get involved in activist work in this city, 'cause it sure never needed it more."

In another example of resisting neoliberalism's individualism and uncaring, social workers spent time sharing their understanding and critique of the problems they encountered. These shared workplace discussions built their collective analyses and nurtured shared, oppositional identities. For example, a long-term immigration settlement worker told us, "Everyone who works here is very progressive. We always talk about everything and learn from each other." Similarly, a veteran domestic violence counsellor noted: "When we talk to each other, we find a new sense of how we can be better than the cutbacks we are now having to impose."

Social workers also turned to existing organisations, such as unions representing social workers, to provide themselves with a collective formal voice in the workplace and to use as a vehicle of social change in and outside their workplaces. In these examples, care undergirds union work, and the unions formed the virtuous site in which care ethics could flourish.

When I have interviewed social workers about why they became active in their unions, they usually said that they wanted a place 'to have a voice' on the social issues that impact them and service users and communities. Many said that the ongoing rounds of restructuring that have accompanied NPM have meant that there are few, if any, opportunities left for them to participate in decision-making in their agencies. Thus, they felt compelled to find new venues, and the unions were waiting and willing.

Unionists wanted voice on issues such as capping caseloads to ensure that workers have enough time to work well with each service user, and providing mechanisms for social worker participation in decisions regarding service changes and agency restructuring so that they can add their 'insider' expertise to agency plans and practices. They also wanted social service agencies to hire more full-time, permanent workers who could really get to know service users and the agency and provide some much-needed continuity. These practices stand in contrast to current practices of hiring disposable, impermanent, part-time contract workers who have to scramble to get up to speed on policies, practices, work culture and service users, often just in time for their contract to end (Cunningham et al., 2016).

Social care workers have also developed new ways of running their local union bodies in order to create a more inclusive and friendly atmosphere for staff participation. For example, one social worker reported that her union always had more people wanting to run for office than positions available. The union decided to create a system of shadow executive positions and shadow stewards wherein two people could share one position, undertaking the roles and responsibilities jointly. In another example, a local initiated a 'buddy system' in which newer activists were paired with experienced ones to share skills, knowledge and companionship, drawing more people into union activities and resistance. In another union, a social worker noted that she and her fellow activists drew on their experience in social movements to create a union committee that 'on paper' filled all the hierarchical executive positions (to meet the parent union's constitution) but operated more or less as a non-hierarchical, consensus-based collective, thus providing opportunities for all members to have a voice and to influence priorities and activities (Baines, 2010).

Most union activists that I interviewed for my studies told me that the main task of the union was to build "an oasis for the members" or positive, supportive space for their co-workers where "they can be themselves." The goal of this space was to provide an alternative to the alienating and uncaring environment they felt they often encountered in their everyday work and in the larger uncaring society. One union president argued that it was very important to maintain a union spirit that was "creative, effective, and very positive; not negative and draggy". The union did this in order to provide a space to develop resistance and to, as the worker said, "take care of each other". In essence, this alternative space embodied an interweaving of virtue and care ethics. It created a space in which being caring and socially conscious were validated and mutually fostered, rather than marginalised and denigrated. In addition to being examples of care and virtue ethics in action, these alternate practices are what Briskin (2011) calls post-heroic politics, in which power is shared, caring relationships are encouraged, voice is rediscovered and authority is downplayed. They are also consistent with the social justice values of full social participation, equity and care.

Representing an additional space where care overlaps with social justice and empowerment to create a virtuous terrain, the Social Work Action Network (SWAN) is a recent initiative in the UK, New Zealand and Ireland where social workers have built grassroots organisations aimed at giving social workers a collective voice on social policy changes, organisational restructures and the neoliberal shift to a less socially caring and equitable society. SWAN works with unions and other social change organisations on issues such as social service funding cuts, poverty, racism, public inquiries and government commissions, domestic violence, child welfare, Indigenous issues, social housing and other social justice issues. It speaks up for social workers in workplaces where workers feel too vulnerable to defend their rights with employers and may not have a union readily available. SWAN also advocates for more socially just practices and protects those who have bent the rules or worked in ways that management sees as too radical. Helping people build and sustain a socially engaged social analysis and skills for activism, SWAN runs conferences to draw people together and nurture them to be brave and hard-working in the defence of social justice.

Conclusion

The preceding analysis shows that in the context of late neoliberalism, managerial models such as NPM make it difficult to practice a social ethic of care. The data presented confirm that despite these difficult conditions, an ethic of care can be seen to exist in the practices of many social workers who work beyond and around the terms of their employment. This ethic of care operates in highly unstable conditions as it is dependent on the commitment, resistance and goodwill of individual social workers rather than a system-wide commitment to social justice. Instead of social care and the social good, the social service system is shaped by neoliberal social policies emphasising austerity, cost saving and valorisation of the private market as the solution to anything human beings need or want. Professionalism operates in a similar manner, undermining social responses to social issues and emphasising personal distance and objectivity between social workers and service users rather than knowledge and practice–informed, social justice–engaged helping relationships that respect and foster the dignity and social inter-connectedness of care providers and recipients.

Rather than assume that the answers to the world's social problems will be found in the global north, which is a neo-colonial and first world supremacist assumption, Connell (2007) urges us to seek solutions in the struggles and knowledge of people in the global south. South Africa was a state that had to reinvent itself in 1994 after many, many years of legalised hate and deep, multifaceted oppression. Despite launching itself during the heyday of neoliberalism, South Africa built a society in which social policy recognises the need for social solidarity, fosters care ethics and attempts to build virtuous contexts where it is easier to behave in ways that advance fairness, community connection and equity. If a country that was steeped in apartheid, racism, hatred and colonialism can place care and social solidarity at the core of its social policy, so can we.

The analysis and data in this chapter confirm care is already central in the aspirations of many social workers and in their resistance practices. Even in the absence of social policies recognising social solidarity and care, social workers and social advocates still draw on the care that is already present in various overt and covert ways in the world of everyday social work. In union work, my data show that social workers also use their unions to build a supportive and caring context in which care/virtue ethics can flourish.

The commitment to care already available in social work workplaces can be nurtured as sources of resistance, replete with ethical social analysis and a promising foundation for building alternative ways of understanding and fostering social justice. Given how deeply neoliberalism has most government and social policy in its grip, our most effective resistance strategies will likely focus on the battle of ideas, or a struggle for the hearts, minds and energies of the population. Building ideas of social care and social solidarity can be deeply transgressive and transformational, challenging the status quo and suggesting more constructive ways for society to grow and flourish. As such, these ideas can contribute significantly to the major shift in thinking and acting that is required to transform social work and the larger society in socially just, caring and equitable ways.

Notes

1 In 1997, the first post-apartheid government, headed by Nelson Mandela, adopted a policy of social welfare that emphasised poverty reduction and social development (Patel, 2015). Cash transfers and community development projects quickly emerged to meet the widespread need for social services and support, generating an expansion of non-government social services (Gray and Mubangizi, 2010). Representing a blending of civil society, social movement and a growing third sector, participatory social and care services, South Africa's model of social work focused on the need to address serious long-term poverty and deprivation and the importance of building on existing community strengths and mobilisation.

   The 'global north' is a political concept denoting industrialised countries identified with European roots and connections (Connell, 2007).

2 This concept recognises gender as a set of social relations of patriarchy and oppression in which those who are perceived as 'male' have cultural, symbolic and material

dominance and privilege while those perceived as 'female' experience the opposite. The term female includes those perceived as women, many trans men, femme non-binary folks and non-women who experience misogyny.

References

Abbott, A. (2014) *The system of professions: An essay on the division of expert labour.* Chicago: University of Chicago Press.

Andersen, M. and Collins, P.H. (2015) *Race, class, & gender: An anthology.* Toronto: Nelson Education.

Armstrong, P. and Armstrong, H. (2004) Thinking it through: Women, work and caring in the new millennium. In: Amaratunga, C., Armstrong, P., Boscoe, M., Grant, K., Pedersen, A. and Wilson, K. (eds.) *Caring for/caring about: Women, home care and unpaid caregiving.* Aurora, ON: Garamond Press, pp. 5–44.

Baines, D. (2010) 'In a different way': Social unionism in the nonprofit social services: An Australian-Canadian comparison. *Journal of Labor Studies*, 35(4), pp. 480–502.

Baines, D. (2015) Nonprofit care work: Convergence under austerity? *Competition and Change.* June, 19, pp. 194–209.

Baines, D. (2017) *Doing anti-oppressive practice. Building transformative, politicized social work.* 3rd edition. Halifax, NS: Fernwood Books.

Bannerji, H. (2000) *The dark side of the nation: Essays on multiculturalism, nationalism and gender.* Toronto: Canadian Scholars' Press.

Briskin, L. (2011) Union renewal, postheroic leadership and women's organizing: Crossing discourses, reframing debates. *Labor Studies Journal.* December, 36, pp. 508–537.

Carey, M. and Green, L. (eds.). (2013) *Practical social work ethics: Complex dilemmas within applied social care.* Farnham, UK: Ashgate.

Carniol, B., Baines, D., Kennedy, B. and Sinclair, R. (2017) *Case critical.* Toronto: Between the Lines.

Connell, R. (2007) *Southern theory: The global dynamics of knowledge in social science.* Melbourne: Allen & Unwin.

Cunningham, I., Baines, D., Shields, J. and Lewchuk, W. (2016) Austerity, 'precarity' and the non-profit workforce – A comparative study of UK and Canada. *Journal of Industrial Relations*, 58(4), pp. 455–472.

Fraser, N. (2010) *Scales of justice.* New York: Columbia University Press.

Glucksmann, M. (2000) *Cottons and casuals. The gendered organization of labour in time and space.* Durham: Sociology Press.

Gray, M. (2010) Moral sources and emergent ethical theories in social work. *British Journal of Social Work*, 40(2), pp. 1794–1811.

Gray, M. and Mubangizi, B. (2010) Caught in the vortex: Can local government community development workers succeed in South Africa? *Community Development Journal*, 45(2), pp. 186–197.

Hankivsky, O. (2014) Rethinking care ethics: On the promise and potential of an intersectional analysis. *American Political Science Review*, 108(2), pp. 252–264.

Held, V. (1995) *Justice and care: Essential readings in feminist ethics.* Boulder, CO: Westview Press.

Lundy, C. (2011) *Social work, social justice & human rights: A structural approach to practice.* Toronto: University of Toronto Press.

Macdonald, K.M. (1985) Social closure and occupational registration. *Sociology*, 19(4), pp. 541–556.

Patel, L. (2015) *Social welfare and social development*, 2nd edition. Cape Town, SA: Oxford University Press.

Pease, B. (2011) Men in social work: Challenging or reproducing an unequal gender regime? *Affilia*, 26(4), pp. 406–418.

Peck, J. (2010) Zombie neoliberalism and the ambidextrous state. *Theoretical Criminology*, 14(1), pp. 104–110.

Robinson, K. (2014) Voices from the front line: Social work with refugees and asylum seekers in Australia and the UK. *British Journal of Social Work*, 44(6), pp. 1602–1620.

Rossi, U. (2013) On life as a fictitious commodity: Cities and the biopolitics of late neoliberalism. *International Journal of Urban and Regional Research*, 37(3), pp. 1067–1074.

Tronto, J. (2015) *Who cares? How to reshape a democratic politics*. Ithaca, NY: Cornell University Press.

van Heugten, K. (2011) Registration and social work education: A golden opportunity or a Trojan horse? *Journal of Social Work*, 11(2), pp. 174–190.

Weinberg, M. (2010) The social construction of social work ethics: Politicizing and broadening the lens. *Journal of Progressive Human Services*, 21, pp. 32–44.

3   Re-imagining social work's engagement with care

Intimations from a progressive and critically connected paradigm

Martyn Jones

Introduction

The time is right for social work to re-imagine its engagement with care. The contention is that this would be beneficial for social work but more importantly for the citizens and communities for whom social work exists. Both social work and care sit at the assembly of public and private issues and assume their form within political economies and social settlements. As these broader societal arrangements change and crystallise, opportunities emerge to re-position in ways that hold promise for realising underlying values and ambitions where people may live richer and fuller lives and environments may flourish. An important opening at present oscillates around care as a pressing and generative space for pursuing moral and political goals that could set a strident way ahead for social work as a future key contributor. But this means that social work's historically compromised relation to care must be confronted. A progressive and critically connected paradigm may offer some valuable prospects.

This chapter argues that through critically connecting social work with diverse constituencies beyond its professional borders, its engagement with care can be re-imagined to enhance its pursuit of a progressive agenda. In this approach, care becomes the contemporary major challenge for social work – and for respectful and equitable social relations at a time when the economy is ever dominant. The latter part of the chapter outlines how this positioning of social work through a critical ethics of care might take shape within a public university setting.

The imperative to re-imagine

Some might argue that a preoccupation with care can only result in social work moving backwards rather than forwards. Surely, care for the needy and vulnerable has been part of the legacy of social work – a legacy, moreover, that is fraught in so many ways. First, the very notion of care, it has long been argued, has required having people who are to be cared for, and hence has encouraged an imputation of need and vulnerability that has created and perpetuated patronising dependency (Healy, 2000). Second, aligning social work with care immediately evokes a counter-proposition that has relentlessly trapped the profession: that social work is in effect as much about control as about care (Dominelli, 2010). Isn't it time that social work shed itself of this tiresome dichotomy? A third problematic of care for social work is that the claim reveals the profession as hypocritical and self-deluded – ask those who have been subject to social work's complicity with institutional abuse, or the excesses of colonial paternalism, or simply a rigid bureaucracy that has denied them their unique personhood.

It is in part the vestiges of care in social work that has propelled an important critical tradition, one which has called into question any complacency by social work about its propensity to harm, oppress and discard (Ife, 1996; Fook, 2002; Allan, Briskman and Pease, 2009). By appropriating analyses of power and justice, this tradition has contributed to a social work that is not only tentative about its capacity to care but reticent to harness itself to a mission of caring. There is some irony, then, in an argument launched from a critical social work philosophy that advocates the merits of embracing a care agenda.

Promoting a positive case for care is immediately in jeopardy of committing an all too familiar error – a well-intentioned but fundamentally naïve and compromised pursuit of a discredited form of elitist professionalism. Perhaps it would be safer to abandon the discourse of care in any attempt to position social work as a politically astute profession attuned to the complex challenges of the contemporary world. Or perhaps, as Meagher and Parton (2004) first mooted over a decade ago, it offers a prime opportunity to confront misguided traditions and create fresh pathways.

The time to re-imagine

Social settlements about 'vulnerable populations', and human and ecological security, appear increasingly precarious. Deepening social and economic disparities, widening cultural divides, mass displacements, an endangered natural world and other compelling challenges all propel us towards moral and political questions in which care can be situated as an important and suitably disruptive consideration (Barnes, 2006; Robinson, 2011; Tronto, 2013). It can assist us to converse over these pressing and perplexing challenges, and re-connect us with the debates and with one another in promising ways (Sennett, 2003; Fine, 2007).

We are likely to enter such conversations from many different starting points. For example, within the Australian context, we are currently seeing the introduction of one of the largest social policy reforms in almost half a century. The National Disability Insurance Scheme (NDIS) is the response to fixing a system of disability services that was declared to be 'underfunded, unfair, fragmented and inefficient' (Productivity Commission, 2011, p. 2). The NDIS, informed by quasi-insurance principles, seeks to harness the power of the market to transform the choice and control exercised by people with disabilities. The funding going into the system is forecast to all but double (Productivity Commission, 2011, p. 3). While 'care' was originally part of the language of the NDIS, the word has since been ejected due to its enduring association with paternalistic welfare, which both policy designers and disability advocates have been determined to transcend.

Meanwhile, also in the Australian context, the attention of policy makers has been fixed for some time on the ageing population. Intergenerational reports have charted the underlying trends related to economic productivity and demands on health and human services (Australian Government, 2015). The 'longevity revolution' has focused minds on the social relations and contributions of older people (Kalache, 2013). Policy responses range from utilising the market mechanisms of 'consumer-directed care' (Australian Government, 2016) to the broader-based movement for 'age-friendly cities and communities' (Buffel, Phillipson and Scharf, 2012; Victorian Government, 2016). Indeed, across continents, elder care has been gaining in prominence (Harper and Hamblin, 2014).

Both these areas are illustrative of increasing interest in future workforce requirements and the organisation of labour in the field of social support and care (King and Meagher, 2009; Australian Institute of Health and Welfare, 2015). The high level of flexibility in staffing arrangements that is implied by consumer-driven services is in tension with safeguarding working conditions to underpin quality provision (MacDonald and Charlesworth, 2016). Minimum qualification levels and regulated credentialing for staff similarly conflicts with aspirations for the untrammelled exercise of choice by consumers (Leading Age Services Australia, 2016). Meanwhile, paucity of service provision intensifies demands on unpaid and family carers. The pressing need to address the situation of carers is at once being recognised but also rendered less visible, or even negated (Australian Institute of Health and Welfare, 2004; Kroger and Yeandle, 2014; Deloitte Access Economics, 2015).

None of these matters will come as any surprise to observers of human services. The forces and fault lines of neoliberalism are well-rehearsed (McDonald, 2006; Harvey, 2010; Baines and McBride, 2014; Duffy, 2016). What is it that an engagement with care can add, and what kind of re-imagining of this may be necessary if it is indeed to have any substantive value? The proposition, put simply, is that we would do well in social work to break from our accustomed ways of construing care – to look outwards and converse with contingent disciplines and perspectives that may assist us to refresh and reclaim a space in the care domain to the benefit of the citizens and communities for whom we exist and the ecologies in which we are embedded.

Building momentum through critical connection

Social work is not alone in its concern with addressing vulnerability, nor in appreciating that to do so through the medium of care risks perpetuating regressive as well as progressive resolutions. Not only is it timely for social work to re-engage with care, but it is also timely for social work to do so by re-engaging with critically allied thinkers, practitioners and community members to build momentum internally and externally. A critical ethics of care invites such connectivity, one through which the political and moral agendas of progressive social work can be further transformed.

As contemporary feminist thinkers on care remind us, much of its potency derives from elevating the relational side of life above the transactional, asserting that vulnerability is part of the human condition, and that it is interdependence rather than individualism that defines us (Sevenhuijsen, 1998; Kittay and Feder, 2002; Held, 2006). These features are not so much an echo of care as *caritas* ('love of humankind' and 'charity') but of care as that which makes us human and binds us together. In that sense, care has long stood in opposition to conceptions that accentuate a rational, impersonal and autonomous approach to life – and consequently, has mostly been sitting at the margins of influence in Western worlds.

The advent of neoliberalism, and its promotion of individualism and competition in a free market, has intensified the oppositional propensity that care represents. It is the fundamentally anti-individualistic tenets of care that recommend it as a vigorous site of resistance to be aligned with progressive politics pursuing cooperative social relations ahead of maximised self-interest (Tronto, 2015). Such a scenario quickly suggests that, wherever care is enacted within an antagonistic political economy, it will likely be at some considerable cost – and that these costs will not be borne equally. The de-stabilising effects of carers' movements emanate from their claims for recognition and rights but perhaps as much from being located at a crucial fissure in neoliberal regimes: their dependence on the subjugated labour of the unpaid – and poorly paid – 'care workforce', and their reliance on the associated, deeply troubled cultures (Fraser, 2016).

The differential costs and benefits of care, and the call for 'affective equality' (Lynch, Baker and Lyons, 2009), afford added depth to a concept of care that would otherwise reify its universality as an inevitable feature of the human condition. An appreciation of care as fused by numerous social divisions can be an antidote to romanticised notions that defy both analysis and the lived experience of care relationships. Care is indeed a contested space – contested by the multiple interests that shape and sustain it, and contested in the intimacies of daily life. And here too, there are intimations of the generative potential of care – for what it means to care, and to organise for care, remain steadfastly vexed questions.

Social work can usefully re-examine its own engagement with these questions and build a new internal momentum around them. But there are compelling reasons why, in doing so, social work would be well-served by also looking beyond its professional borders. First, social work's own conflicted history with care suggests it is vital to cultivate 'critical friends'. While social work may well have among its members many who can inject a critical ethic into the profession, the challenge is such that the contribution of friendly – and at times not so friendly – outsiders (whether professionals, scholars or community members) is vital to building new understandings and practices. Dispensing with paternalistic professionalism requires actively learning from the accumulated knowledge and wisdom that rests with others, crucially so when it comes to the oppressive legacy of care.

Second, a forward-looking concept of care is one that situates its presence (or absence) in a multitude of intersecting contexts. Care is present in the intricacies of interpersonal relationships and kinships. It is also embedded in neighbourhoods, facility design, built environments, transportation, businesses, technologies, aesthetics, natural spaces and landscapes – as well as in the structures and cultures of health, welfare, education and criminal justice (Kellehear, 2005; Goodley,

Hughes and Davis, 2012; Rowles and Bernard, 2013; Williams, 2016). There is a place for a contextual perspective on care that transcends social work's customary 'person-in-environment' and 'micro-meso-macro' heuristics.

Viewing care as inscribed in a multiplicity of intersecting contexts means calling into question a conventional depiction in which the individual is surrounded by ever larger circles of social actors, networks and institutions. Such depictions have informed recent models of care and usefully extended its salience beyond intimate care relationships (World Health Organization, 2007). But despite a certain descriptive appeal these eco-systemic frames offer, they continue to portray an essentially consensual social formation, presuming the smooth, unproblematic and predictable functioning of each part to the benefit of the whole (Houston, MacCallum, Steele and Byrne, 2016). Rather than bypass the place of conflict, domination and uncertainty in the play of multiple intersecting contexts, critical perspectives elicit their presence throughout (Baars, Dohmen, Grenier and Phillipson, 2013; Goodley, 2014).

By synthesising a progressive paradigm with a critically connected one, social work is propelled towards an outward engagement with the multiplicity of contexts through which care is structured and sustained. And in so doing, its contribution is consistently mediated by the equations of rights, recognition and redistribution. Concretely, this implies that a critically informed approach to, for example, the topical movement for 'integrated care' that stops short at 'health and social care' is misleadingly circumscribed. There are many more contextual fields at stake (Nies, 2014). Moreover, it emphasises in any engagement a 'logic of care' that presumes a situated relationality, a concern with the complex exercise of power in the social relations between multiple agents and structures, which stands in stark contrast to the predominant and instrumental market logics of 'choice and control' (Mol, 2008; Dombroski, Mckinnon, and Healy, 2016).

Third, a critically connected, progressive paradigm of care for social work means giving thought to what constitutes the 'social' of the profession. Two distinctive features can be considered. Importantly, the 'social' of social work speaks to the ways in which sense is made of people's lives and the issues confronting them. In appropriating critical social theories that accentuate the significance of structured power relations in understanding the fusion of private troubles and public issues, social work advances its practical action through a progressive program (Gray and Webb, 2013). Such theorising allows, for example, a critical spotlight to be put upon reference to 'social determinants' of health and wellbeing, which can counter a bio-medical orientation but still fall short of penetrating the iniquitous politics at play (Green and Labonte, 2008). Another feature of the social is, however, one that a critically connected paradigm does call into question, namely the perplexing matter of what is taken to be the social context with which the profession seeks to engage.

If in social work, our mindset is one of acting within – and making a claim for – a substantive and separate place that we construe as 'the social', we may overlook important opportunities to advance and transform our progressive agenda. Appending 'social' to issues or contexts is a necessary marker of the way we wish to understand and configure them, and a socially progressive lens is crucial to challenging structures and relationships that constrain and oppress. But in a critically connected paradigm it becomes vital that we do not use the idea of 'the social' to designate the substantive place in which social work is carried out. Rather, 'the social' is pervasive throughout the multiplicity of contexts that shape people's lives and experiences. This is because 'the social', from a progressive perspective, concerns the way inter-connected contexts are organised and structured to serve certain interests above others. And consequently, our mission as social workers is to be active throughout those multiple contexts, resisting and overturning places of injustice and disrespect wherever we may find them. This clearly extends far beyond acting within an aggregation of social and community services, and the allied health and human services to which they are linked. It also reaches into a view of society, community and the person as constituted through a highly complex array of structures, relationships and agents that traditional notions of 'social context' (imbued with the sense of a substantive but highly limited social place) fail to capture.

A final proposition for a critically connected, progressive paradigm is that it assures social work's engagement with care is one that does not re-assert problematic modernist concepts relating to 'the human' (Stengers, 2011). Moving away from prior conceptions of care means a readiness to abandon the tendency to subjugate all to the service of 'mankind' [*sic*]. A progressive understanding of care urges the promotion of radical understandings of interdependency (Whyte and Cuomo, 2017). This includes enabling people to set the conditions of their dependency (Sennett, 2003). But just as care invites us to re-cast how we understand 'the social', it also places a question mark over any assumption about the primacy of 'the human'. Through a critically connected paradigm, we can learn from disciplines that recognise the relevance and action of non-human agents (technologies, geographies, climate systems, built and creative design, landscapes and so on) in the formation of support and care environments (Lorimer, 2012). We can also be much more attentive to the political and ethical requirements of sustaining the wellbeing of natural orders in which the human is but one interdependent part.

These propositions suggest that social work adopt a critically connected, progressive paradigm of care, a paradigm that opens up fresh understandings and wider horizons in its aspirations for a more socially just world. There are hazards associated with such an orientation; particularly that it results in compromising or demoting the social analyses and associated action imperatives of progressive social work in the process of accruing critical friends and forging strong connections with others. However, if there is any merit to the propositions for a progressive paradigm that is critically connected, such challenges cannot be avoided. It may mean that special capabilities will need to be strengthened in forming co-operative relations that serve a progressive agenda. And robust, value-driven collaborative relationships require an investment of time and openness to reflexive learning that may be hard to realise (Jones, 2015). Yet not to embrace these challenges could ultimately leave the progressive social work agenda dis-connected and self-referential, conversing only with itself.

Generating a critically connected approach means active engagement across the complex myriad contexts that give shape to care. And with the presumption that care is embedded in the multiple and interacting domains of people's lives, organised and structured in ways that produce differential benefits and barriers, progressive social work becomes well placed to create new types of collaboration with transformative potential that span sectors, disciplines and community constituencies.

Re-imagining support and care: contributions from a public university

Noticing the advent of the NDIS, new agendas arising from an ageing population, and increasingly unjust demands on unpaid family carers, one public university situated in a large city in Australia decided to adopt 'support and care' as a new strategic priority. While this remains the working title, with support being the currently preferred terminology for many in the disability sector, it is not a phrase that immediately evokes a critically connected, progressive paradigm. Robust discussions centred on the prospects for advancing an initiative that sought to implement a critical ethic and radical agenda for 'support and care'. One advantage in naming the emergent field in this way has been the contrast to dominant categorisations that segregate populations or vulnerabilities or areas of service provision. As such, it has encouraged cross-disciplinary and cross-sectorial engagement – and, it is hoped, constructions of intersectionality that challenge exclusionary privilege and recognise complex identities (Ward, 2015).

Certain conditions were identified as necessary to the pursuit of a critical ethics of care within this public university. The initiative would need to be cross-disciplinary (university-wide) if it was to embrace the multiplicity of contexts through which support and care are produced. It would seek an integrated, cross-portfolio approach (synthesising research, learning and teaching, international and industry engagement). Its learning and teaching would be 'tertiary' (working across a full spectrum of academic qualifications from certificate to PhD). Its research would be both conceptual and applied. Most significantly, it would proceed in all its activities through values-based collaboration and partnership with external constituencies; it would utilise models of co-design, co-production and critical social innovation; and all its operations were to be designed for the ultimate benefit of the 'end user' (citizens and communities).

Developments to date have resulted in the establishment of a new joint entity between the university and the local peak body for the social service sector; the development of partnership agreements with sector organisations; the creation of cross-disciplinary networks of researchers; dedicated PhD scholarships; and the crafting of new vocational education programs for the care workforce. Cross-disciplinary activity has brought together those interested in, for example, critical approaches to human-centred uses of new technologies; locality-based community hubs for older people; dementia design studios; carer-friendly workplaces; living laboratories for innovations in mental health; and training for diversity in care relationships. Partnership agreements have been multi-purpose and relationship-based, with activity to be strongly driven by sector and community interests.

In forming these strategic relationships and specific collaborative projects, much time has been devoted to the orientation underpinning the work. Many from the sector – at executive and frontline levels – have been enthusiastic to join with an initiative that aspires to a progressive agenda. User and carer representatives have similarly been attracted to engage with work that seeks to counter neoliberal ideologies. Dialogue with research and teaching colleagues has ranged from building awareness around a critical ethics of care to strident debate about its pursuit within respective contexts. In one instance, differences could not be reconciled and the collaborative team amicably dissolved and re-assembled with alternate members. Throughout, there has been strong emphasis on the university as a resource that can assist capacity building in knowledge and learning for support and care, rather than presuming it has superior expertise in defining and pursuing a progressive agenda (Nowotny, 2003). While very much a work in progress, strategies and processes have been designed from the outset with a view to people with lived experience in the field of support and care having central influence.

The aspiration is towards not only new political and moral conceptions of support and care but new practices, and the initiative draws on an assumption that these practices are to be designed from the ground upwards through models of critical social innovation. While in many respects the social innovation movement is a capricious companion for progressive social work, it does harbour strands that can provide continuity with radical, emancipatory traditions while being future-oriented in its conception of social change processes and goals. Critical contributors to the movement emphasise its role in 'overcoming conservative forces' (Moulaert, MacCallum and Hillier, 2013, p. 16) and 'fostering inclusion and wellbeing through improving social relations and empowerment processes' (p. 17). Such models require a depth of critical reflexivity for the creation of new practices, conscious of the differential benefits to flow from any innovation. As such, the initiative seeks to draw on principles of co-design and co-production, with end users (community members) engaged centrally in agendas and processes for knowledge creation and learning (Alford, 2009; Social Care Institute of Excellence, 2012). The entitlement bestowed by 'lived experience' has been a constant theme (Beresford, 2013).

While a critical ethics of care, informed by a progressive and critically connected paradigm, has shaped the development of this initiative, the clear challenge is to ensure convergence between its espoused aims and its actual practices and policies. Undoubtedly, these challenges will intensify and many actions will fall short of aspirations. Yet, the opportunity remains an exciting and compelling one, and one to which critically minded social work can make an invaluable contribution.

Conclusion

There is a deep irony in proposing that social work energise its future through promoting and pursuing one of its most historically compromised legacies, that of care. A persuasive argument can be made for social work to divest itself of this tradition. However, rather than sidestep the legacy, by re-imagining its engagement from a progressive and critically connected paradigm social work can be a vital part of fundamentally changing care experiences and values.

Critical connectivity invites much more vigorous collaborative activity, predicated on an understanding of support and care that sees people's lives at the intersection of a complex multitude of contexts. A critical ethics of care requires 'working together' across borders that have traditionally segregated populations, vulnerabilities and services. Implied here is a politics of care that emphasises situated relationality and heightened interdependency. Such an orientation can infuse and enrich progressive social work. It stretches across human and non-human agents, and suggests we focus more on critical social analyses as a point of disciplinary strength for our engagement with care rather than on a substantive domain we seek to claim as distinctively and separately 'social'.

Intimations of how this approach to care might materialise have been considered in relation to an initiative being pursued at one public university in metropolitan Australia. While the greatest challenges are yet to come, early experiences have vindicated the generative potential of a critical ethics of care – not only for social work itself but for the diverse constituencies that a critically connected, progressive paradigm invites into a re-assertion of our life-affirming interdependencies.

References

Alford, J. (2009) *Engaging public sector clients: From service-delivery to co-production.* Basingstoke: Palgrave Macmillan.

Allan, J., Briskman, L. and Pease, B. (eds.) (2009) *Critical social work: Theories and practices for a socially just world.* Crows Nest: Allen & Unwin.

Australian Government. (2015) *2015 intergenerational report: Australia in 2055.* Canberra.

Australian Government. (2016) *Aged care reform.* Department of Health [online]. Available from: https://agedcare.health.gov.au/aged-care-reform [Accessed 4 January 2017].

Australian Institute of Health and Welfare. (2004) *Carers in Australia: Assisting frail older people and people with a disability.* Canberra: AIHW.

Australian Institute of Health and Welfare. (2015) *Australia's welfare 2015.* Australia's welfare series no. 12. Cat. no. AUS 189. Canberra: AIHW.

Baars, J., Dohmen, J., Grenier, A. and Phillipson, C. (eds.) (2013) *Ageing, meaning and social structure: Connecting critical and humanist gerontology.* Bristol: Policy Press.

Baines, D. and McBride, S. (eds.) (2014) *Orchestrating austerity: Impacts and resistance.* Halifax, NS: Fernwood.

Barnes, M. (2006) *Caring and social justice.* Basingstoke: Palgrave.

Beresford, P. (2013) *Beyond the usual suspects: Towards inclusive user involvement.* London: Shaping Our Lives.

Buffel, T., Phillipson, C. and Scharf, T. (2012) Ageing in urban environments: Developing 'age-friendly' cities. *Critical Social Policy*, 32, pp. 597–617.

Deloitte Access Economics. (2015) *The economic value of informal care in Australia in 2015.* Deakin, ACT: Carers Australia.

Dombroski, K., Mckinnon, K. and Healy, S. (2016) Beyond the birth wars: Diverse assemblages of care. *New Zealand Geographer*, 72, pp. 230–239.

Dominelli, L. (2010) *Social work in a globalising world.* Cambridge: Polity Press.

Duffy, S. (2016) *Love and welfare*. Sheffield: Centre for Welfare Reform.

Fine, M. D. (2007) *A caring society? Care and the dilemmas of human service in the 21st century*. Basingstoke: Palgrave Macmillan.

Fook, J. (2002) *Social work: Critical theory and practice*. London: Sage.

Fraser, N. (2016) Contradictions of capital and care. *New Left Review*, 100(July–August), pp. 99–117.

Goodley, D. (2014) *Dis/ability studies: Theorising disablism and abilism*. London: Routledge.

Goodley, D., Hughes, B. and Davis, L. (eds.) (2012) *Disability and social theory: New developments and directions*. Basingstoke: Palgrave Macmillan.

Gray, M. and Webb, S. A. (eds.) (2013) *The new politics of social work*. London: Palgrave Macmillan.

Green, J. and Labonte, R. (eds.) (2008) *Critical perspectives in public health*. London: Routledge.

Harper, S. and Hamblin, K. (eds.) (2014) *International handbook on ageing and public policy*. Cheltenham: Edward Elgar.

Harvey, D. (2010) *The enigma of capital and the crises of capitalism*. New York: Oxford University Press.

Healy, K. (2000) *Social work practices: Contemporary perspectives on change*. London: Sage.

Held, V. (2006) *The ethics of care: Personal, political, global*. New York: Oxford University Press.

Houston, D., MacCallum, D., Steele, W. and Byrne, J. (2016) Climate cosmopolitics and the possibilities for urban planning. *Nature and Culture*, 11(3), pp. 259–277.

Ife, J. (1996) *Rethinking social work: Towards critical practice*. Melbourne: Longman.

Jones, M. (2015) Practice research collaboration in social work: Reflexive knowledge exchange as generative metaphor. *Research on Social Work Practice*, 25(6), pp. 688–696.

Kalache, A. (2013) *The longevity revolution: Creating a society for all ages*. Adelaide: Government of South Australia.

Kellehear, A. (2005) *Compassionate cities: Public health and end-of-life care*. London: Routledge.

King, D. and Meagher, G. (eds.) (2009) *Paid care in Australia: Politics, profits and practices*. Sydney: Sydney University Press.

Kittay, E. F. and Feder, E. K. (eds.) (2002) *The subject of care: Feminist perspectives on dependency*. Lanham, MD: Rowman & Littlefield.

Kroger, T. and Yeandle, S. (eds.) (2014) *Combing paid work and family care: Policies and experiences in international perspective*. Bristol: Policy Press.

Leading Age Services Australia. (2016) *New requirements for our future aged care workforce*. Leading Age Services Australia [online]. Available from: www.lasa.asn.au/news-and-media/media-releases/new-requirements-future-aged-care-workforce [Accessed 4 January 2017].

Lorimer, J. (2012) Multinatural geographies for the Anthropocene. *Progress in Human Geography*, 36(5), pp. 593–612.

Lynch, K., Baker, J. and Lyons, M. (2009) *Affective equality: Love, care and injustice*. Basingstoke: Palgrave Macmillan.

MacDonald, F. and Charlesworth, S. (2016) Cash for care under the NDIS: Shaping care workers' working conditions? *Journal of Industrial Relations*, 58, pp. 627–646.

McDonald, C. (2006) *Challenging social work: The institutional context of practice*. Basingstoke: Palgrave Macmillan.

Meagher, G. and Parton, N. (2004) Modernising social work and the ethics of care. *Social Work & Society*, 2(1), pp. 10–27.

Mol, A. (2008) *The logic of care: Health and the problem of patient choice*. Abingdon: Routledge.

Moulaert, F., MacCallum, D. and Hillier, J. (2013) Social innovation: Precept, concept, theory and practice. In: Moulaert, F., MacCallum, D., Mehmood, A. and Hamdouch, A. (eds.) *The international handbook on social innovation: Collective action, social learning and transdisciplinary research*. Cheltenham: Edward Elgar, pp. 13–24.

Nies, H. (2014) Communities as co-producers in integrated care. *International Journal of Integrated Care*, 14(April–June), pp. 1–4.

Nowotny, H. (2003) Democratising expertise and socially robust knowledge. *Science and Public Policy*, 30(3), pp. 151–156.

Productivity Commission. (2011) *Disability care and support*. Report no. 54. Canberra.

Robinson, F. (2011) *The ethics of care: A feminist approach to human security*. Philadelphia: Temple University Press.

Rowles, G. D. and Bernard, M. (eds.) (2013) *Environmental gerontology: Making meaningful places in old age*. New York: Springer.

Sennett, R. (2003) *Respect: The formation of character in an age of inequality*. London: Penguin Books.

Sevenhuijsen, S. (1998) *Citizenship and the ethics of care: Feminist considerations on justice, morality and politics*. Abingdon: Routledge.

Social Care Institute of Excellence. (2012) *Towards co-production: Taking participation to the next level*. SCIE Report 53. London: SCIE.

Stengers, I. (2011) *Cosmopolitics II*. Translated by Robert Bononno. Minneapolis: University of Minnesota Press.

Tronto, J. C. (2013) *Caring democracy: Markets, equity and justice*. New York: New York University Press.

Tronto, J. C. (2015) *Who cares? How to reshape a democratic politics*. Ithaca, NY: Cornell University Press.

Victorian Government. (2016) *More support for Victorian seniors*. Premier of Victoria [online]. Available from: www.premier.vic.gov.au/more-support-for-victorian-seniors [Accessed 4 January 2017].

Ward, N. (2015) Care ethics, intersectionality and poststructuralism. In: Barnes, M., Brannelly, T., Ward, L. and Ward, N. (eds.) *Ethics of care: Critical advances in international perspectives*. Bristol: Policy Press, pp. 57–68.

Whyte, K. P. and Cuomo, C. (2017, *forthcoming*) Ethics of caring in environmental ethics: Indigenous and feminist philosophies. In: Gardiner, S. M. and Thompson, A. (eds.) *The Oxford handbook of environmental ethics*. Oxford: Oxford University Press.

Williams, C. (ed.) (2016) *Social work and the city: Urban themes in 21st-century social work*. London: Palgrave Macmillan.

World Health Organization. (2007) *Global age-friendly cities: A guide*. Geneva: WHO Press.

4 'Duty *of* care' or 'duty *to* care'

The responsibilisation of social work

Anthea Vreugdenhil

Introduction

Sometimes the smallest of things can lead to big questions. A passing comment from a colleague about social work being one of the 'caring professions' led to a conversation about the meaning of care in social work. Turning to the Code of Ethics (Australian Association of Social Workers [AASW], 2010) for guidance, I discovered that care (or caring) is only mentioned eight times in the 41-page document, with another five mentions of 'careful'. This surprised me, as I thought care would feature more highly given that a key purpose of the Code is to "identify the values and ethics which underpin ethical social work practice" (AASW, 2010, p. 10). The first mention of care in the Code describes how social work "provides humane service, mindful of fulfilling duty of care, and duty to avoid doing harm to others" (AASW, 2010, p. 12). This linking of 'care' with 'duty' was repeated throughout the Code with a focus on 'duty of care' or 'taking due care'. This seemed to suggest that care, beyond a narrow sense of duty, might have little place in contemporary social work. I was not sure what to make of this, but I knew that it warranted further investigation. This chapter is the result and explores the interplay between the growing regulation of the social work profession and the meaning and practice of care in social work.

As a starting point, social work is situated within the neoliberal context, and I argue that the hallmarks of neoliberalism have marked social work as an increasingly regulated profession, with competency-based practice standards and individualistic codes of ethics. I then extend my initial analysis of the Australian Social Work Code of Ethics to examine the location and meaning of care in five other social work codes of ethics (Aotearoa New Zealand, Britain, Canada, the United States and the International Federation). Across all of the Codes, care is rarely mentioned and in the few instances where care does make an appearance, it is predominantly in terms of a social worker's 'duty of care' or 'due care'.

I argue that this coupling of care and duty fits well with the 'responsibilisation' agenda of neoliberalism, where responsibility for care and its consequences are placed squarely with the individual in isolation from the political context (McLeod, 2017). This can be dangerous, as it shifts responsibility for the impact of issues such as inadequate resourcing from the institutional context to the individual social worker (and client). It also ignores how these responsibilities, and their associated privileges and penalties, are unequally allocated to various individuals and groups.

In contrast, the moral element of 'responsibility' in Tronto's ethic of care goes beyond individual duty or obligation to foreground the relational and political aspects of caring as a collective responsibility (Tronto, 2013). This offers the opportunity to consider how social work might be transformed through practices that move beyond the regulated individual to more emancipatory or collectivist approaches. From the smallest of beginnings, this chapter concludes with a 'big question': has social work lost its way, and is it too late for a duty *to* care, rather than a duty *of* care, in social work?

Regulating social work

The impact of neoliberalism on social work has been well-documented (for example, Banks, 2011; Wallace and Pease, 2011; Reisch, 2013). Williams and Briskman (2015, p. 4) describe how a combination of market principles, government cutbacks and ideological shifts "conspire to derail an ethical practice, demoralise workers, shake the very foundations of social work and restructure the relationships of welfare". Moreover, these impacts have intensified over recent years as conditions of austerity result in deep cuts to welfare (Baines and van den Broek, 2017). In particular, New Public Management (NPM) is transforming social work practice, with the marketisation of welfare services, a focus on outcome measurement and the increasing regulation of welfare professionals (Banks, 2011). NPM, coupled with welfare cuts and sensationalised cases of child abuse in many countries, has resulted in increased calls for professional accountability and, in turn, for the increased regulation of the social work profession (for example, the Munro report [2011] in the UK). As a result, in recent years we have seen a trend towards the government regulation of social work and a decline in professional self-regulation (Healy, 2016).

How the social work profession is regulated varies from country to country (Chenoweth and McAuliffe, 2015). For example, Australia does not have a system of social worker registration, but in the US there has long been a system of licensing and certification (Chenoweth and McAuliffe, 2015). The UK has social worker registration but the scope and process has changed markedly in recent years (Furness, 2015; McLaughlin, Leigh and Worsley, 2016). Aotearoa New Zealand has a social workers registration board although the associated 2003 Act is currently under review. Whatever the system, the regulation of the social work profession is contested. For some, the notion of professionalisation is, in itself, antithetical to "the emancipatory values and vision of social work" (Morley et al., 2014, p. 99). For others, there are conflicting views about how social work should be regulated: through professional self-regulation or through external processes (Healy, 2016). Either way, the focus on the conduct of individual social workers raises concerns that workers are being held individually accountable for the consequences of systemic problems such as lack of resourcing (McLaughlin et al., 2016).

Professional codes of ethics are implicated in the increasing regulation of social work, with Banks (2011) observing an expansion in the size of social work codes of ethics over recent decades, particularly in the areas of standards and rules governing the professional conduct of individual social workers. As such, codes of ethics provide a good opportunity to explore the place of care as a value and practice in social work in the context of a regulated profession.

Locating care in social work

I analysed the location and meaning of care in the Codes of Ethics from six social work associations: Aotearoa New Zealand Association of Social Workers (ANZASW, 2007); Australia Association of Social Workers (AASW, 2010); British Association of Social Workers (BASW, 2012); Canadian Association of Social Workers (CASW, 2005); National Association of Social Workers, United States (NASW, 2008) and the International Federation of Social Workers (IFSW, 2012). These Codes were selected as they reflected a range of countries which could be considered as broadly representing Western social work and were written in the English language. While Codes of Ethics are very much a Western construct, it is acknowledged that these selection criteria exclude social work voices from the South and from the non-English speaking West. In a content analysis of the six Codes, I counted the occurrences of the words 'care', 'caring' and 'careful', excluding front matter (such as title pages and table of contents) and also end matter (such as reference lists and appendices). I then analysed the in-text context of these 'care' words to identify how care was positioned and used in the Codes.

Across all of these Codes, care is rarely mentioned. In a total of 110 pages of text across all of the six codes, there were just 21 mentions of 'care', 10 mentions of 'careful' and one of 'caring'. As Table 4.1 shows, the frequency of mentions varied markedly between the Codes with Australia having the most (13) and Britain having the least (1). In one way, perhaps the absence of care in these Codes is not so surprising. Care has not had a good reputation among many social workers (and their clients), with Meagher and Parton (2004) attributing the lack of attention to 'care' in social work more generally to the 'dark side' of care, where social workers have been implicated in the oppression and ill-treatment of others in the name of care.

I identified three main categories of the meaning of care in the Codes: quality of caring relations; duty of care or due care; and standard of care. Of the 32 mentions of care across the Codes, only five were in relation to the ethical or moral quality of our relationships with others. This was in terms of values and principles such as compassion, respect and empathy, as the following quote exemplifies:

> Social workers should act in relation to the people using their services with compassion, empathy and care.
>
> (ANZASW, 2007, p. 19; and IFSW, 2012, section 5)

The other 27 mentions of 'care', 'caring' or being 'careful' were in relation to duty and standards. The majority of these were in the context of a social worker's duty of care in acting in ways that avoid harming others. For example (my italics):

Table 4.1 Frequency of instances of 'care' in social work codes of ethics

Code of Ethics	Number of pages*	Categories of 'care'			Total instances
		Quality of caring relations	Duty of care/due care	Standard of care	
Aotearoa New Zealand Association of Social Workers (2007)	25	1	3	0	4
Australian Association of Social Workers (2010)	41	1	12	0	13
British Association of Social Workers (2012)	15	1	0	0	1
Canadian Association of Social Workers (2005)	12	0	3	2	5
National Association of Social Workers (USA, 2008)	14	1	6	0	7
International Federation of Social Workers (2012)	3	1	1	0	2
Total	110	5	25	2	32

*Excluding front matter, references and appendices.

The social work profession: provides humane service, mindful of fulfilling *duty of care*, and duty to avoid doing harm to others.

(AASW, 2010, p. 12)

Social workers demonstrate *due care* for client's interests and safety by limiting professional practice to areas of demonstrated competence.

(CASW, 2005, p. 8)

Social workers have a *duty* to take necessary steps to *care* for themselves professionally and personally in the workplace and in society, in order to ensure that they are able to provide appropriate services.

(IFSW, 2012, section 5; and ANZASW, 2007, p. 19)

Other instances of the meaning of duty or due care related to more specific concerns such as record keeping and research (my italics):

Social workers will take *due care* to protect the confidences of others when providing clients access to records.

(AASW, 2010, p. 30)

Social workers engaged in evaluation or research should *carefully* consider possible consequences and should follow guidelines developed for the protection of evaluation and research participants.

(NASW, 2008, section 3.06)

Overall, the meaning of care as duty was dominant across the codes. Duty of care has a particular meaning in social work and is understood as a legal obligation which requires a social worker to ensure that in their practice, they provide a reasonable standard of care that does not harm others (McAuliffe, 2014). Such ideas about duty and obligation are founded in deontological ethics, which are based in a logic where professionals such as social workers are duty-bound to follow their code of ethics and comply with practice standards (Gray, 2010). Through a focus on the individual social worker making the right (or wrong) decisions and taking the correct (or incorrect) actions, attention is shifted away from the responsibilities of employing organisations and governments (Liebenberg, Ungar and Ikeda, 2015). But this focus on individual obligations is not just about who is responsible: it is also about who to blame if things go wrong (Weinberg and Campbell, 2014). Extending this line of argument, the coupling of care and duty in social work codes of ethics can be understood in terms of the 'responsibilisation' agenda of neoliberalism.

The 'responsibilisation' agenda

In critiquing responsibility, I am not arguing that the individual has no personal responsibility: of course we all have some level of responsibility for our actions and their consequences. But the balance of responsibility has shifted markedly towards the individual over the last few decades. In the context of neoliberalism, this has been described as the 'responsibilisation' agenda, with the consequent reshaping of social and political relations (McLeod, 2017). In terms of social welfare, responsibilisation has typically involved a shift away from state-led responsibility for collective social provisions (through the welfare state) to individual responsibility for securing the resources required to achieve and maintain wellbeing at even the most basic level (Midgley, 2016). Here, each of us is responsible for meeting our own needs and if we cannot do that, then it is because we did not work hard (or smart) enough.

The question of how responsibility is allocated, and to whom, is of central concern to 'ethics of care' writers such as Tronto (2013), who argues that these questions are at the very core of political and social life. Tronto (2013) describes how the thinking underpinning the allocation of caring responsibilities in society has changed over time, from domesticity, institutionalisation and professionalisation to the current emphasis on the market and self-responsibility. This underlying thinking can make the allocation of responsibility appear natural rather than political. This can be dangerous, as it means that the consequences of responsibilisation also appear natural, and those who fail to meet the requirements of self-responsibility become marginalised and are subject to "coercive techniques and interventions such as shaming, conditionality and sanction to change their behaviour" (Midgley, 2016, p. 613).

An ethic of care approach also highlights that not everyone shares equally in the process of responsibilisation or its consequences. Responsibilisation advantages or disadvantages, depending on one's location at the intersections of race, gender, class and so forth. As McLeod (2017, p. 45) describes, this process works to "exacerbate relations of privilege and poverty; favour cultures that prize autonomy as a virtue; have gendered and classed consequences; and contribute overall to insinuating the divisiveness of neoliberalism into the pores and minutiae of everyday existence". The process not only ties responsibilities to some individuals, it also gives a 'pass out' to others which frees them from those very same responsibilities (because they are doing other things which are seen as more important). Tronto terms this "privileged irresponsibility" and argues that neoliberalism functions as an "irresponsibility machine" (Tronto, 2013, p. 61). The next section explores how this "machine" works not only at the individual level but also at the organisational and institutional levels.

Responsibilising social work

In addition to 'responsibilising' individuals, the neoliberal process of responsibilisation also 'irresponsibilises' governments and other institutions (Liebenberg et al., 2015). This is particularly the case in social work, where discourses of responsibility, independence and choice work to obscure the political and economic roots of social problems (Ferguson and Lavalette, 2013). This has enabled a shift of responsibility for social welfare from the state to the individual. Often social workers are complicit in this shift, readily adopting policies and practices based in rhetoric such as mutual obligation and self-reliance (Liebenberg et al., 2015). For clients, this can have serious consequences, including punitive policies such as welfare-to-work schemes and reduced services or quality of services as a result of cutbacks. This shift has also meant the rise of a culture of blame where those in receipt of government income support (now termed 'welfare dependent') are stigmatised for conditions over which they have no control (Stanford and Taylor, 2013).

This shift of responsibility from the state to the individual also impacts social work practitioners, with much of the responsibility for achieving outcomes with clients (and the consequences of not achieving these) being allocated to individual workers who have little power over the provision of the resources they need. The decisions about resourcing and the organisation of work are largely located with employers and government, with social workers often having little say in these processes (Reisch and Jani, 2012). This impacts on workers' professional autonomy which, in some settings, enables them to work flexibly in the best interests of clients (Harlow, Berg, Barry and Chandler, 2012). At times, social workers shift the consequences of their own responsibilisation to clients, where through "a form of *indirect coercion* or quiet neglect, workers act, often reluctantly, as conduits of the austere state, providing variable care to increasingly frustrated and desperate service users" (Baines and van den Broek, 2016, p. 137).

Increasingly, social workers are performing unpaid work to compensate for having insufficient resources to adequately meet their allocated responsibilities. In a study of UK care providers, Baines and van den Broek (2017) describe widespread practices of unpaid care work such as working through breaks, taking work home and starting earlier or finishing later. Interestingly, many of these workers did not frame this as exploitation but as a way of 'pushing back' against the system. Irrespective of how these practices are framed, the result is often worker stress and burnout (Abramovitz and Zelnick, 2015). And the impacts are felt at the organisational level too, with high rates of staff turnover and difficulties in recruitment (Harlow et al., 2012). Professional supervision and self-care are often proffered as antidotes to these problems, but these too can be understood as part of the responsibilisation agenda, where the responsibility for coping with unreasonable workloads and demands becomes located solely within the individual social worker.

Within social work, responsibilities and their consequences are not allocated to all social workers equally. As Tronto (2013) notes in relation to care more generally, the allocation process is marked by cultural and social formations such as gender, race and class. For social work, the role of gender in particular has been well-documented and it is clear that there is male privilege at work here (Pease, 2011). For example, while the majority of social workers are women, men have benefitted from assumed leadership and technical superiority through rapid progression to management positions or to positions away from the frontline (Baines, Charlesworth and Cunningham, 2015). In addition, female social workers face more precarious work conditions, as they are more likely than men to be employed on a part-time or contract basis (Weinberg, 2010, p. 38). These gendered effects are not allocated equally across all women or all men in social work and, to date, there has been little research exploring the experience of social workers from an intersectional perspective.

Redoing responsibility in social work

In this section, I borrow from Conradi's idea of 'redoing care' (2015) to consider how the concept and practice of responsibility in social work might be reconfigured through Tronto's political ethic of care. In contrast to the neoliberal notion of individualised responsibility, Tronto (2013) argues that responsibility is not located in the individual but is relational, existing in the relationships between people. Responsibility goes beyond formal duty or obligation and involves a willingness to respond to needs and to then allocate responsibility for meeting those needs in a concrete way. This relational view of responsibility fits well with the values and principles of social work, a profession based on the primacy of relationships, respect for others and working in partnership.

There is a gap, however, between this relational view of responsibility and the highly individualised practice of responsibility described so far in this chapter. To address this, we need to find ways to bring the relational back to the forefront of social work practice. Relationships with clients are fundamental to this, in developing meaningful partnerships to identify unmet needs and develop ways to address them. Having the resources to do this can be challenging, and social workers are often overloaded with heavy caseloads which leave little time or energy to create common ground for developing collective approaches (Bertotti, 2016).

Innovative approaches are being developed, however. For example, Calder (2015) reports on social care workshops involving care receivers, caregivers, social care practitioners and academics, with the aim of achieving genuine participation by all in the process of deliberating on care needs. These workshops resulted in contestation rather than 'clean' solutions, but this was viewed as an indicator of real participation rather than as a drawback.

The development of collective processes to ensure that all are included in decision-making about the responsibility for care is central to Tronto's ethic of care (2013). In many instances, social workers are the gatekeepers for the inclusion of clients in these decision-making processes but, as Visse, Abma and Widdershoven (2015) suggest, we first need to work on our own processes within social work before we can meaningfully include others. One strategy is to create opportunities and spaces for transformative dialogue in our workplaces and beyond (Ward and Barnes, 2016). But this needs to go further than dialogue: collective action is also needed. It is not clear how best to go about this, and it seems that there are no easy answers. One avenue might be through existing social work professional associations, such as the AASW and BASW among others. While such associations have been criticised as being exclusive in their quest for professional status, they do provide opportunities for networking though practice groups and events. They also have an active role in advocating and lobbying on social justice issues and, in Australia, for example, the AASW has had a much more visible presence in this area in recent years.

Other kinds of collective social work action are also possible. The UK Social Work Action Network (SWAN) has now been replicated in many other countries and is a social action organisation which includes service users, carers, social workers and other social care practitioners. We must be careful, however, in the way responsibility is allocated in any collective process. For example, while men constitute fewer than 25 percent of social workers in the UK (General Social Care Council figures, cited in the *Guardian*, 25 July 2014), they make up 60 percent of the members of the 2015/16 National Steering Committee of UK SWAN (from SWAN website). Care needs to be taken that patterns of inequality are challenged and not simply reproduced: clearly not a straightforward task, even in highly reflective and critical contexts. Moreover, while this example highlights gender inequality, the experience and consequences of inequality will vary according to one's location at the intersections of multiple axes of privilege and oppression including gender, race, class and sexuality (Hankivsky, 2014).

Has social work lost its way?

In this chapter, I have argued that the responsibilisation agenda of neoliberalism is deeply problematic for social work. Using the example of 'duty of care', I explored how the coupling of care with duty in social work practice reflects and reinforces a highly individualised form of responsibility with often harmful consequences for social workers and their clients. I suggested that critical engagement with the concept of responsibility through a political ethics of care offers some ways forward for the profession which are relational, political and collective. Building on this, I argue here that this presents an opportunity for an alternate conceptualisation of the relationship between duty and care in social work: as 'duty *to* care' rather than 'duty *of* care'. This is not to say that social workers do not care, but the rhetoric of discourses such as 'duty *of* care' disempowers social workers and coerces them into accepting responsibilities that lie elsewhere.

Fenton (2016, p. 209) suggests, perhaps it is time for social workers to do "what they think is 'the right thing' as opposed to simply 'doing things right' (following procedures or instructions)". This is now urgent in the context of growing criticism of Western social work as it struggles to respond to the demands of neoliberalism in conditions of austerity. Reisch (2013) comments on this when he observes that while the profession often talks of empowerment, it has become increasingly apolitical, and cites as evidence recent responses to the implementation of neoliberal policies across the welfare, justice and health sectors. Williams and Briskman (2015) go further, arguing that social work is now too comfortable, and challenge us to be outraged and take action. I agree and suggest that it is time to 'dare to care' (Adler, 2011, cited in Briskman, 2013, p. 62), through the redoing of duty and responsibility in social work.

To conclude, I pose the question: has social work lost its way, and is it too late for a duty *to* care, rather than a duty *of* care, in social work? I am not the first to ask if social work has lost its way, and in some respects this echoes the 'care versus control' tension that has been ever-present in social work (Baines and van den Broek, 2017). So, while we may not yet be able to answer that question, I am hopeful that a duty *to* care, rather than a duty *of* care, might provide some direction for the future of social work.

References

Abramovitz, M. and Zelnick, J. (2015) Privatization in the human services: Implications for direct practice. *Clinical Social Work Journal*, 43, pp. 283–293.

Adler, N. (2011) Cultural sources of newness. Address to the 25th anniversary of the IEDC-Bled School of Management, Slovenia, 14 October. Available from: www.cultural sourcesofnewness.net/articles/nancy-adler-honors-business-school-that-integrates-arts-iedc-bled-school-of-management/

Aotearoa New Zealand Association of Social Workers (ANZASW). (2007) *Code of ethics*. ANZASW. Available from: http://anzasw.nz/wp-content/uploads/Code-of-Ethics.pdf.

Australian Association of Social Workers (AASW). (2010) *Code of ethics*. Canberra: Australian Association of Social Workers. Available from: www.aasw.asn.au/document/item/1201.

Baines, D., Charlesworth, S. and Cunningham, I. (2015) Changing care? Men and managerialism in the nonprofit sector. *Journal of Social Work*, 15(5), pp. 459–478.

Baines, D. and van den Broek, D. (2017) Coercive care: Control and coercion in the restructured care workplace. *British Journal of Social Work*, 47, pp. 125–142.

Banks, S. (2011) Ethics in an age of austerity: Social work and the evolving new public management. *Journal of Social Intervention: Theory and Practice*, 20(2), pp. 5–23.

Bertotti, T. (2016) Resources reduction and welfare changes: Tensions between social workers and organisations. The Italian case in child protection services. *European Journal of Social Work*, 19(6), pp. 963–976.

Briskman, L. (2013) Courageous ethnographers or agents of the state: Challenges for social work. *Critical and Radical Social Work*, 1(1), pp. 51–66.

British Association of Social Workers (BASW). (2012) *The code of ethics for social work*. BASW. Available from: http://cdn.basw.co.uk/upload/basw_112315-7.pdf.

Calder, G. (2015) Caring about deliberation, deliberating about care. *Ethics and Social Welfare*, 9(2), pp. 130–146.

Canadian Association of Social Workers (CASW). (2005) *Code of ethics*. CASW. Available from: www.casw-acts.ca/en/what-social-work/casw-code-ethics.

Chenoweth, L. and McAuliffe, D. (2015) *The road to human service practice*. 4th edition. South Melbourne: Cengage Learning Australia.

Conradi, E. (2015) Redoing care: Societal transformation through critical practice. *Ethics and Social Welfare*, 9(2), pp. 113–129.

Fenton, J. (2016) Organisational professionalism and moral courage: Contradictory concepts in social work? *Critical and Radical Social Work*, 4(2), pp. 199–215.

Ferguson, I. and Lavalette, M. (2013) Crisis, austerity and the future(s) of social work in the UK. *Critical and Radical Social Work*, 1(1), pp. 95–110.

Furness, S. (2015) Conduct matters: The regulation of social work in England. *British Journal of Social Work*, 45, pp. 861–879.

Gray, M. (2010) Moral sources and emergent ethical theories in social work. *British Journal of Social Work*, 40, pp. 1794–1811.

Hankivsky, O. (2014) Rethinking care ethics: On the promise and potential of an intersectional analysis. *American Political Science Review*, 108(2), pp. 252–263.

Harlow, E., Berg, E., Barry, J. and Chandler, J. (2012) Neoliberalism, managerialism and the reconfiguring of social work in Sweden and the United Kingdom. *Organization*, 20(4), pp. 534–550.

Healy, K. (2016) 2015 Norma Parker address: Being a self-regulating profession in the 21st century: Problems and prospects. *Australian Social Work*, 69(1), pp. 1–10.

International Federation of Social Workers (IFSW). (2012) *Statement of ethical principles*. Available from: http://ifsw.org/policies/statement-of-ethical-principles/.

Liebenberg, L., Ungar, M. and Ikeda, J. (2015) Neo-liberalism and responsibilisation in the discourse of social service workers. *British Journal of Social Work*, 45(3), pp. 1006–1021.

McAuliffe, D. (2014) *Interprofessional ethics: Collaboration in the social, health and human services*. Victoria, Australia: Cambridge University Press.

McLaughlin, K., Leigh, J. and Worsley, A. (2016) The state of regulation in England: From the General Social Care Council to the Health and Care Professions Council. *British Journal of Social Work*, 46(4), pp. 825–838.

McLeod, J. (2017) Reframing responsibility in an era of responsibilisation: Education, feminist ethics and an 'idiom of care'. *Discourse: Studies in the Cultural Politics of Education*, 38(1), pp. 43–56.

Meagher, G. and Parton, N. (2004) Modernising social work and the ethics of care. *Social Work and Society*, 2(1), pp. 10–27.

Midgley, J. (2016) Perspectives on responsibility in practice as revealed through food provisioning offers for rough sleepers. *Critical Social Policy*, 36(4), pp. 610–629.

Morley, C. and Macfarlane, S. (2014) Critical social work as ethical social work: Using critical reflection to research students' resistance to neoliberalism. *Critical and Radical Social Work*, 2(3), pp. 337–355.

Munro, E. (2011) The *Munro review of child protection: Final report, A child-centred system*. Available from: www.gov.uk/government/uploads/system/uploads/attachment_data/file/175391/Munro-Review.pdf.

National Association of Social Workers, United States (NASW). (2008) *Code of ethics*. NASW. Available at: www.socialworkers.org/pubs/code/code.asp.

Pease, B. (2011) Men in social work: Challenging or reproducing an unequal gender regime? *Affilia: Journal of Women and Social Work*, 26(4), pp. 406–418.

Reisch, M. (2013) What is the future of social work? *Critical and Radical Social Work*, 1(1), pp. 67–85.

Reisch, M. and Jani, J. (2012) The new politics of social work practice: Understanding context to promote change. *British Journal of Social Work*, 42, pp. 1132–1150.

Social Work Action Network UK (SWAN). Available from: www.socialworkfuture.org/. [Accessed 15 September 2016].

Stanford, S. and Taylor, S. (2013) Welfare dependence or enforced deprivation? A critical examination of White neoliberal welfare and risk. *Australian Social Work*, 66(4), pp. 476–494.

Tronto, J. (2013) *Caring democracy: Markets, equality and justice*. New York: New York University Press.

Visse, M., Abma, T. and Widdershoven, G. (2015) Practising political care ethics: Can responsive evaluation foster democratic care? *Ethics and Social Welfare*, 9(2), pp. 164–182.

Wallace, J. and Pease, B. (2011) Neoliberalism and Australian social work: Accommodation or resistance? *Journal of Social Work*, 11(2), pp. 132–142.

Ward, L. and Barnes, M. (2016) Transforming practice with older people through an ethic of care. *British Journal of Social Work*, 46(4), pp. 906–922.

Weinberg, M. (2010) The social construction of social work ethics: Politicizing and broadening the lens. *Journal of Progressive Human Services*, 21(1), pp. 32–44.

Weinberg, M. and Campbell, C. (2014) From codes to contextual collaborations: Shifting the thinking about ethics in social work. *Journal of Progressive Human Services*, 25, pp. 37–49.

Williams, C. and Briskman, L. (2015) Reviving social work though moral outrage. *Critical and Radical Social Work*, 3(1), pp. 3–17.

5 Care and justice

Two sides of the same coin of a critical care ethics in social work

Jenny Hay

Introduction

Ever since Gilligan (1982) and Noddings (1984) began to talk about an ethic of care as a distinct moral theory that differed from traditional ethics of justice, discussions have continued to be sparked around these ideas. Some scholars argue that there are strong conceptual differences between the two ways of thinking about and enacting ethics, and that they do not align. Others claim that an ethic of care has always been inherent in traditional ethical theory. In this chapter, I examine some of these conflicting ideas and build an argument in support of views held by Meagher and Parton (2004) and Gray (2010), that care and justice are not only compatible, but they are also interdependent ethical concepts that need to be given equal consideration for social work practice.

As a social work researcher, I am fascinated by how ideas about care are constructed in the client-practitioner relationship. My academic and practice interests in this topic were piqued from reading critical literature that questioned the meaning of care in welfare policy that is interpolated by the harsh mentality of neoliberalism (Tronto, 1993, 2013; Bauman and Tester, 2001; Meagher and Parton, 2004; Webb, 2006). I've wondered if 'care' remains and if so, in what forms? My research agenda therefore examines ways that social workers and social work clients conceptualise, enact and experience care in direct social work practice. Recently, I completed a study in Tasmania, Australia, where I interviewed 15 social workers and 15 social work clients to more thoroughly understand how care operates as an ethic in the client-practitioner relationship. I report findings from my research that support my argument for a political ethic of care in social work practice that incorporates a commitment to social justice and trusting relationships. Hence, I argue that care, justice and trust interrelate to inform a complete ethical stance for critical social work theory and practice. First, I begin by outlining theories of justice and care ethics.

Explaining justice and care approaches

The Kantian ethic of justice has been the most influential moral theory since the time of the Enlightenment. Kant's (1964, p. 67) approach viewed ethical principles as abstract and universal, applying equally and impartially to everyone in the same situation. An ethic of justice promotes independence and autonomy. It is from Kantian ethics, along with utilitarian approaches, that formalised codes of ethics have been developed, and they are a defining feature of most helping professions (Hugman, 2005, p. 6). The valuable contribution of Kantian ethics cannot be overlooked, as it resulted in an enhanced humanitarian concern by acknowledging the rights and needs of disadvantaged and marginalised members of society and the recognition of slavery as a moral wrong (Tronto, 1993, p. 58).

Concerns have been raised that justice ethics commonly privilege a dominant construct of justice that advantages the most privileged members of society, including those who are white, middle class, from Western backgrounds, male, and heterosexual (Ife, 2010; Reisch, 2016). Additionally, the ethic of justice has been criticised for failing to take into account the relational ontology of human beings – that individuals exist in relation to others (Tronto, 1993; Sevenhuijsen, 1998). Incorporating an ethic of care into a social justice approach considers differences between and within groups and acknowledges interdependence.

The ethic of care was first proposed as a viable moral theory in the 1980s by feminist theorists Gilligan (1982) and Noddings (1984), who questioned whether something was missing in the traditional Kantian approach to morality. According to ethic of care theorists, it is always through relationship that care occurs (Gilligan, 1982; Noddings, 1984; Tronto, 1993; Noddings, 1995; Gilligan, 2002; Held, 2006). Noddings (1984) placed great importance on listening when engaging in a caring relationship and referred to this type of listening as 'engrossment', which requires the carer to put aside his or her own biases and judgments, and to attempt to understand the other's point of view, emotions and particular circumstance. According to Noddings (1984), understanding another person entails positioning oneself in a place of care, love, empathy, compassion and emotional sensitivity. She argues that understanding requires respecting the unique experience of the other rather than making assumptions based on the carer's own life.

Tronto (1993) originally suggested that an ethic of care comprises four phases and five ethical dimensions. The four phases consist of caring about, taking care of, care-giving and care-receiving (Tronto, 1993, pp. 105–107). Caring about involves the recognition of suffering or need and making an assessment of how needs may be met. 'Taking care of' involves recognition of actions required to meet caring needs. 'Care-giving' is carrying out those actions. And 'care-receiving' involves recognition of responses to care. Tronto claims that observing and seeking responses to care is important as it provides a way of evaluating whether caring needs have been met. Tronto (2013) recently added a fifth phase – 'caring with', which carries the moral elements of solidarity and trust. The five ethical dimensions of an ethic of care consist of attentiveness, responsibility, competence, responsiveness and integrity (Tronto, 1993, pp. 127–137). Attentiveness requires the carer to suspend one's own goals and concerns in order to recognise and be attentive to others (Tronto, 1993, p. 127). Tronto (1993, p. 132) distinguishes between responsibility and obligation, arguing that obligation arises from a sense of duty, whereas responsibility comes from an inclination to do 'the right thing'. From a perspective of responsibility, care is viewed as an end in itself, rather than simply as a means of achieving certain outcomes (Tronto, 1993, p. 133).

Competence involves drawing on knowledge, skills and abilities to meet caring needs whenever possible (Tronto, 1993, p. 133). Responsiveness necessitates considering the position of the other and remaining aware of the power held by the carer and possibilities for abuse of that power (Tronto, 1993, p. 136). Finally, integrity demands that the four phases of care and the first four dimensions of an ethic of care are integrated into a complete whole (Tronto, 1993, pp. 136–137). Tronto (1993, 2013) promotes an ethic of care that constitutes an equitable and democratic use of power that operates within relationships. While much more could be said about the power dynamics of caring relationships, further discussion of this topic is beyond the scope of this chapter. Before I report some of my findings, I discuss the criticisms of ethic of care theory, along with responses to these.

Acknowledging the 'dark side' of care

One of the most common critiques of incorporating an ethic of care into the helping professions is that it may result in a paternalistic/maternalistic approach that can create co-dependency and remove peoples' autonomy (Nelson, 1992; Curzer, 1993; Allmark, 1995). This criticism is particularly raised by disability rights activists (Wood, 1991; Morris, 1997; Finkelstein, 1998). Morris (1997, p. 54) argued that care is a form of oppression against disabled people and is not compatible with ideas of empowerment:

> Care – in the second half of the twentieth century – has come to mean not caring about someone but caring for in the sense of taking responsibility for . . . People who are said to need caring for are assumed to be unable to exert choice and control. One cannot, therefore, have care and empowerment, for it is the ideology and the practice of caring which has led to the perception of disabled people as powerless.

It is for these same reasons that Finkelstein (1998) and Wood (1991) rejected the idea of an ethic of care, preferring a justice model that focuses on self-determination, rights and autonomy. In response to such concerns, Clement (1996, p. 24) and Tronto (1993) contended that it is through relationship that self-determination is developed. They have claimed that by supporting and valuing the needs of the other, care can facilitate a shift, where the recipient of care moves from feeling powerless to feeling more powerful and in control. Many people who require care have limited autonomy, and it is through caring that autonomy is increased and levels of independence are reinstated (Tronto, 1993; Gray, 2010). Amber, a social worker who participated in my research, supported these ideas when she said: "I have this notion that the social worker is like a bridge. It's okay for you to be the arch that supports people until they get to the other side and reach a level of independence again."

None of the participants in my research supported paternalistic/maternalistic forms of care. Social workers were adamant that such practice was antithetical to ethical practice, and clients expressed disdain for practitioners who took an 'I know what's best for you' approach. However, as Noddings (1995) asserted, there are no grounds for having to defend an ethic of care against criticisms relating to paternalism and autonomy if it is approached in the 'right' way. Reflecting the findings from my research, she claimed that true care is enacted from a position of genuine interest and concern for the other person, and with consideration for their needs as expressed by them.

Critics of an ethic of care also raise concerns that it results in practice that is parochial and biased. Tronto (1993) accepted that this can be viewed as problematic when justice is not considered when applying a caring approach. She acknowledges that an ethic of care necessarily involves engaging with each particular person and their unique needs, and argues that approaches that take a broad, abstract view can potentially result in failure to recognise needs, as well as broader societal issues. In order to minimise parochialism and favouritism that are to be expected in the private realm of family life, she advocates for a 'political' ethic of care that is connected to a theory of justice and that is approached in a democratic manner. Tronto (1993, p. 169) states her version of an ethic of care as

> a political concept that requires that we recognise how care – especially the question, who cares for whom? – marks relations of power in our society and marks the intersection of gender, race, and class with care-giving . . . These facts must be judged according to what a just distribution of caring tasks and benefits might be . . . There is a danger if we think of caring as making the public realm into an enlarged family. Family is a necessarily private and parochial understanding of caring . . . Care need not be associated with family in order to become a political ideal.

At the same time, proponents of a political ethic of care (Barnes, 2006; Held, 2006; Tronto, 2013) have challenged the individualistic ethos promoted by neo-liberalism, arguing that people are all interdependent to at least some extent and rarely completely autonomous. The degree to which each individual relies on others varies throughout the lifespan. Requirements for care and support may change depending on circumstances, age and health status, yet care and support remains a necessary requirement to some degree or another in everyone's life (Hankivsky, 2004; Barnes, 2006). Individuals hold some level of autonomy over their own lives, yet once again, this can vary widely. According to Ververk (2001, p. 291), a distinction can be made between autonomy being about self-sufficiency and independence and autonomy as having the power to make one's own choices in life. She argued that the latter does not necessarily preclude an ethic of care, whereas the former may. Next, I outline the history of care in the social work profession, explain how it is currently conceptualised in codes of ethics, and argue for a critical ethical approach that combines both care and justice.

Bringing care and justice together in critical social work practice

Care was at the heart of much of early social work practice. Both the Charity Organisation Society and Settlement House Movement workers of the early twentieth century held a strong care ethos (Dybicz, 2012, p. 271). Relationship-based practice, informed by the work of Carl Rogers (1951), was highly valued during the 1950s and 1960s. Humanist values such as empathy, compassion, unconditional positive regard and genuineness have remained constant, although arguably they have become increasingly devalued as evidence-based practice has become more prominent and as a focus on challenging inequalities and addressing macro issues has increased (Lymbery, 2001). At the same time, it can be difficult for social workers to maintain care in the current political climate that promotes a context driven by neoliberal ideals and New Public Management – a context that imposes constraints on caring social work practice (Parton, 2003; Gray, 2010; Dybicz, 2012).

The 2010 edition of the Australian Association of Social Workers (AASW) Code of Ethics briefly mentions care in its glossary of terms when defining 'competence' (2010, p. 42). The British Association of Social Workers (BASW) Code of Ethics (2012, p. 11) states that social workers should "treat people with compassion, empathy, and care". Yet, no further explanations of what this means in terms of ethical practice are provided, further indicating the taken-for-granted nature of the term 'care'. A commitment to social justice, human rights, dignity and worth, self-determination, respect, integrity and competence are the common values and principles stated in social work codes of ethics, all of which align more with an ethic of justice than an ethic of care (Gray, 2010, p. 1796).

Like the notion of care, 'duty of care' is another taken-for-granted concept with no definition provided in codes of ethics, and minimal explanations of its meaning are provided elsewhere in the social work literature. This is in spite of its ubiquity in social work and policy documents. McAuliffe (2014, p. 123) describes duty of care as "a legal obligation imposed on an individual and that requires that they adhere to a reasonable standard of care when engaged in the performance of actions that could potentially harm another". The Social Care Institute for Excellence (2014, p. 1) in the UK defines duty of care as "a legal obligation to always act in the best interest of individuals and others, to not act or fail to act in a way that results in harm, and act within competence". These definitions indicate that a duty of care is very different to an ethic of care, the aims of which extend far beyond safety and avoidance of harm to creating connections with people through deep listening, understanding the unique experiencing of the other, and attempting to meet individual and unique needs. Chenoweth and McAuliffe (2014, p. 16) have more closely aligned the idea of 'duty' with an ethic of care in their definition of social work when they say: "They (social workers) are further charged with the duty to respond with passion, hope and care, to human need wherever and however it is manifested."

What does the research say?

Findings from my research have supported conceptualisations of care posed by critical ethics of care theorists, with empathy and compassion, deep listening, genuineness, non-judgment, understanding, trust and respect constituting the main features of caring social work practice. These features of care culminate in caring practice that demonstrate a general 'valuing of the other'. For example, social worker Cloudy Bay explicitly supported this idea when he said, "Care is about valuing the other as an important human being." Several clients echoed this view when they spoke about care as "making me feel like I mattered".

I identified that the views and experiences presented by participants in my research supported arguments posed by theorists (Tronto, 1993, 2013; Jagger, 1995; Heckman, 1999; Held, 2006) who contend that care and justice are logically compatible and indispensable to one another, and that a political ethic of care does not preclude an ethic of justice. In line with this, the social workers in my study argued that an ethic of care for direct social work practice must incorporate an ethic of justice. They spoke about care as a response to injustice, inequality and unfairness. Clients indicated that being treated in a just and fair manner required an understanding of their unique position in the world and recognition of their individual struggles and strengths.

Narratives of care were often intertwined with considerations of justice. Some social workers talked about care as a natural response to suffering and injustice. Witnessing the suffering of others due to discrimination, stigma, marginalisation and structural inequalities evoked feelings of care. For example, Sally asserted that as a social worker she held a responsibility to recognise injustice and to address the injustice, but to do so in a caring way that respected the client's self-determination. She stated:

> I feel that 'fire in my belly' that I experience when I recognise injustice. I ask what they need, how I can help, what I can offer, because I can't know that without asking; I am not in their shoes, so I can't assume anything. In doing all of that, I am coming from a place of social justice and care.

Jade shared a similar passion for caring about inequality and indicated that care extended beyond the individual, even when working in direct-practice roles. She said: "It is deep in my blood that people deserve to be treated fairly and equally, and that is as much about care as social justice."

Similar findings are evident in other empirical research on care in social work practice. The participants in Gregory's (2010) research in the field of criminal justice argued that there are ways of providing care for offenders while at the same time supporting and protecting victims as well. They remained committed to balancing the demands of both justice and care. Holland (2010, p. 1678) interviewed young people involved in the child protection system about their relationships with social workers. He identified that participants focused on issues of fairness and rights along with relationships and care, indicating that an ethic of justice also played a role in the young people's discussions about their experiences. Just as an ethic of care is not a complete moral theory without justice, justice cannot be properly served without care, and without paying particular attention to the situation and needs of individuals through relationships with them (Tronto, 1993).

Merging care and justice with 'care respect'

The language used by both social workers and clients in my research has reflected the intersection between care and justice. 'Respect' has featured in descriptions of care, indicating that while respect is a principle of deontological ethics it is also viewed as a form of care. In much of the literature on ethic of care theory (Gilligan, 1982; Tronto, 1993; Held, 2006), care and respect are viewed as separate but complementary concepts, with respect being aligned with an ethic of justice. The findings from my research fit most closely with Dillon's (1992, pp. 116–119) idea of 'care respect', which he describes as follows:

> Care respect thus involves viewing persons simultaneously in the abstract and in the particular, valuing this person as the fully specific concrete individual 'me' she is because she is a particular individual and human 'me'. Care respect, we might say, sees at the same time both the person in the individual and the individual in the person.
>
> (Dillon, 1992, p. 118)

Dillon (1992, p. 113) describes this version of respect as being about valuing another person simply because they matter as a feeling, thinking human being. This differentiates her version from general notions of respect that suggest that a person must 'earn' the right to be valued. She argues that 'care respect' differs from the type of respect that applies as a universal principle, with everybody being treated the same, without consideration of their unique character and circumstances. Instead, 'care respect' embraces the individual person and the differences that exist between people involved in caring relationships. Similar to the findings in my research (Hay, 2015), Dillon (1992, p. 115) argues: "What matters about each of us is not (only) some abstract capacity but the fact that we are the specific concrete individuals that we are."

Dillon (1992) asserts that 'care respect' helps build trust. In the next section I report findings from my research that show how the construct of trust relates to issues of power in social work practice. I argue that trust-building is a crucial aspect of just and caring practice that requires significant emphasis for social work practice.

Trust as a core component of just and caring practice

In my research, while clients mostly shared common views with social workers about the features of just and caring practice, one of the main differences between the social workers' and the clients' accounts relates to the importance clients placed on trust. According to Mollering (2006) trust involves a process of reasoning used to overcome vulnerability in the face of uncertainty. Mistrust occurs when a person suspects that the worker does not have the client's best interests at heart and/or is following their own agenda that does not align with the client's wishes or needs (Williams, 2007). Trust is more likely to be built when the trustee shows that they are invested in understanding and meeting the interests of the 'truster' (Williams, 2007). Brown, Calnan, Scrivener and Szmukler (2009) viewed trust in human service settings as a communicative, relational process that facilitates the service user perceiving the professional as both competent and caring. Like care, trust cannot be taken for granted. Levels of trust are often dependent on past relational experiences with others, particularly with those who hold significant degrees of power (Mollering, 2006).

Only a couple of social workers mentioned trust in passing, whereas 11 of the 15 clients who participated in this research spoke specifically about what they perceived to be an important link between justice, care and trust. The findings showed that an approach that was consistent with an ethic of justice, including basic respect, the valuing of their self-determination, and being treated in a fair manner was important to clients. Yet, it was a genuine demonstration of care and a commitment to building a trusting relationship that added to and enriched the clients' experiences of social work interactions. These findings were congruent with conclusions drawn from studies conducted by Beresford, Adshead and Croft (2007, 2008), who indicated that negative views of social workers as using their power in ways that were manipulative, controlling, threatening and intrusive signalled a lack of trust. Clients who participated in my study were strong in their claims that social workers need to understand that it can take time for clients to trust and to feel secure enough to be open and honest about their problems and feelings. Trust-building requires social workers to value their clients and to be patient. The findings showed that clients were more likely to trust their social workers when they felt that their social worker believed in and trusted them in return. Luke commented:

> It takes a while to feel comfortable and to trust. You know, you need to get to know them and feel that you won't be criticised or judged. My social worker is really good though. I tell him a lot of stuff I have never spoken about to anyone because I can trust him.

Eve believed that social workers need to know how important trust is to clients – that trust can be broken in an instant. She relayed an experience from a past social work interaction:

> It took a year of trust building with this particular social worker, and one sentence, one sentence was all it took to break that. It was nothing about me; I knew that and I understand that we all have those bad days, but if you have a bad day, perhaps you ring up later and apologise and explain. That would have been the right thing to do, and the caring thing to do. She didn't do that. I got up and walked out and never went back.

Eve's comment demonstrates how justice, care and trust link together to 'make or break' a social worker-client relationship. She speaks about the 'right' thing to do, the 'caring' thing to do, and the crucial role of 'trust'. Guttman (2006, p. 146) argued that trust is "the central nucleus in social worker-client relationships", particularly in regard to issues of privacy and autonomy. All too often social workers expect to be trusted, simply by virtue of their professional role (Brown et al., 2009). Yet, my research reveals that trust must be earned; it is not a social worker's right to be trusted, but a privilege.

Conclusion

A commitment to social justice is a core value of critical social work, and the espoused principles that underpin professional codes of ethics are congruent with this ethos. Yet, care is a taken-for-granted and devalued aspect of social work practice that has been overridden by a focus on evidence-based knowledge and practice and the neoliberal context that the profession is now situated in. My research has highlighted the interdependent nature of both care and justice in ethical decision-making and the all-important social worker-client relationship. Respect, justice, self-determination, trust, and care can all be integrated into an ethical stance that addresses the rights and needs of social work clients. A critical ethical position requires consideration of both care and justice. There are times when the moral and ethical thing to do is to make a decision based on care and other times when the decision should be based on justice. Often the caring thing to do is the most just thing to do and vice versa. As Gilligan (2002, p. 683) claimed, the two ways of thinking are simply "two sides of the same coin". While critical social workers are committed to working towards social justice, this cannot be genuinely realised without also recognising the value of an ethic of care – an ethic of care that values the role that trust plays in building and maintaining caring relationships. The inclusion of a political ethic of care in social work theory and practice may address an important gap in the social work profession. It is time that care is returned to the heart of the social work profession. Ultimately, I argue for an ethic of care that uses a critical approach by placing an emphasis on trust, incorporates the concept of 'care respect', follows a social justice approach that does not privilege dominant groups, and disrupts the neoliberal ideology and its individualistic focus that informs social policy and contemporary social work practice.

References

Allmark, P. (1995) Can there be an ethics of care? *Journal of Medical Ethics*, 21, pp. 19–24.

Australian Association of Social Workers. (2010) *AASW code of ethics*. Barton: Australian Association of Social Workers.

Barnes, M. (2006) *Caring and social justice*. Houndmills: Palgrave Macmillan.

Bauman, Z. and Tester, K. (2001) *Conversations with Zygmunt Bauman*. Cambridge: Polity Press.

Beresford, P., Adshead, L. and Croft, S. (2007) *Palliative care, social work and service users*. London: Jessica Kingsley.

Beresford, P., Adshead, L. and Croft, S. (2008) We don't see her as a social worker: A service user case study of the importance of the social worker's relationship and humanity. *British Journal of Social Work*, 38, pp. 1388–1407.

British Association of Social Workers. (2012) *The code of ethics for social work: statement of principles* [online]. Birmingham: British Association of Social Workers. Available from: http://cdn.basw.co.uk/upload/basw_112315-7.pdf [Accessed 22 October 2016].

Brown, P., Calnan, M., Scrivener, A. and Szmukler, G. (2009) Trust in mental health services: A neglected concept. *Journal of Mental Health*, 18(5), pp. 449–458.

Chenoweth, L. and McAuliffe, D. (2014) *The road to social work and human service practice*. Melbourne: Cengage.

Clement, G. (1996) *Care, autonomy and justice: Feminism and the ethic of care*. Boulder, CO: Westview Press.

Curzer, H. (1993) Is care a virtue for health care professionals? *Journal of Medicine and Philosophy*, 18(1), pp. 51–69.

Dillon, R. (1992) Respect and care: Towards moral integration. *Canadian Journal of Philosophy*, 2(1), pp. 105–132.

Dybicz, P. (2012) The ethic of care: Recapturing social work's first voice. *Social Work*, 57(3), pp. 271–280.

Finkelstein, V. (1998) Doing disability research. *Disability and Society*, 14(6), pp. 859–867.

Gilligan, C. (1982) *In a different voice*. Cambridge: Harvard University Press.

Gilligan, C. (2002) In a different voice. In: Pojman, L. (ed.) *Ethical theory: Classic and contemporary readings*. 4th edition. Belmont, CA: Wadsworth, pp. 682–688.

Gray, M. (2010) Moral sources and emergent ethical theories in social work. *British Journal of Social Work*, 40, pp. 1794–1811.

Gregory, M. (2010) Reflection and resistance: Probation practice and the ethic of care. *British Journal of Social Work*, 40, pp. 2274–2290.

Guttman, D. (2006) *Ethics in social work: A context of caring*. New York: Hawthorn Press.

Hankivsky, O. (2004) *Social policy and the ethic of care*. Vancouver: University of British Columbia Press.

Hay, J. (2015) *Shining a light on care in direct social work practice*. PhD thesis, University of Tasmania.

Heckman, S. (1999) *The future of differences: Truth and method in feminist theory*. Cambridge: Polity.

Held, V. (2006) *The ethics of care: Personal, political and global*. New York: Oxford University Press.

Holland, S. (2010) Looked after children and the ethic of care. *British Journal of Social Work*, 40, pp. 1464–1680.

Hugman, R. (2005) *New approaches in ethics for the caring professions*. New York: Palgrave Macmillan.

Ife, J. (2010) Human rights and social justice. In: Gray, M. and Webb, S. (eds.) *Ethics and value perspectives in social work*. Basingstoke: Palgrave Macmillan, pp. 148–159.

Jagger, A. (1995) Caring as a feminist practice of moral reason. In: Held, V. (ed.) *Justice and care: Essential readings in feminist ethics*. Boulder, CO: Westview, pp. 179–202.

Kant, I. (1964) *The moral law: Groundwork of the metaphysics of morals*. Translated by H. J. Paton. London: Routledge.

Lymbery, M. (2001) Social work at the crossroads. *British Journal of Social Work*, 31, pp. 369–384.

McAuliffe, D. (2014) *Interprofessional ethics: Collaboration in the social, health and human services*. Port Melbourne, VIC: Cambridge.

Meagher, G. and Parton, N. (2004) Modernising social work and the ethics of care. *Social Work & Society*, 2(5), pp. 10–27.

Mollering, G. (2006) *Trust: Reason, routine, reflexivity*. Oxford: Elsevier.

Morris, J. (1997) Care or empowerment: A disability rights perspective. *Social Policy & Administration*, 31(1), pp. 34–60.

Nelson, N. (1992) Against caring. *Journal of Clinical Ethics*, 3(1), pp. 8–15.

Noddings, N. (1984) *A feminine approach to ethics and moral education*. Berkeley: University of California Press.

Noddings, N. (1995) Caring. In: Held, V. (ed.) *Justice and care: Essential readings in feminist ethics*. Boulder, CO: Westview Press, pp. 7–30.

Parton, N. (2003) Rethinking professional practice: The contributions of social constructionism and the feminist ethics of care. *British Journal of Social Work*, 33, pp. 1–16.

Reisch, M. (2016) Social justice. In: Hugman, R. and Carter, J. (eds.) *Rethinking values & ethics in social work*. London: Palgrave Macmillan, pp. 33–48.

Rogers, C. (1951) *Client-centred therapy: Its current practice, implications and theory*. Boston: Houghton Mifflin.

Sevenhuijsen, S. (1998) *Citizenship and the ethics of care*. London: Routledge.

Social Care Institute for Excellence. (2014) *Understanding common induction* [online]. Available from: www.scie.org.uk/workforce/induction/standards/cis01_role.asp [Accessed 22 October 2016].

Tronto, J. (1993) *Moral boundaries: A political argument for an ethic of care*. New York: Routledge.

Tronto, J. (2013) *Caring democracy: Markets, equality and justice*. New York: New York University Press.

Ververk, M. (2001) The care perspective and autonomy. *Medicine, Health Care and Philosophy*, 4(3), pp. 289–294.

Webb, S. (2006) *Social work in a risk society*. Houndmills: Palgrave Macmillan.

Williams, R. (2007) *Tokens of trust*. Norwick: Canterbury Press.

Wood, R. (1991) Care of disabled people. In: Dalley, G. (ed.) *Disability and social policy*. London: Social Policy Institute, pp. 199–202.

Part II
Situating care

6 The risks of care and caring about risk in mental health

Anne-Maree Sawyer and Sonya Stanford

Introduction

Sonya sat at Claudia's two-seated kitchen table in her sunny, small kitchen, talking about Claudia's experience of mental illness and what it was like to access recovery-oriented community mental health services. Sonya was talking with people who had been diagnosed with severe mental illnesses as part of a qualitative study in Tasmania, Australia. She was interviewing people about how they experienced recovery as an ethos and practice. At that time (2011), 'recovery' was a relatively new focus for mental health policy in Australia (Bland et al., 2009).

Sonya recalls the interview in the following terms:

> Together, Claudia and I shared a pot of tea in her small unit. I sat near the window and as I looked at Claudia and listened to her speak, I had a vision of her life and sense of self as contracting from the impact of mental illness. Whereas her life before being diagnosed was wide and expansive, the illness and responses to it by others had squeezed her into a much smaller life where her movements were restricted (Claudia was regularly hospitalised). Who she was as a person was also squeezed into a smaller sense of self where she was required to be a constantly well person. She grieved her lost sense of self. Claudia felt hurt by how mental health practitioners seemed to ignore the daily heartbreak she endured from living what she saw as a diminished life. Instead, they focused on the risk of her becoming unwell and emphasised her personal responsibility for achieving recovery.
>
> Visions of finger wagging, sterile clinicians brought to life in so many lived experience accounts of mental illness sprung into my mind. I imagined a clipped and authoritative voice saying to her: "This is your last chance Claudia. No more help for you if you fail again young lady." Indeed, Claudia broke through my reverie by sharing with me her secret fear that reflected my auditory vision:

> > And one of the things I'm worried about is . . . what happens if I get sick again? . . . And if I go backwards that's my failing, you know, and that'll be my fault because I've gone through all the resources and used them. I've been taught ways to deal with things.

Recovery could be gentler and kinder; I thought surely recovery workers would be caring when people dreaded the likely misery of their days. Claudia, in her quiet way and looking into her cup, explained how she 'did' recovery from time to time when it was possible:

> Recovery just feels good at the time . . . Like in the morning I have a cup of coffee and I go sit outside and just watch the birds, you know, and it's just nice just to be. It's just to be and not to have that torture day in, day out.

We have used this example from Sonya's research to immediately draw attention to the social suffering of people with mental illness and, specifically, to a very particular form of suffering that usually remains tacit, unrevealed. Social suffering encapsulates the idea that "human misery, no matter how deeply interior to the individual, is often a collective experience resulting from large-scale societal forces" (Wilkinson and Kleinman, 2016, p. viii). In this chapter, we examine the torment arising from the effects of 'risk-thinking' that is a feature of neoliberal welfare regimes (Webb, 2006). This form of social suffering is rarely acknowledged, requiring a view that looks beyond the symptom-based effects of mental illness. For example, Claudia's story highlights how the rationality of risk that pervades mental health services (Stanford, Sharland, Heller and Warner, 2017) exacerbated her daily anguish. She understood that practitioners saw her as someone who was at risk of 'failing' recovery. As Claudia explained, "recovery sort of makes it sound like you're recovered, you're better," and for Claudia this meant that mental health workers were telling her they would shun her if she became unwell. She would be left on her own; in other words, she risked their withdrawal of care. This caused her pain.

Explicating how risk-focused thinking compromises an ethics of care and caring practices as a response to suffering associated with mental illness is the moral and practical story of this chapter. We critically analyse the ways in which various models of 'person-centred' community-based mental health care are interpolated with formal rationalities of risk (Sawyer, 2017). At face value, person-centred approaches encapsulate the moral qualities of an ethics of care described by Tronto (2013, pp. 22–23): caring about, caring for, care-giving, care-receiving and caring with. However, person-centred care is delivered in a neoliberal welfare paradigm that is dominated by the logic of risk-thinking that ultimately values economic security (Webb, 2006). In this context, the value and practice of 'care' is distorted through the market.

Using the concept of social suffering, we examine the social misery that is generated and often disguised by risk-thinking in the provision of person-centred mental health care. We draw attention to the subjective experience of abjection that derives from these risk-dominated practices: experiences of living with loss, humiliation and heightened anxiety. Significantly, we demonstrate that the lived reality of suffering, engendered by risk-focused responses and procedures, both creates and compounds the pain of inequality and injustice. This understanding provides us with an opportunity to consider changes to organisational and practice strategies of care that could address the wounded 'self' of people experiencing mental health problems. We set the scene for this discussion by first explaining how the neoliberal welfare risk regime distorts and silences social suffering.

Silencing social misery through neoliberal risk rationalities

From the late twentieth century, rationalities of risk began to pervade the institutional logic of neoliberal welfare (McDonald, 2006) across the whole spectrum of community-based human services, including juvenile justice, family violence, aged care and mental health. It is now impossible to speak of mental health issues without evoking ideas of risk (Kemshall, 2002; Green, 2007). Neoliberal welfare risk rationalities (Stanford and Taylor, 2013) dominate how mental health problems are understood, which in turn informs responses to these problems (Stanford et al., 2017).

The rise of 'risk-thinking' (Rose, 1998) developed in the context of several interrelated socio-political processes:

- Deinstitutionalisation and the growth of community-based care, which generated a range of new and intensified risks for practitioners, service users and their families, and the general public (Rose, 1998; Kemshall, 2002);
- Neoliberalism, which transformed the public sector of Western democracies from the 1980s with the introduction of market-based models into health and welfare services and new demands for accountability, including formal procedures to reduce, transfer and eliminate identified risks (Munro, 2004); and, more recently,
- Policy initiatives focused on the provision of 'individualised' or 'person-centred' care, tailored to reflect "what is of subjective significance to the client" (Yeatman, 2009, p. 27).

With the marketisation of health and welfare services, which coincided with deinstitutionalisation, governments reduced their roles as direct service providers, contracting out many of their services to other agencies who competed for government funding to deliver them. Increasingly, governments assumed a regulatory role in monitoring these contracted services, albeit from afar, relying on a plethora of accountability measures – key performance indicators, risk management systems (including critical incident logs), quality assurance, and the like – to audit their performance (Munro, 2004). In the context of these institutional imperatives focused on performance, economic efficiency and risk management, Rose (1998, p. 186) argued that community mental health professionals are "governed through . . . a bureaucratic nexus of reports, forms, monitoring, evaluation and audit, under the shadow of the law . . . according to logics which are not their own, in the interests of community protection".

Moreover, the "cost-and-effect calculations . . . and other free market commandments" driving neoliberalism (Bauman, 2000, p. 9) demand an emphasis on 'outputs' (occupied bed days, length of community care episodes and competitive tendering processes). This leaves services and practitioners "largely outcome-blind with regard to the health, economic and social impact of mental health care" (Crosbie, 2009, cited in Rosenberg and Hickie, 2013, p. 3). In other words, it helps to foster a social imaginary that obfuscates the effects of public policy on the lived experiences of people who receive mental health services (Hall and Lamont, 2013).

Consequently, the practices and procedures utilised in community mental health programs are now shaped not only by service objectives and philosophies, professional knowledge and disciplinary values, but also – increasingly – by the imperative to manage identified risks (Green, 2007). Risk management and person-centred care, which represent different paradigms of contemporary practice, now come together in the everyday worlds of frontline community care. Practitioners must negotiate and reconcile these apparently competing policy imperatives in making contextually specific judgments that consider *both* risk management and risk-taking (Sawyer and Green, 2013). However, because of increased demand, particularly for acute mental health services, collaborative and 'healing' work with clients may be passed over in order to meet the more pressing demands of the moment.

We are concerned that "the language of risk . . . conceal(s) more than it explains about the painful social realities of human experience" (Wilkinson, 2006, p. 4). Risk-thinking has become so dominant as a way of interpreting mental health problems that other ways of thinking about the risks associated with mental health problems have been screened out, including caring about the lived experience of social suffering. We are alarmed by how the hurts associated with the structural formation of societies, institutional arrangements and the exercise of power through the mentality of risk (Wilkinson and Kleinman, 2016) are disguised and, in some cases, rendered redundant and inconsequential in policy, service and practice responses to mental health problems.

Frost and Hoggett (2008, p. 441) succinctly explain: "Social suffering draws attention to what those without power endure." To focus on suffering is to catalogue "a moral register of political and economic processes that leave people materially disadvantaged, culturally undernourished, and socially deprived" (Wilkinson and Kleinman, 2016, pp. 3, 14). We recognise this can be an agonising confrontation for those professionals who seek out how to best care for people tormented by everyday and extraordinary forms of social misery. The moral sensibility of what it means to care for people in extreme distress bumps up hard against the brutish logic of neoliberal welfare. Practitioners realise – crushingly – that their risk practices are part of the structural violence wrought by neoliberal welfare (McDonald, Postle and Dawson, 2008; Stanford, 2010). Scripted into a plot of safeguarding the future (Rose, 1998; Culpitt, 1999; Webb, 2006), 'care workers' have been recast as 'risk workers' (Horlick-Jones, 2005) and they feel the anguish of being morally diminished in this production (Stanford, 2010; Fine and Teram, 2012; Smith et al., 2016). Thus the potentially disparate and, sometimes, contradictory responsibilities demanded by organisational risk management regimes, emphasising 'safety first', and those demanded by the provision of individualised care (efforts to enable the service user's aspirations and rights to self-determination, along with attention to their safety) must be negotiated by frontline practitioners at the sites of everyday service delivery (Sawyer and Green, 2013).

George's story, presented in the next section of the chapter, highlights how this conundrum impacts in real ways in his lived experience of mental illness. He spoke with Anne-Maree as part of a large qualitative study, in which people were interviewed about their experiences of 'risk' and risk management in the context of community-based care in Victoria, Australia (Green, 2007, p. 407). George's struggles illustrate the urgent need to remove the harms caused by risk logics that are entangled in person-centred care in community mental health services. Anne-Maree now tells us about George's lived experience of the pain he suffered when risk-focused interventions were applied to him.

George's story: the lived experience of pain arising from risk-focused person-centred care

George was a middle-aged man, widowed and living alone in a small, rented flat on the outskirts of a regional town, with "no really close friends". He had been diagnosed with paranoid schizophrenia and depression some 10 years earlier. George explained that his illness had developed fast on the heels of "a complete mental breakdown" after the deaths of his daughter and, six months later, his mother:

> I lost my Dad when I was 11, I lost my wife when I was 28, I just turned 34 and I lose my daughter and I lose my Mum, that's the only family I knew . . . I don't get attached to people anymore. They're okay as acquaintances but I don't let people in close. The psychiatrist and everybody like that says, "Oh you should let people in," but . . . when you lose so many people so close to you it doesn't matter what people say . . . "oh well you've got to make friends, you've got to trust in people" – but the risk to myself is the panic of losing that person.

When I met George, he was facing imminent discharge from the community mental health service where he had been a client for seven years. He didn't know when the separation would take place, only that it would probably occur after his next appointment with the psychiatrist. As he explained, he had not been in hospital for two years and "felt okay at the moment". But earlier on, he was "in and out of hospital so many times, it was like my second home". Although George had learned over the years to recognise some of the 'signals' of a looming relapse, he was patently aware that many of his relapses had arrived without warning:

> Sometimes I can go to bed and wake up in the morning and feel absolutely wrecked, no good. And people say, "Oh you were okay yesterday – why do you feel like that?" I don't know. I've got no idea. I've got no idea why I was happy and laughing the day before and the next day I feel like I'm a piece of

shit. I don't know why, and that's a risk because when you feel like that the risk is you can go into deep depression . . . and with me it sometimes triggers off my paranoia, schizophrenia, so then eventually – it all starts again.

The interview offered an occasion for George to reflect on his experiences as a service user, especially the frequency and quality of contact with his case managers. In the past, he had seen his case manager twice each week in the months following discharge from hospital; once he was 'settled' at home, the visits were reduced to weekly or fortnightly. However, as he observed: "as time's gone on and with different workers, the time frame changes." He saw his current case manager very 'infrequently', less than every six weeks: "it's just a quick chat at the door and then she's got to go." These 'quick chats' appeared to function as surveillance activities, specifically to monitor 'risks', whereas in the past the case managers "used to come in and *talk to me*". Clearly engaged in relationship-building, George recalled that his first two case managers had worked with him to explore and help him implement several strategies, including the use of a mood diary and focused efforts to deconstruct negative thinking and 'turn' these thoughts 'into positives', along with plans to structure his day, all in an effort to 'control' the 'illness'. To George, these workers were "much more understanding" than his current case manager. His experiences reflect the moral dimensions of an ethics of care (Tronto, 2013, pp. 22–23). According to the logic of neoliberal risk society, helping relationships that may be inherently healing tend to be redefined in terms of dependency. George's history as a service user encapsulates the shift, so clearly articulated by Culpitt (1999, p. 39), as "a movement away from the validation of the 'helping relationship' " as "an aspect of governance . . . by which welfare clients, collectively, are 'disciplined' away from dependency towards risk".

George confessed that it had been particularly difficult to negotiate the frequent changes in case managers and the reduced contact with them:

it's very hard that way . . . and I think that is one part of the system that breaks down . . . They can't spend as much time as they would like with the client, so they don't get to know the client . . . [or] their illnesses that well.

Thus the case manager, operating from a distance, is limited in their understanding of the client's "experiential situation" and in exercising "both relational and contextual awareness", capacities that are fundamental to caring with and caring for another person (Borg and Kristiansen, 2004, p. 501). George felt that he was not recognised, not treated as a self; he carried the risks of self-management, which he argued, generated further risks: "My old case manager knew when I was getting sick . . . He knew when I was depressed, so he could then try and get me a bed." However, his current case manager was unfamiliar with his ongoing needs:

The thing that scares me is . . . I'm okay at the moment, but because it's so infrequent – they don't see me every week. I do have days where I'm a bit down and the thing that scares me and why I feel at risk is not having that support.

In case of a future relapse, George had been advised to call the ambulance or the local psychiatric crisis team. This floored him, fearful of possibly not recognising he needed help until it was too late. George argued that he may not be able to self-regulate, to take steps to manage the risks he posed to himself and others: "My main concern is that I might hurt somebody or do something stupid." In this context, he also understood, very insightfully and reflexively, that his capacity to self-manage was tied to the availability of hospital beds. This is a systemic problem, well beyond his control, but one that demonstrates how the management of risk is devolved from services to frontline workers and, subsequently, to clients. It also shows how devolution operates in a hierarchical way, with 'risk' transferred lower down the chain to parties and persons with progressively fewer resources and power to manage it. Earlier in the interview, George had explained that when he had not been able to get into hospital in the past because of bed pressure, he felt "frustrated" and "more at risk because"

> For me as a paranoid schizophrenic, I then start feeling unsafe about my surroundings and I feel like people are after me . . . and it just snowballs so the risk then starts to get real high for me . . . I feel like, I have actually gone up to people and yelled and screamed at them and felt like attacking them because I feel like they're going to attack me and when I'm at that risk I should be in hospital but because there is not enough beds I can't get into hospital.

George was cognisant of his risk history and how he might best manage these risks; however, this knowledge, and his fears about his upcoming discharge, appeared to have no place in the service's discharge planning. His suffering remained hidden, unrecognised.

Yet, George's sense of abandonment by the service was palpable as he spoke to me:

> They've just said if you feel like you're depressed or something, get yourself to Emergency or phone up [the crisis service] . . . It just feels like part of your left arm and your left leg have been cut off . . . I know I'm doing okay and but I still think I should have a case manager, even if it's every three months [to remain connected to the service] . . . instead of just being like put on a life-boat: "Oh you're doing so well, here's your life boat, off you go on your own." And that's very scary for somebody [like me].

George was "reclassified" (Bauman, 2000, p. 7) as not a client because he no longer met the risk-based criteria for service provision. However, the risk paradigm screens out the human 'being' (as emotional self, and relational self); we see only the agentic, autonomous, responsibilised self. From the standpoint of the service, George seemed able to future-proof himself. So, he was cast "adrift", as he put it, left to his own devices, to decide when and how to refer himself to emergency services. But in this calculation, the poignancy of George's earlier losses and traumas are effaced. The hurt he felt and the heightened anxieties are surely compounded by his past experiences of abandonment. These are the injuries – the psychic wounds – generated by the neoliberal risk paradigm. Hall and Lamont (2013, p. 59) argue that social relations provide people with such "social resources" as a sense of belonging, recognition, support and identity that can be used "to cope with life's challenges". George recognised the value of staying 'connected' to the service in some way, if only to have contact with a case manager every three months, especially in light of his sustained social isolation. The imminent 'cut-off' from mental health services seemed to violate one of the most deeply felt aspects of his inner world: his identification as a person with paranoid schizophrenia and his personal history of living with the wear and tear of a serious and persistent mental illness. Here we can see, in the lives of both George and Claudia, how the substantive and formal rationalities of risk in neoliberal welfare policy can distort a person's capacities for shaping their selfhood.

Conclusion: advancing critical caring practices through a focus on social suffering

Risk-thinking is captivating. In the context of the ongoing bureaucratisation of health and welfare services, neoliberal welfare risk rationalities are like car headlights on high beam, drawing managers' and practitioners' attention to checklists, form filling, reporting requirements and compliance measures. As George's story illustrates, care work that is embodied in the face-to-face work of relationship-building with clients and their families is often peripheral in this night-vision, cast in shadow. Both George and Claudia suffered profound losses: they were personally and socially bereaved. They feared and experienced the withdrawal of care justified by equations of their riskiness and the moral judgements that accompanied these calculations. For George and Claudia, this meant the "social constitution of (their) humanity was at stake" (Wilkinson and Kleinman, 2016, p. 9). However, Alaszewski (2006, p. 43) explains, it is common in health care for people's feelings of fear and distress "to be overlooked or even airbrushed from the record because they are inconvenient or difficult to deal with". In such circumstances, mental health workers, particularly in statutory services, can become heavily reliant on routines and administrative procedures "rather than working proactively and creatively" (McDonald et al., 2008, p. 1374) with risks that cause acute social misery. As George's and Claudia's stories attest, such practice causes considerable anxiety and sorrow, and compounds people's vulnerabilities.

The core technologies of risk work – monitoring, management and surveillance – de-emphasise the need for therapeutic skills and other caring practices to respond to the emotional impacts of the inequalities and injustices that are so prevalent for people experiencing mental health problems. In this way, risk-focused practice fosters the de-skilling of mental health professionals such as social workers (McDonald et al., 2008; Munro, 2010). However, as argued in recent research (Sawyer and Green, 2013; Smith et al., 2016), an organisation's risk culture is critical to successfully balancing an ethos of care in the delivery of person-centred practices alongside responsibly managing risks of personal and social hurts. If management of the risks that create social suffering can be understood and approached as part of, and integrated with, the practice of person-centred care, we claim that practitioners are more likely to develop and advance their professional skills of relationship-building, engagement and collaborative care. As Robertson and Collinson (2011, p. 147) suggest, in the absence of a caring, organisational risk culture that gives primacy to the psycho-social dimensions of mental health suffering, workers can often feel isolated and unsupported in their attempts to engage with caring practices that feature positive risk-taking. Assuming the need to control risk (and the person), some mental health workers may "see themselves as gambling" (Robertson and Collinson, 2011, p. 147), and others may seek security by resorting to conservative and procedurally bound responses. Both responses can hinder therapeutic relationships and increase risks over a longer period of time (Munro, 2010; Roberston and Collinson, 2011). Certainly, this is how George and Claudia spoke about how they understood their 'risk futures'.

The way that we have written this chapter draws attention to experiences of abjection of people who are diagnosed with mental illness. We know there is a risk involved in doing this: it emphasises despair and can impede hope. However, there is a purpose to our construction of this narrative of suffering: while the experience of mental illness (including recovery) is particular to an individual, the distress arising from mental illness and the conditions that cause it is also socially and politically experienced. Arguing a similar point, Frost and Hoggett (2008, p. 455) state: "We believe the negative has an important place, particularly for a critical social policy . . . to illuminate the ugliness of social injustice and to illustrate just how deeply it affects human experience."

There is a need to care about what neoliberal risk rationalities do to people who experience mental illness. Following Wilkinson and Kleinman's (2016, p. 3) vision of reinstating " 'care for the human' as a social priority", we claim the merit of focusing on social suffering to inform caring actions on and in mental health policy and practice. A focus on social suffering can help practitioners hold fast to a critical ethics of care and to caring practices that help ameliorate how risk-focused policies (explicit and tacit) and structured risk practices assault the personhood of those living with mental illness. In this way, social suffering can be used as a lens to understand the effects of risk regimes that corrupt care and damage people. Nevertheless, we also understand that such an enterprise is wrought with difficulty, as good intentioned attempts to relieve suffering can also create suffering (Wilkinson and Kleinman, 2016, p. 16). This knowledge alerts us to the need for a critical praxis between research on suffering and learning how to care – as best we can – in ways that honour the dignity of people with mental illness. This remains a task for critical social work committed to creating social interventions aligned to care.

Acknowledgement

This chapter is based on research funded by an Australian Research Council Linkages Grant, no. LP0667485, and an Institutional Research Grant Scheme from UTAS, no. S0018196.

References

Alaszewski, A. (2006) Diaries as a source of suffering narratives: A critical commentary. *Health Risk & Society*, 8(1), pp. 43–58.

Bauman, Z. (2000) Special essay: Am I my brother's keeper? *European Journal of Social Work*, 3(1), pp. 5–11.

Bland, R., Renouf, N. and Tullgren, A. (2009) *Social work in mental health: An introduction*. Sydney: Allen & Unwin.

Borg, M. and Kristiansen, K. (2004) Recovery-oriented professionals: Helping relationships in mental health services. *Journal of Mental Health*, 13(5), pp. 493–505.

Crosbie, D. W. (2009) Mental health policy – Stumbling in the dark? *Medical Journal of Australia*, 190(4), pp. S43–S45.

Culpitt, I. (1999) *Social policy and risk*. London: Sage.

Fine, M. and Teram, E. (2012) Overt and covert ways of responding to moral injustices in social work practice: Heroes and mild-mannered social work bipeds. *British Journal of Social Work*, 43(7), pp. 1312–1329.

Frost, L. and Hoggett, P. (2008) Human agency and social suffering. *Critical Social Policy*, 28(4), pp. 438–460.

Green, D. (2007) Risk and social work practice. *Australian Social Work*, 60(4), pp. 395–409.

Hall, P. A. and Lamont, M. (2013) Why social relations matter for politics and successful societies. *Annual Review Political Science*, 16, pp. 49–71.

Horlick-Jones, T. (2005) On 'risk work': Professional discourse, accountability, and everyday action. *Health, Risk & Society*, 7(3), pp. 293–307.

Kemshall, H. (2002) *Risk, social policy and welfare: Introducing social policy*. Buckingham: Open University Press.

McDonald, A., Postle, K. and Dawson, C. (2008) Barriers to retaining and using professional knowledge in local authority social work practice with adults in the UK. *British Journal of Social Work*, 38(7), pp. 1370–1387.

McDonald, C. (2006) Institutional transformation: The impact of performance measurement on professional practice in social work. *Social Work and Society*, 4, pp. 25–37.

Munro, E. (2004) The impact of audit on social work practice. *British Journal of Social Work*, 34(8), pp. 1075–1095.

Munro, E. (2010) Learning to reduce risk in child protection. *British Journal of Social Work*, 40(4), pp. 1135–1151.

Robertson, J. P. and Collinson, C. (2011) Positive risk taking: Whose risk is it? An exploration in community outreach teams in adult mental health and learning disability services. *Health, Risk and Society*, 13(2), pp. 147–164.

Rose, N. (1998) Governing risky individuals: The role of psychiatry in new regimes of control. *Psychiatry, Psychology and Law*, 5(2), pp. 177–195.

Rosenberg, S. and Hickie, I. (2013) Managing madness: Mental health and complexity in public policy. *Evidence Base*, 3. Available from: https://journal.anzsog.edu.au/publications/6/EvidenceBase2013Issue3.pdf [Accessed 24 October 2016].

Sawyer, A. (2017) Negotiating the interface between risk management and human rights-based care. In: Stanford, S., Sharland, E., Heller, N. and Warner, J. (eds.) *Beyond the risk paradigm in mental health policy and practice*. London: Palgrave, pp. 103–120.

Sawyer, A. and Green, D. (2013) Social inclusion and individualised service provision in high risk community care: Balancing regulation, judgment and discretion. *Social Policy and Society*, 12(2), pp. 299–308.

Smith, M., Cree, V. E., MacRae, R., Sharp, D., Wallace, E. and O'Halloran, S. (2016) Social suffering: Changing organizational culture in children and families social work through critical reflection groups – Insights from Bourdieu. *British Journal of Social Work* [online]. Available from: https://doi.org/10.1093/bjsw/bcw087. [Accessed 20 December 2016].

Stanford, S. (2010) 'Speaking back' to fear: Responding to the moral dilemmas of risk in social work practice. *British Journal of Social Work*, 40(4), pp. 1065–1080.

Stanford, S., Sharland, E., Heller, N. and Warner, J. (eds.) (2017) *Beyond the risk paradigm in mental health policy and practice*. London: Palgrave.

Stanford, S. and Taylor, S. (2013) Welfare dependence or enforced deprivation? A critical examination of white neoliberal welfare and risk. *Australian Social Work*, 66(4), pp. 476–494.Tronto, J. (2013) *Caring democracy: Markets, equality, and justice*. New York: New York University Press.

Webb, S. (2006) *Social work in a risk society: Social and political perspectives* Houndmills: Palgrave Macmillan.

Wilkinson, I. (2006) Health, risk and 'social suffering'. *Health Risk & Society*, 8(1), pp. 1–8.

Wilkinson, I. and Kleinman, A. (2016) *A passion for society: How we think about human suffering*. Oakland: University of California Press.

Yeatman, A. (2009) *Individualisation and the delivery of welfare services*. New York: Palgrave Macmillan.

7 I've got your back

Learning with homeless people about care, mutuality and solidarity

Anne Coleman

Introduction

In 1990, I began work as the social worker/welfare coordinator at a homelessness inner city drop-in centre. This chapter is a reflection on, and a critical examination of professional care in this context with a focus of two themes: mutuality and solidarity. First, to establish the contextual factors that shaped care, I give a description of the drop-in centre, the people who accessed it and my role. I then relate the story of one interaction which illustrates mutuality, and shows the significance of solidarity when working with marginalised and socially excluded groups. I then reflect back on its significance for a critical ethics of care for social work practice. Throughout the chapter, I have taken pains to unsettle the notion of professional care by presenting a view of relationally based social work and by privileging the views of the homeless people I have learned from, and whose views are seldom acknowledged.

For much of our lives, we are engaged in reciprocal relationships of interdependence (Lynch, Lyons and Cantillon, 2007, p. 6). We give and receive care in a relational dance; we practise care in a chorus with others; and we navigate receiving and giving care in our personal and professional lives. Featherstone and Morris (2012, p. 345) remind us that care is a mutual endeavour and that "no one is just a giver or receiver of care." Bozalek (2013, p. 391) draws attention to Iris Young's (2011) idea of 'asymmetrical reciprocity' that allows for mutual but fluid caring relationships that are dynamic, rather than fixed and rigid.

Professional carers, however, are often unaware of, or discomforted by clients' desires to demonstrate care, and either blind or resistant to their actual demonstrations of care. These demonstrations are understood as invitations to transgress boundaries or as attempts to manipulate them. Increasing and inflexible interpretations of professional codes of conduct and standards can reinforce the discomfort felt by workers offering professional care (Banks, 2013, p. 366). Clearly intended to improve the standard and transparency of social work services, they can equally inhibit social work's willingness and capacity to recognise and engage in mutual relationships. I argue that this diminishes both the nominal carer and the cared for, and restricts the possibility of dialogical relationships (within and through which social change can be achieved).

Tronto (1993) identifies professional caring as an inherently political activity, arguing that who cares for whom mirrors and reinforces existing power relations.

Professional caring is equated with power, autonomy and legitimacy, and encompasses "multiple relations of power" (Williams, 2001, p. 476). Professional care gives relative power to social work but also presents it with a challenge: how to show and enact care in a way that is guided by the people with whom we work and directed to achieving justice on their terms.

Solidarity provides an alternate way of framing relationships between professional carers and the people with whom we work. It signifies a willingness to stand beside and with people who are marginalised and socially excluded to achieve a common purpose. Empathic solidarity is identified by Banks (2013, p. 370) as one of six essential values in "a situated ethics of social justice in social work" (Bozalek, 2013, p. 391). Critchley (2007, p. 132) argues that ethical practice itself is "driven by a response to situated injustices and wrongs" framed by an ethics of commitment and a politics of resistance. The focus of solidarity work is on those situated injustices and wrongs rather than the designated 'client'.

The chapter is an acknowledgement of the many things I have learned, personally and professionally, about care with and from people experiencing homelessness. Knowing them has touched and changed my life. My relationships with people who are homeless have shaped my understanding of care, and my practice of care professionally and personally. I owe to each of these people a great debt.

The following section of the chapter provides a description and analysis of the drop-in centre, my role there and the people who were members of the 139 Club.

The 139 Club

Three days after completing my final placement, I started as the social worker/welfare coordinator at the 139 Club, a homelessness drop-in centre on the boundary of two inner city suburbs of Brisbane. Homeless people had lived in the area since colonisation, and early histories of the area documented their presence. When I started at the 139 Club (or The Club as it was locally known), public space dwellers were still a visible presence in the area, and acknowledged as locals. The public spaces where they lived and gathered were imbued with significant life events and personal histories, which transformed these spaces into places that held particular meanings for homeless people, and served as their de facto homes.

My arrival at The Club coincided with the start of an urban renewal process that promised to transform the area from a decaying inner city area to a hub of commerce. This posed a threat to the continued presence of the homeless community which was blamed for the area's failure to thrive economically. The dynamic and highly politicised context generated by urban renewal changed the way homeless people experienced daily living and their sense of being a legitimate part of the local community. It also changed the way I thought about my work at The Club and transformed my ideas about social work and professional caring.

The Club owed its existence to the persistent lobbying of inner city public space dwellers. It was not intended to be a welfare service but a place homeless people could call their own, and where they could access the basic amenities and services that provided a measure of dignity (such as access to showers, toilets and a laundry). It was also a place where people's individuality and legitimacy as community members were recognised and supported. The only signage on the building was deliberately enigmatic: it stated simply *139 Club*. The Club had an open-door policy and aimed to accept all members unconditionally.

This approach was consistent with the clubhouse model (which was familiar to Club members and had been influential in the establishment and development of the 139 Club). The model emphasised shared worth and shared responsibility for organisational roles and tasks, the exchange of skills and knowledge, and the deliberate minimisation of hierarchical distance between workers and the people with whom they worked. People accessed clubhouses as members of the club, not clients.

The Club aimed to be, and was understood by its members as being a sort of third space: one that was inherently unstable, a kind of "borderland zone between different modes of action . . . a dynamic in-between space" (Routledge, 1996, p. 406). It was a borderland where housed and homeless communities came together, where the rules and norms of each rubbed up against each other and were negotiated daily. Club members were generally respectful of the few rules The Club sought to impose (no drugs or alcohol, no weapons and no fighting on the premises), but at tense moments they were unable to understand why they could not do at The Club exactly what they would have done on the street.

On a busy day, between 75 and 100 members accessed The Club. The majority were men, but between one-quarter and one-third were women. Their ages ranged from late teens to late sixties. Most members were single, with little or no contact with families, although there were a few couples of long standing. Around a third of Club members identified as Aboriginal or Torres Strait Islander people. There was a small but growing number of people from culturally and linguistically diverse backgrounds. Most members were categorised by workers as 'chronically' homelessness and had been homeless for extended periods of time.

The majority had been in foster or institutional care as children. Most had left school early and many had difficulty with reading and writing. Work histories were patchy at best, with a significant number never having worked. Those who had had generally been semi-skilled or unskilled workers whose jobs had disappeared. They were survivors, but survivors who were wounded, marginalised and frequently dismissed as having nothing to contribute to the community.

They had a range of health conditions either associated with public space dwelling (e.g. skin rashes, scabies, lice, foot problems, back problems, colds and flu) or exacerbated by it (e.g. diabetes and hepatitis C). People were often reluctant, because of previous encounters with services, to seek treatment quickly. Their ability to complete a treatment regime on the streets also impacted negatively on their health. There was an over-representation of people with mental health issues (some diagnosed and others not) ranging from people with, for example, anxiety disorders through to people experiencing psychosis. There was also a disproportionate number of people with either an intellectual disability (generally a mild intellectual disability) or an acquired brain injury. Poly drug use was common, and overdoses, reactions to a mixture of drugs, and withdrawal related symptoms were dealt with regularly.

Violence was part of the lives of Club members. Most had come through violent homes, alternative care (that had failed to provide care), and early homelessness with a wealth of experiences (as wards of the state, in juvenile detention and later in prisons) of systems that seemed unconcerned about or oblivious to their potential. Their visibility as public space dwellers meant they were regularly subjected to verbal insults, and sometimes physical assaults. The world as they had experienced it had taught them that disagreements were solved by physical force, that hope was a pointless exercise and that their value as people was minimal.

The tolerance and generosity people with so little regularly showed to one another balanced this. The Club brought together a mix of people whose histories and immediate issues would have been difficult to manage consistently under ideal circumstances. On most days though, The Club exemplified 'unconditional acceptance'. Good outcomes were achieved. People shared and cooperated. There was laughter, rest and sharing.

In addition to the challenges of working with what was effectively a distinct sub-cultural group in a third space, with fluid norms and rules, The Club's opening hours made professional distance impossible to maintain. I spent every working day primarily in the company of homeless people. I knew about their lives and how they were faring: who was sick, who was having a bad day, who was in hospital or prison and wanted a visit. I knew about people's foibles, and the things that worried them at night. I knew who was hiding out to avoid a beating, who owed who money and what drugs were on the street. I heard about who'd helped out, given someone shelter, kept someone safe. I'd seen them *busted up* and *buggered up*, raped and humiliated – but still somehow defiantly themselves.

They had seen me cry, and argue vehemently on their behalf with Centrelink, hospitals and prisons. We'd been to funerals and wakes and celebrations together. I'd helped organise weddings and birthday parties. And my contact with people in working hours extended inevitably into public spaces and shopping malls in the area whenever I met up by chance with people after hours. These relationships had an intimate closeness that opened my eyes and my heart to caring on a different level. It allowed me to see and know people as individuals. It also allowed me to understand them as part of a community that gave and shaped their identity, and that bound them together in regular performances of care.

When I started at the 139 Club, the need for care was evident to me. People lacked housing (and many lacked even basic shelter). Their health status was poor. They had problems storing and preparing food. They couldn't read a newspaper and they didn't know their local member (in either local council or state parliament). They were bored and had few opportunities to feel good about themselves. At The Club, I learned that there were needs that, while less visible, were of more importance to members: the need to be recognised as a unique individual; the need to be seen as fully human with the capacity to give and receive care; the need to be listened to and heard; and the need to be understood and accepted by the wider community. The following story helps to illustrate what homeless people cared about, and how they understood care.

A mile in my shoes

The following story is a simple one and represents the day-to-day requests and interactions that were part of an ordinary day at The Club. I chose it from among many examples of care because of its apparently mundane nature. On the surface, it is an interaction between a worker and a client in an unsuccessful attempt to find housing. The story, however, captures the key themes in this chapter: mutual care and solidarity. I also chose this particular incident because of its personal significance and its lasting impact on my social work practice. The interaction between PJ and I represented the moment when it first occurred to me that I was involved in reciprocal relationships of care, and my first conscious awakening to the possibility of solidarity with people with whom (superficially) I had little in common.

My first winter at The Club was about six months after I had started work there. It was an unusually wet, cold winter, and it rained every day and most nights for 40 days straight. The people who slept without shelter in my neighbourhood were no longer invisible to me. I knew them from the 139 Club. They had names and stories, and while my privilege meant I was safe and warm, I had some restless nights imagining people I knew by name outside, wet and cold, their belongings saturated.

One of the members came to talk to me one afternoon. He was an older man whom I knew was sleeping out – I'll call him PJ. Sleeping out was PJ's preferred option, but he came to talk to me at a time when he was unwell and the inclement weather made sleeping out tough going. He asked for my help to find a place to stay – something short-term, maybe a boarding house room, while he got strong again and the weather started to improve. He looked poorly and it concerned me that he had no shelter. I also understood that this was clearly something that was within my role and something I felt confident I could achieve. I said I was happy to help and started to make suggestions about boarding houses in the area he could try.

At this stage, PJ interrupted gently to give me an overview of his recent attempts to get accommodation himself. He'd made a few calls to be told that, yes, there was a vacant room but each time he showed up (often mildly intoxicated, smelling of unwashed clothes and unkempt) he was told that the room had already been let. As well as these disappointments, he'd responded to a hand-lettered sign outside a boarding house advertising a room. The manager was happy to show him a room. PJ's estimation was that the room (and the place generally) was not as desirable a residence as the park. PJ was proud, but clearly these experiences, at a time when he was feeling low, had made him feel small. He wanted a room but he wanted no more humiliation.

We agreed that I would try to find a place in the next day or so, phone in my role to say I had a client interested in the room, and confirm it was still available. If PJ was turned away when he went to inspect the room, and wanted to challenge it, he could bring me back into the interaction. We parted company, agreeing that PJ would get back in touch with me before the weekend (when the drop-in centre would be closed and PJ would be on the streets for another two days).

As it turned out, all my efforts to find him a room were unsuccessful. Despite the fact that this was a small and relatively uncomplicated task, I had failed to get an outcome even though I cared deeply that PJ should access shelter, be safe, get some rest and gather up his energy. I was embarrassed at the thought of our next meeting when I would have to explain this to him. I was worried that he'd think that either I didn't care enough to make it happen or that I was inefficient and inept. When PJ showed up he asked for me. I interpreted this as a clear sign that PJ was anticipating a positive response from me, and a room of his own for the next few weeks.

After we sat down beside each other we talked generally for a few minutes – how he was, how I was, where he'd slept last night – as I gathered my nerve. After a while, I steered the conversation to the matter that was preoccupying my mind. I confessed to PJ that I had been no more successful finding accommodation than he had. I provided details of the efforts I'd made and the responses I'd got. He flicked his eyes in my direction and looked down. I could see (I thought) how disappointed he looked. My emotions were hard to sit with. PJ gave a long sigh, looked up and thanked me for *really* trying for him. For an instant I thought he was mocking me and then I looked at his face: calm, free of anger or disappointment and touched by what he saw as my care and efforts on his behalf.

The moment was loaded with emotion, and our connection to each other was on the basis of two people engaged in a mutual endeavour and in which the most important element was care. With the distance of years, I have come to understand this moment as a gift to me as a human being and as a social worker. PJ reframed my ideas about what care in my role as social worker/welfare coordinator meant. For him, I was solid with him: I'd tried on his behalf. I'd shared for a minute his experiences of rejection and his inability to get what he needed. And I'd done what I said I would even if there was no visible outcome. Now, what moves me most is that while I was demonstrating care for PJ, it seems clear to me that he demonstrated care for me by finding the emotional balance and sensitivity to reassure *me* when he was in a difficult place himself. It is also a pinnacle moment in the development of my practice framework, pushing me to question the notion of care as the core of my practice.

Reflections on my learning with and from homeless people and implications for critical social work

I felt that the moments shared between PJ and I were somehow special, and that PJ had given me a gift. I was aware of his care in the moment. Over time, this story has provided me with opportunities to view it in greater depth, and from different perspectives. The lessons from this single example of care are simple ones.

The preceding story shows that professional care can be tentative, and relationally based. PJ and I both demonstrated care for one another by paying attention to one another's needs and vulnerabilities, being reliable and being able to share a humiliating experience. We shared the tentativeness of people navigating differences in world views and expectations in a way that would allow us both to give and receive the care we felt for one another. We connected as two people caring about and caring for one another.

The story encapsulates my shift from thinking care was mine alone to dispense to a beginning understanding that homeless people too wanted to give as well as receive care. The interaction between PJ and me moved me from professional pride in what I knew and what I could do, to the humbling realisation that while I had skills, homeless people had much to teach me. My immersion in the homeless community revealed to me their unexpected desire to be of use, and to demonstrate care. Assumptions about the nature of homelessness and the character people experiencing homelessness made these realisations especially poignant. Much has been written about homeless people's social disengagement, their apparent indifference to social norms and values, and their lack of social capital beyond the homeless community (Caplow, Bahr and Sternberg, 1968; Department of Social Security, 1973; Bahr and Caplow, 1974). Little has been written about their loyalty, their grief at the loss of family and former friends, and their continuing desire to care when there were few legitimate ways they could demonstrate this care. The exceptions to this silence have been ethnographic studies like Liebow's (1993) study of homeless women, and more recently research into social capital in homeless communities (Stablein, 2011).

My developing relationship with PJ (and with other Club members I was getting to know) was the beginning of a solidarity I developed with this community and that has extended, over time, to all those without shelter. The shared interest PJ and I had in finding accommodation motivated me to use whatever privilege I had as a professional to stand and speak up against inequality. At The Club, this initially entailed advocating on issues Club members had identified collectively and individually as important. Over time, members set the agenda and became effective self-advocators. A deliberate program of introducing Club members to local members of council and parliament connected them to people whose decisions influenced their access to public space, community perceptions of them, and the way they felt about themselves.

The apparently small incident with PJ was also the catalyst for what would emerge as a radical framework for my practice, and my understanding of my work as political activity directed to changing not the people I worked with, but the structures that excluded and judged them, and the policies that affected them daily. My work at The Club was the start of a working life devoted to homelessness issues. I have always understood this work as political, and I have intentionally created spaces (through research and policy work) where the values and beliefs of public space dwellers can be heard and responded to (Coleman, 1997; Drew and Coleman, 1999; McAuliffe and Coleman, 1999; Coleman, 2001; Coleman, 2002; Coleman, 2007; Coleman, 2016). I have been able to use what I have learned from PJ and others at The Club to challenge assumptions about homelessness (and the people experiencing it). Each piece of work has been a statement of my solidarity with homeless people, and I have been constantly reminded of and motivated by what hooks (1994, p. 54) describes as "an ethics of struggle". This concept encapsulates for me the merging of an ethics of care with an ethics of justice.

My time with homeless people also taught me how very differently care can be understood and demonstrated. The care that was most valued by the people I worked with was not the professional care they would rightly expect from a social worker (or the sort of care a social work degree had prepared me to give). They appreciated most the genuine interest, empathy and care I showed to them as unique individuals *and* as part of a unique group. I was initially not always able to recognise or see their care for me for what it was: a genuine interest in me as a person. To give and receive care as workers, we need a generous view of what care looks (and feels) like, and an understanding of homeless people's genuine desire to care – and the limited chances they have had to observe, and develop their capacity to care.

My work at the 139 Club also raised some broad questions for social work. The focus of the chapter is not on these issues, but I raise them for consideration in the hope that other practitioners (and the people they work with) might continue to discuss and practice care as part of reciprocal relationships, and as a demonstration of solidarity with people in the margins.

The first of these issues relates to what an ethics of care means for professional work in the human services, and for critical social work specifically. Banks (2013) makes a case that care is inherent in a radical approach to social work. She argues that social work must reclaim its mission by attending to the fair distribution of resources (such as public space) while also questioning and challenging power and vested interests (for example, developers in Fortitude Valley). Acknowledging this work as inherently political, Banks reframes the social work project as ethico-political (2013, pp. 364–365). My opportunity to work with and get to know homeless people at the 139 Club confirmed for me the political nature of social work, and the role solidarity with these groups plays in our ability to expose injustices and to enter into care that is meaningful to them.

In an environment where neoliberal views predominate, the matter of whether an ethics of care involves (or should involve) a political stance is related to the question of whether the care social work provides will be improved by what Banks (2013, p. 357–358) calls the "ethics boom". Her fear is that empathy and a willingness to engage with other world views will be sacrificed for efficiency and equity. As she concludes, there are two views on whether the increasing focus of ethics and standards gives social work a platform from which to resist neoliberal ideas of individual responsibility, or merely another way to regulate and standardise the profession.

Of personal concern is the question of the relevance of radical/structural frameworks of practice in the present climate. Banks (2013, pp. 354–355) reveals the concepts of care that in radical politics are "deeply embedded in the analysis" although not explicitly articulated. A radical framework for practice can provide a sound platform for an ethics of care which includes interrogating power, oppressive structures and the role of social work itself. Like Banks (2013), I see a pressing need for radical theory and practice in any social work ethics of care, and a particular need in the present context. Banks identifies the narrow view of social work endorsed by neoliberalism as "being divorced from people with personalities and from political debates about what counts as fairness or equality" (Banks, 2013, p. 367).

Conclusion

Writing this chapter has brought to mind many examples of care shown to me at the 139 Club, and the connection I have with The Valley and the people I worked with there. My time at The Club was full of daily examples of people finding ways to show me they cared for, and about me. As a researcher doing field work in The Valley some years after I'd left my role as the social worker/welfare coordinator, homeless people provided advice and guidance that kept me safe on the streets, and offered me information and tips. Some relationships begun at The Club turned into friendships that are a continuing reminder to me that there are many views of the world, and many ways to be in the world.

The story that is central to this chapter illustrates what can happen when we see and acknowledge our strengths and vulnerabilities as professionals, as well as those of the people with whom we work. It also shows that social work, at its heart, is a political activity. Homelessness is the product of structures that distribute opportunities unequally, as is social work. A social work response to homelessness requires social work not to further monitor or stereotype the people experiencing it, but to engage in a sustained critique of inequality and injustice and a willingness to be with, and learn from the people who experience it most sharply. My professional qualification gave me a voice that was seen as legitimate and could (and has) been used to raise homelessness issues, to advocate for the people with whom I worked (and others in similar situation whom I will never meet). A critical and empathic approach to social work practice has enabled me to challenge policies and practices that further isolate and disadvantage homeless people. For me, this work continues to be a way of showing ongoing care for and solidarity with people experiencing homelessness and a way of enacting my commitment to (and celebrating) the values I learned with and from homeless people: mutuality, solidarity and resistance.

References

Bahr, H. and Caplow, T. (1974) *Old men drunk and sober*. New York: Oxford University Press.

Banks, S. (2013) Reclaiming social work ethics: Challenging new public management. In: Ferguson, I. and Lavalette, M. (eds.) *Critical and radical debates in social work* [online]. Bristol: Policy Press, pp. 352–374. Available from: www.worldcat.org/title/critical-and-radical-debates-in-social-work/oclc/862050022?referer=di&ht=edition [Accessed 8 January 2017].

Bozalek, V. (2013) Reframing social work ethics through a political ethic of care and social justice lens. In: Ferguson, I. and Lavalette, M. (eds.) *Critical and radical debates in social work* [online]. Bristol: Policy Press, pp. 387–392. Available from: www.worldcat. org/title/critical-and-radical-debates-in-social-work/oclc/862050022?referer=di&ht=ed ition [Accessed 8 January 2017].

Caplow, T., Bahr, H. M. and Sternberg, D. (1968) Homelessness. *International Encyclope- dia of Social Sciences*, 6, pp. 494–499.

Coleman, A. (1997) Empty streets: Current policy relating to long term homelessness. In *States, markets and communities: Remapping the boundaries conference.* Proceedings of the National Social Policy Conference, Sydney, November 1997, pp. 59–71.

Coleman, A. (2001) *Five star motels: Spaces, places and homelessness in Fortitude Valley, Brisbane.* PhD thesis, School of Social Work and Social Policy, University of Queensland.

Coleman, A. (2002) *Sister it happens to me every day: An exploration of the needs of Indigenous women in inner city Brisbane.* Brisbane: Brisbane City Council, Department of Families, Youth and Community Services, Department of Aboriginal and Torres Strait Islander Policy and Development and Office of Women.

Coleman, A. (2007) *Art or science? Sustaining housing for people experiencing long term homelessness.* Brisbane: Queensland Department of Communities, Housing and Home- lessness Services.

Coleman, A. (2016) Through the looking glass: Other ways of thinking about community development and homelessness. *Parity*, 29(6), p. 9.

Critchley, S. (2007) *Infinitely demanding: Ethics of commitment, politics of resistance.* London: Verso.

Department of Social Security. (1973) *Report of the Working Party on Homelessness to the Minister for Social Security.* Canberra: Australian Government Printing Service.

Drew, B. and Coleman, A. (1999) This place here is our home: Defining homelessness beyond housing. *Parity*, 12(2), pp. 16–17.

Featherstone, B. and Morris, K. (2012) Feminist ethics of care. In: Grey, M., Midgley, J. and Webb, S. A. (eds.) *The Sage handbook of social work.* Los Angeles: Sage, pp. 341–354.

hooks, b. (1994) *Teaching to transgress.* New York: Routledge.

Liebow, E. (1993) *Tell them who I am: The lives of homeless women.* New York: Basic Books.

Lynch, K., Lyons, M. and Cantillon, S. (2007) Breaking silence: Educating citizens for love, care and solidarity'. *International Studies in Sociology of Education*, 17(1–2), pp. 1–19.

McAuliffe, D. and Coleman, A. (1999) Damned if we do and damned if we don't: Expos- ing ethical tensions in field work. *Australian Social Work*, 52(4), pp. 25–31.

Routledge, P. (1996) The third space as critical engagement. *Antipode*, 28(4), pp. 399–419.

Stablein, T. (2011) Helping friends and the homeless milieu: Social capital and the utility of street peers. *Journal of Contemporary Social Capital*, 40(3), pp. 290–317.

Tronto, J. (1993) *Moral boundaries: A political argument for an ethic of care.* New York: Routledge.

Williams, F. (2001) In and beyond New Labour: Toward a new political ethics of care. *Critical Social Policy*, 21(4), pp. 467–493.

Young, I. 2011. *Responsibility for justice.* Oxford: Oxford University Press.

8 From state to market

Reclaiming a critical ethics of elder care

Sharon Moore

Introduction

In this chapter I examine the nature of caring and care work and argue that caring is a normative, community issue requiring social analysis, based on gender and power. It cannot be described as just a women's issue, a family concern or commercial opportunity. Intersectionality offers an important theoretical and strategic resource to extend our exploration of care ethics particularly by developing analyses of diversity and power relations. This analysis is useful in understanding the move to the marketisation and commodification of elder care in Australia and internationally, including China and the Asian region.

The global privatisation of human services, increased reliance on commercial services and public-private partnerships have radically altered social discourses around care. Care work in Australia, as elsewhere, is being regulated and bureaucratised as care managers adopt the latest new management private solutions (Australian Government Productivity Commission, 2011). While service users and their families may be consulted, they are often treated as objects, not subjects, in the development and delivery of their care services. In the midst of these shifts, we are left with the question of who actually 'cares' in newly privatised care systems, and this is the guiding question of this chapter.

Aged care: Australian and international perspectives

Aged care is emerging as a significant domain of Australian contemporary social policy due in part to the ageing of the population, the growth of health and social security budgets, and baby boomers' expectation of a better ageing future from that experienced by their parents. So the rapid expansion of private markets to deliver care is perhaps not surprising, coming as it does after the extension of publicly subsidised non-profit services which were central to post-war welfare state development in Australia. In recent times, the costs of care to the public have been portrayed by government as prohibitive, and the need for choice for consumers is an increasingly popular policy message (Department of Health and Ageing, 2010). Private care solutions are promoted as an appropriate response by government as part of welfare pluralism and the new mixed economy of care.

In the UK, Fiona Williams (2010, 2012) reminds us of the contribution of feminist theory, the women's movement and pensioner organisations to promoting state-provided services. In this analysis, the state is seen as recognising its rights and responsibilities to its senior citizens and supporting women by supporting families and thus offering service choices. However, a social commitment to aged care as the moral touchstone of the welfare state has been increasingly challenged over recent decades. Public welfare has been increasingly replaced by global enthusiasm for neoliberal ideas about choice and competition together with increased pressures on public finances, leading Australian governments of different political persuasions to promote policies that foster markets in care, including for-profit care providers, for over two decades.

A more critical, gendered analysis of this domain of social policy is losing its primacy as markets have been promoted and defended, alongside a new push towards care users being portrayed as consumers where care is increasingly framed as a commodity. The new care consumer is often assumed to be a self-interested individual embedded in primarily economic relationships, which is at odds with the reality of the typical consumer being a frail older, low- to middle-income woman, with her primary carer being her middle-aged daughter. The reframing and redefining of care relationships as primarily economic relationships, the promotion of for-profit care services and the discourse of the well-resourced independent care purchaser consumer sit uneasily within a wider discourse of care based on relational models and interdependence.

Post-war Australia had a strong tradition of delivering elder care through publicly subsidised non-profit organisations, rather than private for-profit providers. However, care markets operate according to a different logic than other health and caring systems. Since 2000, the balance of formal care for frail older people in Australia has changed from predominantly residential care to home-based care services with an increasing reliance on family care (Department of Health and Ageing, 2010). The use of privately purchased services has increased markedly during the same period (King and Martin, 2009). Interestingly, the situation in many Asian countries is the reverse, as residential care has become more common, especially in countries such as China (Moore and Wen, 2016). The use of privately purchased services has also increased during the same period throughout the region with increased wealth and women's increased participation in the economy and paid work force (Moore and Wen, 2016).

Family care values and models still predominate in most countries while coexisting alongside a private care market for many frail elderly people and their families (Howe and Healy, 2005). Market-oriented policies construct care users as consumers, and care as a commodity to be bought and sold, and the reality of care relations is overshadowed by the image of the consumer as a self-interested individual embedded primarily in economic relationships. This contrasts with feminist notions of elder care in social work and health, traditionally based on a care ethic and care rationality first proposed by Nel Noddings (1984, 2002) and Kari Waerness (1984) in the 1980s in both Anglo-American and Nordic countries, and firmly situated in critical gender theory. An ethic of caring in the West, however, has been severely tested by the privatisation and marketisation of care work and an increasing reliance on regulations and risk management to improve quality and manage costs. Privatisation provides ample evidence of this phenomena at work.

Aged care privatisation

Privatisation of care is reshaping service models globally in many different welfare systems and states as well as throughout Australia. A host of questions has been raised by this development. What kinds of market reforms are being carried out? What are the impacts on older people and their families, care workers and aged care services? Are they adding to social inclusion, and consumer rights and empowerment, or the reverse? The policy rhetoric focuses on the ability to increase access to services through targeting and a new focus on consumer rights (Hodge, 2010), but is this actually occurring? We also need to ask whether market reforms are gendered or gender-neutral, given that such a high proportion of caring remains informal, done mainly by women as daughters and mothers (King and Martin, 2009). In addition, most paid care work is done by low-paid women workers, particularly in aged care and in domestic support roles. Do these shifts from public to private and informal care reflect social values and rights-based welfare ideologies or a more conservative, uncaring view of human services? (Howe and Healy, 2005). This chapter explores these questions and attempts to find answers to them. However, as the reforms are complex and far-reaching, the answers must be tentative.

In this part of the chapter, I outline the marketisation and privatisation trends in aged care and other community services in Australia and the Asian region, and highlight common themes, including the expansion of the for-profit share of the market, as well as increased bureaucratic regulation. To date, most of the privatisation research data are from the global north – that is, first world research. So this chapter encourages comparative research in the Asian region, arguably the most interesting region in the world in terms of emerging responses to social and economic globalisation, as well as economic and welfare liberalism. Asia can be seen as the future site of new and emerging trends in social policy and practices in pursuit of economy, efficiency and effectiveness, which are all part of New Public Management theory and economic liberalism. My research in China between 2003 and 2013 indicated that many women in China struggle to manage their paid and unpaid family care work, exacerbated by privatisation of formerly state-provided social infrastructure (Moore and Wen, 2016).

Privatisation of aged and community care services research has been critiqued by radical social work as well as contributions from the consumer movement including the carers and disability sectors, and critical research into the co-creation and co-production of person-centred care. Care researchers often argue that consumer-led care is naïve because of the power differential between the professional or manager and the older person. It can be seen as misleading or false consumerism, and consultation at best, rather than real choice and care partnership in action. Further, it has been argued that the administration or management fees in aged care packages built around the individual consumer can use up much of the total aged care budget, leaving little to actually pay for care services (Baxter, Wilberforce and Glendinning, 2011).

Rather than providing services for the many, they appear to be 'gold-plated' services for the very few, moving care into a specialist and individualised direction rather than as more general service to support many frail older people continuing to live at home. Since 2015, the previous preventative focus of Home and Community Care (HACC) funding has been increasingly directed from general home care support for many towards individualised care packages for relatively few. This has resulted in most HACC programs being subsumed under the Commonwealth Home Support Program.

The Australian experience of increasing home care to replace some residential care generally mirrors the Anglo-American experience as a way of meeting care needs without the psychological and financial cost/burden of residential care. When privatisation of both home and residential care has been the response, the outcomes are often negative for workers and care users. It could be argued that an increased focus on regulation of aged care management can reduce a focus on quality in the pursuit of for-profit, efficiency-driven outcomes (Hancock and Moore, 1999). Indeed, it appears that rules have at times come to replace quality of services, as aged care staff often complain that they get 'rules rather than resources'. Similarly, the work organisation of care workers has changed significantly with a move from team-work or relational care models to more bureaucratic systems. Quality of care is not being linked to quality of working life for care workers in the new care order. The nexus between quality of care and service, and the quality of the caring work was being recognised in some Australian states and nationally as being at the heart of successful care planning and service prior to the privatisation experience. This was based on international experience, especially the contributions of UK and European care researchers. Profits rather than quality of care and service seem to be the new mantra, and the profits in some cases are huge. Private for-profit organisations are rapidly taking over home care as well as residential care services, as they are predicated on guaranteed public funding (Australian Productivity Commission, 2011).

The government role as purchaser and regulator of services has also radically changed the role and responsibility of the state. Public sector abrogation is evident as the state contracts its planning and delivery role to the private sector, including large multinational health providers and insurance companies as well as large charitable organisations. The government's role is increasingly to provide the bulk of funds and monitor the regulatory environment, resulting in a major shift towards regulation and standardisation as the new order of the day. However, the Nordic experience of increased regulation of care work is that it may actually detract from quality of care provision (Brennan, Cass, Himmelweit and Szebehely, 2012). This is a challenge for governments which need to assert their role in planning and developing aged care and ensuring that the conditions and resources for aged care work are present.

Veteran Canadian social work researcher Pat Armstrong alerted us 20 years ago to the fundamental flaw in the private model: private operators looking to maximise profits are tempted to reduce the investment needed to provide the best possible care for the most vulnerable people in their charge (Armstrong, 1999). Her words remain pertinent today.

The introduction of contracting in aged care is making government reshape itself to reflect the structure of 'big business'. Ernst and Glanville (1997) first characterised this as the shift to more bureaucratic, technocratic service management, and it is clearly so today. Seminal Australian research on privatisation and public sector abrogation detail an evaluation of the outcomes of the contracting out and competitive tendering of public sector services in over 240 cases, sourced from international literature (Hodge, 2010). Hodge emphasises the lack of data and experience around the contracting of human services and argues that if services are social (or any other of the less profitable services), standards may reduce. Hard data on the effectiveness of contracting health and human services are scant, and it is debatable whether the contracting of such services is always effective. Governance requires a willingness to lead while resolving political and community conflict through notions such as democracy, fairness, openness and due process (Hodge, 2010).

Early research into privatisation and public-private partnerships identified factors which make human services such as community, aged and disability services, as well as services for families, children and youth, different from other areas of government activity (Ernst and Glanville, 1997). These factors are still relevant today (Hodge, 2010). Care services are personal and individual and generally involve direct interaction between service provider and recipient. An ongoing relationship is established and continuity of care service provision is important to its quality, as services deal regularly with sensitive areas of people's lives, where people may feel particularly vulnerable. The "technology" used is different and this has implications for the design and delivery of services. The issues involved are not technical but value-laden, as service users are active agents. Power is a critical issue and the power imbalance between service provider and service user is important to acknowledge and address. Activities are also relatively unpredictable and non-routine, requiring individual judgement, flexibility, adaptability and the use of discretion on the part of the service provider, which may present particular challenges in the task of drawing up contract specifications.

Care services operate most functionally in an environment of co-operation, as they are people services and relationally based. A dynamic of co-operation may be threatened by the movement towards a competitive model, along with equity principles which are central to the formulation of human services policy and the provision of human services. Women remain the major users and providers of social and human services in our communities. They are much more likely to be located in the private realm performing the tasks of caring for and nurturing in the area of social reproduction, as both paid and unpaid informal carers and also as care recipients. In these respects, women are intimately and particularly affected by the changing role of government. This is most currently evident in the privatisation policy and the privatisation impacts on the women who manage and work in care services. In summary, Meagher and Szebehely (2010) posit 10 most frequently mentioned gendered disadvantages of the competitive tendering: heavier workloads; loss of job security; general increase in unfair treatment and favouritism; negative impact on health (physically and in terms of stress); loss of respect and appreciation; unclear processes and avenues for complaint; loss of job satisfaction; and a reduction in conditions of service and entitlements such as superannuation, long service and sick leave.

Redeveloping a feminist care rationality for aged care

Norwegian feminist sociologist Kari Waerness (1984) first developed her gendered analysis of the concept of caring by focusing on women caring in the Nordic or Scandinavian context. This research was significant in redirecting feminist care researchers in Europe, and Western countries more broadly, to caring as critically important and valuable women's work. She claimed caring work should be based on a specific kind of care rationality. A rationality of caring, Waerness argued, is essentially female and is different from a more male-focused rationality which is often instrumental or transactional, as opposed to emotional and expressive care. This critique has been viewed as essentialist, and links are now made with new models of care systems focusing on the specific qualities inherent in everyday caregiving work (Williams, 2010).

Waerness's seminal research, despite its essentialist tendencies, formed the basis of a gendered critique of the modernisation of elder care in the 1980s, and many other feminist authors have developed her caring discourse themes. In the United States, Nel Noddings (1984, 2002) was exploring a feminist care ethic or rationality located in philosophy about the family and social care which echoes many of later feminist care themes. While Noddings has also been criticised for being essentialist, Nordic researchers have developed a theory of caring which characterises aged care workers' involvement in their work with older people as a rationale or caring orientation (e.g. Meagher and Szebehely, 2010). Their focus on paid care work is a useful antidote to the more essentialist critique of Waerness and Noddings.

Carers, both paid and unpaid, often operate according to a rationality which is difficult to organise according to strict economic technical rationality, and the positive results reflect their enjoyment and involvement in their work. Care workers often act according to a rationality which is not formal or abstract as they pay attention to the immediate needs of the elderly and fulfil these in their daily practices (Meagher and Szebehely, 2010).

Feminist research into aged care utilises a similar everyday gaze, noticing actions and relationships, and ascribing cultural and subjective meanings, being influenced by progressive research into the importance of caring by both family carers (usually women) as well as paid carers increasingly presented as partners in the caring relationship (Baines, 2017). A social or community-based view of caring and its importance to the state and society were adopted as part of the social policy and advocacy mandate of the Carers' Movement which was very successful in putting caring and family carers on the Australian public policy agenda. Their advocacy, supported by feminist research into the actual costs of care and importance of community support for carers, led to the carers' strategy, carers' pension and allowance, and relatively generous carers' policy and program responses in all Australian states and territories. The Australian Carers' Movement, under strong female leadership, has been instrumental in contributing to support for progressive care policies and services.

Institutionally based aged care can be analysed in terms of the ways it is integrated into a patriarchal, ageist, bio-medical system and also reflects the low value typically placed on care work in general. Aged care services are often located in medically focused workplaces where the dominant culture focuses on maintenance in people's functioning as part of the late stages in the ageing process rather more than a social or quality care orientation. Recent research by the author into the work/life challenges facing women in contemporary China, the largest global economy and a leading economic power in our region, indicates that China, among other developing economies, is less inclined to privilege age and experience as older family members are increasingly separated from their extended family. "There has to be more than Ma Jong and Tai chi in my life" is a common plea I heard from older people in China interviewed for this research (Moore and Wen, 2016, p. 13). This needs more exploration, as China rapidly develops its own mixed economy of care, and embraces private for-profit care service solutions, particularly the use of aged care institutions. At this point in our history, the health care or hospital model seems more acceptable than home or community care services in many large cities in China (Moore and Wen, 2016).

Returning to the situation in Australia, it is increasingly difficult to produce sufficient formal evidence that care rationality is more effective than the economic-technical hospital-style efficiency rationality which dominates the privatisation of aged care in recent decades (Meagher and Szebehely, 2010). Care rationality and a feminist perspective are not being incorporated and reflected in policy and practice research, although many workers and service users attest to its central importance and relevance to quality care (Moore and Wen, 2016). Quality of care has long been identified as integral to successful care relations and caring outcomes (Baines, 2017). When feminist notions of caring are formally neglected, there are stressful dilemmas in everyday care work from both worker and service user perspectives, as the relational aspects are replaced by commercial or more technical approaches to the work (Hancock and Moore, 1999). The concept of care rationality is in striking opposition to the way care work is organised under New Public Management theory. This style of work is characterised by an instrumental routine or industrial view of production where emotional labour is overlooked and ignored (Meagher and Szebehely, 2010). "A social worker with a mop" is how one older woman described her overworked, exhausted care manager whose work organisation and management reflected an industrial production line process, rather than a complex, relational approach to the work (Hancock and Moore, 1999).

Conclusion

Increasingly, Australian government rhetoric can be interpreted as "what's there not to like about introducing more choice and competition in areas in which governments fund and/or deliver human services?" This appears to be the starting point of the Australian Productivity Commission's recent inquiry (2011) into competition and choice in human services, which came out strongly supporting private for-profit services funded by public monies. In contrast, Hodge's (2010) analysis of an extremely comprehensive privatisation dataset heavily critiqued the privatisation agenda as ill-conceived and heavy-handed. This is clearly contested terrain, and caring services may give Australia another opportunity to show global leadership in a significant social policy area by offering a spirited critique of privatised care – as in the days of economic reform from 1980 until 2000, when uniquely within the Anglo-American world, Australia pursued neoliberal economic efficiencies while also strengthening the social safety net (Garnaut, 2016).

There are powerful challenges from privatisation to a rationality of caring, which sees an ethic of care as fundamental to quality of care and caring relationships as well as supporting the social safety net function inherent in former welfare state thinking. Economic liberalism as applied to aged care privatisation lacks an understanding of the difficulties of delivery – and is often applied without entering the world of those on the ground, which in aged care is potentially all older people, their families and care workers. It is a normative experience and everyone has a mother or other family member attempting to deal with aged care and primary health systems as service users/consumers. Too often 'the market' can appear as a machine, somehow absolving the policy maker and national funders from their fundamental responsibilities to service users, family members and care workers.

Even more conservative management theorists are starting to argue publicly that the master narrative for care should not be contracting out, competition, choice or even market design, but rather the management of a corporate supply chain with all of those phenomena being part of the supply chain technical business repertoire (Garnaut, 2016). This is radical, even dangerous language in health and human services, as these services can mean life or death for older people, who are not cars or widgets but vulnerable people with complex and varying support needs. Concepts from industrial production have limited relevance, yet are increasingly used in economic liberal policy and program discourse. They appear to be diametrically opposed to feminist care theory and its relational focus.

We need to reclaim a feminist rationality of caring so that services are meaningful and continue to make a real difference to people's quality of life. There is current widespread dissatisfaction with the privatisation of formerly government services in health, education and social care, precisely because the tendering processes are seen to have resulted in poorer service outcomes and widespread public sector abrogation (Moore, in press). There is growing acknowledgement of the effects of lack of regulation and the power of vested interests which go against Australia's traditional support for a fair go and commitment to social equality. Caring can be viewed as part of this ethical value commitment. A caring community is greatly valued in Australia, and Australians appreciate and value publicly provided services and the welfare safety net. Unlike the United States, for example, Australians use and trust publicly provided services over privatised services. Australia has had a tradition of universal, tax-financed elder care services centred on public provision. Yet it has not escaped the influence of the global wave of privatisation in recent years. Market-inspired measures such as competitive tendering and user choice models have been introduced in community care services, and there has been an increase of private for-profit provision of care services. In this process, the voices and experience of care workers, service users and their families have been overlooked and ignored despite their central role in providing quality of care and service. The voice and experience of women as carers and service users is integral to the provision of quality caring services. A critical ethics of care is fundamental to care analyses and caring practices.

References

Armstrong, P. (1999) *Feminist political economy and the state*. Toronto: University of Toronto Press.

Australian Government Productivity Commission. (2011) *Caring for older Australians, draft report*. Canberra: Australian Government Productivity Commission.

Baines, D. (ed.) (2017) *Doing anti-oppressive practice: Social justice and social work*. 2nd edition. Halifax, NS: Fernwood.

Baxter, K., Wilberforce, M. and Glendinning, C. (2011) Personal budgets and the workforce implications for social care providers. *Social Policy and Society*, 10(1), pp. 55–65.

Brennan, D., Cass, B., Himmelweit, S. and Szebehely, M. (2012) The marketisation of care: Rationales and consequences in Nordic and liberal care regimes. *Journal of European Social Policy*, 22(4), pp. 377–391.

Department of Health and Ageing. (2010) *Report on the operation of the Aged Care Act 1997, 1 July 2009–30 June 2010*. Canberra: Commonwealth of Australia, DOHA.

Ernst, J. and Glanville, L. (1997) Coming to terms! The initial implementation. In: Ernst, J., Glanville, L. and Murfitt, P. (eds.) *Breaking the contract? The implementation of compulsory competitive tendering policy in Victoria*. Melbourne: Outer Urban Research and Policy Unit.

Garnaut, R. (2016) Vested Interests are killing our capitalist democracy. *Australian Financial Review*, May 23, pp. 1–6.

Hancock, L. and Moore, S. (1999) Caring and the state. In: Hancock, L. (ed.) *Health policy and the market state*. Sydney: Allen & Unwin, pp. 265–287.

Hodge, G. (2010) *The Australian public private policy experience: Observations and reflections*. Cheltenham: Edward Elgar.

Howe, A. and Healy, K. (2005) Generational justice in aged care policy in Australia and the United Kingdom. *Australasian Journal on Ageing*, 24(Supplement), pp. S12–S18.

King, D. and Martin, B. (2009) Caring for profit? The impacts of for-profit providers on the quality of employment in paid care. In: Meagher, G. and King, D. (eds.) *Paid care in Australasia: Politics, profits, practices*. Sydney: Sydney University Press.

Meagher, G. and Szebehely, M. (2010) *Private financing of elder care in Sweden*. Stockholm: Institute for Future Studies.

Moore, S. (in press) Public private partnerships: The Australian and international experience. In: W. Lei Huang (ed.) *Corporate social responsibility and global business*. Guang Zhou, PRC: GDUFS Publishing House.

Moore, S. and Wen, J. (2016) Women managers in China speak out. Unpublished paper.

Noddings, N. (1984) *Caring: A feminine approach to ethics and moral education*. Berkeley: University of California Press.

Noddings, N. (2002) *Starting at home: Caring and social policy.* Berkeley: University of California Press.

Waerness, K. (1984) The rationality of caring. *Economic and Industrial Democracy*, 5(2), pp. 185–211.

Williams, F. (2010) *Claiming and framing in the making of care policies: The recognition and redistribution of care.* Geneva: United Nations Research Institute for Social Development (UNRISD).

Williams, F. (2012) Converging variations in migrant care work. *Journal of European Social Policy*, 22(4), pp. 363–376.

9 Protecting children within a relationship-based feminist care ethic

Maria Harries

Introduction

At national as well as international levels, challenges in the practice of protecting and caring for children have catapulted this important area of labour yet again into the public eye and consolidated it firmly as a major social problem in public, political and professional spheres. Multiple inquiries and investigations of failures have led to numerous demands for changes in professional practice, public and social policy, legislation and organisational arrangements (Featherstone et al., 2014). Included in these recent and proliferating demands has been the call to re-consider the place of ethics in the decision-making about how we protect children and ensure their wellbeing, while at the same time ensuring the wellbeing of their families and communities which constitute their vitally important 'relational environment' (Lonne et al., 2016).

The work of protecting children

The need to protect children is politically, professionally and publicly non-controversial: we must ensure their safety from abuse and neglect. However, concealed in the folds of the virtuous intention of systems aimed at protecting children are myriad ethical and practical complexities that, as Featherstone et al. (2014, p. 370) so cogently argue, "mask the moral nature of the work" and defy simple organisational solutions. Among the folds of practice is the place of compassion and care and, in particular, where that care and compassion is located – singularly, towards children, or, more organically, towards them within the relational and cultural environment into which these children are born and reared.

Practitioners working to protect children function in risk-saturated environments where relationships are fractured, care is fragile and sometimes frightening, and value-based practice with a broader focus than the safety of a child unit is particularly difficult. There is a high intensity of emotional labour demanded of those protecting children and 'doing care' in such an environment. Unarguably, emotion is at the centre of this work. A consequence of the high-risk profile of the work amid the sensitivity to failure to assess well and protect appropriately is that the rationality represented in particular by the requirements of legal decision-making and duties have been privileged and the significance of emotion and relationships marginalised. Notifications, assessments, risk screens, decision-making templates and 'dutiful recording' are instituted as the mechanisms for guarding against engagement and ensuring as much impartiality as possible.

The question addressed in this chapter is how, if at all, a feminist ethic of care with its attendant and complex view of morality and the centrality within it of relationship, can provide better understanding of how the caring professions can work more 'care-fully' in this contested area of practice. In this chapter, I place child protection practice within an historical context in terms of ethical thought and consider the promises that a feminist ethic of care may provide to our thinking about how to rise to the challenges that have been articulated in the public and policy domains.

A personal context

The thinking in this chapter is that of a practitioner and teacher, not of a moral philosopher or feminist scholar, and it is not based merely on academic reviews of theory or the myriad challenges presented in scholarly discourse and inquiries into service failures. Instead, it engages with observations I and others have made over years of practice and teaching as well as, parenthetically, on ideas that have emerged from research with children and families who have had the misfortune to find themselves involved with the statutory child protection system due to their experiences of a variety of forms of adversity. The ideas herein are also heavily influenced by discussions around power and ethics held with postgraduate students and practitioners in various disciplines and jurisdictions. All of these people have struggled with the nexus between action, theory and values, that is, the complex space where ethics and moral decision-making collide in their often highly bureaucratised world of work including that of protecting children from harm. Making sense of ethical theories in all their domains of work has itself been challenging to these practitioners, particularly as many of them had held fast to the principle-based ethical theories of their discipline training which they were no longer finding sufficient.

At the centre of my reflections is the inescapable core value I hold of the uniqueness and dignity of every human being and the associated need to care for them within a relational framework – theirs and mine. This value was seeded in a family committed to justice in my birthplace – a racially torn but deeply relational Africa. It appeared syntonic with some of the early social work values espoused by writers such as Biestek (1957), Teicher (1967) and Gottschalk (1974). Indeed, Biestek (1957, p. 18) called relationship "the soul of casework". Recent scholars have justifiably and usefully critiqued this early work as being historically embedded within a simple Western casework context, and note that our contemporary practice context is now globalised and challenged in 'turbulent times' that Biestek could not ever have conceptualised (Harlow, Berg, Barry and Chandler, 2013; Cheung, 2015; Hugman and Carter, 2016). However, the importance of relationship has continued to inform my commitment to the broader world of social justice and has always fuelled a family life committed to racial equality. An ethic of practice that has the capacity to embrace a relational paradigm has been essential to my professional work. As with so many other practitioners with whom I have had the privilege to ponder the challenges of our work, relational care in practice has sat uneasily but steadfastly for 50 years embedded in a tense disjuncture with the demands of practice. Legal duties, ethical principles and organisational directives as well as indispensable bureaucratic requirements have provided endless obstacles to the expression of care in professional practice that Biestek and his colleagues promoted within their principles of good practice and that were foundational to my professional education.

The landscape of ethics

Various ethical perspectives offer characteristic ways of understanding what we should care most about, what we should do and how we should approach the decisions about what to do – in this case, about the safety and welfare of children. In very simple terms, principle-based or deontological ethics follows a code of practice based on the 'premises' or 'rules' that should inform decisions (e.g. the duty to protect). Outcome-based or teleological/utilitarian ethics focus on achieving the best outcomes (e.g. safety of the child). On the other hand, virtue ethics focuses on the disposition or character of the decision-maker as a moral agent who needs to be a person of virtue and who has the required characteristics to make the best decision in the circumstances – which might well include the incorporation of thinking about principles and outcomes as well as the value of care itself (Oakley and Cocking, 2001, p. 139). As noted in a recent text on ethics and child protection (Lonne et al., 2016), a virtue ethics approach can sit coherently with the need to balance principles and outcomes when making decisions about the lives of children and families. It acknowledges the significance of the complex interpersonal context for decision-making as well as the primacy of the role of the integrity and personhood of the worker.

More recently, newer approaches such as discourse ethics and the feminist ethic of care – together sometimes called 'relational ethics' (Noddings, 2003) – have emerged as welcome additional approaches to ethics (Held, 2006). It is important to acknowledge these newer approaches, particularly the feminist ethic of care, have been seen by a number of scholars as alternative rather than additional approaches to ethics (Morrow, 2005).) As Furrow (2005, p. 67) argues, at the heart of the disagreements is the question of whether care is foundational or whether it derives from other ethical principles or positions. This is an arena of deep philosophical controversy between scholars and one that is beyond the scope of this more practical analysis. However, a simple examination suggests that historically virtue ethics has been seen for some as anti-feminist, and more importantly, there are complex and interesting philosophical differences in views about how we frame the lens of care and how we apply reason to this (Halwani, 2003; Sander-Staudt, 2006).

It is my deeply practical view that a virtue ethics framework that embraces the relational ethics of discourse ethics and care ethics, is ideally suited to improving ethical practice in child protection. Held (2006, p. 19) asserts the ethic of care has been seen by many philosophers as "a form of virtue ethics" although she does not accept this position herself. Her criticism of this position is based on a number of factors including the limited attention at that time of the significance of caring relations within the theoretical understanding of virtue ethics, its "patriarchal past", and its more limited focus on the 'disposition' of the individual rather than on the "social practices and values that sustain them" (2006, p. 20).

Care and justice

While care has been considered a universalist principle in social work, it is also seen as and is fundamental to the struggle for justice (Rummery and Fine, p. 326). With due respect to the views of Held, and embracing the challenge to ethical pluralism as encouraged by Houston (2010), it is through a virtue ethics lens on child protection practice that an ethic of care is viewed in this chapter. Although care and justice are often counterposed in theoretical writings (Held, 1995), if we dive into the meaning of caring, we find ourselves involved in the political world of social justice in which we encounter the strongholds of power and power relationships that undermine fair dealings and that sabotage dreams and hopes for a flourishing world. There is no doubt that power imbalances are at the core of the work of people involved in the care and protection of children. Let there be no doubt that the majority of families caught up in the exchange with statutory child protection systems are economically and socially on the periphery of 'mainstream society' (Bywaters et al., 2015).

Care ethics is indeed political and places care itself at odds with the prevalent and burgeoning values of autonomy, power and conflict. In this light, Meagher and Parton (2004, p. 17) comment that we need to "integrate thinking about ethics of care with political theory". An ethic of justice focuses on individual rights, fairness and equality: care focuses on relationship, interdependence, trust, and, "it disrupts the boundaries erected between the public and the personal" (Holland, 2010, p. 1665). Again, as Parton (2003, p. 23) asserts, "justice and care are logically compatible and indispensable to each other." Similarly, Hoggett (2000) affirms the centrality of both an ethic of justice and an ethic of care.

Challenges in contemporary practice

Prior to the 1980s, the work of protecting children was generally contained within the mantle of child and family welfare – albeit mired in accusations of punitive paternalism and not necessarily a period of ethically robust relationship-based practice either (Lonne et al., 2016, p. xii). The now named field of child protection itself emerged following the important work of Kempe and his colleagues in the United States during the 1960s. During this period, the requirements of legal decision-making, mandated reporting, organisational obligations and stringent assessment criteria have increasingly privileged rationality based on duty that is captured within a paradigm of risk (Beck, 2009).

Many authors comment on the 'prevailing objectivist paradigm' that developed and which has continued to shape child protection practice since that time. Arguably, this paradigm sits uncomfortably if not illogically with care ethics or any relational or relationship based, inter-subjective practice of engagement. Downie and Telfer (1980, p. 90) prophetically anticipated this contemporary situation, stating "personalness [the ideal attitude of the caring worker], so far from being desirable, is logically incompatible with the caring worker's situation." In the area of child protection the dominant discourse is one of duty – the duty to protect children using the process and outcome of the paramount principle of 'best interests'. Having disengaged from placing care at the centre of child protection work and succumbed to the demands of managerial imperatives and deontological ethics, the question is how if at all we can place care again at the centre of our practice?

Almost universally, care and protection orders are adopted in legislation in order to enable children to be removed from their families and placed in what is generally called 'alternative care'. Many service users who were removed from their parents are unequivocal in their condemnation of what they call 'the no care system'. They argue that neither care nor respect is what they experienced during their engagement with authorities, but that care is simply a bureaucratic term used to define the outcome of legal proceedings that removed them from family. In the contemporary public policy environment, we are indeed witnessing a call from multiple stakeholders, including these adults who have been in statutory care to stop what they see as oppressive practice in child protection, to work differently, and to reform and 're-imagine' the work involved in protecting and caring for children (Scott, 2006; Featherstone et al., 2014; Lonne et al., 2016). Central to this call at the present time are families who experience themselves as marginalised, dismissed and despised by the care system involved in ensuring the protection of their children (Harries, 2008). Importantly, also present is the voice of Indigenous people and practitioners from across disciplines who call for new ways of incorporating the centrality of relationships in the work of protecting children and caring for their families and communities (Strega and Esquao, 2009; Young, McKenzie, Schjelderup, Omre and Walker, 2014). Many of the accusations about current practice and outcomes in child protection practice highlight the injustices perpetrated in the name of protecting children. Arguably, attention to these injustices is central to an ethic of care. In a different voice is not just the voice of women but of poor and ethnic minorities (Roberts, 2002).

What is apparent in the contemporary environment is the evident failure of the objectivist, risk-saturated paradigm dominated by the almost solitary rule of duty despite the dedication, commitment and carefulness of so many people who have worked in the face of systemic hurdles to retain the essence of care and love in their work (Hudson, 2003). Elaborate protocols and strict guidelines in bureaucratised institutional structures that enforce rules do not permit the acknowledgement let alone the prioritisation of the relationships so important to children, families and communities. Here, as Froggett (2002, p. 111) so cogently explains, "although remaining part of a personal emotional repertoire that enables welfare professionals to tolerate the pain and rage of others," compassion and care "sit uneasily within a discourse of contractual or procedural rights, or of performativity". Here, it is demanded of them that they remain objective, detached and 'distant' while they grapple with working in an area of work unparalleled in its emotional intensity and complexity. As Featherstone et al. (2014, p. 37) observe, in this environment, the moral nature of the work of caring for and protecting children, respecting family relationships and culture becomes concealed and the place of ethics becomes perilous.

Re-locating care in professional practice

While the nursing profession readily accepts care as "central to nursing theory and practice" and "comprises nursing's specialised knowledge base" (Froggett, 2002, p. 203), other professions, including (for me quite paradoxically) social work, appear to have had a more ambivalent relationship with it. Observing the tensions inherent in the work worlds of caring professionals who work in formalised bureaucratic structures, Parton (2003, pp. 10, 21) talks of care being devalued in social work and associated with a past that social work may be trying to avoid. Weick (2000) refers to this as the "hidden voice" in social work. Adopting the tenets of an ethic of care provides an opportunity for social work and other helping professions to reinstate and reassert the value of the concept of care within the centre of practice again. In the words of Dybicz (2012), ethics of care provides insights that enable us to recapture "social work's first voice" – the voice of care – but, he adds, it can also locate this alongside the voice of justice, autonomy and rights. No one suggests this will be easy!

Care is not an untroubled notion and as Froggett (2002, p. 119) has suggested, the concept itself has "become corrupted". However, it is beyond the scope of this chapter to do what Cloyes (2002, p. 204) asks us to do, and that is to develop a more critically robust conception of care. In simple terms, the concept of care embraces active concern, love and other-centredness. Care is both a moral and a political concept – relational and pluralistic (Parton, 2003, p. 14). Among other emphases is its focus on "meeting the needs of the particular others for whom we have responsibility" (Held, 2006, p. 10). Care is at the core of relational and family life and so needs to be at the centre of work we do with children and families – however we define family. Care is not simply a feeling or a set of activities. As Tronto (1993) and many other feminist women and profeminist men have argued so powerfully, care is a deeply moral concept that counters the self-interest and individualism characterising Western society and relationships today as well as much that sits in social and public policy. Importantly, and in the light of the challenges presented about it being central to a virtue ethics approach, Rummery and Fine (2012, p. 323) agree that the concept of care has become corrupted but in essence is "a feeling or emotion involving a disposition towards others" that is crucial to ethical practice.

The tension in the contemporary world of welfare practice was highlighted in a recent exchange with a relatively new graduate in social work, who explained that the term used to describe her work team in the organisation is 'care bears'. The designation was explicitly derogatory and clearly not complimentary. The message for the team was clear: their 'soft' caring welfare role is only tolerated in the real work of the organisation, the real and important role of which is to manage people. Similarly, I recall a much less recent plaintive question by a social work student in the 1980s, who in the final week of the course asked why at no stage had any lecturer used the concepts of 'care' or 'love' to frame the work of social work. "Presumably" he suggested, "it is all about social work laying claim to being objective and eschewing emotion!" On graduation, this young man became a highly successful international aid worker where, he found, 'care' and 'love' were the crucible of the work organisation. The observations of these two social workers are connected by a web of meanings about the place of care in social work – how it is taught, how it is sustained and how it can be defended.

In this context, care and its deeply relational essence is at the fulcrum of the disposition to think, dialogue and behave ethically – an activity which involves balancing principles such as the duty to protect and ensure fairness and justice, acknowledging and respecting the rights of all stakeholders, and maintaining an authentic position of integrity and 'compassionate concern' for all involved (Bilson, 2007). Scholars such as Sommerville (2006, p. 38) have called for us to find common ground in ethics and to develop ways forward that respect all life and balance conflicting priority values within differing ethical approaches. Inviting us to use 'ethical imagination' and asserting that the way we treat one another day by day "matters deeply" (Sommerville, 2006, p. 232), she acknowledges the significant place of feminist ethics of care and the place of compassion for the future of all humanity. Utilising the idea of human nature embedded in the ethic of care enables us to move from the many 'restrictive theories' (Sevenhuijsen, 2016) such as those embedded in so much child protection policy and practice. Froggett (2002), along with so many others such as Meagher and Parton (2004), focus this call to an ethic of care directly on the practice of the helping professions and assert that a revival of the importance of care and compassion so central to the discourse of ethics of care offers "ways of conceiving and representing the relational dimensions of social work that are obscured by the rational-technical focus of managerialism" (Froggett, 2002, p. 11). As Sevenhuijsen (2003, p. 185) asserts, the starting point is to accept the significance of relationship, in this case, in the lives of children as well as adults and look at their lives using a lens that is relational. He states, "The most important contribution of the ethic of care in this respect is it invites us to think in terms of relationality" (2003, p. 191). In so doing, adopting an ethic of care also recognises the significance of intersectionality – "the intersections of difference and their relationships to power" (Hankivsky, 2014, p. 252).

The normative assumptions embedded in policies on family are abundant. These include the embedding of assumptions based on individualistic notions of family and parental responsibility that are discordant with the cultural experiences of contemporary life in multicultural communities and certainly at odds with the relational culture of family in most Indigenous communities. There are numerous accounts wherein it is evident that the focus on parenting failure and strategies to overcome these centre on the ineptitude or neglect by mothers (Swift, 1995). As Murray and Barnes (2010, p. 534) comment, there are many other "neglected dimensions in understanding family" in social and public policy, and certainly in the demanding area of child protection practice where there is little time for doing other than responding to 'notifications of abuse' by using templates designed in a culturally context-free vacuum. For example, the concept of the 'detached carer', which is not defined by proximity, is well appreciated in the lives of families with family members and close friends spread across the globe but is alien to most conceptual policy and practice in child protection. Murray and Barnes (2010, p. 535) observe: "the practices of family are predicated on shared and situated relationships of care" and children as well as the range of people with whom families interact are "integral to wider relationships of care". In differentiating between 'substantive' and 'active' discourses on family, they argue that a non-normative concept of family is rhetorically present but not generally applied within an appreciation of the lived experience of families.

An ethic of care situated within a virtue ethics framework provides a timely opportunity to re-position the work involved in protecting children. As Tronto (1987) states, the ethic of care is 'grounded' in the daily life and experiences of real people. It recognises children and families as embedded in a complex web of relationships and takes a contextual approach to appreciating the meaning of individual lives and relationships. In its interrogation of arrangements of care and responsibility in particular contexts, it has the marked potential to create the conditions for non-exploitative caring (Robinson, 2006, p. 7). Importantly, it acknowledges the tangled and complex link between the wellbeing of the children and the wellbeing of their carers and eschews the notion that the protection of children can be reduced only to duty based on 'rights talk'.

In this vein, Kelly (2005, p. 377) suggests that conceptualising children as diminished beings "vulnerable to both harm and deviance" in need of protection or individual holders of human rights leads to paternalism and protectionism and denies children agency. She argues that this conceptualisation must be challenged because it places rights and rules above relationship and assumes an atomistic, autonomous and rational individual. Furthermore, she reasons, this approach "essentialises children" and "assumes a universal child rather than one embedded in a cultural context" or indeed of an idiosyncratic relational or family context. In arguing for an ethic of care approach rather than one limited to the rights of the child for protection, she asserts that a feminist ethic of care does not eschew a rights approach but de-centres it and in so doing de-centres adults "as the exclusive source of information about children". She does not reject a rights approach but suggests we supplement it within a context of relationship (2005, p. 391).

An ethic of care, adopted in its broadest sense, incorporates the possibility of caring for adults in order for them to be able to care for other adults and children. It acknowledges that caregivers and care receivers are non-dualistic concepts as well as the inter-dependency of giving and receiving. Care receivers in child protection work are also caregivers. Children and young people provide care and, as many children in the care of statutory authorities assert, they continue to care deeply for family and community when they are removed from family.

Theorising about the significance of an ethic of care in child protection practice must take us beyond theorising because the work required is deeply practical and profoundly important for children, families, communities and practitioners. As Tronto (1987) argues so potently, care is central to human existence and engages with notions of interdependence and relationality rather than individualism and impartiality. Sevenhuijsen, Boalek, Gouws and Minnaar-McDonald (2003) provide a compelling analysis of how such an ethic of care can be useful in a social policy context. In utilising the lens of a feminist political ethic of care as enunciated by Tronto, they draw attention to the original key elements of such an ethic. 'Attentiveness' would require that we pay attention to the problems as actually experienced by families and 'reduce the objectifying and stereotyping' of them. Attention to 'responsibility' would require that we pay attention to a broader level of understanding about the various resources that are needed in order for families in trouble to care for and protect their children. The notion of "competence" requires us to work to ensure that the skills of people (families) are enhanced to enable them to 'optimally develop their capabilities'. Finally, the value of "responsiveness" demands that we construct professional practices in relational terms that convey an appreciation of the ubiquity of vulnerability and the passive but potent power differentials that so easily disguise the presence of paternalism.

Conclusion

There have been multiple demands to address the failures of the child protection system, and as Lonne et al. (2016, p. xiii)) assert, the answer to the ethics problems in the Child Protection Services is nothing more ambitious than "a new system that is ethically coherent and responsive to current realities" and must incorporate a deep commitment to care, compassion and relationship. On an even more expansive scale, Sevenhuijsen (2003, pp. 179, 180) argues that care has to become part of "active citizenship" wherein "the public sphere is interpreted as a special location for beginning new things by acting together." The almost generic motto 'child protection is everyone's business' suggests such a citizenship approach to the care and protection of children rather than resorting to the now acknowledged paternalistic set of oversights ingrained in contemporary public policy practice.

Froggett (2002, p. 119) challenges us to understand that contemporary organisational cultures that are instrumental and narcissistic cannot sustain and nourish relations of care. She argues that developing, let alone sustaining any capacity for incorporating an ethic of care in the face of the complex intersection of justice and care requires "formidable ethical and emotional resources" (Froggett, 2002, p. 121). I agree, but I hold hope that practitioners can continue to value the centrality of relationship and care and remind themselves and others at all times of the moral and ethical imperatives involved in the care and protection of children and their families and communities.

References

Beck, U. (2009) *World at risk*. Cambridge: Polity Press.

Biestek, F. (1957) *The casework relationship*. London: Allen & Unwin.

Bilson, A. (2007) Promoting compassionate concern in social work: Reflections on ethics, biology and love. *British Journal of Social Work*, 37(8), pp. 1371–1386.

Bywaters, P., Brady, G., Sparks, T., Bos, E., Bunting, L., Daniel, B., Featherstone, B., Morris, K. and Scourfield, J. (2015) Exploring inequities in child welfare and child protection services: Explaining the 'inverse intervention law'. *Children and Youth Services Review*, 57, pp. 98–105.

Cheung, J.C.S. (2015) A letter to the late Felix Biestek: Revisiting the seven principles of The Casework Relationship with contemporary struggles. *Ethics and Social Welfare*, 9(1), pp. 92–100.

Cloyes, K. (2002) Agonizing care: Care ethics, agonistic feminism and a political theory of care. *Nursing Inquiry*, 9(3), pp. 203–214.

Downie, R. and Telfer, E. (1980) *Caring and curing: A philosophy of medicine and social work*. London: Methuen.

Dybicz, P. (2012) The ethic of care: Recapturing social work's first voice. *Social Work*, 57(3), pp. 271–280.

Featherstone, B., White, S. and Morris, K. (2014) *Re-imagining child protection: Towards humane social work with families*. Bristol: Policy Press.

Froggett, L. (2002) *Love, hate and welfare*. Bristol: The Policy Press.

Furrow, D. (2005) *Ethics: Key concepts in philosophy*. New York: Continuum.

Gottschalk. (1974) Toward a radical reassessment of social work values. *Journal of Sociology & Social Welfare*, 2(4). Available from: http://scholarworks.wmich.edu/jssw/vol2/iss2/4.

Halwani, R. (2003) Care ethics and virtue ethics. *Hypatia*, 18(3), pp. 161–192.

Hankivsky, O. (2014) Rethinking care ethics: On the promise and potential of an intersectional analysis. *American Political Science Review*, 108(2), pp. 252–264.

Harlow, E., Berg, E., Barry, J. and Chandler, J. (2013) Neoliberalism, managerialism and the reconfiguring of social work in Sweden and the United Kingdom. *Organisation*, 20(4), pp. 534–550.

Harries, M. (2008) *The experiences of parents and families of children and young people in care*. University of Western Australia, Perth: Centre for Vulnerable Children and Families.

Held, V. (1995) The meshing of care and justice. *Hypatia*, 10, pp. 128–132.

Held, V. (2006) *The ethics of care: Personal, political and global*. New York: Oxford University Press.

Hoggett, P. (2000) *Emotional life and the politics of welfare*. Basingstoke: Macmillan.

Houston, S. (2010) Discourse ethics. In: Gray, M. and Webb, S. (eds.) *Ethics and value perspectives in social work*. Basingstoke: Palgrave, pp. 95–107.

Hudson, B. (2003) *Justice in the risk society: Challenging and re-affirming justice in late modernity*. London: Sage.

Hugman, R. and Carter, J. (2016) *Rethinking values and ethics in social work*. Basingstoke: Palgrave Macmillan.

Kelly, F. (2005) Conceptualising the child through an 'ethic of care': Lessons for family law. *International Journal of Law in Context*, 1(4), pp. 375–396.

Kempe, C., Silverman, F., Steele, B., Droegemueller, W. and Silver, H. (1962) The battered-child syndrome. *Journal of the American Medical Association*, 181(1), pp. 17–24.

Lonne, R., Harries, M., Featherstone, B. and Gray, M. (2016) *Working ethically in child protection*. New York: Routledge.

Meagher, G. and Parton, N. (2004) Modernising social work and the ethics of care. *Social Work & Society*, 2(1), pp. 10–27.

Morrow, D. (2005) *Ethics: Key concepts in philosophy*. New York: Continuum.

Murray, L. and Barnes, M. (2010) Have families been rethought? Ethic of care, family and 'whole family' approaches. *Social Policy and Society*, 9(4), pp. 533–544.

Noddings, N. (2003) *Caring: A feminine approach to ethics and moral education*. 2nd edition. Berkeley: University of California Press.

Oakley, J. and Cocking, D. (2001) *Virtue ethics and professional roles*. Cambridge: Cambridge University Press.

Parton, N. (2003) Rethinking professional practice: The contributions of social constructionism and the feminist ethics of care. *British Journal of Social Work*, 33(1), pp. 1–16.

Roberts, D. (2002) *Shattered bonds: The color of child welfare*. New York: Basic Civitas Books.

Robinson, F. (2006) Care, gender and global social justice: Rethinking 'ethical globalization'. *Journal of Global Ethics*, 2(1), pp. 5–25.

Rummery, K. and Fine, M. (2012) Care: A critical review of theory, policy and practice. *Social Policy & Administration*, 46(3), pp. 321–343.

Sander-Staudt, M. (2006) The unhappy marriage of care ethics and virtue ethics. *Hypatia*, 21(4), pp. 21–39.

Scott, D. (2006) Towards a public health model of child protection in Australia. *Communities, Families and Children Australia*, 1(1), pp. 9–16.

Sevenhuijsen, S. (2003) The place of care: The relevance of the feminist ethic of care for social policy. *Feminist Theory*, 4(2), pp. 179–197.

Sevenhuijsen, S., Boalek, V., Gouws, A. and Minnaar-McDonald, M. (2003) South African social welfare policy: An analysis using the ethic of care. *Critical Social Policy*, 23(3), pp. 299–321.

Sommerville, M. (2006) *The ethical imagination: Journeys of the human spirit*. Melbourne: Melbourne University Press.

Strega, S. and Esquao, S. (2009) *Walking this path together: Anti-racist and anti-oppressive child welfare practice*. Halifax, NS: Fernwood.

Swift, K. (1995) *Manufacturing bad mothers: A critical perspective on child neglect*. Toronto: University of Toronto Press.

Teicher, M. (1967) *Values in social work: A re-examination*. New York: NASW.

Tronto, J. (1987) Beyond gender difference to a theory of care. *Signs, Special Issue: Within and Without: Women, Gender, and Theory*. University of Chicago Press, 12(4), pp. 644–663.

Tronto, J. (1993) *Moral boundaries: A political argument for an ethic of care*. New York: Routledge.

Weick, A. (2000) Hidden voices. *Social Work*, 45(5), pp. 395–402.

Young, S., McKenzie, M., Schjelderup, L., Omre, C. and Walker, S. (2014) What can we do to bring the sparkle back into this child's eyes? Child rights/community development principles: Key elements for a strengths-based child protection practice. *Child Care in Practice*, 20(1), pp. 135–152.

10 Caring in an uncaring context

Towards a critical ethics of care in
social work with people seeking
asylum

Sharlene Nipperess

Introduction

The number of people seeking asylum worldwide has more than doubled in the last two years. What is being described daily as a humanitarian crisis is being responded to by governments with increasingly punitive measures, aimed to deny people the right to cross borders and claim asylum. This chapter explores what it means to care in such an uncaring context with a focus on social work practice with people seeking asylum. It begins by exploring the history of the concept of asylum and the development of the much more recent right to asylum, which is intimately related to the establishment of the United Nations, the Universal Declaration of Human Rights, and the Convention and Protocol Relating to the Status of Refugees. Then the contemporary experience of seeking asylum is examined, with particular attention paid to the Australian context, which has some of the harshest policies directed at asylum seekers in the world. The chapter next shifts to an analysis of what it means for social workers to care in such a context. The chapter concludes with the argument that caring is not enough, and that for an ethics of care to have value for social work practice with people seeking asylum, it needs to move towards a critical ethics of care. Such an orientation pays attention to the principles of human rights and social justice as well as the caring relationship, incorporates an intersectional analysis and a commitment to critically reflective practice, and pays attention to self-care.

Caring and the concept of asylum

Scholars such as Linda Rabben (2011) and Philip Marfleet (2011) argue that asylum is a universal institution. They argue that refuge has been provided to those escaping from persecution for millennia, and that evidence of this can be found in the historical records of ancient Greece, Rome, Egypt and India; in the Jewish, Islamic and Christian traditions; and in numerous traditional societies across the world, from the Arunta of central Australia through to the Ovambo of southwestern Africa (Marfleet, 2011; Rabben, 2011). Why is this institution so widespread and enduring? Rabben (2011, p. 44), an anthropologist, argues that "giving asylum or sanctuary can be seen as one of the basic manifestations of altruistic behavior and human morality." To care for and care about strangers seems to be the very basis of sanctuary.

Almost every major religion values the practice of sanctuary, and there is evidence to suggest that religious texts have codified customs that had already been in place since ancient times (Rabben, 2011). Although the custom of sanctuary can be seen to be universal, Ancient Greece and Rome seem to have had the most influence on modern practices (Marfleet, 2006). The word 'asylum' entered the English lexicon in the fifteenth century via Latin but originally came from the Ancient Greek word *asylon*, which means inviolate – a place of safety, of refuge that cannot be violated. The word 'sanctuary' comes from the Latin word *sanctus* which means holy or sacred place – a place where protection and safety is provided.

The provision of sanctuary entered Canon Law in the fourth century when the Roman Emperor Constantine declared Christianity the religion of Rome. The religion spread with the Roman Empire throughout Europe and over time refuge was increasingly associated with, and under the protection of, the Church (Marfleet, 2011). By the eleventh century, "the ideas of sacred space, protection and inviolability or immunity of ordinary people in distress were powerful ideas with popular currency, so that all manner of people (but overwhelmingly men) made use of sanctuaries" (Marfleet, 2011, pp. 446–447). Examples of not so ordinary people claiming sanctuary can also be found in the historical record and include the English Queen Elizabeth, Queen Consort of King Edward IV, who claimed sanctuary for some months on two occasions in Westminster Abbey. The experience of English King Henry II, whose knights murdered Thomas Becket in Canterbury Cathedral, which was greeted with outrage across Europe, demonstrates the consequences – even for a king – of breaking sanctuary.

According to Rabben (2011), widespread abuse of sanctuary resulted in the eventual abolition of sanctuary, although Marfleet (2011) contends that it was more about the monarchy attempting to limit ecclesiastical authority. For example, successive kings of England tried to put limits on sanctuary until finally it was abolished by the British Parliament in 1624. Although it ended over 1,000 years of church sanctuary, it did not stop the custom of providing sanctuary or asylum which transitioned to a more secular institution by the end of the seventeenth century.

The right to asylum

The concept of asylum has gone from an ancient custom codified in major religious teachings to one that is firmly embedded in the nation state and international law. From providing sanctuary to murderers, escaped slaves and people fleeing wars, asylum now has a very specific and narrow meaning.

It was not until after the horrors of World War Two that the humane treatment of refugees and asylum seekers was officially and internationally articulated in the United Nations (UN) Universal Declaration of Human Rights (1948), in particular Article 14, which states that everyone has the right to seek asylum from persecution. The Declaration was followed by the UN Convention Relating to the Status of Refugees (1951) and the UN Protocol Relating to the Status of Refugees (1966) (United Nations High Commissioner for Refugees [UNHCR], 2010). According to the Convention a refugee is a person who,

> owing to a well-founded fear of being persecuted for reasons of race, religion, nationality, membership of a particular social group or political opinion, is outside the country of his nationality and is unable or, owing to such fear, is unwilling to avail himself of the protection of that country; or who, not having a nationality and being outside the country of his former habitual residence as a result of such events, is unable or, owing to such fear, is unwilling to return to it.
>
> (UNHCR, 2010, p. 14)

According to the Convention therefore, refugees are people who owing to their well-founded fear of persecution have fled to another country and have successfully applied for protection under the Convention. Asylum seekers, on the other hand, have not yet had their application or refugee status determined. There are 142 state parties to both the Convention and Protocol (UNHCR, 2015a).

In this chapter I use the term 'asylum seeker' which is widely used in legislation, policy and research. However, I also use the phrase 'people seeking asylum', which emphasises the person rather than the label and acknowledges the diversity and multiple identities of people who seek asylum throughout the world (Zetter, 2007; Nipperess and Clark, 2016).

The Convention and Protocol established the minimum standards for the treatment of refugees and, following World War Two and the Cold War, many hundreds of thousands of people claimed and were granted asylum in countries throughout the world. The numbers of refugees and asylum seekers decreased to a low of 2.9 million in 1975 (Lamey, 2011). However, since the late 1970s, refugee numbers have grown again to the current figure of over 16 million (UNHCR, 2015b).

Refugees and asylum seekers have become a major political issue throughout the world. Even though 142 'state parties' have signed one or both of the Convention and Protocol since 1951 (UNHCR, 2015a), increasingly they are abandoning their responsibility for refugees. Underpinned by racism and age-old notions of who is deserving or undeserving of state protection and support, many countries are becoming increasingly hostile to refugees and asylum seekers. Political rhetoric attacking refugees and asylum seekers has increased, and since the 1990s restrictive immigration policies have been introduced with the aim of preventing entry. In the context of globalisation, the nation state has asserted its right to determine who can become its citizen. Over the last 30 years, and particularly in Western countries, the refugee regime has been fundamentally transformed from welcome to exclusion (Castles and Miller, 2009).

The experience of asylum

In 2015 there were a total of 16,121,427 refugees and 3,219,941 people seeking asylum worldwide (UNHCR, 2015b). These numbers have dramatically increased, especially in relation to the number of asylum seekers, which has more than doubled in two years. According to the UNHCR (2015b, p. 6), "the world again witnessed record levels of forced displacement in 2015. More than 65 million people were uprooted by war, conflict, persecution or human rights abuses by year end." By the end of December 2015, 1,159,702 asylum seekers were in Southern Africa and 1,075,781 were in Northern, Western, Central and Southern Europe. The war in Syria was a significant cause of displacement, with over four million Syrians escaping the conflict to seek asylum in neighbouring countries (UNHCR, 2015b).

The UNHCR (2015b, p. 8) notes that

> despite socio-economic challenges, numerous countries kept their border open, generously welcoming large numbers of refugees. But in many parts of the world we also witnessed threats to the international protection regime, sometimes fuelled by dangerous anti-foreigner rhetoric giving rise to xenophobic attitudes.

Many countries introduced increasingly restrictive legislation, and indeed many constructed fences and other obstacles along borders, all with the purpose of discouraging and preventing people from crossing borders (UNHCR, 2015b, p. 8).

People seeking asylum have experienced significant hardship. They have escaped from unimaginable circumstances of trauma and sometimes torture in their home country. They have survived perilous journeys across seas and continents. Upon arrival, many have experienced further trauma in relation to detention and an unwelcome reception, as they go through the refugee determination process. Resettlement presents yet more challenges (Leach and Mansouri, 2004; Austin, Silove and Steel, 2007). At the same time, people seeking asylum are incredibly resilient, complex and diverse based on their experiences of both oppression and privilege (Pease, 2010) in relation to social identities such as class, gender, race/ethnicity, sexuality, ability, religion, age, language, national origin and so on, as well as other experiences related to the refugee journey (Nipperess and Clark, 2016).

Australia's cruelty to people seeking asylum

Australia's response to refugees and asylum seekers has been contradictory and highly controversial. While it is not possible to provide a detailed account of Australia's refugee policy here, a brief overview demonstrates that despite Australia ratifying the *Refugee Convention* in 1954 and the *Protocol* in 1973 and settling hundreds of thousands of refugees since then, its policies towards asylum seekers have become more and more punitive and continue to be widely and trenchantly criticised (Australian Human Rights Commission, 2015; Amnesty International, 2016; Human Rights Watch, 2016; Maguire, 2016a). Indeed, there are many who argue that Australia's policies are nothing short of cruel (Maguire, 2016b; Manne, 2016).

In particular, Australia's policies of mandatory detention of asylum seekers, the many abuses associated with offshore processing and the outsourcing of refugee obligations to other countries have received continued criticism. Amnesty International (2016), for example, in a report on the conditions of Nauru, a remote island in the Pacific Ocean, details the numerous abuses that asylum seekers experience due to the policy of offshore 'processing'. These include high levels of mental illness and self-harm caused by devastating uncertainty about their future. Refugees and asylum seekers experience high levels of violence, including verbal and physical attacks and sexual assaults. Health care is inadequate, meaning that people have to wait months to receive appropriate treatment for serious illnesses. The report discusses the "countless daily humiliations that have cumulatively served to dehumanise them and violate their dignity" (Amnesty International, 2016, p. 6), including calling asylum seekers by the number of their boat instead of their name, referring to people by their refugee identification number if they have obtained refugee status, and practices that serve no purpose such as expelling people from the shower after two minutes. Children are subject to abuse, again both verbal and physical, and as a result do not attend school. Amnesty International concludes by stating:

> In furtherance of a policy to deter people arriving in Australia by boat, the Government of Australia has made a calculation in which intolerable cruelty and the destruction of the physical and mental integrity of hundreds of children, men and women, have been chosen as a tool of government policy.
>
> (2016, p. 7)

The response by the Australian government to the criticism from United Nations experts, international human rights organisations, foreign governments and even Australia's own Australian Human Rights Commission (AHRC) has been largely dismissive. Efforts have even been made to discredit the organisations involved, such as the AHRC and the UN, and to personally criticise people involved with these organisations such as Professor Gillian Triggs, president of the AHRC (Maguire, 2016a).

Amnesty International suggests that the extent of abuse on Nauru "is demolishing Australia's international reputation" (2016, p. 7), and yet the Australian government is unmoved (Jakubowicz, 2016; Maguire, 2016a). Indeed, it would appear that many countries are actually following Australia's lead, especially in Europe (Loewenstein, 2016).

Australia's policies were not always so cruel, but over time they have become more and more punitive. In 1976 the first asylum seekers, five Vietnamese men, arrived on Australia's shore by boat. These men represented the first challenge to asylum seeker policy because after decades of Australia carefully controlling its immigration program, suddenly people were arriving directly on Australia's shores without going through the refugee application processes established in other countries. This would not have been unusual in many other countries in the world – countries that share one or multiple borders – but Australia is surrounded by ocean and is very difficult to get to safely. The other challenge was directly related to the ethnicity of the new arrivals – they were Vietnamese, and the fear of Asians invading this largely unpopulated country was an idea in the living memory of many Australians at that time. Marr (2011, p. 241) notes that "the five men on the *Kien Giang* have been followed by less than 30,000 [asylum seekers] in the years since, 35 years in which Australia has taken in three and a half million immigrants." Despite these relatively small numbers, asylum seekers have received an increasingly hostile reception from politicians and the public alike.

Since then, the rhetoric has gradually become harsher and the policies more restrictive, from the introduction of mandatory detention in 1992 through to the most recent proposal to ban asylum seekers who attempt to reach Australia by boat (Foster, 2016; Reilly, 2016). How did Australia's asylum seeker policies become so cruel? Robert Manne suggests that a history of Australia's asylum seeker policy would reveal

> the process whereby the arteries of the nation gradually hardened; how as a nation we gradually lost the capacity to see the horror of what it was that we were willing to do to innocent fellow human beings who had fled in fear and sought our help.
>
> (Manne, 2016, para. 26)

Manne draws on Hannah Arendt's idea of the 'banality of evil' to explain why Australia's policies towards asylum seekers are so cruel. He argues that politicians allow the suffering of people in detention and the continued anxiety of those in the community

> because they no longer possess, in the Arendtian sense, the ability to see what it is that they are doing, and because the majority of the nation has become accustomed to thinking of what we are doing as perfectly normal.
>
> (Manne, 2016, para. 30)

Caring in an uncaring context

Social workers have a long history of working with refugees in Australia, in a range of specialist and generalist agencies, although arguably it has not been part of mainstream practice (McMahon, 2002; Williams and Graham, 2014; Nipperess and Clark, 2016) or indeed social work education (Danso, 2016). In contrast, very few agencies provided services to asylum seekers until relatively recently, meaning that social workers have not had many opportunities of working with people seeking asylum. However, the release of people from detention in 2010 meant that numerous agencies accepted funding to work with asylum seekers, and as a consequence many more social workers are now working with asylum seekers in a range of non-government and faith-based organisations.

What does it mean to care in such an uncaring context? I argue that this is one of the few fields of social work practice where social workers are working in a policy context that is antithetical to the values of the profession. While there is a developing literature that explores the demanding nature and ethical challenges facing social workers working with asylum seekers (see, e.g. Bowles, 2005; Fiske and Briskman, 2013; Robinson, 2013, 2014; Nipperess and Clark, 2016), the experience of caring in the specific policy context described earlier is underexplored. I will now explore the literature on how an ethics of care has been used to inform practice with people seeking asylum.

There is very little literature that discusses an ethics of care in relation to practice with asylum seekers. In an Australian study, Zion, Briskman and Loff (2009) explored the ethics of care in relation to nursing practice with asylum seekers in detention. The authors interviewed nurses who had worked in detention and explored how an ethics of care might assist ethical health care practice. They concluded that "it is clear that actions congruent with an ethics of care could not compensate for the inhuman conditions in which asylum seekers found themselves. Such changes required political action" (2009, p. 550). They found that while actions by nurses consistent with an ethics of care – a focus on the relationship between nurse and person seeking asylum (patient) and the responsibility of the nurse for the wellbeing of the person seeking asylum – failed to restore autonomy, these actions instead provided some hope and "drew asylum seekers back into the human circle" (Zion et al., 2009, p. 550). Some nurses, however, moved beyond this micro-level of care to a more activist position of acting witness to their experiences, often at some personal cost. They spoke at inquiries, to the press and to researchers, which had the result of breaking down some of the secrecy in relation to detention, as well as the stigmatisation of people seeking asylum.

Ottosdottir and Evans (2014) published one of the few articles that considers the ethics of care in relation to social work practice with disabled forced migrants, which encompasses asylum seekers. The authors' research was based on interviews with disabled forced migrants, their family care-givers and social care workers. The authors note that the legal and policy context dominates care and this has detrimental effects on disabled forced migrants, their family and professionals. They identified that "disabled forced migrants and informal care-givers associated 'good care' with individual personalities, a willingness to act, persevere and advocate on their behalf, empathic understanding, attitudes and ethics of care and respect" (Ottosdottir and Evans, 2014, p. 166).

Caring is not enough

What these two studies show is that caring is not enough in the context of practice with people seeking asylum. As Featherstone (2010, p. 80) notes, "care is not only personal, it is an issue of public and political concern whose social dynamics operate at local, national and transnational levels." A critical ethics of care acknowledges the importance of personal caring relationships between social workers and people seeking asylum, but it also embraces the necessity for political change. I will now explore five principles of social work practice with asylum seekers informed by a critical ethics of care.

A critical ethics of care that pays attention to the principles of human rights and social justice can provide a way forward for social work practice with people seeking asylum (Nipperess, 2016). As demonstrated earlier, the right to asylum is clearly enshrined in the Universal Declaration of Human Rights, specifically in Article 14 and further developed in the Convention and Protocol for the Status of Refugees. It is imperative that social workers understand the international human rights context and Australia's obligations and engage in political as well as personal practice. In such a hostile environment, having a clear conception of rights is essential for a socially just practice.

The importance of the relationship is fundamental to an ethics of care (Hugman, 2005; Banks, 2012; Featherstone and Morris, 2012). As Banks (2012, p. 77) notes,

> while 'care' or 'caring' can be regarded as a quality of character and features in lists of virtues for social care and health, it is care as a *relationship* and/or as a *practice* that is the main focus of attention of care ethicists.

The relationship between social worker and asylum seeker is important and valued by people seeking asylum, as Ottosdottir and Evans's (2014) research demonstrates. Restoring hope and dignity cannot be underestimated, even though it may not restore autonomy (Zion et al., 2009). The caring relationship is therefore just as important in a critical ethics of care as are attention to human rights and social justice.

Incorporating an intersectional analysis into a critical ethics of care is integral. People seeking asylum are often treated as a homogeneous group but, as I have already discussed, this is far from reality. While asylum seekers share significant experiences of trauma in their own country, on their journey to Australia, upon arrival and eventually, for many, resettlement, they are also incredibly diverse. Hankivsky (2014, p. 262) suggests that

> if care ethics is to deliver on the promise of opening new ways of seeing human beings, their social problems, and their needs, and to critically assess how governments respond to these, theorising around social locations, differences, experiences of inequality, and power need to be further developed.

Research with asylum seekers more broadly is beginning to develop a much more nuanced understanding of the diversity of people seeking asylum, and social work practice informed by a critical ethics of care should embed this understanding in its practice.

Social work practice with asylum seekers informed by a critical ethics of care should be underpinned by a commitment to critically reflective practice. Critically reflective practice enables social workers to interrogate their own practice – their values, beliefs and assumptions – as well as the profession of social work itself. Critically reflective practice goes hand in hand with an intersectional analysis that does not just identify oppression but identifies privilege as well, in relationship to the people with whom social workers work and in relation to social workers themselves (Pease, 2010).

Attention to care is another key principle of a critical ethics of care. One of the themes that Robinson (2013) identified in her research with social workers working with asylum seekers in Australia and the UK was sustaining effective practice. She notes that

> interviewees reported that the motivation for working with the client group emerged from their own personal experience and political commitment. They identified the hardships the service users experienced and that regular exposure to these posed a challenge for their own emotional well-being.
>
> (Robinson, 2013, p. 96)

Social workers who work with both refugees and asylum seekers are highly motivated personally and politically, but caring in an uncaring context can impact on social workers in a number of ways. Paying attention to self-care in such a context is vital (Briskman and Cemlyn, 2005; Nipperess and Clark, 2016).

Conclusion

Providing asylum for people escaping persecution has a long history. It is based on caring for and caring about the stranger. Principles of welcome, hospitality, inclusion and indeed love underpin this ancient custom. However, for contemporary asylum seekers and for social workers working with them, the social and political context in Australia and internationally is the very antithesis of care. The policies are increasingly hostile, punitive and cruel. A critical ethics of care offers much to social work practice with people seeking asylum in this context. A critical ethics of care is underpinned by a twin focus on rights and care, informed by an intersectional analysis, committed to critically reflective practice and pays attention to self-care. Such practice has the potential to further the social justice aims of the profession.

References

Amnesty International. (2016) Island of despair: Australia's 'processing' of refugees on Nauru. *Amnesty International* [online]. Available from: https://static.amnesty.org.au/wp-content/uploads/2016/10/ISLAND-OF-DESPAIR-FINAL.pdf?x66249 [Accessed 8 November 2016].

Austin, P., Silove, D. and Steel, Z. (2007) The impact of immigration detention on the mental health asylum seekers. In: Lusher, D. and Haslam, N. (eds.) *Yearning to breathe free: Seeking asylum in Australia.* Leichhardt, NSW: Federation Press, pp. 100–112.

Australian Human Rights Commission (AHRC). (2015) *The forgotten children: National Inquiry into Children in Immigration Detention 2014.* Sydney: AHRC.

Banks, S. (2012) *Ethics and values in social work.* 4th edition. Basingstoke: Palgrave Macmillan.

Bowles, R. (2005) Social work with refugee survivors of torture and trauma. In: Alston, M. and McKinnon, J. (eds.) *Social work: Fields of practice.* 2nd edition. South Melbourne: Oxford University Press, pp. 249–267.

Briskman, L. and Cemlyn, S. (2005) Reclaiming humanity for asylum-seekers: A social work response. *International Social Work*, 48(6), pp. 714–724.

Castles, S. and Miller, M. (2009) *The age of migration: International population movements in the modern world*. 4th edition. Basingstoke: Palgrave Macmillan.

Danso, R. (2016) Migration studies: Resuscitating *the* casualty of the professionalization of social work. *British Journal of Social Work*, 46(6), pp. 1741–1758.

Featherstone, B. (2010) Ethic of care. In: Gray, M. and Webb, S. (eds.) *Ethics and value perspectives in social work*. Basingstoke: Palgrave Macmillan, pp. 73–84.

Featherstone, B. and Morris, K. (2012) Feminist ethics of care. In: Gray, M., Midgley, J. and Webb, S. (eds.) *The SAGE handbook of social work*. London: Sage, pp. 341–354.

Fiske, L. and Briskman, L. (2013) Working with refugees and asylum seekers. In: Connolly, M. and Harms, L. (eds.) *Social work: Contexts and practice*. 3rd edition. South Melbourne: Oxford University Press, pp. 151–162.

Foster, M. (2016) Turnbull's asylum seeker ban violates Australia's human rights obligations. *Conversation* [online]. Available from: https://theconversation.com/turnbulls-asylum-seeker-ban-violates-australias-human-rights-obligations-68475 [Accessed 14 November 2016].

Hankivsky, O. (2014) Rethinking care ethics: On the promise and potential of an intersectional analysis. *American Political Science Review*, 108(2), pp. 252–264.

Hugman, R. (2005) *New approaches in ethics for the caring professions*. Basingstoke: Palgrave Macmillan.

Human Rights Watch. (2016) *World Report 2016: Events of 2015*. Human Rights Watch [online]. Available from: www.hrw.org/sites/default/files/world_report_download/wr2016_web.pdf [Accessed 8 November 2016].

Jakubowicz, A. (2016) European leaders taking cues from Australia on asylum seeker policies. *Conversation* [online]. Available from: https://theconversation.com/european-leaders-taking-cues-from-australia-on-asylum-seeker-policies-66336 [Accessed 8 November 2016].

Lamey, A. (2011) *Frontier justice: The global refugee crisis and what to do about it*. St Lucia: University of Queensland Press.

Leach, M. and Mansouri, F. (2004) *Lives in limbo: Voices of refugees under temporary protection*. Sydney: UNSW Press.

Loewenstein, A. (2016) Australia's refugee policies: A global inspiration for all the wrong reasons. *Guardian* [online]. Available from: www.theguardian.com/commentisfree/2016/jan/18/australias-refugee-policies-a-global-inspiration-for-all-the-wrong-reasons [Accessed 8 November 2016].

Maguire, A. (2016a) Why does international condemnation on human rights mean so little to Australia? *Conversation* [online]. Available from: https://theconversation.com/why-does-international-condemnation-on-human-rights-mean-so-little-to-australia-53814 [Accessed 8 November 2016].

Maguire, A. (2016b) Accusations of deliberate, cruel abuse of refugee children must prompt a more humane approach. *Conversation* [online]. Available from: https://theconversation.com/accusations-of-deliberate-cruel-abuse-of-refugee-children-must-prompt-a-more-humane-approach-67154 [Accessed 8 November 2016].

Manne, R. (2016) Robert Manne: How we came to be so cruel to asylum seekers. *Conversation* [online]. Available from: https://theconversation.com/robert-manne-how-we-came-to-be-so-cruel-to-asylum-seekers-67542 [Accessed 26 November 2016].

Marfleet, P. (2006) *Refugees in a global era*. Basingstoke: Palgrave Macmillan.

Marfleet, P. (2011) Understanding 'sanctuary': Faith and traditions of asylum. *Journal of Refugee Studies*, 24(3), pp. 440–455.

Marr, D. (2011) *Panic: Terror! invasion! disorder! drugs! kids! blacks! boats!* Collingwood, VIC: Black.

McMahon, A. (2002) Writing diversity: Ethnicity and race in Australian Social Work 1947–1997. *Australian Social Work*, 55(3), pp. 172–183.

Nipperess, S. (2016) Towards a critical human rights-based approach to social work practice. In: Pease, B., Goldingay, S., Hosken, N. and Nipperess, S. (eds.) *Doing critical social work: Transformative practices for social justice*. Crows Nest, NSW: Allen & Unwin, pp. 73–88.

Nipperess, S. and Clark, S. (2016) Anti-oppressive practice with people seeking asylum in Australia: Reflections from the field. In: Pease, B., Goldingay, S., Hosken, N. and Nipperess, S. (eds.) *Doing critical social work: Transformative practices for social justice*. Crows Nest, NSW: Allen & Unwin, pp. 195–210.

Ottosdottir, G. and Evans, R. (2014) Ethics of care in supporting disabled forced migrants: Interactions with professionals and ethical dilemmas in health and social care in South-East of England. *British Journal of Social Work*, 44(Supplement 1), pp. i53–i69.

Pease, B. (2010) *Undoing privilege: Unearned advantage in a divided world*. London: Zed Books.

Rabben, L. (2011) *Give refuge to the stranger: The past, present, and future of sanctuary*. Walnut Creek, CA: Left Coast Press.

Reilly, A. (2016) Same old rhetoric cannot justify banning refugees from Australia. *Conversation* [online]. Available from: https://theconversation.com/same-old-rhetoric-cannot-justify-banning-refugees-from-australia-67923 [Accessed 8 November 2016].

Robinson, K. (2013) Supervision found wanting: Experiences of health and social workers in non-government organizations working with refugees and asylum seekers. *Practice*, 25(2), pp. 87–103.

Robinson, K. (2014) Voices from the front line: Social work with refuges and asylum seekers in Australia and the UK. *British Journal of Social Work*, 44(6), pp. 1602–1620.

United Nations (UN). (1948) *Universal Declaration of Human Rights*. UN [online]. Available from: www.ohchr.org/EN/UDHR/Documents/UDHR_Translations/eng.pdf [Accessed 16 November 2016].

United Nations High Commissioner for Refugees (UNHCR). (2010) *Convention and protocol relating to the status of refugees*. UNHCR [online]. Available from: www.unhcr.org/en-au/protection/basic/3b66c2aa10/convention-protocol-relating-status-refugees.html?query=convention and protocol relating to the status of refugees [Accessed 16 November 2016].

United Nations High Commissioner for Refugees (UNHCR). (2015a) *State parties to the 1951 Convention Relating to the Status of Refugees and the 1967 Protocol*. UNHCR [online]. Available from: www.unhcr.org/protection/basic/3b73b0d63/states-parties-1951-convention-its-1967-protocol.html [Accessed 16 November 2016].

United Nations High Commissioner for Refugees (UNHCR). (2015b) *Global report 2015*. UNHCR [online]. Available from: www.unhcr.org/gr15/index.xml [Accessed 16 November 2016].

Williams, C. and Graham, M. (2014) 'A world on the move': Migration, mobilities and social work. *British Journal of Social Work*, 44(Supplement 1), pp. i1–17.

Zetter, R. (2007) More labels, fewer refugees: Remaking the refugee label in an era of globalisation. *Journal of Refugee Studies*, 20(2), pp. 172–192.

Zion, D., Briskman, L. and Loff, B. (2009) Nursing in asylum seeker detention in Australia: Care, rights and witnessing. *Journal of Medical Ethics*, 35, pp. 546–551.

11 Humanitarian aid and social development

A political ethics of care view of international social work practice

Richard Hugman

Introduction

In the field of international social work in recent times there has been increased attention to the areas of humanitarian aid provision and social development practice (Healy, 2008; Hugman, 2010, 2016; Cox and Pawar, 2012; Midgley, 2014; Pawar, 2014). Although these two areas can be distinct, they may be connected and they certainly share many of the challenges for social workers in thinking about how to approach involvement in such activities, both practically and ethically. In particular, there are many political and moral issues that affect how and even whether social work has a role in humanitarian aid and social development interventions.

This chapter considers these broad questions. Using the framework of the ethics of care it explores ways in which a progressive focus on such practice can be conceptualised and argues for a critical ethics of international social work. Using the example of responses to 'natural disaster', the chapter considers how a 'political ethics of care' approach (Tronto, 1993) can inform practice in the provision of immediate humanitarian aid and ongoing social development.

The nature of the problem: aid, development and 'caring'

Social work has had an international focus since its earliest days (Healy, 2008). Despite political and practical differences between them, there was often an exchange of ideas between various strands of social work. For example, the development around the beginning of the 1900s of formal university level education for social work brought together caseworkers and community workers through international exchanges of people and ideas (Payne, 2005).

However, it is important to note that all these practices and those involved in them originated in those countries that now are seen as the global north (Gray, 2005; Hugman, 2010). These are the countries of North Western Europe, Scandinavia and Northern America. Not only were these the first countries to industrialise, but also they did so partly through colonising the rest of the world on a scale not seen before in human history. Therefore, social work's gradual spread across international borders must be seen in this colonial context. The global growth of social work is not a neutral, objective process but one that is embedded in the dynamic of unequal relationships between countries, cultures and individuals. More widely, colonisation produced what the development theorist Frank (1966) termed 'the development of underdevelopment', as colonised countries were stripped of assets, had their economies distorted and were turned into markets for goods produced in the global north. Frank's work also revealed that aid often is delivered in such a way as to promote the interests of donors rather than recipients, while development could frequently be seen as causing more harm than good in relation to whether or not goals such as the alleviation of poverty, greater personal freedom, dignity and participation in culture and society were achieved.

In this analysis, many of the contemporary concerns of the humanitarian and social development fields must be seen as the products of earlier colonial relationships and even of previous development practices and policies – consequently we may ask critical questions about 'neo-colonialism' in current practices and systems. The impact of this history still echoes in the often unequal relationships between institutions and the wider profession in the global north and the global south (Gray, 2005; Hugman, 2010).

Yet this history also contains many contradictions. While the dominance of the global north in the worldwide formation of social work has to be understood in relation to colonialism, at the same time the practices and values that social work represents are also sought as part of the processes of social development in many parts of the global south. The pursuit of social justice and human rights as the value goals of social work and social welfare (see e.g. IFSW/IASSW, 2004) are often contributors to concrete improvements in human life, including access to clean water, health care and education. These are social goods that are often welcomed as tangible benefits. One example of this can be seen in the improvement of human life expectancy (from birth) and general levels of health that have occurred around the world in recent decades, including declines in infant mortality, achieved through development in public health and education (Midgley, 2014). Not everyone shares equally in these gains – there are continuing disparities between countries and also between socio-economic classes and other stratifications within countries – but on average such measures show a healthier and longer life for many people.

Ideas of 'aid' and 'development' that dominate in the international sphere convey a sense of contributing to the wellbeing of others, which is often a motivation for social workers to enter this broad type of practice. From this perspective, aid is synonymous with assisting or helping at times of emergency or crisis, while development suggests ongoing assistance to achieve the betterment of human life. So both might be seen as expressions of 'care' by their proponents, insofar as that in turn is understood in terms of supporting people and communities in situations where they are unable to accomplish all they need on their own. However, while care may be an expression of intention ('caring about') that in itself does not guarantee good practices follow ('caring for') (Tronto, 1993, pp. 118–22; compare with Hugman, 1991; Barnes, Brannelly, Ward and Ward, 2015). Intentions are one thing while the actual impact of practices may be entirely different.

In other words, we must ask if these practices help people to move out of poverty, achieve freedom and dignity, and be able to engage actively in their own communities. If not, then other measures such as a country having greater total economic wealth can mask the failure of aid and development goals. This is particularly the case when such statistics are aggregates that disguise ways in which the large proportion of benefit is enjoyed by only a small proportion of the population in the form of wealthy elites. Midgley (2014), for example, calls this 'distorted development'.

An example: post-disaster humanitarian aid and social development

To explore these issues in greater depth and consider their implications for international social work, let us consider responses to 'natural disaster' to illustrate how practice can unfold. The term 'natural disaster' is highlighted as problematic, because although the physical events such as earthquake, winds, flood or drought can be thought of as natural phenomena, their impact on human life is shaped by human society (Park and Miller, 2006). The devastation of such events is not shared equally across societies, because factors of poverty, age, disability, race, gender, levels of education and so on create differing opportunities. For example, as Park and Miller argue, the events of Hurricane Katrina were experienced very differently by Black and White Americans, those who were poor and those who were well-off. This included the way the built environment impacted the effects of the natural environment, such as who lived in which parts of New Orleans, Louisiana, as well as which services were available for whom and what personal resources could be used to escape in the immediate situation and then to rebuild lives afterwards.

What can be observed from Hurricane Katrina in 2005 concerning the social constructions of 'natural' disasters has also been observed with regard to the Indian Ocean Tsunami in 2004, Typhoon Haiyan/Yolanda in 2013, and earthquakes in Iran in 2003, China in 2008 and Nepal in 2015 (Park and Miller, 2006; Javadian, 2007; Dominelli, 2013; Wang and Lum, 2013; Ii Untal and Guinto, 2016; Nikku, 2016). In particular, the issues that are repeatedly portrayed are:

1   Existing social development challenges prior to a humanitarian crisis;
2   The multi-dimensional impacts of a disaster and the way in which these intersect as both 'natural' and 'social';
3   The characteristics of immediate humanitarian aid and its implications for local society;
4   Complexities in longer term post-disaster reconstruction and development, including imbalances of power between local communities and national institutions and the international donors.

While in reality the interests and actions of people at local, national and international levels are diverse, both within and between various historical situations, there is an identifiable pattern across all these instances that requires a critical response as the basis for creating more progressive practice.

Problems of care: power and inequality in social development

At the centre of these concerns about humanitarian aid and social development practice is the question of social power. In the aforementioned cases, it was the members of local communities that had the least overt capacity to exercise power, while at the same time they were the most seriously impacted by the immediate and longer-term consequences of devastation. In each of these situations, the international donors and practitioners exercised considerable power, in relation both to local communities and the national governments, although governments also exercised some power.

Power here should be understood as the capacity for a person, a group or a community to act within the context of particular social structures and relationships (Hugman, 1991, p. 38). It involves both the assertion of interests against opposition, but it also is often seen in the many ways that actions and decisions are regarded as normal ('business as usual') even though the interests of everyone involved may not be reflected equally in processes or outcomes. For this reason we can say that all professional action is political, even though in most situations the overt intention is to provide assistance and care.

Care is defined by Tronto and Fisher as "a species activity that includes everything we do to maintain, continue and repair our 'world' so that we can live in it as well as possible" (1991, p. 40). The actions of social workers and others in humanitarian aid and social development are directed to ends that can indeed be understood in these terms. The overt goal of such work is to enable and support the 'repair' of damaged communities so that life can continue as well as possible. Yet, as Tronto (1993) later argued, care both as an action and as a disposition to act involves imbalances of power between people as individuals and members of social groups. For example, particular forms of care are often socially constructed as 'women's work', or in terms of 'racial' and ethnic differences, social class differences, and so on (also see Hugman, 1991). Thus, Tronto proposes that the ethics of care is political as well as moral. Moreover, Hankivsky (2014) identifies that these different oppressions do not simply 'stack up' as if in an arithmetic sum, but intersect dynamically so that the benefits and costs of caring are experienced in diverse ways. This makes the task of understanding and responding to the appeal of 'care' as a moral value highly complex.

Tronto's conception of an ethics of care is discussed in different ways in other chapters in this volume. For the purposes of this discussion, we can particularly note that her model is based on an understanding of the distinction between care as a disposition and care as a practice (Tronto, 1993, p. 118). This point draws on wider debates about care from a feminist and profeminist perspective that distinguish care as 'love' and as 'labour' (e.g. Finch and Groves, 1983; Kittay, 2001). Tronto concludes that care must be regarded as a practice because to focus solely on the disposition so easily leads either to sentimentality or to privatisation, both of which reinforce unequal power relations. To this can be added that while care as practice without disposition potentially becomes power of dominance, care as disposition without practice is disempowered (summarised in Hugman, 2005, pp. 75–76). In the instances cited earlier, what mattered was that the needs of the people in these different communities were addressed promptly and appropriately. However, the problem is seen quite clearly as being that while some (although not all) responses were prompt, whether or not they were appropriate to local culture and other needs is much more questionable. Some disposition is required for action to occur at all, but this may be felt only by some of those who are involved towards the needs and interests of local communities; alternatively it may equally be a reaction to a sense of legal obligation, political expedience and so on, in which questions about what is appropriate locally may never be asked. Indeed, even thinking about that question may never occur as national and international social development professionals can easily assume that their knowledge and skills are universally valid. An even greater social distance and expression of power occurs when individual practitioners are motivated to work in this field to advance their careers (such as 'doing time overseas to get a promotion to head office'), to have an opportunity to undertake overseas travel as part of their work or for other reasons not directly associated with the needs of the end beneficiaries of their work.

Ethics of care in humanitarian aid and social development

A political ethics of care approach provides the basis for examining these issues critically, in order to understand more effectively the connections between the political and moral bases of humanitarian aid and social development. The major elements in the practice of care identified by Tronto are:

1   attentiveness – recognition of need, that also combines with it the recognition and acceptance of the moral claims of the people or groups to a response;
2   responsibility – acceptance that care should be provided and of one's own role in that, which is different from obligation because it does not concern formal rules but is a combination of cultural and moral practices that shape recognition of need;
3   competence – attentiveness and responsibility on their own are not sufficient for the practice of care, rather it requires that those who provide care (whether face to face or through management, setting policy and soon) ensure that care can be provided appropriately;
4   responsiveness – recognition that those who receive care are part of the set of the interdependent social relations of care, not simply objects to be attended to but subjects with their own ideas and values; and
5   integrity of care – that the four 'phases' of care (attentiveness, responsibility, competence and responsiveness) must fit together as a suitable whole, including addressing conflict that may occur as different participants' interests collide, and be based on sound judgement that brings together personal and political dimensions.

(Tronto, 1993, pp. 126–137)

More recently, Tronto (2013, p. 28) has also argued that the fifth element of care is that of 'caring with', emphasising the relational nature of care and the way in which both cared-for and carer are interdependent actors, rather than only one or the other having agency. While Tronto's focus in this is on the marketisation and privatisation of individual care in the global north, her analysis emphasises the social and political contexts of care as constitutive of care relationships. Of great importance in humanitarian aid and social development practices, therefore, is that a political ethics of care approach does not focus exclusively on the morality of individual action or on socio-political structures and systems. Rather, it examines both together, placing action in structural context and considering structural contexts in terms of the actions that are supported or held back.

So, from a political ethics of care perspective, the needs and interests of local community members should be at the forefront of the way in which practitioners, managers and policy makers approach the tasks of immediate aid and ongoing development. The studies of specific disaster responses noted earlier have identified that, for example, there is frequent failure by those from the global north to recognise and respect local culture and customs in the ways in which both short and long-term projects are set up and operate. For example, Dominelli (2013) documents how in Sri Lanka a project initiated by the International Association of Schools of Social Work (IASSW) floundered because of shifting commitments by the international participants, the lack of local social work infrastructure through which to form partnerships and the long-standing disinterest on the part of the national government towards disadvantaged communities. In addition, attempts by local officials to manage the large number of international organisations who were intervening ironically amplified the problems of such organisations in working together to maximise the benefit of the resources that they had. Dominelli (2013, p. 55) suggests that this control at national level led to the voices of local people being silenced in the processes of providing assistance. Similarly, in Bam (Iran), Javadian (2007, p. 337) noted that social workers involved in the relief effort following a massive earthquake were hampered by the lack of systems, the uncertainty of leaders, poor instructions, chaotic bases from which to work, uncertainty of roles and the mishandling of aid resources by various agencies.

Even in a global northern country such problems are evident. Park and Miller (2006, p. 19) summarise key issues faced after Hurricane Katrina in New Orleans as including blanket responses (rather than recognising and responding to localities of high need), Eurocentric provision (ignoring diverse cultures and languages) and the socio-economic class bias of service providers. In the longer term, social workers have been involved in the reconstruction of New Orleans. One of the outcomes of listening to and working with local communities is that previous assumptions about the importance of trauma counselling have been revised as community members have emphasised that this is often less valued than practical assistance in rebuilding homes and restoring education and health services, at least in the immediate post-crisis period (Smith, 2012).

The implications of these critiques for humanitarian aid and social development can be summarised in the following ways. First, in what ways can international aid and development organisations be attentive? From a political ethics of care perspective, this would require that engagement with local communities should be a dialogue that starts by listening, and their encultured ways of living should be the centre of planning for immediate and longer-term responses. But more than this, both the national government and international organisations should be seeking to involve the local communities in framing the ways in which questions are asked and how needs are to be understood. Although there is ample argument among community development practitioners that participation is not a panacea, nor free from issues of inequality in power relations (Cleaver, 2001), practitioners can use strategies to ensure that everyone who is affected has a voice (Larsen, Sewpaul and Hole, 2014).

Second, careful thought must be given to who should carry which responsibilities. Although necessary, it is not sufficient for practitioners, managers, members of boards, or governments to feel responsible. There must be planning in how such responsibility is shared among the various participants, including local community members. If local areas or regions in particular and countries more generally are to avoid the extremes of large-scale duplication of effort or of resources being blocked from reaching communities in need, as reported by Dominelli (2013) among others, then attentiveness to those needs must be shaped deliberately. This includes international organisations respecting the sovereignty of national and regional governments as well as co-operating with mechanisms to prevent wasteful competition between aid and development organisations seeking to take the lead or to dominate in particular aspects of intervention or of localities being chosen to receive assistance to suit the needs of the professional helpers. Placing the needs and interest of local communities at the centre of practice does not absolve professionals of responsibility but is potentially a way of achieving it.

Third, an ethic of competence suggests that everyone who is involved must exercise self-awareness and restraint to avoid over-reaching in terms of commitments to the communities in need. Several studies of both humanitarian aid in disaster situations and ongoing social development practice identify examples where people and agencies who lack appropriate training or experience are able to become involved because they have resources available, irrespective of their capacity to work appropriately (Park and Miller, 2006; Javadian, 2007; Cox and Pawar, 2012; Dominelli, 2013; Wang and Lum, 2013; Midgley, 2014; Hugman, 2016). For example, in disaster situations the immediate needs are usually for clean water, food and shelter, followed closely by medical attention. In the longer term, the needs of communities may well be for rebuilding of homes, schools and health services, as well as roads and other infrastructure. However, often there is also a need for paid work, so if the value of competence is not to be turned against local people in addressing these very important issues, then this also points to the provision of employment and possibly of training as key needs. It may be seen as quicker and cheaper for all the necessary skills to meet these ongoing needs to be brought in from elsewhere, perhaps because aid and development donations are tied to 'in kind' provision of expert labour (as, for example, happened in Aceh in response after the Indian Ocean Tsunami of 2004). However, practice that does not directly involve local people and meet all their needs (in this case for employment) fails to meet the wider values of attentiveness and responsibility and perpetuates neo-colonial relationships between recipient countries and international donors.

Fourth, to address the value of responsiveness, all practitioners, international organisations and government agencies must ensure that they continue to consider the impact of their interventions on local life. This includes having appropriate ways to ensure that feedback is listened to throughout the process. However, for this to happen requires that thought is given to ensuring that there are ways for people to voice their responses and that practitioners, managers, donor organisation board members, local and national policy makers and others all exercise empathy and reflexivity in considering how their actions are impacting on the lives of the local community members. Achieving this while trying to ensure that progress is made in immediate aid, reconstruction and ongoing development is made more difficult by the myriad voices of any community. However, if it is not addressed then interventions remain at the level of doing things 'for' and 'to' recipients rather than 'with' beneficiaries.

Finally, these four aspects of intervention must be integrated, so that the overt objective of meeting the needs of local people and communities may be achieved. As indicated earlier, for example, attentiveness interconnects with responsibility and also with responsiveness, in working with community members to identify needs and find ways of intervening that enable community participation. As also noted, concerns with competence must not be enacted in a way in which some local needs (for example, training to support local employment and income generation) are masked by the covert interests of donors. In this sense the international social development field replicates at an international level the same type of moral response that was seen in the early days of social work, and which can continue in uncritical practice, that of assuming that those who are in need must be incapable of making decisions or expressing their needs appropriately (compare with Payne, 2005; also, Kittay, 2001). In the example of "natural" disasters provided earlier, the risk is that international experts in construction, economics, agriculture, fishing, communications and even social development will set the agenda and the local communities will be excluded from active involvement in their own reconstruction and future planning.

Caring justly: achieving care in justice and justice in care

How then can a political ethics of care approach assist more generally in overcoming major problems in providing practices, systems and structures that are both effective and anti-oppressive? Gasper and Truong (2008) argue that, along with attention to a humility concerning humanity's place in the world, care offers the dispositional dimension to balance the risks in the exercise of power by practitioners and agencies. They connect the political and moral aspects of care in relation to international social development through the integration of disposition and practice, arguing that:

> Care as a moral orientation for global social justice must understand the sufferings of those who are denied care as not only a discrete tragedy of persons

and groups, but as [an] outcome of systemic forces which sustain the functioning of care systems for richer others.

(Gasper and Truong, 2008, p. 27)

More than this, practice must be guided by such an understanding so that it is
competent and responsive.

In addition, Hankivsky (2014) directs our attention to the ways in which an
intersectional understanding of care is necessary to avoid the pitfalls both of power
silencing the values (dispositions) that Tronto has spelled out, for example, in
compassion becoming oppressive, and of care becoming distorted in other ways,
such as by implicitly privileging particular sections of a society. The communities
in which social workers practice in humanitarian aid and social development are
richly diverse. So, for example, in planning and project implementation, making
sure that the diversity of interests is attended to and that marginalised groups in
particular are not excluded or disadvantaged.

One ethical quality that has been identified by several contributors to these
debates but which is as yet largely under explored is that of 'humility' (Gray,
2005; Gasper and Truong, 2008; Hugman, 2010). This does not require the denial
of the knowledge and skills of practitioners – indeed, if they do not possess these,
then why are they there at all – but begins with a *cultural* humility that involves
a critical reflexivity on the part of practitioners, individually as people and collectively as agencies. So much theory and practice in international social work
still retains the colonial assumptions out of which it emerged, and these must
constantly be questioned and rethought.

An early debate regarding an ethics of care concerned its apparent location
of care in the private sphere (Held, 2006). In contrast, a political approach to an
ethics of care integrates care and justice as foundational moral values, connecting
the private and public domains (Tronto, 1993; Sevenhuijsen, 1998; Held, 2006;
Gasper and Truong, 2008). Care is compromised in situations of injustice; likewise, justice cannot be attained without the elements of care. Crucial though they
are, the values of human rights and social justice that are claimed by social work
internationally (IFSW/IASSW, 2004) may risk constructing human life as autonomous, ignoring its relationality. When care and justice are integrated, it is possible
to see justice as social and not simply as abstract or contractual.

The challenge this poses for international social work, whether in humanitarian
aid or social development, is to demonstrate these values in all aspects of practice.
Social workers and their agencies operate in relationship with members of communities that are in particular types of need. Therefore, it can be argued that a relational ethics provides a stronger framework for critically reflexive practice than
one based in abstract principles. For this to be realised requires social workers to
gain both an understanding of ourselves as situated, with our own world views
seen alongside an empathic grasp of the world views of those who we are there to
serve. It points to the relationality of social work macro-practices of assessment,
planning, advocacy, negotiation, resource finding, reviewing, research and policy
development. And it necessitates that we take seriously the value of humility, not

as self-effacement or false modesty, but through an embodiment of attentiveness, responsibility, competence and responsiveness integrated in the practices of international social work in humanitarian aid and social development.

References

Barnes, M., Brannelly, T., Ward, L. and Ward, N. (2015) *Ethics of care: Critical advances in international perspective*. Bristol: Policy Press.

Cleaver, F. (2001) Institutions, agency and the limitations of participatory approaches to development. In: Cooke, B. and Kothari, U. (eds.) *Participation: The new tyranny?* London: Zed Books.

Cox, D. and Pawar, M. (2012) *International social work: Issues, strategies and programs*, 2nd edition. Thousand Oaks, CA: Sage.

Dominelli, L. (2013) Empowering disaster affected communities for long-term reconstruction: Intervening in Sri Lanka after the tsunami. *Journal of Social Work in Disability and Rehabilitation*, 12(1–2), pp. 48–66.

Finch, J. and Groves, D. (eds.) (1983) *A labour of love: Women, work and caring*. London: Routledge & Kegan Paul.

Frank, A. G. (1966) The development if underdevelopment. *Monthly Review*, 18(4), pp. 17–31.

Gasper, D. and Truong, T.-D. (2008) *Development ethics through the lens of caring: Gender and human security*. ISS Working Paper 459. The Hague: Institute of Social Studies.

Gray, M. (2005) Dilemmas of international social work: Paradoxical processes of indigenisation, universalism and imperialism. *International Journal of Social Welfare*, 14(3), pp. 231–238.

Hankivsky, O. (2014) Rethinking care ethics: On the promise and potential of an intersectional analysis. *American Political Science Review*, 108(2), pp. 252–264.

Healy, L. M. (2008) *International social work: Professional action in an interdependent world*. New York: Oxford University Press.

Held, V. (2006) *The ethics of care: Personal, political and global*. Oxford: Oxford University Press.

Hugman, R. (1991) *Power in caring professions*. London: Macmillan.

Hugman, R. (2005) *New approaches in ethics for the caring professions*. Basingstoke: Palgrave Macmillan.

Hugman, R. (2010) *Understanding international social work: A critical analysis*. Basingstoke: Palgrave Macmillan.

Hugman, R. (2016) *Social development in social work*. London: Routledge.

Ii Untal, M. and Guinto, E. (2016) Family integration: Displaced Yolanda survivors and receiving families of Davao City in focus. Paper presented at the *Joint World Conference on Social Work, Education and Social Development*, Seoul, 27–30 June 2016.

International Federation of Social Workers/International Association of Schools of Social Work (IFSW/IASSW) (2004) *Ethics in Social Work, Statement of Principles*. Available from: http://ifsw.org/policies/statement-of-ethical-principles/ [Accessed 18 August 2016].

Javadian, R. (2007) Social work responses to earthquake disasters: A social work intervention in Bam, Iran. *International Social Work*, 50(3), pp. 334–346.

Kittay, E. F. (2001) When caring is just and justice is caring: Justice and mental retardation. *Public Culture*, 13(3), pp. 557–579.

Larsen, A. K., Sewpaul, V. and Hole, G. O. (2014) Participation in community work: International perspectives. In: Larsen, A. K., Sewpaul, V. and Hole, G. O. (eds.) *Participation in social work*. London: Routledge.

Midgley, J. (2014) *Social development: Theory and practice*. London: Sage.

Nikku, B. R. (2016) Social work, disasters and community engagement praxis: Case of the Nepal School of Social Work. Paper presented at the *Joint World Conference on Social Work, Education and Social Development*, Seoul, 27–30 June 2016.

Park, Y. and Miller, J. (2006) The social ecology of Hurricane Katrina: Rewriting the discourse of 'natural' disasters. *Smith College Studies in Social Work*, 76(3), pp. 9–24.

Pawar, M. (2014) *Social and community development practice*. New Delhi: Sage.

Payne, M. (2005) *The origins of social work: Continuity and change*. Basingstoke: Palgrave Macmillan.

Sevenhuijsen, S. (1998) *Citizenship and the ethics of care: Feminist consideration on justice, morality and politics*. London: Routledge.

Smith, S. L. (2012) Coping with disaster: Lessons learned from executive directors of nonprofit organizations (NPOs) in New Orleans following Hurricane Katrina. *Administration in Social Work*, 36(4), pp. 359–389.

Social Work (IFSW/IASSW). (2004) *Ethics in social work, statement of principles*. Available from: http://ifsw.org/policies/statement-of-ethical-principles/ [Accessed 18 August 2016].

Tronto, J. (1993) *Moral boundaries: A political argument for an ethic of care*. New York: Routledge.

Tronto, J. (2013) *Caring democracy: Markets, equality and justice*. New York: New York University Press.

Tronto, J. and Fisher, B. (1991) Towards a feminist theory of care. In: Abel, E. and Nelson, M. (eds.) *Circles of care: Work and identity in women's lives*. Albany: State University of New York Press.

Wang, X. and Lum, T. Y. (2013) Role of the professional helper in disaster intervention: Examples form the Wenchuan earthquake in China. *Journal of Social Work in Disability and Rehabilitation*, 12(1–2), pp. 116–129.

Part III
Unsettling care

12 Speaking of care from the periphery

The politics of caring from the post-colonial margins

Ann Joselynn Baltra-Ulloa

> Postmodern culture with its decentered subject can be the space where ties are severed or it can provide the occasion for new and varied forms of bonding. To some extent, ruptures, surfaces, contextuality, and a host of other happenings create gaps that make space for oppositional practices which no longer require intellectuals to be confined to narrow separate spheres with no meaningful connection to . . . the everyday . . . a space is there for critical exchange . . . this may very well be the 'central' future location of resistance struggle, a meeting place where new and radical happenings can occur.
>
> (hooks, 1990, p. 31)

No doubt, bell hooks, as an African American cultural critic, seeks in this introductory quotation to rescue from the ashes of modernity the new possibilities of the post-colonial era. To me, she challenges intellectual elitism: the thinker that embraces all things 'post-modernity' but from the comfortable chair of Western epistemological privilege. She fundamentally challenges the accepted norm. Through this quotation, hooks states that to truly embrace diversity, we have to let go of our Western need to make all things neat and tidy. Her words affirm that diversity, by its nature, is a mess-making process. In this chapter I attempt to make a mess of what have become accepted ideas about care and the ethic of care. I do so by welcoming the post-colonial. Post-colonial theory has entered social work thinking not as a demand for inclusion of all that has been excluded but for what Raghuram et al. (2009) say is a demand for not becoming the same. Inclusion on the basis of *being* different and that difference being about the ambiguous, the contradictory and the in-between space results from being ruptured from accepted norms. I engage in a dialogue about the politics of care, a dialogue that will sound unfamiliar, non-normative, uncomfortable, precarious, but nevertheless a dialogue that in an age of privilege by few at the cost of many I argue is essential to social work's relevance. West (1990) argued that this 'gesture' of speaking about the non-normative is not just about a new history of critical thinking; it is also about a cultural politics. It is about an attempt to speak of what makes up difference, what disorders our accepted and unchallenged understandings of difference, what representation is given and not given to the intersections of cultures, colonies, colonialists, classes, races, gender, sexuality, age, ethnicities, power and privilege. This introductory commentary is my setting of the scene, my revealing of my position-ality in the discussions I offer in this chapter. It is my nervous jump into the abyss from the precipice of the politics of caring from the margins. Like many scholars of colour, as a First Nations woman of refugee background living and working in the West, I am nervous because I know what I am adding to this book disturbs the epistemological and ontological privileging of Euro-Australian perspectives. Moreover, these kinds of contributions from people like me have historically been considered as contributions from the 'other' – an 'other' that is 'made special room for' but is seldom valued and heard from as equal (Walter and Baltra-Ulloa, 2016).

The aims of this chapter

This chapter is not about seeking special room in the reconstitution of what it means to care from a 'different' perspective. The chapter constitutes a cultural politics founded on a belief that multiple ways of knowing, being and doing can have equal value in understanding care and the critical ethics of care in social work. I also believe that the perceived scarcity of room to speak with validity has been created to keep "different" views as alternatives and continue to affirm "a norm", an undisturbed "mainstream bench mark" that struggles against a para-digm shift (Walter and Baltra-Ulloa, 2016). As I write these words, I echo the feelings expressed by Narayan (1997). She too felt strange and annoyed that for many 'Southern theorists' we must again and again be the ones to highlight and account for our differences, explain our location, find ways to tell our stories so that the West hears us. We want to be heard for our differences, for our split from the accepted and unchallenged Western norms and not merely be heard as "prob-lematic products of our Westernization" (Narayan, 1997, p. 3).

This chapter begins with some mess-making about accepted ways of thinking about the ethic of care in Western social work. I explore how care is conceptualised in the West, from the *centre* of privileged knowledge, and how these conceptu-alisations from the centre, even when they claim to be culturally and politically progressive, retain a blind spot. There is no consideration of Western privilege; the taken-for-granted ways of thinking that are the foundations of cultural practices that reinforce Western epistemological and ontological superiority remain unsettled. Essentially, even when thinking about care and the ethic of care is disrupted, these disruptions retain an unspoken assumption that thinking from anywhere else is thinking from the margins. Much like the section in this book, "Unsettling Care", in which this chapter is located, I wonder: is there an assumption that '*unsettling care*' can only come from perspectives that are different from the norm? What is lost, what is never truly seen by this unsettled *centre* is the essence of marginality, is the value of epistemologies that offer completely new ways to understand care. The wisdom that other worlds, other ways of thinking and being in the world offer is omitted and placed on the margins as though its true value is only as periphery to the accepted and unchallenged norm. This omission serves a purpose: for social work, it helps the profession to retain its role as a *helping* and *caring* profession, prodded to make room for differences but essentially unchanged at its roots.

I tell a story about my social work practice with Hope, 'the client', the person I thought I was *helping and caring for*. This story unfolds during the unravelling of my practice, during my unlearning and letting go of what I had learnt in social work about care. It is a story of re-engaging with the *periphery*, my ancestral feminine knowledge, with the *ordinary*, realising that caring is about doing, being and knowing ordinary things with extraordinary love (Westoby and Dowling, 2013, p. 100). In sharing this story, I attempt to speak of care from the post-colonial periphery.

I end this chapter with more questions than answers. I offer a perspective where words like 'tangible' and 'clear' seem confusing, where caring happens in relationships founded in humble vulnerability, where unlearning becomes about transforming, where all that is considered marginal is norm and where care is an act of refusing, resisting and reframing the complexity and simplicity of our shared humanity. There is no complex theory or formula to follow and no straight answers in what I offer. This chapter aims to contribute to an ongoing dialogue in social work. This dialogue is born in deep listening, in believing and trusting one another and in de-privileging much of what has afforded Western social work such power and unearned privileges (Pease, 2010).

Care from the *centre*

The concept of care in the West is primarily understood as the foundation of relationships. It has been understood as a socio-moral practice involving the fundamentals of the human condition – our trust for each other, our mutual respect, the feelings we share and the values we treasure (Featherstone, 2010). The ethic of care delves into the moral compass we use to judge how and why we act in interactions with others. Different theoretical perspectives have added a range of aspects to consider in our understanding of this moral compass, but fundamentally the ethic of care wrestles with how humans approach relationships in ways that contribute to a positive interdependency (Featherstone, 2010).

In Western social work, ways of thinking about the ethic of care have built from Kantian deontological concerns. These concerns lead the profession to consider its role and purpose in society, how social work practice can facilitate individuals' capacity to access their rights to self-determination and act from their sense of duty and obligation. More recently, thinking has shifted to concerns over pluralist ethics where social work is about acknowledging and accepting that cultural differences result in people holding an array of values and ways of seeing the world that are sometimes "incompatible and incommensurable" (Hugman, 2013, p. 75).

Ideas about care from outside of social work may not have been detrimental in shaping the practice of care within social work, but they have intensified the relevance of exploring how care is thought about and how it is practiced within social work. Gilligan's 1982 work, from a feminist perspective, began framing the ethic of care as a gendered relational issue requiring considerations beyond modernist ideas about morality, rights, responsibilities, laws and rules (Featherstone, 2010). Gilligan (1982) began the project of thinking about care from a relational perspective, self in relation to other, shifting discourse about care towards an engagement with ethics as an issue negotiated in and through relationships. Further, these relationships take place and are negotiated through a web of contexts including balancing questions about how to care, how we connect, how we retain individual freedom and yet remain connected (Hirschmann, 1997, p. 170).

How directly the work of Gilligan has influenced social work is debatable. However, this work was noticed by other ethic of care writers and thinkers in its suggestions that care and caring had political implications. Tronto (1993) and Sevenhuijsen (2000) lead the way in considering care as both a moral orientation and a social activity (Sevenhuijsen, 2000, p. 14), as both about a *being* and a *doing* intricately linked to the social, political and cultural world we live in. It is here that caring began to be considered as a practice and as a product of power. Care and caring were being theorised as requiring not just a disposition and a moral imperative, but also considerations of the needs of people. The socio-cultural, political and economic positionality of those *doing* the caring was being considered as a possible interference in the capacity to hear and respond to the needs of those requiring care. Tronto (1993) directed attention to the need to not solely focus on meeting caring needs and addressing power differentials in caring but also to engaging with the complexities of socio-political and cultural contexts that inevitably shape how care needs are identified and expressed and how caring is ultimately practiced.

Sevenhuijsen (2000) expanded on these ideas by critically exploring the work of *The Third Way* by Anthony Giddens (1998). Giddens (1998) suggested a middle ground be found in the provision of social welfare and social policy development by fusing elements of neoliberalism with "old-style social democracy" (Sevenhuijsen, 2000, p. 6). However, Sevenhuijsen (2000) suggested that there is no middle ground or *Third Way* possibility without a consideration of care and the ethic of care as elements of how social justice is achieved. For her, care is about a democratic practice and citizenship, a socio-political process that makes sure everyone can actively participate in society and benefit from it by being able to receive and give care equally. Sevenhuijsen's work (2000) offers social work the chance to bring together care and justice as key elements of a socially just and human-focused practice.

Almost parallel to these developments in thinking about care and the ethic of care was the work being done around issues of intersectionality. The literature in this area is extensive and explores how different social, cultural and economic contexts give way to multiple ways of understanding relationships, how care occurs and how power interacts with ethics. A detailed exploration of this literature here is not possible. However, in relation to what this literature offers debates in social work around ideas of care and the ethics of care, Featherstone (2010) describes the work by Williams (2001) and Daly and Lewis (2000) as standout and summarises their contributions as follows:

> We are neither just givers nor receivers of care . . . in the right conditions of mutual respect and material support, [we] learn the civic responsibilities of

responsibility, trust, tolerance for human limitations and frailties and acceptance and diversity. Care is part of citizenship . . . Inequalities in care giving
and care receiving are exposed through questioning who is and is not benefit-
ing from existing policies.

(Featherstone, 2010, pp. 79–80)

These ideas flag the need to think beyond essentialist notions about gender, class,
age, able-bodiedness, race and sexuality and communicate the need for social work
to think about the complexity that issues like globalisation, cultural diversity, the
experiences of colonisation, forced migration, poverty and climate change present
for social work practice. In this context, care expands beyond borders of selfhood
and political spaces and beyond social workers just being carers doing the caring.
Care becomes about all that is personal, relational, political, cultural, social, local,
national and transnational. It becomes about the tensions that exist in a globalised
world where humans are interdependent and where multiple ways of knowing,
being and doing are inescapable. In the face of these debates, pluralism is born.

Hugman (2013) has explored pluralism and ethics in social work. He argues
that pluralism accepts that as a result of cultural diversity and the complexities,
intersections and multiplicities of post-modern life, the values that people hold are
often "incompatible . . . in conflict with each other" (Hugman, 2013, p. 74). Quot-
ing Kekes (1993), Hugman (2013, p. 75) states that values can even be "incommensurable. That is, it may be impossible to achieve all shared values at the same
time and impossible to compare them in such way that an order of priorities can be
established". If this is the case, then theories that explain ethics are also conflicting
and cannot be compared, and thus our understanding of ethics may well require
a fundamental revisiting. What pluralism offers social work is the message that
to understand an ethic of care, to engage in what care means inter-culturally and
cross-culturally in this post-modern era of globalisation, we need dialogue. We
need to find ways to learn from one another's differences, to discover what our
values are and find ways to care and be cared for that are neither right nor wrong
but rather relevant in context, to those in caring relationships.

This perspective inspires a process of learning in and through practice. In
relationships, we learn about values and morals from different standpoints. This
suggests social work practice is about wrestling with all contexts that shape the
understandings held about care, caring and the ethics of care. Hugman (2013),
again citing Kekes (1993), suggests differentiating between primary and secondary values in order to put to practice a pluralist approach to ethics (pp. 77–79).
Primary values refer to widely agreed values across cultural contexts, including
things like the need for food, water, shelter and safety. Secondary values are in
essence the detail of how we give meaning to primary values, including how we
conduct relationships and how we approach family life. Identifying and distinguishing between these categories of values is said to assist the social worker in
engaging with the process of making practice choices. These choices are never
singularly 'right and ethical' but rather are based on relational processes that value
pluralism and facilitate mutual understanding (Hugman, 2013, p. 79). Intersecting

these relational processes are the law, systems and policies that, for social workers, cannot be overlooked. Hugman (2013) states that for the pluralist, caring is in being able to bring all elements together. First, finding commonalities through primary values discussions and then wrestling with the detail of secondary values where most of the cultural differences are found. Key to this process is learning to accept that disagreement is inevitable and indeed positive in the pursuit of mutual understanding.

I argue that despite the diversity in points of view regarding care and the ethics of care, there is still a blind spot. All of this theorising emerges from one way of seeing the world, that of the West. The epistemological and ontological foundations of all this work remain unsettled and unidentified as the product of Western culture. If there is to be an ethic of care derived from multiple ways of knowing, being and doing in social work, there needs to be a new geography of care (Raghuram et al., 2009).

Despite more recent critiques and discussions about care, reinforcing the importance of relationships to understanding how we make sense of each other, our actions, thoughts and differences, thinking continues to favour a hierarchical method of settling what care and caring are. Ways of thinking still talk about the need to identify categories of values, to establish some level of order and to come up with concrete suggestions for how we do care in a diverse world. To me, this is problematic and it derives from the privilege and the superiority Western culture exercises over everyone else.

In the following sections I share my practice story and I make links to how I see caring from the periphery in this post-colonial time.

Care from the periphery

Thirteen years ago, I met Hope and her family. They were newly arrived refugees from the continent of Africa and I was their assigned re-settlement worker. We spent much of that first year getting to know each other and making room for my ignorance and my attempts at assimilating them to Australian life. One day, I was left alone with Hope and her siblings while her parents attended a computer course. I helped get breakfast and saw the younger kids off to school. In the car, Hope asked me if she could stay home because she wanted to talk with me about life. We argued about her not going to school until she said: "It's time we talk aunty Jos." Thinking this could be a breakthrough in talking about torture and trauma issues, I drove us back to her house and we went to the kitchen where Hope wanted to learn how to make empanadas. As I gathered the ingredients to start the cooking, thoughts came about how I would react to a possible disclosure of abuse, neglect or violence, who I would need to ring and what I would do to take care of such situation. Hope noticed I was distracted in thoughts and she said to me: "Aunty Jos have you seen my feet?" Her words hauled me out of my head and back into the moment. I responded: "No Hope, why?" Hope proceeded to tell me how she'd lost three toes after the rebels held her upside down as a baby to force her father to join them, when he refused the rebels cut her toes off as vengeance.

I sat in silence listening to Hope. I remember vividly feeling that something had drastically shifted and changed but I couldn't identify what. We talked all morning and never got to the cooking. Hope told me how much she wanted to tell me that story, how much she wanted me to know what had happened to her family and how much she and her family had waited for me to be ready to hear it.

I have written countless reflections about this one experience because it was a pivotal moment in my practice that challenged and changed everything I had learnt about helping and caring for people as a social worker. The first year in this relationship with Hope and her family was a whirlwind of activity, mostly dedicated to meeting the needs of bureaucracy and systems and not necessarily the needs of the family. It was also a year filled with teaching me and waiting for me to work out how to be in this relationship. I had convinced myself that I was critically aware, good at critical self-reflection and that I was doing the caring for this family labelled by everyone involved in *helping* them as vulnerable. I was the practitioner with the specialised skills and knowledge acutely aware of ethical practice, of my power as social worker and my role in making sure Hope and her family could re-settle in Australia. I had inklings that the family would also *care* for me in the relationship because there was much to learn about African families and cultural differences.

This experience made me think about the distance we create in social work between our real selves and our professional selves and from the 'clients' we work with. Hope and her family have taught me to question this distance, to examine who defines this distance and who gets to be near and far and in between by virtue of these definitions of distance. Caring for them and being cared for by them has transpired through being and doing in the ordinary – cooking and sharing a meal, talking around the table, discussing politics and our journeys to Australia, being in each other's lives. Also, letting each other down, arguing, disagreeing, and confronting each other on issues we see differently. This has meant we've learnt to face conflict and work through our differences, and most importantly we've had to find ways to lean comfortably on the constant discomfort of vulnerability.

How do I begin to put 'theory' around these relational processes when so much of what I've learnt about care, caring and the ethic of care in these practice contexts has come from the being and the unlearning of what I assimilated to in my life here in Australia? I begin by describing that I believe we are all colonised, colonised to ways of thinking about social work practice that have emerged from epistemologies of fear. Fear has had a great role in an illusion being created in social work that control is possible, necessary and results in avoiding the *wrong* social work practice. Many post-colonial thinkers agree that the influences of neo-colonialism have convinced us that our differences preclude us from belonging in each other's worlds, that acknowledging our interdependence, the mutuality of our human condition risks losing our individuality, our freedom to make independent decisions. Through a post-colonial perspective, all this is challenged to argue that we are never distant from each other because lines of caring and being cared for are always implicated in each other's lives.

A post-colonial care and caring

A key fundamental characteristic of post-colonial thought is that it questions socio-political-cultural relationships; it seeks to understand how the past has shaped the present and influences the future. Care and the ethic of care from a post-colonial perspective are seen as representations of complex lines of connections, responsibility, raptures and disconnections. This post-colonial perspective sees everyone as part of each other, in each other's world, at the same time as there is distance and withdrawal from one another. People are seen as responsible and accountable for both how connected and disconnected they may be (Raghuram et al., 2009).

This means caring and being cared for is the product of how much we ask ourselves what spaces we occupy and not, why do we occupy them, who do we care for and why, what are the limits of our caring? When is not caring an act of caring? Is caring good for the carer and the cared for? When is caring actually an irresponsible act? (Raghuram et al., 2009, p. 9).

Post-colonial thought also challenges the way history is treated. Bhabha (1994) explains that for a post-colonial the dominant version of history is problematic. This dominant version of history has privileged the version where the West tells the story of the South, with reference to what the South does not have that the West does. De Sousa Santos (2014) agrees and adds that this way of telling and privileging a history told by the West about the rest has created absences of knowledge. There are dismissed wisdoms and misleading linear tellings of how the South and the West have developed separate from each other, and they ignore the conjoined nature of the relationship between the West and the South.

Post-colonial thinking challenges us to imagine an "unlinear map of human progress" (Raghuram et al., 2009, p. 9), a messy past, parts of which have been selectively chosen to be left in or out of what has become accepted centre-mainstream know-how. Our shared humanity has been obscured and with it the understanding of the importance of the past and how it has shaped present forms of knowing, being and doing. This complex messy world has been homogenised, past injustices have been denied and forgotten, and important lessons and wisdoms have been ignored. Post-colonial thinking is concerned about how we speak back to this misbalance, how we find ways for people from everywhere in the world to speak for themselves about care and the ethic of care with equal validity (Raghuram et al., 2009).

The implications of speaking of care and the ethic of care from this post-colonial political perspective are that we begin to see how important it is not to seek universal definitions for anything. The ultimate aim is to have no centre or periphery, no single writer and teller of stories, and no preferred practice model other than splintering and unsettling all that we know while we honour the messiness of what we learn from each other. So, the politics of caring from this post-colonial 'margin' and the ethic of care are always open to multiple meanings derived from multiple places. Critics may well suggest this leaves everything up for interpretation, no clarity on where the moral ground lays and no firm foundation on issues of human rights and social justice. The history of knowledge from the *centre* already captures so much knowledge. We know relationships work; we know dialogue is crucial; we know a democratic citizenship includes the ability to care and be cared for; we know power differentials make caring a political activity; we know enough. The critical terrain of post-colonial thought says "learn to unlearn"; "learn to listen from other wisdoms"; "learn to step off the pedestal of superiority to let others speak for themselves". This is not an era of post-colonisation but of an era where we work against ongoing colonisation.

My experiences with Hope and her family have evoked many unanticipated emotions in me. I have felt the power of trust in the ordinary, the power of caring and being cared for through the mundane, the everydayness of connecting and building relationships around a simple being in each other's life. I have learnt to value mistakes, getting things wrong like offending and being offended. I have felt anger that I was taught to think I had the answers, the skills, the knowledge and the resources to care for other people and define what that care should look like. Unlearning all that has been taught to me as valuable social work knowledge has been difficult because I've had to get used to being vulnerable. It has felt unfair that Hope and her family had to wait for me to be ready to hear their story. It has felt shameful to realise that these feelings of unfairness come from a deep way of thinking about Hope and her family as more vulnerable than me, and thinking of myself as superior in my capacity to self-care. Accepting fear as a constant companion has been difficult; I have felt fear of crossing boundaries, of being judged as unethical, of being called unprofessional. Fear is seductive and it generates a belief that the ways we are taught to care in the West are the only safe and ethical ways to care.

Hope and her family showed me the ethics of care are in the fragility of the web of relationships we co-create. How we come to these relationships is important. We come as learners and deep listeners; who we are in them is critical. We are genuine, vulnerable, emotional beings and what we do in these relationships is always emergent. What shifted in me the day Hope told me her story was my spirit self. It came back to join heart, head, hands and feet. It brought back my ancestors, their wisdom, their voices and messages. Messages I had heard from childhood were validated. It was ok to love; it was ok to make mistakes; it was ok to not know; it was ok to trust instincts; and, it was ok to share your real self. Hope and her family entered my heart and that complicated everything.

To conclude, the politics of caring from the margins is about anti-colonial practice. It is a painful 'alternative' and direct challenge to the centre norm. It is a demand for inclusion on the basis of difference, an energy for change that recognises the world could be a better place if we accepted that not becoming the same is in our best collective interest. This politics is about making a mess of all that we've learnt thus far about care and caring in Western social work. It involves unlearning, de-privileging Western ways of knowing, being and doing to enter the space of whom we call *other,* *hear* them speak about themselves while they formulate what care is in their language. The ambivalence and ambiguity this politics suggests is at the heart of an epistemological and ontological disrupting we can lead and engage with bravely through social work and social work practice.

References

Bhabha, H. K. (1994) *The location of culture*. London: Routledge.

Daly, M. and Lewis, J. (2000) The concept of social care and the analysis of contemporary welfare states. *British Journal of Sociology*, 52(2), pp. 281–298.

De Sousa Santos, B. (2014) *Epistemologies of the South: Justice against epistemicide*. Boulder, CO: Paradigm.

Featherstone, B. (2010) Ethic of care. In: Gray, M. and Webb, S. (eds.) *Ethics and value perspectives in social work*. London: Palgrave Macmillan, pp. 73–84.

Giddens, A. (1998) *The third way. The renewal of social democracy*. Cambridge: Polity Press.

Gilligan, C. (1982) *In a different voice: Psychological theory and women's development*. Cambridge, MA: Harvard University Press.

Hirschmann, N. (1997) Feminist standpoint as postmodern strategy. *Women and Politics*, 18, pp. 73–92.

hooks, b. (1990) *Yearnings: Race, gender and cultural politics*. Boston: South End Press.

Hugman, R. (2013) *Culture, values and ethics in social work*. London: Routledge.

Kekes, J. (1993) *The morality of pluralism*. Princeton, NJ: Princeton University Press.

Narayan, U. (1997) *Dislocating cultures/identities, traditions, and third world feminism*. New York: Routledge.

Pease, B. (2010) *Undoing privilege: Unearned advantage in a divided world*. London: Zed.

Raghuram, P., Madge, C. and Noxolo, P. (2009) Rethinking responsibility and care for a postcolonial world. *Geoforum*, 40(1), pp. 5–13.

Sevenhuijsen, S. (2000) Caring in the third way: The relation between obligation, responsibility and care in Third Way discourse. *Critical Social Policy*, 20(1), pp. 5–37.

Tronto, J. C. (1993) *Moral boundaries: A political argument for an ethic of care*. New York: Routledge.

Walter, M. and Baltra-Ulloa, A. J. (2016) The race gap: An Indigenous perspective on whiteness, colonialism and social work in Australia. *Social Dialogue*, 4(15), pp. 29–32.

West, C. (1990) The new cultural politics of difference. *October*, 53, pp. 93–109.

Westoby, P. and Dowling, G. (2013) *Theory and practice of dialogical community development: International perspectives*. London: Routledge.

Williams, F. (2001) In and beyond New Labour: Towards a new political ethics of care. *Critical Social Policy*, 21(4), pp. 467–493.

13 Aboriginal people and caring within a colonised society

Sue Green[1]

Introduction

This chapter explores the meaning of care within Aboriginal communities prior to colonisation and the impact of colonisation upon Aboriginal people and their ability to provide this care. As Aboriginal people do not see the environment and people as being separate, this chapter will talk about care of being inclusive of the environment and will present two fundamental concepts, Yindyamarra[2] and Wirimbirragu Ngurambanggu[3] from the Wiradyuri people of western New South Wales (NSW). The chapter concludes by considering the importance of these concepts for social work practice both within Aboriginal and non-Aboriginal peoples and communities.

Yindyamarra and Wirimbirragu Ngurambanggu

'Yindyamarra' means respect, honour, go slowly, go gently, and 'Wirimbirragu Ngurambanggu' means 'caring for country' in the Wiradyuri language and culture. While the English translation does not give the full depth of meaning, it can give the readers some level of understanding of these two concepts. Yindyamarra and Wirimbirragu Ngurambanggu are more than just words or phrases – they are the foundation to Wiradyuri culture and way of life. In order to understand Aboriginal systems of caring, one needs to have insight into these key concepts and how they formed and informed Aboriginal society.

Yindyamarra is a concept that is much more than just the concept of respect within the English language. It is a way of living. While Yindyamarra is about being respectful of each other and of the environment, it is also about how we live within our communities and the world. Yindyamarra talks about going slowly and going gently. By going slowly, Yindyamarra does not mean going so slow that you get nothing done or you always put off things to another time. What Yindyamarra is saying is that you are to take your time to do things fully and properly. If you don't do things slowly you will miss so much. If we think about how we live in today's world, we are always rushing, always too busy to take time to be fully aware of everything around us. It is like when you got up this morning: how much did you notice what was happening around you? What did you see? What did you hear? Were you so focused on getting to your destination that you did not see that dragonfly or hear that cricket? In your search for happiness and fulfilment, what simple pleasures do you miss? Today we rush around so much and are so stressed trying to achieve and be successful that we forget to live in the moment and enjoy the beauty that is all around us, and that beauty is what gives us joy and creates that happiness that we are so desperately searching for. Furthermore, that stress we create within our body creates many health problems. If we just took more time, went a bit more slowly, our health, both physical and psychological, would benefit greatly and we would be happier with our lives. As well, Yindyamarra also asks us to go gently. This means we need to be conscious of the impact that we have on the earth, on each other and also on ourselves, which brings us to Wirimbirragu Ngurambanggu.

Wirimbirragu Ngurambanggu encompasses all, including land, plants, animals and people. However, it is also about buyaa,[4] the lore. Buyaa outlines the manner in which Wiradyuri are to live with each other and with every other aspect of life. Often people hear 'caring for country' and they think of land, plants and animals and the only consideration given to people is the actions of people upon the land. They do not consider that caring for country is also about caring for people. Western thought deems people as separate from land, animals and plants and not as part of the ecosystem. However, people are just as important to the environment as everything else. People are made up of the same elements that all other living things such as land, animals and plants are made up of. We are reliant on the same elements in order to live, and we rely on each other in order to live. People do not live without sunlight, without water and without food. All other living things rely on each other. I am not fully convinced that the environment would not live without us and in fact do much better without the existence of people. However, regardless of my doubt about the value of people to the environment, people were placed here for a purpose. Biama (the creator) gave people the responsibility for looking after the land and for all other beings. It is our sacred duty to care for land, for plants, for animals and for each other. If we do not care for the environment, not only does the environment suffer but also so do we. Despite this we still do not take care of the environment. If we were to practice Yindyamarra for everything, we would be looking after the environment. Yindyamarra tells us how to look after the environment: be gentle. We need to ensure that our impact upon the environment is one that is gentle and is as minimal as possible. People are impacted along with the environment; so to care for people is also to care for country – Wirimbirragu Ngurambanggu.

Prior to colonisation

Each person within Aboriginal societies was an important part of their family, community and nation. Not only were individuals valued for who they were, they also carried important information. Each individual was the carrier of a particular part of the knowledge contained within the Aboriginal world view. That world view was made up of stories, songs, designs and roles that individuals played.

These stories, songs, designs and roles were handed down from individual to individual, but not just any individual or at any time. Certain people were deemed to be the correct person to hold that particular piece of knowledge, through their positioning at birth and also their learning and by demonstrating their readiness to hold that knowledge. Not one person was seen as incapable but was given what they were ready to know. Every person was an important part of their family and community and everyone worked together to Wirimbirragu Ngurambanggu, as this was the sacred role of people. Prior to colonisation Aboriginal communities operated on the concept of reciprocity and sharing and that each person has an important place and role within the family and community (Bourke and Bourke, 1995). Furthermore, Aboriginal families are based on the extended family model rather than the smaller nuclear family, and responsibility for the family and family members does not sit with just one person but is shared across different family members (Wirimbirragu Ngurambanggu and Yindyamarra). Hence the role of caring was not just situated with one person and an individual was not seen as being someone who was specifically cared for, but rather everyone was cared for and everyone played a role in the caring and nurturing of the family and community. Caring for each other also meant ensuring Wirimbirragu Ngurambanggu. It was important to ensure that the land was healthy; the same with water and food sources. It was equally as important to manage the supply and that nothing was ever damaged or used to extinction.

Aboriginal people handed down what are now called 'dreaming stories' about how to Wirimbirragu Ngurambanggu. Many people have thought of these stories as myths or stories for children. However, these stories contained knowledge about how to look after the environment and how to ensure the wellbeing and safety of all. There are creation stories, stories about events over time and stories about dangers if certain actions were to occur. Today, non-Aboriginal people are starting to realise that these stories are not just children's stories or stories of fancy. The evidence of the giant animals that are within many of the stories is starting to be discovered and hopefully now the message within those stories will be listened to and acted upon. We have stories that tell us not to mine, stories that tells us the dangers of mining certain minerals from the ground, the sickness that these minerals can cause to people. We have stories that tell us how to survive certain natural disasters. We have stories that are about public health and also for public order. We have stories for how to deal with conflict and that govern human relationships. These stories are the bases for our buyaa (lore). Basically our buyaa is the key for Wirimbirragu Ngurambanggu and Yindyamarra.

Through buyaa, Aboriginal society and life was highly structured and was based on an interconnection with the environment, with humans not being seen as more important or dominating any other part of the environment (Green, 2014, p. 129). Thus the health of the environment was a fundamental part of Aboriginal life. Additionally, under Aboriginal lore it was an offence (lore is based on the dreaming and therefore unchangeable, in comparison to Western law which can be and is changed frequently by politicians) not to provide for others (Bourke and Cox, 1994, pp. 50–51, in Green, 2014, p. 129). Essentially everything is connected and nothing exists outside of its connection with everything else, and that includes people. Aboriginal people always knew that they existed as part of the environment and that to survive they had to ensure Wirimbirragu Ngurambanggu and Yindyamarra were practiced and maintained. Due to following Wirimbirragu Ngurambanggu and Yindyamarra, Aboriginal people lived successfully within the Australian environment and the environment with people until relatively recently. Aboriginal life and society were heavily impacted upon by colonisation.

Impact of colonisation

While there is debate about the length of time Aboriginal people have lived upon the lands now known as Australia, it is widely accepted how well Aboriginal people were living prior to British arrival and colonisation (Franks, Smith-Lloyd, Newell and Dietrich, 2001; Bussey, 2013). Furthermore it is also widely accepted that the arrival of the British impacted heavily upon the structure of Aboriginal societies and upon the lives of Aboriginal people. Aboriginal societies went from being highly structured and organised to being disturbed and forced into dependency upon the coloniser (Green, 2014). As stated earlier, everyone had a role within their community and people existed within an extended family network. However, colonisation heavily impacted upon people's roles and upon the structure of Aboriginal communities and societies.

Following the arrival of Captain Phillip and the first fleet in 1788, the ability of Aboriginal people to continue to live in the manner that enabled them to live within the Australian environment was quickly and severely disrupted. At first it was the taking of land and preventing access to food and water. Next was the introduction of new diseases that had a devastating effect on the Aboriginal people in the Sydney region. Within a few short years came the massacres of Aboriginal people and also what was to become a long-term policy and practice of removing children (known as the Stolen Generations). The children were taken from their families and their way of life. The justification for this was to protect Aboriginal children from the moral corruption of their families and communities. Further to this, Aboriginal people were forcibly removed from their lands and incarcerated onto missions and reserves. This allowed for the control of Aboriginal people and also disconnected Aboriginal people from their land.

In addition to the disruption caused to communities through the removal of people and the breaking up of families and communities, there was also the disruption to culture and cultural knowledge. As discussed earlier, each individual holds a particular part of Aboriginal knowledge and this knowledge is kept by being handed down. When you remove children, this prevents knowledge from being handed down. In addition, under government policies and legislation, it became illegal for Aboriginal people to practice their cultures. Aboriginal people were punished for speaking their language or performing any cultural practices. Language is a very important part of culture, as outlined in this chapter through the use of the key concepts of Yindyamarra and Wirimbirragu Ngurambanggu. You cannot simply translate every meaning of these terms into English. English simply does not have the ability to translate the full meaning or the depth of either of these concepts. Further to this, these concepts by themselves have little meaning. Without the stories, the songs, the designs and the buyaa that go with these concepts there is no direction of how to follow them. How do I know how to care for country, when I don't know the information about what this country needs and when it needs it? I have outlined the importance of caring for country, but what I have not provided is all the information required to care for country. One example of this is fire. Fire is a very important part of Wirimbirragu Ngurambanggu. However, fire itself can be very dangerous if not managed correctly. Buyaa gives us the information about how to manage and use fire to Wirimbirragu Ngurambanggu. Buyaa also tells us how to keep safe if there is a fire that is out of control. The Australian environment is one that needs fire as part of its management but also fire creates much loss and destruction due to the nature of the Australian environment. Aboriginal people know how to manage and use fire, but Aboriginal people were prevented from using and passing on this knowledge for many years.

Colonisation is not just a single act that happened more than 200 years ago. It is also seen and re-enacted through the legacy that the act of colonial occupation has left behind. The continuing removal of Aboriginal children and adults from their families and homes, the experiencing of racism and discrimination against Aboriginal people, and the poverty and disadvantage that the majority of Aboriginal people live with are all ongoing examples of both the impact of the event and the ongoing legacy of colonisation. The intent was to destroy Aboriginal society and culture, and to this very day the practice continues (in forms differing from the early colonial period) as well as the devastating effects and impact. Many Aboriginal people today do not know where they are from, who their family is or what their culture is. The majority of Aboriginal people do not speak their language and while there are some attempts to address this situation, the actions that created the disruption to identity and culture continue. Aboriginal people continue to be removed from families and communities. Currently Aboriginal children are almost 10 times more likely to be in care than other children (AIFS, 2016); the numbers of Aboriginal people being imprisoned is extremely high, at 27 percent of the prison population (ABS, 2015), and we see governments continuously attempting to force Aboriginal people from their homes and off their land (Kagi, 2014).

The impact of colonisation has not only disrupted Aboriginal societies and the ability to pass on knowledge and practice culture but has also had a massive impact upon the ability to Wirimbirragu Nguramanggu. Colonisation has prevented Aboriginal people from practicing and living Wirimbirragu Ngurambanggu and Yindyamarra but both of these practices have not completely gone away. Today, Aboriginal people are working to redevelop and strengthen their cultures through language revitalisation programs. Language itself does not sit separately from culture – everything is connected. So the first steps of living Wirimbirragu Ngurambanggu and Yindyamarra is to bring people back home and to restore language and, in turn, restoring language is Wirimbirragu Ngurambanggu and Yindyamarra. As a Wiradyuri elder Uncle Stan Grant senior has pointed out, our language, our culture is not lost but is within us, it is just waiting to be remembered (2016).

Today the sacred duty of Aboriginal people within Wirimbirragu Ngurambanggu and Yindyamarra is to remember and relearn their language. With language comes learning of culture and the ways to Wirimbirragu Ngurambanggu and to live Yindyamarra. However, today Wirimbirragu Ngurambanggu and Yindyamarra is not only for Aboriginal people but also for all people who now live on and in Aboriginal nations.

What does this mean for caring in social work?

The principles and values of the social work profession in Australia place it in a position where it has an obligation to work with Aboriginal people in a culturally appropriate and responsive manner. The Australian Association of Social Workers (AASW) states that the 'Principles of human rights and social justice are fundamental to social work' and outlines that this means subscribing to United Nations human rights documents (AASW, 2010, p. 7). These documents include the Declaration on the Rights of Indigenous Peoples, which provides Indigenous peoples with the right to their land and to practice their culture. Also, the Association commits the profession to 'working with Australian's First Peoples' (AASW, 2010, p. 7). This places social workers in a position where they need to know and be able to work within the concepts of Wirimbirragu Ngurambanggu and Yindyamarra. However, what does this mean for social work profession and for individual social workers?

Social work as a profession already defines social work as being underpinned by theories that include Indigenous knowledges (AASW, 2013, p. 4). As well, the AASW also outlines that social workers need to be able to demonstrate knowledge and understanding of Aboriginal 'cultures, protocols and practices within the local context' (AASW, 2013, p. 11). This means that the profession has a responsibility to ensure that all social workers have access to, and participate in, learning about Aboriginal people and the land on which they live and work. Unfortunately at this time, what is being taught within social work programs is limited to knowledge of historical and contemporary issues and some cultural awareness. Social work students are not being taught the concepts and foundations of Aboriginal culture in the area in which their programs are being taught. If social workers do not know and understand Wirimbirragu Ngurambanggu and Yindyamarra, then how can they have knowledge and understanding of the local culture and protocols? This might sound as if it is extremely difficult and maybe even too hard; however, social work does have some starting points upon which to build.

Social work does acknowledge that people are part of systems and social workers need to work with people within their environment (AASW, 2010, p. 7). However, the concept of environment is limited to that of human environments rather than a wider view of the larger ecosystem. This is illustrated by McKinnon (2008, p. 257), who points out that in social work 'the environment' has primarily been referred to as the "sociocultural or psychosocial environment". However, all is not without hope, as there is a growing awareness within social work that 'the environment' needs to include the ecosystem as well (Norton, 2012). Even so, the current focus is very much on how we deal with ecological disasters and environmental distress rather than the environment being a continuation of the social and cultural dimensions of life (McKinnon, 2008; Gray and Coates, 2012). While there is some acknowledgement of the importance of the environment to human survival, there is still a lack of awareness of the interconnection between people and the environment and that people are part of the ecosystem.

In the same way that Indigenous populations have been colonised, so has the environment. Moreover, non-Aboriginal people have also been colonised and this is evident through Western thinking and priorities. One way in which this colonisation of non-Aboriginal people is illustrated is through the disconnect with the environment and the exploitation of the environment for capital gain at the expense of the future. Colonisation is about exploitation, and this has included both people and land (Green, 2014, p. 118). As much of the difficulty that we are faced with today within Australia is due to colonisation and the colonial legacy, there is a need to find ways to decolonise. Decolonisation is not just a term of fantasy or something that belongs in the far past. In fact the United Nations has the 'Committee of 24', the Special Committee on Decolonization (United Nations, 2016). While this committee does not appear to recognise countries that are settler colonies, the United Nations does recognise the 'inherent rights' of Indigenous people to have control over their land via the Declaration on the Rights of Indigenous Peoples (United Nations, 2008, pp. 2–3). Therefore the United Nations is clearly stating that Aboriginal people have the right to their lands and what happens on their lands. For social workers, all United Nations documents are relevant to them and their practice. It is essential that social workers join with Aboriginal people in Wirimbirragu Ngurambanggu and look for ways in which to decolonise. There is a growing body of work on decolonisation and social work both within Australia and internationally (Sinclair, 2004; Muller, 2007; Green and Baldry, 2008; Briskman, 2008; Green and Baldry, 2013; Adamson, 2014; Cunneen and Rowe, 2014; Rowe, Baldry and Earles, 2015). Given the work both on decolonisation and on eco-social work, in conjunction with the AASW Code of Ethics, social work within Australia is well-situated to further develop a practice that is embedded within Wirimbirragu Ngurambanggu and Yindyamarra and hence to advance understanding of care and caring practices. To do this, social work as a profession and individual social workers need to engage with their local Aboriginal communities and start the process of truly learning Aboriginal life.

Conclusion

To care for others is to care for all, and that includes land, animals and plants. People are not separate from any other form of life on this planet: we are not just interconnected and dependent for our survival; we are created from the same elements. Without true Yindyamarra, in all meaning and sense of this word, then we cannot practice Wirimbirragu Ngurambanggu. If we do not practice Wirimbirragu Ngurambanggu and realise that in caring for people, we must also care for the ecosystem which people are a part of, then we do not care at all. To live in a place such as Australia, there must be an awareness and a willingness to practice the ways of Aboriginal people, who managed to live here for many thousands of years successfully. Our country is suffering and because of that suffering, so are people. If one is sick, then all are sick. The time has come for a return to the old ways, the only ways of living on these lands: Wirimbirragu Ngurambanggu and Yindyamarra.

Notes

1 The author acknowledges Uncle Stan Grant senior, Wiradyuri elder and custodian language.
2 Yindyamarra is a Wiradyuri word – translation can be found in Grant and Rudder (2010).
3 Wirimbirragu Ngurambanggu – translation can be found in Grant and Rudder (2010).
4 Buyaa is a Wiradyuri word – translation can be found in Grant and Rudder (2010).

References

Adamson, C. E. (2014) Decolonizing social work. *Social Work Education*, 33(7), pp. 979–980.

Australian Association of Social Workers. (2013) *Practice standards*. Canberra, ACT: AASW.

Australian Association of Social Workers. (2010) *Code of ethics*. Canberra, ACT: AASW.

Australian Bureau of Statistics (ABS) (2015) *Prisoners in Australia 2015*. Aboriginal and Torres Strait Islander Prisoner Characteristics. Available from: www.abs.gov.au/ausstats/ abs@.nsf/Lookup/by%20Subject/4517.0~2015~Main%20Features~Aboriginal% 20and%20Torres%20Strait%20Islander%20prisoner%20characteristics~7 [Accessed 10 December 2016].

Australian Institute of Family Studies. (2016) *Child abuse and neglect statistics*. CFCA Resource Sheet – October 2016. Available from: https://aifs.gov.au/cfca/publications/ child-abuse-and-neglect-statistics [Accessed 10 December 2016].

Bourke, E. and Bourke, C. (1995) Aboriginal families in Australia. In: Hartley, R. (ed.) *Families and cultural diversity in Australia*. Sydney: Allen & Unwin.

Bourke, C. and Cox, H. (1994) Two laws: One land. In Bourke, C., Bourke, E. and Edwards, W. (eds) *Aboriginal Australia: An introductory reader in Aboriginal studies*. St Lucia: University of Queensland Press, pp. 49–64.

Briskman, L. (2008) Decolonizing social work in Australia: Prospect or illusion. In: Gray, M., Coates, J. and Yellow Bird, M. (eds.) *Indigenous social work around the world: Towards culturally relevant education and practice*. Aldershot: Ashgate Press.

Bussey, C. (2013) Food security and traditional foods in remote Aboriginal communities: A review of the literature. *Australian Indigenous Health Bulletin*, 13(2). Available from: http://healthbulletin.org.au/wp-content/uploads/2013/06/bulletin_review_bussey_ 2013_v2.pdf [Accessed 12 February 2017].

Cunneen, C. and Rowe, S. (2014) Changing narratives: Colonised peoples, criminology and social work. *International Journal for Crime, Justice and Social Democracy*, 3(1), pp. 49–67.

Franks, A., Smith-Lloyd, D., Newell, S. and Dietrich, U. C. (2001) *Aboriginal Health Promotion of Self-Determination Project: Background paper*. Prepared for Health Promotion Unit, Northern Rivers Area Health Service, Lismore, NSW.

Grant, S. (2016) *IKC Wiradjuri language*. Graduate Certificate in Wiradjuri Language, Culture and Heritage. Charles Sturt University, Wagga Wagga. February 2016.

Grant, S. (2016) *IKC Wiradjuri language*. Graduate Certificate in Wiradjuri Language, Culture and Heritage. Charles Sturt University, Wagga Wagga.

Grant, S. and Rudder, J. (2010) *A new Wiradjuri dictionary*. English to Wiradjuri, Wiradjuri to English. Restoration House, Wagga Wagga.

Green, S. (2014) *The history of aboriginal welfare in the colony of NSW 1788–1856*. PhD thesis, University of New South Wales.

Green, S. and Baldry, E. (2013) Indigenous social work education in Australia. In: Bennett, B., Green, S., Gilbert, D., Bessarab, D. (eds.) *Our voices: Aboriginal and Torres Strait Islander social work*. Melbourne: Palgrave Macmillan, pp. 114–135.

Gray, M. and Coates, J. (2012) Environmental ethics for social work: Social work's responsibility to the non-human world. *International Journal of Social Welfare*, 21(3), pp. 239–247.

Green, S. and Baldry, E. (2008) Building Indigenous Australian social work. *Australian Social Work*, 61, pp. 389–402.

Kagi, J. (2014) Plan to close more than 100 remote communities would have severed consequences, says WA Premier. *ABC News*. Available from: www.abc.net.au/news/2014-11-12/indigenous-communities-closures-will-have-severe-consequences/5886840 [Accessed 2 February 2017].

McKinnon, J. (2008) Exploring the nexus between social work and the environment. *Australian Social Work*, 61(3), pp. 256–268.

Muller, L. (2007) De-colonisation: Reflections and implications for social work practice. *Communities, Children and Families Australia*, 3(1), pp. 80–87.

Norton, C. (2012) Social work and the environment: An ecosocial approach. *International Journal of Social Welfare*, 21(3), pp. 299–308.

Rowe, S., Baldry, E. and Earles, W. (2015) Decolonising social work research: Learning from critical Indigenous approaches. *Australian Social Work*, 68(3), pp. 296–308.

Sinclair, R. (2004) Aboriginal social work education in Canada: Decolonizing pedagogy for the seventh generation. *First People's Child & Family Review*, 1(1), pp. 49–61.

United Nations. (2008) *United Nations Declaration on the Rights of Indigenous Peoples*. United Nations.

United Nations. (2016) *The United Nations and decolonization*. Available from: www.un.org/en/decolonization/index.shtml [Accessed 8 February 2017].

14 'No sex, please . . .'

Applying a critical ethics of care perspective to social care provision for older lesbian, gay and bisexual (LGB) adults

Michele Raithby and Paul Willis

Introduction

Social care provision for older lesbian, gay and bisexual (LGB) people remains a predominantly heteronormative preserve, reflecting the cultural saturation of heterosexual norms and values in contemporary social and political life (Warner, 1993; Berlant and Warner, 1998). In addition, assumptions can be made that older people are asexual (Bauer, Nay and McAuliffe, 2009; Doll, 2012) or heterosexual, disregarding sexual diversity or continuing desires and activity. Older LGB people can thus experience dual discrimination through the conjunction of heterosexist assumptions of care providers with ageist beliefs within LGB communities themselves (Clarke, Ellis, Peel and Riggs, 2010). Within research communities, Brown (2009) has noted that ageing studies have unintentionally silenced the voices of sexually diverse older people in its body of research, while queer theorists are guilty of not taking into account the dynamics of ageing in their critique of sexual and gender dichotomies. Long-term care settings can be sexualised spaces, even if unacknowledged, but the recognition of older LGB people's intersecting identities, biographies and sexual citizenship (Richardson, 2017) is a domain that can be undervalued, denied or avoided.

This chapter draws on our findings from a social work study conducted in Wales on affirmative, dignified social care with older LGB people in residential and nursing care homes[1] (Willis, Maegusuku-Hewett, Raithby and Miles, 2016a; Willis, Raithby and Maegusuku-Hewett, 2016b).[2] Our research adopted a cross-sectional, mixed-methods approach to explore and examine current elements of long-term care provision for older LGB people from different stakeholder perspectives. This encompassed examination of care home reports produced by the Care and Social Services Inspectorate Wales (CSSIW) to identify any content about sexual diversity, sexual health and older LGB people; a survey of attitudes and knowledge of 121 care staff through self-administered questionnaires; nine focus groups with practitioner and policy stakeholders, which included groups with care staff and managers; and interviews with 29 older LGB-identifying people (aged 50–76 years) who were living independently, on their hopes and wishes for their own future care. In this chapter, we focus on thematic findings from focus groups with care staff and managers employed in residential and nursing homes across Wales (five focus groups; three with care staff [$n = 14$] and two with members of management [$n = 27$]), and from interviews with older LGB people living in Wales ($n = 29$).

Building on these findings, we argue that an ethic of care framework can enhance recognition of older LGB adults' life histories and sexual identities and relationships. The perspective of an ethics of care has increasingly been adopted by social work and social policy in the UK (Orme, 2002; Lloyd, 2006; Koggel and Orme, 2010; Ward and Barnes, 2016). However, there has been little exploration of how a critical ethics of care perspective can be applied to provision of social care for older LGB people. Such a framework can enhance the recognition of older LGB people's social care needs, sexual lives and histories by addressing the dynamics of intersecting identities, including the co-construction of ageing and sexual orientation. We also contend that this approach can be further extended through fostering a deeper understanding of sexual rights as a rights-based framework for advancing everyday care.

Our research was located in Wales, a small, devolved nation in the UK which is rapidly developing its own distinctive health and social care agenda. In a major development, the Welsh government has implemented its own social care legislation under the Social Services and Well-being (Wales) Act 2014, which came into force in 2016. This adopts a more community and rights-based direction that diverges from the more individualistic and market-oriented legislation and policy in England. The Welsh government recognises the differing care needs of older LGB people within its broader strategy for older people (Welsh Government, 2013), but there is limited discussion on how these needs may diverge from other ageing populations and how they may be met within available, albeit limited, resources. The requirement for public and private care services in Wales to provide anti-discriminatory services to older LGB citizens is reiterated in the UK Equality Act 2010, which recognises both age and sexual orientation as protected characteristics. Thus, our research aligns with the equality agenda for older people of diverse sexual backgrounds in Wales, but it also locates the discussion within a critical ethics of care framework. As Ward (2015) notes, a sole focus on justice can obscure intertwined intersectional identities by focusing on one dimension at a time, or privileging one above another.

Theoretical orientation

Applying a critical ethics of care: attentiveness and responsiveness

Gilligan's (1982) first-wave conception of an ethic of care posed an alternative to a masculinised model of justice-based ethics, grounded in responses to the needs of others and mutual relationships. This laid the foundations for emphasising the necessity and value of care relations (Tronto, 1994), placing them at the centre of human life (Ward and Barnes, 2016). In an early application to social work, Orme (2002, p. 802) applied Gilligan's gendered ethical framework to the domain of care as a 'practical moral activity', while cautioning against essentialising care as a natural function of being female. Hankivsky (2014) also criticises the prioritisation of gendered relationships of care in care ethics, with insufficient attention paid to power relations and intersectionality. Nevertheless, care provided both inside and outside the home remains a gendered activity, as we found in the care homes surveyed in Wales.

Tronto's (1994) articulation of the components of caring as attentiveness, responsibility, competence and responsiveness link emotional and practical aspects of care-giving. According to Tronto (1994), attentiveness requires being attuned and receptive to the needs of others; to notice others who require care and to avoid actions that do not take into account their concerns. Responsiveness is the capacity of the care-giver to be receptive to and consider the recipient's world view with the recognition that the other person's experiences and needs differ to the caregiver's self. Both elements have informed our reading of the reflections of staff and their managers on how best to meet the needs of older LGB residents.

The delivery of professionalised care to older people needs to be located in a wider rights-based context in which care staff and managers situate their practice within a frameworks of rights and responsibilities to older people. Within Welsh social policy, some advances have been made in this direction through the introduction of a Declaration of Rights for Older People (Welsh Government, 2014). The Declaration sets out universal expectations for providers of services to older people while aiming to make older citizens more conscious of their rights and the value placed on their participation in Welsh society. However, there is further scope for integrating recognition of *sexual rights* for older people.

Recognition of sexual rights

While the notion of sexual rights is difficult to neatly define, Richardson (2000) identifies three common strands: (1) rights to participate in sexual activities and practices; (2) rights to self-define, claim and express individual identities, inclusive of LGB identities; and (3) rights recognised by public and social institutions, such as the state recognition of sexual and intimate relationships. The latter is frequently captured in global debates and campaigns for recognition of same-sex marriages on equal footing with heterosexual relationships. Sexual rights as a rights-based agenda emerged from international lobbying efforts for women's reproductive rights and protection from sexual violence in the 1970s. The UN International Conference on Population and Development in Cairo 1994 is cited as a more recent seminal event in which reproductive rights and sexual health were acknowledged as areas for action under the banner of 'reproductive rights and responsibilities' (Altman and Symons, 2016). Another pivotal document is the 'Declaration of Sexual Rights' (World Association for Sexual Health (WAS), 2014) which developed from the 13th World Congress of Sexology in Valencia, Spain, in 1997. This declaration encompasses WHO's working definition of sexual health, acknowledges wellbeing and sexuality as located within human rights discourse, and maintains that sexuality 'is a central aspect of being human throughout life, encompasses sex, gender identities and roles, sexual orientation, eroticism, pleasure, intimacy, and reproduction' (WAS, 2014, p. 1). Emphasis is given to sexuality as 'a source of pleasure and wellbeing'. The Declaration outlines 16 rights in total. Like human rights, sexual rights are described as universal and integral to the maintenance of health, inclusive of the right to enjoy sexual pleasure.

In parallel with contemporary discourse on sexual rights, sociological authors have discussed the notion of *sexual* citizenship. Sexual citizenship can be understood through the degrees to which social groups have differential access to rights within nation states – the recognition and denial of rights according to gender and sexual status. Claims to sexual rights are bound with the emergence of sexual subjectivity as a new way of being in late modernity (Weeks, 1998). Weeks argues that akin to other definitions of citizenship, sexual citizenship 'is about belonging, about rights and responsibilities, about ending social exclusion and ensuring social inclusion' (p. 113). In these respects it shares common ground with other forms of citizenship; however, it extends historical understanding of what constitutes citizenship (Weeks, 1998). Wilson (2009), in response to Weeks, argues that too much emphasis is given to the making of claims for sexual rights without sufficient recognition of the responsibilities of state bodies to recognise such claims; claims for rights are voiced in a field of power relations in which rights are legitimised through state recognition. Plummer (1995) locates emerging claims for sexual rights and recognition within a wider societal proliferation of sexual storytelling – stories about the diversification of family structures and forms, identity claims for equal recognition, narratives about erotic experiences in sub-cultural groups and communities of interest, and debates about gender, rights and the body in discussions of reproductive politics.

Writing in 1998, Richardson argued for a sexualisation of citizenship to critique the ways in which citizenship, and the associated rights that accompany it, recognise some social groups to the exclusion of others. Lesbians and gay men are granted 'partial citizenship' through which they are denied equal protections and rights under the law in contrast to heterosexual citizens, for example the privileges of heterosexual marriage (Richardson, 1998). Within the UK, this partial status has receded with recent legislative gains in anti-discrimination and equality measures, for example the recognition of same-sex marriage (Marriage (Same-sex Couples) Act 2013) and the Equality Act, discussed earlier. However, what remains unclear is the extent to which the expansion of these legal rights, such as marriage equality, enhances notions of equal citizenship and social inclusion for older LGB people. We now turn to some of the findings from our research.

Different but the same? Responding to sexual identities in care settings

Contrasting views on achieving equality in care practice

For the care staff and managers who participated in the focus groups, equality primarily equated with sameness; in other words, treating older LGB adults as having the same needs and wishes as heterosexual residents. Emphasis was laid on the provision of equal care regardless of sexual identity and social background:

> Well I'd just be normal . . ., everyone's the same, so you're just being the same with everyone.
>
> (Care staff)

However, this was to the detriment of recognising individual differences in sexual identity and biography. This is a familiar discourse in care settings for older people. Other authors have noted the ways in which this discourse compresses recognition of social difference and inequality across residents' life histories and identities and can represent a 'sexuality-blind' approach to care (Leyerzapf, Visse, De Beer and Abma, 2016; Simpson, Almack and Walthery, 2016). Moreover, the dominant discourse of 'equal-same treatment' can blinker employees and managers from being more attentive to the sexual histories of LGB residents in their care.

In contrast, older LGB adults in interviews regarded equality as receiving equal treatment to heterosexual residents, encompassing respect and recognition for individual dignity, identity and the role of significant others, including same-sex partners. Older participants discussed respect and privacy as being intertwined with the recognition of LGB identities, whereas care staff and managers discussed these principles predominantly in reference to other residents' wellbeing. To initiate discussions about sexual identity ran the risk of causing offence to the individual resident or infringing privacy. LGB identities were relegated to the private sphere and therefore not for public discussion. In one example, a manager raised her concern about the rights of other residents to express their personal views, regardless of whether their views could be experienced as homophobic or racist:

> You can't make people behave themselves. It's their home they're living in, and they have to be able to say what they want to say. And I think we have to sort of pick up the pieces and support the person they've upset, maybe.
>
> (Manager)

While supporting the offended party is evident, it does not clarify how the derogatory comments would be addressed. From this standpoint, older residents are perceived as 'stuck in their ways', holding fixed beliefs and unwilling to rethink how their views may impact on others. Furthermore, the right of LGB residents to feel safe in their home environment is superseded by the right of other residents to express their views freely.

Limited knowledge of older LGB lives and histories

Some of this lack of understanding of specific LGB needs or histories may stem from staff lacking encounters with LGB people of any age, whether in working or private lives. Across the focus groups, staff and managers struggled to articulate knowledge of residents who identified as LGB or had been in same-sex relationships. The absence of discussion about LGB lives and identities stood in stark contrast to discussions about residents' marital partners, or the ways in which married heterosexual couples were accommodated, for example provision of adjoining rooms, and the inclusion of partners and children as visitors. One staff member indicated that this information was not included in residents' care plans when older people were transitioning into the home, making it difficult to establish this history when building rapport with new residents. LGB identities and relationships were equally absent from staff development activities. No one recalled receiving training about issues of sexuality, identity and equality, apart from some training on managing sexualised behaviours exhibited by residents with dementia. Some managers felt 'bereft of information' and 'lacking in expertise'.

Nevertheless, managers wanted to learn from care staff in other organisations about their experiences of working with LGB residents and they sought guidelines on how to 'work with' LGB older adults as a minority group. Older staff members communicated some awareness of historical discrimination and indicated their understanding that the socio-legal status of LGB people in the UK had improved over the last five decades. However, some staff discussed discrimination in the past tense and implied it was no longer a problem in the contemporary world:

> And it's [LGB identity] been accepted better now than it did years ago. So it's not as bad as it was years ago . . . It's not a problem is it? It's not a problem anyway but you just wouldn't say it when we were young would you? It was, not a bad word, but you just didn't say it and I think that's because it was hidden.
>
> (Care staff)

Separating sexuality from everyday care

The absence of recognisable LGB residents was also actively sustained by separating sexuality from care. Several staff members and managers referred to a resident's sexual identity as separate and subsidiary to their care or health needs:

> and they're normal people and there is nothing wrong with them but when you're in a nursing home it's, you really have to think about their illnesses and why it's happening, you know.
>
> (Care staff)

Sexual orientation was located as an extraneous factor that was not relevant to providing good care to others, as well as being a potential subject for 'judgement':

> You are nursing these people and we're all human, maybe gentlemen or lady, you know it's part of, you sort of, you don't think about it actually. You know it's just part of everyday life when you're nursing someone. Yeah, you know

you are looking after people's needs and what's best for them and what would help them rather than judge them for what they are.

(Care staff)

While seeking to locate sexual orientation as separate to the provision of care, staff and managers equally relayed their desire to be 'doing more' to ensure the inclusion of LGB residents:

Yeah, I think we've got an awful long way to go on meeting people's sexuality needs in care homes, full stop. That means man-woman relationships as well, you know, we've got to get it all right.

(Manager)

Thus, there was an open acknowledgement of the case for change and the need to enhance knowledge and understanding about LGB lives. Staff were open to more information about LGB lives and increased knowledge about ageing and sexual functioning in later life.

Older LGB people's voices: life history outside the heteronorm

Homophobic encounters, past and present

LGB adults participating in our study were no strangers to homophobic encounters across their social worlds. Nearly all participants reported either first-hand experiences or anecdotal cases of discrimination during their earlier life history. The majority of participants had hidden lesbian and gay identities in one or more public arenas to protect themselves from anticipated discrimination, including those who lived a predominantly 'out' life. Many of the participants had 'come out' later in life, typically in their mid to late thirties, and did not feel safe to discuss their sexual attractions and relationships during young adulthood. Homophobic treatment had been experienced within familial, social and community networks:

My mother found out when I was 13 that I was gay, screamed the house down and made me promise never to do anything about it. So, I didn't. And she died when I was 23 and I just sort of existed . . . I always thought that I'd never do anything about it [being gay], because I'd promised my mother that I would never do anything about it . . . I was 38 coming out.

(Gregory, 53)

Participants relayed stories of negative interactions with health and social care professionals where they had received homophobic and heterosexist responses, or where elements of their sexual lives were not acknowledged. One participant, Amy, recalled accompanying her girlfriend to see a hospital-based psychiatrist in the 1970s. The psychiatrist had advised her girlfriend to marry her fiancé in spite of her relationship with Amy and described her attractions to women as deviant. Another lesbian, Angela, described the 'double life' she had applied as a college student in her interactions with general practitioners (GPs). She had accepted prescriptions for the contraceptive pill from GPs without taking any, to avoid any discussion of her sex life and relationships. These experiences may be explained by the historical, legal and medical context in which they are situated. Sex between men had only been decriminalised partially in 1967 in England and Wales, leaving behind a long wake of criminal charges, and in some cases prison sentences. Medical and psychological treatments to 'cure' same-sex desire were frequently prescribed and sought in the 1960s and 1970s, and 'homosexuality' was only removed from the International Classification of Diseases in 1992 (Smith, Bartlett and King, 2004; Fish, 2012).

Interviewees also shared examples of more recent healthcare practice within the last 15 years, during which they had experienced exclusion of their partners from medical decision-making and consultation. Managing homophobia in healthcare settings can also encompass having the confidence to deal with the discriminatory views of other patients:

> When I was in hospital for a gall bladder operation, because I don't wear girly pyjamas in bed and have a short haircut one of the women on the ward asked me to be moved to a men's ward. She asked a nurse, why I was on the ward if I was a bloke? Now I don't know if she asked for me to be moved to a man's ward because she continued to believe I was a man, because the nurse said 'she's a woman,' but she still wanted me to be moved, and I don't know whether that's because she didn't believe the nurse or she did believe the nurse and didn't care and she thought it was inappropriate. I was only in overnight, lucky . . . When you're in that minority position you have to put up with [it] really to some extent don't you.
>
> (Jennifer, 58)

Sarah, and other women interviewed, reiterated the importance of being in a civil partnership that provided a legal basis for equal recognition of same-sex partners. However, having this legal recognition, and the confidence that accompanies it, does not necessarily abate the strain of having to repeatedly come out to medical professionals:

> Just even when three or four weeks ago when I went to the doctor about my shingles I said I was a bit concerned because my partner's got MS and her immune system is obviously sort of low. And the doctor, who wasn't the usual doctor anyway, just said: 'Oh I think he will need to.' And I said: 'Oh she's a woman,' and she was absolutely fine. She didn't bat an eyelid. But it's always this assumption unless you prove otherwise, and you have to show otherwise that you're not. So I think this is about age, that it increasingly could be really difficult for older people.
>
> (Sarah, 59)

Anticipating unequal care provision

Given prior experiences of discrimination, it was unsurprising that many participants anticipated negative treatment from residential and nursing staff if having to
live in long-term care environments. Concerns ranged from fears of physical and
verbal abuse to being separated from partners and significant others, or having
restrictions placed on their privacy. Annie (61) discussed her feelings of vulnerability as a lesbian:

> to be somewhere where nobody speaks to you is a horrible thought. To be
> somewhere where somebody was greasing the top step to get rid of you
> would be worse. I know it's extreme, but that sort of thought is there. To
> have somebody involved in personal care who didn't like you because of
> your orientation, that doesn't sound good either . . . You hear about people in
> care homes who are mistreated . . . Are they going to be worse towards you?
> Scary – the way you are going to be treated is scary; it scares me.

While speculative, these concerns were genuinely felt for older adults when
reflecting on future 'care anticipated', or more accurately, 'care dreaded'.

Older LGB men and women expressed their concerns about the prevailing
assumption of heterosexuality, and how this assumption might shape future care.
Similarly, several individuals relayed their anxieties about having to go 'back into
the closet' if they moved into a care home, or having to make invisible aspects of
their sexual lives and histories they had grown accustomed to sharing with others:

> I suppose I can't imagine being in a place where everybody around you
> would not know that you had spent all of your life as a lesbian. I mean that
> would be, there is no point in living, that would be the worst thing for me if
> you had to be completely in the closet with nobody knowing about you and
> you couldn't talk about your life.
>
> (Sarah, 59)

Alongside worries about declining health and mobility, several women relayed
their dread of losing control over their personal dress and appearance while in
the receipt of care. These anxieties stemmed from a deeper concern about having
conventional gender roles and feminine attributes enforced upon them by care
staff without their consent or control; for example being dressed in skirts or other
feminine apparel, sharing living spaces with male residents or receiving bodily
care from male carers.

Conclusions: dismantling heteronormative attitudes and enhancing care practices

In their Australian study, Tolley and Ranzijn (2006) asserted that exposure to lesbian and gay lives will assist in dismantling heteronormative attitudes among care

staff. In our research, some participating staff members had already experienced a degree of exposure to LGB lives through colleagues or personal networks. In addition, the increasing representation of LGB lives and relationships through popular media brings another layer of cultural exposure. An alternative question to ask is how attentive are staff members to facets of LGB adults' biographies when they do have contact with LGB individuals, including older adults? Within an ethic of care, White and Tronto (2004) frame care as a public and a political matter; the need for and the provision of care is a universal principle and a 'public activity' that involves all members of society. It is difficult to recognise the care needs of older LGB people as a shared responsibility when organisations work to relegate socio-sexual dimensions of their lives to the private sphere: LGB identities are represented as unspeakable topics. Care staff communicate their motivation to be more attentive and responsive to the wishes of LGB residents; however, they lack the communication tools and confidence to be attuned to differences in sexual identity and life history. Moreover, the dominant discourse of 'equal-same treatment' hinders employees and managers from being more attentive to the sexual histories of LGB residents in their care.

Older LGB adults need to have trust and confidence in service providers before sharing aspects of their sexual biography. This requires staff and managers alike to have the confidence to initiate ongoing discussions with residents about their sexual histories. Initiating these conversations is an equally important aspect of providing person-centred care to older adults. Care staff and management need to stay attentive to non-normative sexual lives, be mindful of the world views of individual residents, and be prepared to challenge oppressive views expressed by other residents or staff, particularly when these expressions compromise the rights of LGB adults to feel safe in their home environments. This also challenges ageism by recognising that older residents may be receptive to rethinking their beliefs when their views may cause emotional injury to others. Respecting individual personhood involves recognising preferences and wishes such as choice of clothing, gender of carers, and language used to describe identities and relationships.

Tronto (2010) poses the question of how 'good' care can be recognised within institutions, concluding that the purpose of such care provision must be addressed through a political process that considers the contributions, needs and futures of different actors including those providing and those receiving care. Older LGB people from our study conveyed in equal amounts their fears and hopes for future care in long-term care environments. Participants emphasised the importance of 'equal treatment' in relation to heterosexual residents, and accentuated a sense of common humanity by alluding to shared values of respect and dignity. However, this apparently common vocabulary of equality did not correspond to the care home staff conception that treating people equally was equivalent to treating everyone in the same way. The older LGB participants expected care homes to demonstrate equalities by such positive initiatives as welcoming partners and friends and upholding the privacy of residents by facilitating private time together; displaying visual signs of LGB affirmation such as rainbow signs on entrances and pictures of same-sex couples; and making LGB residents feel comfortable to discuss their personal and sexual lives with other residents and staff. Fundamentally, older participants hoped that staff would be mindful that some residents might identify as LGB, be sexually active and have experienced same-sex relationships.

Although there is work still to be done to meet such expectations in Wales, the wider UK, and other countries with legacies of LGB oppression, care staff and managers' expressed willingness to learn more about LGB lives and histories is promising. A critical ethics of care perspective that emphasises attentiveness and responsiveness to individual biographies that include the intersections of sexual and gender identities, age and ethnicity can enhance the capacity of care environments to promote the wellbeing of all their residents.

Finally, recognition of sexual rights can help underpin and extend this care agenda. To fully realise notions of attentiveness and responsiveness in everyday care, a deeper appreciation of older people's rights as sexual beings with a social history and subjective sense of sexual self is required. We made earlier reference to the WAS Declaration of Sexual Rights (2014) – while all 16 rights statements are relevant, several of these statements are particularly pertinent here, including 'the right to equality and non-discrimination', 'right to autonomy and bodily integrity' and 'right to freedom of thought, opinion and expression'. If older people are to be fully recognised as sexual beings, care staff and their managers need an appreciation of their sexual rights and their responsibilities in providing care that encompasses respect and advancement of these rights. Furthermore, there is scope in professional development activities for discussion about the ways in which sexual rights overlap with broader rights-based frameworks for advancing the recognition of older citizens' voices, needs and wishes in social care and social work. With a social justice orientation, social workers providing services to older people are well-situated to help advance this agenda.

Notes

1 The two-year research project was funded in Wales by a National Institute for Social Care and Health Research (NISCHR) Social Care Award; Principal Investigator, Paul Willis.
2 Some of the chapter contents have been previously published in the following article: Willis, P., Maegusuku-Hewett, T., Raithby, M. & Miles, P. (2016) Swimming upstream: The provision of inclusive care to older lesbian, gay and bisexual (LGB) adults in residential and nursing environments in Wales. *Ageing and Society*, 36(2), pp. 282–306.

References

Altman, D. and Symons, J. (2016) *Queer wars: The new global polarization over gay rights*. Cambridge: Polity Press.

Bauer, M., Nay, R. and McAuliffe, L. (2009) Catering to love, sex and intimacy in residential aged care: What information is provided to consumers? *Sexuality and Disability*, 27(1), pp. 3–9.

Berlant, L. and Warner, M. (1998) Sex in public. *Critical Inquiry*, 24(2), pp. 547–566.

Brown, M. T. (2009) LGBT ageing and rhetorical silence. *Sexuality Research and Social Policy*, 6(4), pp. 65–78.

Clarke, V., Ellis, S., Peel, E. and Riggs, D. (2010) *Lesbian, gay, bisexual, trans and queer psychology: An introduction.* Cambridge: Cambridge University Press.

Doll, G. (2012) *Sexuality and long-term care: Understanding and supporting the needs of older adults.* Baltimore, MD: Health Professions Press.

Fish, J. (2012) *Social work and lesbian, gay, bisexual and transgender people: Making a difference.* Bristol: Policy Press.

Gilligan, C. (1982) *In a different voice: Women's conceptions of voice and morality.* Cambridge, MA: Harvard University Press.

Hankivsky, O. (2014) Rethinking care ethics: On the promise and potential of an intersectional analysis. *American Political Science Review*, 108(2), pp. 252–264. doi:10.1017/S0003055414000094.

Koggel, C. and Orme, J. (2010) Editorial: Care ethics: New theories and applications. *Ethics and Social Welfare*, 4(2), pp. 109–114.

Leyerzapf, H., Visse, M., De Beer, A. and Abma, T.A. (2016) Gay-friendly elderly care: Creating space for sexual diversity in residential care by challenging the hetero norm. *Ageing and Society*. doi:10.1017/SO144686X16001045. Published online: 8th November 2016.

Lloyd, L. (2006) A caring profession? The ethics of care and social work with older people. *British Journal of Social Work*, 36(7), pp. 1171–1185.

Orme, J. (2002) Social work: Gender, care and justice, *British Journal of Social Work*, 32(6), pp. 799–814.

Plummer, K. (1995) *Telling sexual stories: Power, change and social rights.* London: Routledge.

Richardson, D. (1998) Sexuality and citizenship. *Sociology*, 32(1), pp. 83–100.

Richardson, D. (2000) Constructing sexual citizenship: Theorizing sexual rights. *Critical Social Policy*, 20(1), pp. 105–135.

Richardson, D. (2017) Rethinking sexual citizenship. *Sociology*, 51(2), pp. 208–224.

Simpson, P., Almack, K. and Walthery, P. (2016) 'We treat them all the same': The attitudes, knowledge and practices of staff concerning old/er lesbian, gay, bisexual and trans residents in care homes'. *Ageing and Society*. Published online: 29th December 2016. doi:10.1017/S0144686X1600132X.

Smith, G., Bartlett, A. and King, M. (2004) Treatments of homosexuality in Britain since the 1950s – an oral history: The experience of patients. *BMJ*, 328, p. 427.

Tolley, C. and Ranzijn, R. (2006) Heteronormativity amongst staff of residential aged care facilities. *Gay and Lesbian Issues and Psychology Review*, 2(2), pp. 78–86.

Tronto, J. (1994) *Moral boundaries: A political argument for an ethic of care.* London: Routledge.

Tronto, J. (2010) Creating caring institutions: Politics, plurality and purpose. *Ethics and Social Welfare*, 4(2), pp. 158–171.

Ward, L. and Barnes, M. (2016) Transforming Practice with older people through an ethic of care. *British Journal of Social Work*, 46(4), pp. 906–922.

Ward, N. (2015) Care ethics, intersectionality and poststructuralism. In: Barnes, M., Brannelly, T., Ward, L. and Ward, N. (eds.) *Ethics of care: Critical advances in international perspective.* Bristol: Policy Press, pp. 57–68.

Warner, M. (1993) Introduction. In: Warner, M. (ed.) *Fear of a queer planet: Queer politics and social theory.* Minneapolis: University of Minnesota Press, vii–xxxi.

Weeks, J. (1998) The sexual citizen. *Theory, Culture and Society*, 15(3–4), pp. 35–52.

Welsh Government. (2013) *Strategy for older people in Wales 2013–23.* Available from: http://wales.gov.uk/docs/dhss/publications/130521olderpeoplestrategyen.pdf.

Welsh Government. (2014) *Declaration of rights for older people in Wales*. Cardiff: Welsh Government. Available from: http://gov.wales/topics/health/publications/health/strategies/rights/?lang=en.

White, J. and Tronto, J. (2004) Political practices of care: Needs and rights. *Ratio Juris*, 17(4), pp. 425–453.

Willis, P., Maegusuku-Hewett, T., Raithby, M. and Miles, P. (2016a) Swimming upstream: The provision of inclusive care to older lesbian, gay and bisexual (LGB) adults in residential and nursing environments in Wales. *Ageing & Society*, 36(2), pp. 282–306. doi:10.1017/S0144686X14001147.

Willis, P., Raithby, M. and Maegusuku-Hewett, T. (2016b) 'Everyday advocates' for inclusive care: Perspectives on enhancing the provision of long-term care services for older lesbian, gay and bisexual adults in Wales. *British Journal of Social Work*. First published online: January 12, 2016, doi:10.1093/bjsw/bcv143.

Wilson, A. (2009) The 'neat concept' of sexual citizenship: A cautionary tale of human right discourse. *Contemporary Politics*, 15(1), pp. 73–85.

World Association for Sexual Health (WAS). (2014) *The WAS Declaration of Sexual Rights*. Prague: WAS. Available from: www.worldsexology.org/resources/declaration-of-sexual-rights/ [Accessed 31 March 2017].

15 Critical engagements with the politics of care and disability

Russell Shuttleworth

Introduction

Within disability studies, the care relationship between carer and disabled person has historically been viewed as an asymmetrical relation with power inevitably in the hands of the former. This critique was an impetus for the development of a consumer, user-directed model of care in the US, UK, Canada and now Australia. Drawing from the feminist ethics of care, counter critiques have charged that the latter is instrumentalist and masculinist and does not take into account the relational aspects of care (e.g. Shakespeare, 2000; Hughes, McKie, Hopkins and Watson, 2005). There have, thus, been several attempts to incorporate a relational ethics into the understanding of care and disability; these attempts have focused on notions of mutual recognition (e.g. Hughes et al., 2005; Fisher, Robinson, Graham and Johnson, 2015; Banks, 2016) and a relational ethics of intercorporeality (Fritsch, 2010), among others. Recently, Kelly (2013, 2016) has presented an argument to bridge the various positions on care. What she terms "accessible care" is the awareness and maintenance of an unstable tension between competing care perspectives.

The concept of care is a major concern of social work and the tension between care and control has long been a key topic of reflection for social workers whose role can often balance these seemingly conflicting values in their work with clients and communities. However, social work has often failed to acknowledge or confront this tension in their work with disabled people (Meekosha and Soldatic, 2013). Moreover, disability has generally not been considered a prioritised field of social work practice, either in clinical work, policy studies or community practice. Critical social work has likewise only sporadically included disability in its discourse on structural oppression, anti-oppressive practice and political advocacy for and in alliance with marginalised groups (e.g. Hiranandani, 2005; Meekosha and Dowse, 2007; Meekosha and Soldatic, 2013). Similar to disability studies critiques of care, however, critical social work until recently has tended to be suspicious of this concept, and has focused on "the shadow side" of care; that is, care as control (Meagher and Parton, 2004). Some scholars writing within critical social work have begun to recognise the potential of the feminist ethics of care. Meagher and Parton (2004), for example, argue that framing social work with the feminist ethics of care can act as a counter to the advancement of neoliberal and managerialist reforms. Lloyd (2006), discussing social work with older people, draws out what an ethics of care might mean for models of empowerment with this population: caring as listening to older people's voices with competence, skill and sensitivity (p. 1781). While the issue of disability does enter into Lloyd's discussion, it is nevertheless peripheral to her main concern, social work practice with older adults. It is thus overdue to present an assessment of the issue of care and disability and its relevance for critical social work.

My aim in this chapter is to argue that critical social work, with its renewed interest in care discourse within a neoliberal environment and a marketised approach to human service delivery, must critically think through the issue of care and disability, especially within the current changing dynamics of care for disabled people in Australia (for example, the National Disability Insurance Scheme, or NDIS). I also argue that critical disability studies (CDS) can provide critical social work with important perspectives with which to inform their reflections on politicised and ethical practice with this diverse and marginalised group.

Care and control in social work

'Care' has been a central theme in social work since its inception (Meagher and Parton, 2004) and can be first linked with the activities of charitable organisations that helped 'poor' people and in the settlement house movement which aimed to alleviate the social problems associated with industrialisation and urbanisation through engagement and political action within the community (Hardy, 2015). One of the abiding principles of the settlement house movement was that student activists lived with the 'poor' rather than simply administered to them. The settlement movement in Sydney was seen as building bridges between Aboriginal and non-Aboriginal communities (Meekosha, 15 January 2017, personal communication). The work of activist reformers such as Jane Addams in the United States, advocated what Hamington and Miller (2006) call "socializing care: systematically instantiating the habits and practices of care in social institutions" (p. 4). Hamington (2001) maintains Addams approached care in her work as an active embodied process; the cultivation of caring habits was the caregiver's responsibility (p. 109). He further argues that Addams effectively integrated a political sensitivity into an embodied ethics of care (2001, p. 109). This understanding of care is deeply connected to social work's response to the individual's unique experience and circumstances and commitment to progressive social change.

The concept of 'care' in social work, however, has as its shadow side the control of subjects through administration and human governance; what Webb (2003), employing a Foucauldian perspective, calls a "technology of care" (pp. 223–224). Care has often been conditional on whether certain criteria were met by those being assisted and also whether certain rules and regulations were followed or not. Not abiding by the rules could result in some form of 'control' being exercised. This shadow side, up until the last several decades of the twentieth century, had tended to be obscured by "the maintenance of the fiction of non-directiveness"

(Day, 1979, p. 206). With the advent of radical and then critical social work, this fiction has become much more difficult to sustain. The controlling side of social work has also become much more acknowledged with the influence of Foucauldian analysis on the profession. Foucault's concepts radically de-familiarise modern institutions and practices, including social work, as caring and benevolent and reveal technologies and procedures that classify, normalise, manage and control body-subjects (Foucault, 1978; Burchell, Gordon and Miller, 1991).

Chambon (1999, p. 64) observes that Foucault's work "raises the important question of how the functions of control and caring can actually coexist within a single context, how they are separate or joined in professional practices". Within the current neoliberal context, the rise of the concept of risk has made the relationship between care and control much more complicated; operationalisation of this concept in strategies of risk assessment and risk management highlights the tension between care and control. On the one hand, a service may be rendered to qualifying persons in order to assist them. But any assistance needs to control for risk; cost-efficiency and the status quo must be maintained. It could be asked to what extent an ethics of care can be sustained in a risk-aversive society? Needless to say, critical social work has for the most part tended to focus on this shadow side of care, that is, control and the oppressive structures that social work can reinforce in individualised practice contexts (Meagher and Parton, 2004).

Meagher and Parton (2004) are concerned that the neoliberal implementation of managerialism within the administration and delivery of social services threatens the long-held social work commitments to caring and emancipatory practice. These authors argue for restoring and rehabilitating the concept of care in social work, engaging with feminist work on the ethics of care to productively participate in the discourse and arguments within critical social theory. Drawing on poststructural ideas and by highlighting local dialogical relations, practitioner reflectivity and client needs instead of immediately focusing on the macro-structural processes, Meagher and Parton (2004, p. 19) envision social work practice contexts as "sites of transformative action". Similarly Dybicz (2012) calls for revisiting the client-worker relationship of Charity Organisation Society workers, which accords with recent postmodern practices that are grounded more in an ethics of care that critically works against sterile applications of scientistic evidence-based practice (p. 271).

A pertinent question at this point in the chapter is: how has social work historically and currently responded in practice to the issues of disabled people? And given the insight of Meagher and Parton, are there opportunities for social workers to revisit the ethics of care in their work and, in addition to their structural critique, approach the contexts they work in with disabled people as sites of transformative action?

Social work and disability

For much of its history, disability has been a low priority for social work or has been attended to within an individualised, medical understanding of disability

(Oliver, Sapey and Thomas, 2012). The social model of disability (SMD) was introduced in 1983 by Michael Oliver, a disabled social worker in the UK, but this groundbreaking idea was not taken up much by social workers who, similar to other human service and allied health professionals, continued to filter their approach to disability through the lenses of individual tragedy and the medical model. Reflecting recently on the lack of attention to this notion in the UK, Thomas and Sapey (2012) observe that over the past quarter of a century, there has been minimal progress in incorporating the SMD within social work practice (pp. i–ii).

There has been a similar lack of social work prioritisation of disabled people's issues and concerns in other national contexts. Mackelprang (2010), writing about social work in the United States, argues that because the medical model often underlies approaches to disability in mental health and social service organisations, this makes the issue of disability more difficult for social workers to perceive as a diversity issue (pp. 88). Raske (2005) notes that social workers even when sympathetic to more socio-politically oriented approaches are often "compelled to structure services to fit the medical model" (p. 102). For example, "rules that regulate placement of clients in various levels of residential settings typically require differing sets of functional limitations" (p. 100). Obviously medicine can be appropriate for health-related issues, but these assumptions about disability embedded in the structure of health and many non-health-related services mean that social workers may be implicitly emphasising control over care.

Writing from an Australian perspective, Meekosha and Soldatic (2013) note that historically, "disabled people were characterised by their deficiencies and practical intervention amounted to control with some limited assistance, although often assistance has been traditionally given to the family and/or carers of the disabled person" (p. 145). While involved in the processes of institutionalisation and deinstitutionalisation as they affected disabled people, social workers did not effectively challenge the socio-political structures that kept disabled people apart from the community. This is not to say that social workers never provided important services for this population. Bigby and Atkinson (2010), in a study of women social workers in the UK and Australia, document the contributions to the field of intellectual disability made by social work up to the mid-1980s. These social workers had facilitative roles in both institutional contexts as "conduit[s] between the institution and community" (p. 11), and in community care, where they were often the core support for families. The authors note that while this "facilitative work" by social workers made significant contributions, it has gone unrecognised and hidden within the social history of intellectual disability.

In contemporary Australian social work practice, disability is not a major area of concern in comparison to, for example, children in care, which may be easier to link to current risk assessment and management practices. As the population ages, an interest in social work in the area is developing. However, impairment as a result of ageing is motivated by a different politics than early and midlife onset impairment and disability. In terms of clients with physical impairments, beyond assessment and managing services, social work has distanced itself from everyday care (Lloyd, 2006, p. 1178). Bigby and Atkinson (2010) also note that with the move to generic work positions such as "client coordinator", "social welfare worker" and "case manager", those individuals who had identified as intellectual disability social workers became "invisible in most government welfare services" (p. 5). This kind of invisibility in the field is not the best way to promote disability as a focus for practice among social work students.

The low priority of disability in social work practice is reflected historically and currently by its minimal inclusion in social work education and accreditation (see, e.g. Meekosha and Dowse, 2007; Thomas and Sapey, 2012; Moyle, 2016). Further, Thomas and Sapey (2012) maintain that the individual model of disability is still the dominant perspective and that social model principles have not been effectively integrated into social work education. Meekosha has argued consistently that disability as a human rights and a social justice issue should be a central concern in social work education (e.g. Meekosha and Dowse, 2007; Meekosha and Soldatic, 2013). Moyle (2016) in fact has recently argued persuasively for the inclusion of disability in the Australian Social Work Education Accreditation Standards core curriculum areas alongside child protection, mental health, cross-cultural and Aboriginal and Torres Strait Islanders.

Within the discourse of critical social work, disability also has not been a primary concern, albeit a few authors have raised relevant concerns (see, e.g. Hiranandani, 2005; Soldatic and Meekosha, 2012a, 2012b; Meekosha and Soldatic, 2013). Working with disabled people in the disability movement is an important arena for critical social workers to contribute in the struggle for access and participation for this highly marginalised population. There has been some political advocacy for and alliances made with disabled people on various issues. For example, in the Australian context community practitioners, including social workers, have worked hard with People with Disability Australia (PWDA) for disabled people to be released from institutions and nursing homes to live in the community (Meekosha, Wannan and Shuttleworth, 2016). On a theoretical level, disability can also be marginalised – for example, Ife's (2012) relegating disability below that of other categories of difference.

The low priority of disability in social work practice and theory has historically meant there has been no effective discussion of disability and the concept of care in the social work discourse. Thus, even those social workers who do work with disabled people in some capacity such as an allied health role, case manager or in the case of NDIS local area coordinator, are likely unaware of the changing dynamics of the concept of care within the disability movement and CDS literature. Certainly an important step is to integrate the SMD into all levels of social work practice as a critical tool. The SMD can be especially useful in advocacy work and developing alliances with disabled people as they struggle for full access to social participation. However, there are dangers to completely buying into the SMD's vision. Its separation of impairment from disability while being an effective political and analytical tool to combat structural and socioeconomic oppression is less effective in analysing cultural and embodiment issues. Similarly, its understanding of care and its uncritical promotion of consumer user-directed care has been critiqued by a range of CDS scholars as fitting neatly into an individualised, neoliberal approach (e.g. Hughes et al., 2005; Fritsch, 2010; Soldatic and Meekosha, 2012a, 2012b). The market approach to care can be critiqued as offering a dubious 'choice' to the disabled person, while at the same time being driven by the need to make financial profits out of the care transaction. In Australia, the sale of state care services to private for-profit companies is rarely mentioned, nor has it come under the scrutiny of the social work profession or received much attention in critical social work.

The concept of care within the disability movement and CDS has shown increasing complexity. Originating with the historical perception of a lack of power in the care/recipient dynamic, the notion of care has expanded to include a sense of relationality and interdependence, as well as negotiations between these seemingly contradictory positions. Social workers need to be aware of the complexities of this discourse in order to work in a sensitive, caring and effective way in their support of disabled people, whether in clinical, policy, community, advocacy or alliance contexts. Social workers need to be cognizant of the multiple meanings of care in the current socio-political environment and how these different views can affect not only the carer/disabled person dynamic but might also affect how they might engage with disabled clients.

Care in critical disability studies

The disability movement and disability studies has long criticised the concept of care. As Hughes et al. (2005, p. 261) emphasise, disability studies have viewed the language of care as constructing disabled recipients as having a deficit of agency – that is, as dependent and "associated with institutional confinement, limited social engagement, partial citizenship, disempowerment and exclusion". Within a neoliberal environment, social policy constructs those who receive care as "a burden and a drain on scarce resources" (2005, p. 261). Disabled recipients of care have traditionally had no decision-making power over their own care process. For disability studies and social model advocates, the concept of care and its highlighting of dependence and control is seen as conflicting with their emancipatory project.

In the United States, the politics and language of care changed dramatically in the 1970s and 1980s with the advent of the Independent Living Movement (ILM). The ILM, based on consumerist principles and the move towards direct payments, ushered in the notion of the personal assistant (PA), hired and managed by their disabled employer. Beginning in the mid-1990s, this model was increasingly taken up in the UK. User- or consumer-directed care, borne of the disability rights movement, thus attempts to empower the recipient by putting them in control of their own care. In Australia, the NDIS reflects this critique of the organisation of care. For example, persons with long-term impairments who are among the relatively small proportion to receive Individualised Funding Packages or their carers will be able to choose among competing services. There are different levels of support available for disabled people and their carers to make informed decisions. At the most general level, local area coordinators will work with disabled people to locate and engage relevant resources, support and services. Not all disabled people will choose to fully go the route of direct payments; nevertheless this implementation of decision-making autonomy and consumer choice reflects the original principles of the ILM.

Consumer, user-directed care, however, has garnered many critics in CDS. Tom Shakespeare (2000, p. 81) argued that while disabled people's management of their assistance remains key to the reformation of the caring dynamic, a narrowly defined independence should be jettisoned and replaced by the notion of a negotiated autonomy. This perspective needs also to be tempered by feminist ethics of care, interdependence and recognition of the "frailty of the human condition". Hughes et al. (2005) contended that user-directed care organised as simply an instrumental service errs by extracting the relational aspect from the care dynamic and is masculinist and narrowly instrumental at the expense of interdependence. While providing disabled people with a sense of empowerment, fully buying into this model simply reverses the hierarchical social relations of care and marginalises both the disabled recipient of care and the primarily female and ethnic or migrant care workforce. "It might also mean that the ethical imperative of recognition of the other is left out of the moral equation" (Hughes et al., 2005, p. 268).

These are important insights that should counterbalance any wholesale embrace of the neoliberal and consumer values that underlie the NDIS. In this sense, the move to educate and train social workers capable of filling the various roles necessary in the full implementation of NDIS requires critical reflection. Incorporating an understanding of the care discourse in CDS in critical social work can provide impetus for analysing both structural constraints and the local dynamics of care in this area. For example, the following questions might be asked. What kind of care will social workers provide in their practice within the NDIS? Will they recognise the necessity of cultivating a critical but embodied caring response in their practice? In what ways do local contexts of care articulate with the neoliberal and managerialist principles that drive these kind of initiatives? Despite the rhetoric of person-centred care and choice, will there be vestiges of the shadow side, that is, control, in social workers' practice in this area?

There have been recent attempts in CDS to incorporate an ethics of care into an understanding of care and disability. There is a move to conceptualise care in a more nuanced, contextual and mutually enhancing way. Hughes et al. (2005) suggest that a post-feminist perspective emphasising embodied interdependence and reciprocity within the caring relationship would work, not only to undermine the hegemonic masculinist agenda, but also the hierarchical structure within the current dynamic of care (also see Williams, 2001). Others such as Fisher et al. (2015) and Banks (2016) have explored the notion of the enhancement of relations through mutual recognition within the caregiving relationship. Fritsch (2010) has proposed an ethics of intercorporeality between disabled people and their PAs. These studies are all useful for providing variations on the relational approach to care and disability in the current neoliberal context.

The most concerted effort to productively conceptualise the divide between consumer user-directed model of care and the relational feminist ethics of care is that proposed by Christine Kelly (2013, 2016), who conducted research on user-directed care in Canada. She presents a complex argument for what she terms "accessible care". According to Kelly, "accessible care is an unstable tension among emotions, actions and values, simultaneously pulled toward both empowerment and coercion" (2016, p. 36). For Kelly, unstable tension also exists among competing definitions of care, most notably disability studies power relational critique of care as a form of oppression and the feminist ethics of care relations analysis. She further argues that care is "a tension between among all . . . definitions, none to be disregarded . . . [and] the critical concept of access is necessary to reveal the links among discourse, material environments, and social inequalities" (2016, p. 36).

Implications for critical practice with disabled people

Engaging with the complex discourse on care in CDS can effectively enhance critical social work practice with disabled people. Critical social workers often employ multiple theoretical perspectives (for example, sociological and psychological theories) in their practice. Social workers are also familiar with managing the tension between competing perspectives and values in their work, not the least of which is between care and control. Engaging with the different perspectives within CDS discourse would seem like a natural expansion of their critical approach. Kelly's conceptualisation of the unstable tensions that divide care perspectives and the productive possibilities of accessible care might be especially useful for social workers to explore in their practice with this population.

Ardoino's understanding of a multireferential approach to research and educational practice (Castoriadis, 2007; Alhadeff-Jones, 2012) can complement Kelly's work and enhance its applicability to social work practice. Multireferentiality is about identifying the complexity and multiple perspectives that frame social situations and practices. For Ardoino, this involves a plural or heterogeneous reading of the objects of analysis, that is, practices or theories; each reading not being reducible to any of the others as they derive from different reference systems (Ardoino in Alhadeff-Jones, 2012); these different readings are held in productive tension. And, as Alhadeff-Jones (2012) argues: "From a practical point of view such a perspective invites practitioners and researchers to distinguish what is constitutive of heterogeneous realities . . . in order to interpret their relationships" (p. 185).

Critical social workers interpret and critically reflect on the values, issues and problems of clients and communities from diverse conceptual angles. However, when the purpose is problem-solving, epistemological assumptions and disciplinary or theoretical references often remain in the background. It is especially important to reflect on the complexities of a client's care situation, how it can be conceptually framed in different ways by both the worker and the client. In the case of working with disabled people on their care and support needs, it may be perfectly legitimate for a disabled person to view care with suspicion of its oppressive side given the historical perspective and power relational critique of this concept. One reason that a person might choose to manage their own care and direct their own PAs is to maintain a sense of control and decision-making autonomy. Alternately, some clients may prefer that an agency take on these tasks. For some clients, it may be more appropriate for the social worker to ally with a client's relational needs in planning their care. What makes the issue more complex is the unstable tension between perspectives that can underlie even a staunch claiming of a particular point of view by a client or community. For example, even those disabled people who advocate a strict user-directed approach to their care will invariably have some sort of relationship with their support worker. Then again, as Kelly's (2016) research shows, there may be many disabled people who reject the notion of care as a description of the support they receive. It is thus often not appropriate for the social worker to impose either the term care if is not recognised by the client or a particular perspective of care that is at odds with how the client views their own care. However, it may sometimes be necessary to enhance a client's understanding of their own care if that understanding is perceived as being self-detrimental or to challenge care perspectives that would diminish the client's wellbeing. A flexible ability to move between diverse references and meanings of care is necessitated by client's particularities and perspectives and the local and national contexts of practice.

A multireferential approach can also incorporate the fluidity of changing meanings of care as this concept expands into other domains. For example, some disabled people require assistance and support in sexual expression and participation, which under the hegemony of sexual autonomy has traditionally not been legitimated, but increasingly can be analysed within the politics of care and disability (e.g. Earle, 2001; Kulick and Rydstrom, 2015). Indeed, depending on the socio-political and cultural context, various forms of sexual support (for example, facilitated sexual support, sexual assistance, sexual surrogacy or sex worker services) may or may not be available for disabled people's sexual wellbeing (Shuttleworth and Taleporos, forthcoming). Given that these practices are highly controversial in most countries, including Australia, it may necessitate that social workers advocate or form alliances with disabled people for their inclusion in social policy and the practice agenda within a particular local context. This political stance can be viewed as an effort to expand the sense of care into related areas which have heretofore been taboo. On the other hand, in Denmark, which has a progressive policy on sexuality and disability, it is often social workers who manage clients' use of the PAs who facilitate clients' sexual expression and participation (Kulick and Rydstrom, 2015); albeit in recent years progress on this issue has to some extent rolled back.

In conclusion, the current neoliberal environment and marketised approach to care that many countries are adopting make it paramount that social workers engage with critical and nuanced perspectives on disability and care within CDS. While critical social workers already reference multiple disciplinary and theoretical perspectives in their practice, they have for the most part neglected to engage with the different conceptualisations of care in CDS discourse. This discourse can productively inform critical social workers who work with disabled people in diverse policy and practice contexts. Recognising how different perspectives on care can result in different outcomes, will work to ensure that social workers in each case critically reflect on how care is being framed in their work with disabled clients and communities.

Acknowledgements

I want to thank Helen Meekosha for providing critical feedback on this chapter.

References

Alhadeff-Jones, M. (2012) Transformative learning and the challenges of complexity. In: Taylor, E., Cranton, P. & Associates (eds.) *Handbook of transformative learning: Theory, research and practice*. San Francisco: Jossey-Bass, pp. 178–194.

Banks, S. (2016) *'Becoming people to each other': How practice and meaning intersect in the delivery of aged care and disability support*. Unpublished doctoral thesis, University of Tasmania.

Bigby, C. and Atkinson, D. (2010) Written out of history: Invisible women in intellectual disability social work. *Australian Social Work*, 63(1), pp. 4–17.

Burchell, G., Gordon, C. and Miller, P. (eds.) (1991) *The Foucault effect: Studies in governmentality*. Chicago: University of Chicago Press.

Castoriadis, C. (2007) Psyche and education. In: *Figures of the thinkable*. Translated by Helen Arnold. Stanford, CA: Stanford University Press, pp. 165–187.

Chambon, A. (1999) Foucault's approach: Making the familiar visible. In: Chambon, A., Irving, A. and Epstein, L. (eds.) *Reading Foucault for social work*. New York: Columbia University Press, pp. 51–82.

Day, P. (1979) Care and control: A social work dilemma. *Social Policy & Administration*, 13(3), pp. 206–209.

Dybicz, P. (2012) The ethic of care: Recapturing social work's first voice. *Social Work*, 57(3), pp. 271–280.

Earle, S. (2001) Disability, facilitated sex and the role of the nurse. *Journal of Advanced Nursing*, 36(3), pp. 433–440.

Fisher, K., Robinson, S., Graham, A. and Johnson, K. (2015) Recognition between people with intellectual disability and support workers. Paper presented at *The Australian Sociological Association Annual Conference*, Cairns, Queensland, November.

Foucault, M. (1978) *The history of sexuality, Volume I: An introduction*. Translated by R. Hurley. New York: Pantheon.

Fritsch, K. (2010) Intimate assemblages: Disability, intercorporeality, and the labour of attendant care. *Critical Disability Discourse*, 2, pp. 1–14.

Hamington, M. (2001) Jane Addams and a politics of embodied care. *Journal of Speculative Philosophy*, 15(2), pp. 105–121.

Hamington, M. and Miller, D. (2006) Introduction. In: Hamington, M. and Miller, D. (eds.) *Socializing care: Feminist ethics and public issues*. Lanham, MD: Rowman & Littlefield.

Hardy, M. (2015) *Governing risk: Care and control in contemporary social work*. Basingstoke: Macmillan.

Hiranandani, V. (2005) Towards a critical theory of disability in social work. *CriticalSocial Work*, 6(1). Available from: http://uwindsor.ca/criticalsocialwork/towards-a-critical-theory-of-disability-in-social-work.

Hughes, B., McKie, L., Hopkins, D. and Watson, N. (2005) Love's labours lost? Feminism, the Disabled People's Movement and an ethic of care. *Sociology*, 39(2), pp. 259–275.

Ife, J. (2012) *Human rights and social work: Toward a rights-based practice.* Cambridge: Cambridge University Press.

Kelly, C. (2013) Building bridges with accessible care: Disability studies, feminist care scholarship and beyond. *Hypatia: A Journal of Feminist Philosophy*, 28(4), pp. 784–800.

Kelly, C. (2016) *Disability politics and care: The challenge of direct funding.* Vancouver: University of British Columbia Press.

Kulick, D. and Rydstrom, J. (2015) *Loneliness and its opposite: Sex, disability and the ethics of engagement.* Durham, NC: Duke University Press.

Lloyd, L. (2006) A caring profession? The ethics of care and social work with older people. *British Journal of Social Work*, 36(7), pp. 1171–1185.

Mackelprang, R. (2010) Disability controversies: Past, present, and future, *Journal of Social Work in Disability & Rehabilitation*, 9:2–3, 87–98.

Meagher, G. and Parton, N. (2004) Modernising social work and the ethics of care. *Social Work and Society*, 2(1), pp. 28–39.

Meekosha, H. and Dowse, L.M. (2007) Integrating critical disability studies into social work education and practice: An Australian perspective. *Practice*, 19, pp. 169–183.

Meekosha, H. and Soldatic, K. (2013) Disability-inclusive social work practice. In: Beddoe, L. and Maidment, J. (eds.) *Social work practice for promoting health and wellbeing: Critical issues.* Oxon: Routledge, pp. 144–156.

Meekosha, H., Wannan, A. and Shuttleworth, R. (2016) The politics of diversity in Australia: Extending the role of community practice. In: Meade, R., Shaw, M. and Banks, S. (eds.) *Politics, power and community development.* Bristol: Policy Press, pp. 139–157.

Moyle, J. (2016) Including disability in the social work core curriculum: A compelling argument. *Australian Social Work*, 69(4), pp. 503–511.

Oliver, M., Sapey, D. and Thomas, P. (2012) *Social work with disabled people.* 4th edition. Basingstoke: Macmillan.

Raske, M. (2005) The disability discrimination model in social work practice. In: May, G. and Raske, M. (eds.) *Ending disability discrimination: Strategies for social workers.* Boston: Pearson Education, Allyn & Bacon, pp. 99–112.

Shakespeare, T. (2000) *Help: Imagining welfare.* Birmingham, UK: Venture Press.

Shuttleworth, R. and Taleporos, G. (forthcoming) Disability, facilitated sex and sexual participation. *Sexuality and Disability*.

Soldatic, K. and Meekosha, H. (2012a) Disability and neoliberal state formations. In: Watson, N., Thomas, C. and Roulstone, A. (eds.) *Routledge handbook of disability studies.* London: Routledge, pp. 195–210.

Soldatic, K. and Meekosha, H. (2012b) Moving the boundaries of feminist social work education with disabled people in the neoliberal era. *Social Work Education*, 31(2), pp. 246–252.

Thomas, P. and Sapey, B. (2012) Preface. In: Oliver, M., Sapey, B. and Thomas, P. (eds.) *Social work with disabled people.* 4th edition. Basingstoke: Palgrave Macmillan, pp. i–ii.

Webb, S. (2003) Conclusion. In: Harlow, E. and Webb, S. (eds.) *Information and communication technologies in the welfare services.* London: Jessica Kingsley, pp. 223–238.

Williams, F. (2001) In and beyond new labour: Towards a new political ethics of care. *Critical Social Policy*, 21, pp. 467–493.

Part IV
Transforming care

16 Conceptualising mothers' care work as maternal practice

Implications for feminist practice with mothers

Sarah Epstein

Introduction

Feminists theorising motherhood have moved from describing this institution as oppressive and implicated in the perpetuation of unequal gender relations to considerations of maternal agency and the potential for women's caretaking to actively inform relations of power. The chapter starts by tracking some of these shifts and then moves into a description of the ethical component of maternal activity, conceptualised here as a maternal ethics of care and referred to in feminist literature as maternal practice. It is the position of feminist scholarship, adopted here, that feminist maternal practice should be valued as a political ethic of care that forms part of wider feminist work towards social transformation. The chapter concludes with emphasising how the concept of maternal practice can alert social work practitioners to new conversations and social work practice responses in their work with women who mother. Through attending to women's intentions and experiences of mothering, the social work focus can better support them to reveal political practices. Thus maternal subjectivities are configured as dynamic, agentic and capable of informing social change.

From motherhood to maternal practice

The notion of motherhood has been critiqued throughout feminist history as a culturally constructed discourse that is given form through the institution of marriage (O'Reilly, 2004). At the same time, within this discourse, women's identity becomes connected to her potential for reproduction (Rich, 1976) and the social expectation that marriage and motherhood are what women aspire to (Friedan [1963] 2001). Before I explore what this has meant to feminists who have engaged with the notion of 'motherhood', it is prurient to employ a definition of this discourse as:

> The belief that children's optimal growth and development are directly and exclusively related to the quality and quantity of maternal care they receive, and caring mothers always put children's needs ahead of their own.
>
> (Tucker, 2008, p. 210)

Feminist theorists writing about women's experience of being mothers have historically defined this discourse as the Institution of Motherhood (O'Reilly, 2004; Rich, 1976).

The relationship between motherhood and feminism has shifted and turned in a dynamic process often revealing conflict (Kinser, 2010) and demanding repudiation (Friedan [1963] 2001). However, all seem in agreement that the parameters of motherhood as it exists within patriarchal discourse constrains women through the determinants that equate her womanhood with motherhood (Kinser, 2010; Hughes et al., 2016).

In 1963 Betty Friedan argued in her book *The Feminine Mystique* that the prevailing social view of motherhood meant that women's identity was solely connected to her potential for reproduction and the social expectation that marriage and motherhood were what women aspired to. She argued that it was only by breaking this oppressive link to marriage and childbirth that women's liberation could be found. Thus, this discourse compromises women's identity as separate to that of her child. She is allocated all responsibility but imbued with no power. The Institution of Motherhood denies women the "authority and agency to determine her own experiences of mothering" (O'Reilly, 2008, p. 10). By relegating the role of mother to the domestic realm, rendering her work non-public, women's effect on social change is restricted (O'Reilly, 2008).

Feminist's theorising maternity have been greatly influenced by Adrienne Rich's (1976) influential book *Of Woman Born* and the description of herself and her sons as "conspirators, outlaws from the institution of motherhood" (p. 195). She argues that motherhood is both 'institution' *and* 'experience' and that Motherhood as Institution is shaped and constrained by patriarchal ideas about women. Rich's (1976) critique joined the voices of other second-wave feminists who were able to reveal some of the key issues for women within the patriarchally defined and prescribed role of 'mother'. However, what was groundbreaking was her distinction between the Institution and women's lived experiences of being mothers. Her emphasis on the experience of mothering attends to a woman's own experience that is necessarily female-centred and disconnected from male definition. Rich's distinction is so important because it is an attempt to reclaim motherhood and allow women to define the terms.

Feminist social work practice with mothers would do well to take up this distinction in interactions with, and practice responses to, working with mothers as service users. Motherhood is a discourse that women are positioned in relation to and thus it has a central place in feminist theory.

Through the late second wave of feminism and continuing through the third wave to the present day, feminists shifted focus from the child to focus on the mother, exemplified by Rich's (1976) articulation of motherhood as experience. Consequently, women's experiences as mothers became the subject of feminist investigation and research (Everingham, 1994). This marks the introduction of women's standpoint into a patriarchally defined domain.

While feminist critique of the institution of motherhood recognises the political and structural inequalities that are thrust upon women, feminists also seek to encompass the possibilities for women within their mothering (Kinser, 2010). This reflects a feminist drive to reinstate the notion of empowerment and agency in women's lived experiences as mothers, wives and partners. One of the strategies for doing so is the requalification of mothers' experiences and their 'care work' as legitimate activity.

Maternal practice as a feminist ethic of care

Sara Ruddick's ([1989] 1995) book *Maternal Thinking: Toward a Politics of Peace* was an attempt to move mothering away from something that is naturally occurring and must necessarily be provided by women only. Ruddick's argument is that mothering is an activity, as distinct from 'birthgiving', because it is something that can be carried out by a man or a woman. Her book was an attempt to undermine the notion of maternal instinct by positing that women develop both a set of skills and way of thinking that is honed through interaction with their children. Through 'care work' they establish a craft of child-rearing borne of the applied (unpaid) labour in caring for their children.

In separating 'birthgiving' from mothering, she contends "to be a mother is to take upon oneself the responsibility of child care, making its work a regular and substantial part of one's working life" (Ruddick, 1995, p. 17). Mothering work is a commitment to responding to the demands of looking after children and is not dependent on identity or a "fixed biological or legal relationship" (Ruddick, 1995, p. xi). Her conceptualisation of mothering rejects the idea that women, by virtue of their physiology, are naturally suited to nurturing and caring for children. The notion of mothering does not accept that a woman's social status relegates her and her alone to being the primary caregiver. As well, mothering thus presupposes women's right not to mother (Forcey, 1987).

Placing an emphasis on mothering as work draws attention to what is being *done* rather than *felt*. Ruddick's ([1989] 1995) shift of focus challenges the patriarchal discourse of maternal instinct that links women's biology and gendered subjectivity to the role of mother. By employing the concept of maternal logic she theorises mothering as a discipline, a set of maternal practices, which involves a sense of judgement of success and failure. Further, moving mothering away from essentialism, she argues that these disciplined acts are intellectual, not emotional. Similarly, and more broadly, the ethic of care as a general concept also configures care as activity. Configuring care as activity is an important foundation from which to rethink the concept of 'human nature' and the essential self (Tronto, 1994).

The concept of maternal thinking stems from maternal practice, which dictates certain interests that are guiding the mother's judgement (Everingham, 1994). The areas of interest are related to nurturing and socialisation of children. However, it is important to emphasise that the forms that such interest takes are not universal. For example, women from diverse cultural or class backgrounds may foreground different areas of concern and prioritise particular emphasis on areas of socialisation (Muhonja and Bernard, 2016; O'Reilly, 2016).

Maternal practice is also relational as "different pairings of individuals and circumstances produce differently nuanced knowledges, which subsist in lifeworlds where the natural, spiritual, and social worlds interface" (Muhonja, 2016, p. 1). Tronto (1994) reminds us that what we care about, that is what a mother might determine as needing care, depends on position, culture and context. Thus the manifestation of care work is always contextually contingent and as such women contextualise their care taking of their children differently. The importance of recognising this is emphasised by Hankivsky's (2014) urging for a critical ethics of care to demonstrate its ability to "develop more nuanced and complex accounts of power" (p. 259). Motherwork *is* complex involving both iteration and reaction to context and discourse (Muhonja, 2016).

The raising of boys to adulthood is a key task for all of those who are mothering sons, and is a good example of the way that maternal practice involves iteration and reaction to context and discourse. The social expectations of manhood intrude on all mothers' maternal practice in different ways. Normative gendered standards hold both mother and son accountable and inextricably constitute the relationship. As Ruddick ([1989] 1995) asserts, the primary externally imposed constitutive demand of mothering is the expectation that we will train our children "in the behaviour acceptable to their social and cultural group" (p. 110). Women caring for sons negotiate mothering in oppressive conditions. As women, their "secondary status is enforced in both the gender arena (service to men) and in the maternal realm (service to children). Mothers must, if they hope to raise non-sexist men who reject traditional masculinity, challenge both patriarchal imperatives" (O'Reilly, 2016, p. 20). For feminist mothers raising sons, in particular, this presents significant conflict. However, it is experienced in different ways, depending on how intersectional social locations interact with subjectivity, tradition, culture and psychology (Ferdinand, 2016).

The expectations, norms and surveillance of masculinity practice operate differently for black mothers' sons and these differences inform everything. In Australia, for example, Aboriginal and Torres Strait Islander mothers enact maternal practice within a broader white context that stigmatises rather than valorises their sons' masculinity, putting them at significant risk of incarceration and death. First Nations mothers, as well as refugee, immigrant and Muslim mothers, will be raising their sons within their own cultural locations with diverse expectations and ideas about masculinity while simultaneously being positioned within a white Australian society where their boys are at significant risk.

Within Anglo-American culture, white feminist mothering challenges the sons' community of identification, the male peer group and patriarchal culture. A study of white, middle-class, heterosexual, able-bodied and tertiary-educated women in Australia (Epstein, 2014) found their feminist assessment of the demands that maternal practice must meet is the risk that male privilege presents to who they are as women but also how male privilege seeks to hegemonise their sons' masculinity. They talk about enacting maternal practice that supports boys to recognise male privilege *and* white privilege in order to accept some responsibility for addressing inherited privilege (Epstein, 2015).

For many feminists, their practices are "simultaneously embedded and woven into their efforts against racism, classism, and other threats to their access to equal opportunities and social justice" (Samuels and Ross-Sheriff, 2008, p. 5). Returning then to Hankivsky's (2014) concern for a critical analysis of the ethical context of care, it is possible that maternal practice as a concept is capable of revealing the ways that mothering is economically, racially, culturally and geographically determined (O'Reilly, 2016).

Maternal practice as moral position

Everingham (1994) has critiqued Ruddick's ([1989] 1995) theory for lacking analysis of how maternal thinking is socially constructed and constrained. She suggested that maternal thinking be considered as a moral attitude "adopted by mothers amongst any number of possibilities" (p. 32). This suggestion paves the way for a paradigm that provides context and form for moral attitudes mothers enact with their children.

Ruddick ([1989] 1995) suggests that mothering, if considered as practice, promotes empowerment. Tronto (1994) extends this notion of practice, arguing that recognising care as practice also allows for consideration of the assessment required to enact practice as an interdependent yet agentic activity. The exploration of women's experience of mothering, that is the naming and thinking about their mothering, challenges the invisibility of women's work and lays foundations for social transformation. Rendering oneself visible within the mothering process is antithetical to patriarchal motherhood yet vital as a tool for women's empowerment and role as social change agents.

The maternal subject

One of the important differences within the theory of feminist maternal practice is the taking up of ideas about power as relational. As feminist maternal practice considers the maternal subject as mutable, multiple and constituted through discourses, mothering has been wrested from a structural location where it is a result of and acted on by external forces of power. Instead, poststructural feminist ideas about power allow the concept of maternal practice to form a part of, be responsive to and inform relations of power.

One of the ways that maternal practice informs relations of power is to reconsider structural accounts of autonomy (Everingham, 1994). Such accounts rely on binary structures that essentialise women's position as mother. This both relegates them to the primary role as birth giver and care taker as well as trivialising her work because it is socially and politically isolated and unpaid. Everingham (1994) argues that autonomy can be configured to include maternal activity as agentic caring activity.

Everingham (1994) seeks to theorise autonomy as a form of subjectivity that is constructed through relationship to another's claim to autonomy within concrete social situations that are saturated with power. Autonomy is rejected as a stand-alone achievement rather it is an activity where the "child's autonomous subjectivity is constructed in relation to the (m)other's own claim to autonomy during this activity" (Everingham, 1994, p. 6).

Like Everingham (1994), Jeremiah (2006) tracks the shift in feminist thought from essentialist constructions of motherhood to the more poststructural terminology of mothering. Within this, she argues that motherhood is no longer taken as fixed or biologically driven but conceptualised as a set of ideas and practices that change across time and context. For Jeremiah (2006), the maternal subject first emerges through a consequence of engaging in maternal practice. The maternal subject emerges as a consequence of conscious decision-making.

Jeremiah (2006) critiques structural feminist accounts of mother and maternity as if it exists outside of culture. Instead, maternal subjectivities are constituted through discourses about gender difference, mothers, maternity, the body and motherhood. She proposes a poststructural feminist engagement with mothering where there are explicit feminist discourses that constitute maternal subjectivities that are removed from an essentialist foundation and which recognises a maternal subject who enacts maternal practice. In this way, mothering involves the taking up of maternal practice imbuing the subject as active, interactive and part of an exchange (Jeremiah, 2006).

One of her main arguments is that despite feminists being aware of the social construction of gender, they have not conceptualised maternity, as it is constituted through relations of power and dominant discourse. Jeremiah (2006) uses Rich's (1976) notion of motherhood as experience to argue that the maternal subject is in relationship to, and constituted by, multiple ideologies and discourses about maternity. The emphasis in feminist maternal practice is her agency that works to disrupt motherhood discourse. This means that the mother's experience and knowledge has authority and her agency is legitimated. The concept of the maternal subject represents a shift in thinking because she is constituted through activity and practice.

The maternal subject as agentic

Contemporary feminist theorising about motherhood considers the private domestic domain as a valid location for disrupting dominant discourse. Rather than being considered as sequestered from the public domain and thus the arena where power is held and exercised, feminist maternal practice draws on poststructural notions of power as dispersed, everywhere and relational. In this way, the exercise of maternal practice within the private domain is not exempt from relations of power. Rather maternal practice is directly in response to and forms part of the relations of power.

Power as relational considers the agentic activity of all subjects, the mother and child included. The reconfiguration of power in this way fits well with the reconceptualisation of mothering as activity. Both Muhonja (2016) and Jeremiah (2006) suggest that maternal practice is a combination of performance and action. This practice is performed over and over and is likely to be varied. Butler (1992) argues that this variation is an effect of agentic activity and constitutive of sub-jectivity. This is an important idea to consider because of the traditional mother-hood discourse that positions women as being powerless and constrained within a patriarchal structure.

While it is the private sphere where agency is enacted, mothering practice is still context bound and historically specific. The reason for action may be taken from a response to basic necessity; feeding, changing nappies, picking a child up from school and so forth. When mothering is relegated to meeting basic require-ments alone, this activity can be considered as responsive, as a passive role. How-ever, feminist maternal practice draws on ideals, values and aims of feminism that are given expression through interaction and activity enacted with our children.

Taken from a feminist perspective, maternal activity traverses the personal and political, the ideological, philosophical, the private and the public domain. This sees the mother moving "into focus as a subject (and) a creator of cultural meanings and human value systems" (Everingham, 1994, p. 7). Maternal practice operates within a theoretical structure, one that contextualises personal narratives positioning them as political rather than merely an expression of individualism. In this way, the enacting of maternal practice fits with the feminist tradition of cast-ing a critical lens on dominant discourse, their institutions and cultural practices (Muhonja and Bernard, 2016; O'Reilly, 2016).

The progressive potential of maternal practice

I have thus far argued that moving the mother into focus as a maternal subject honours and reveals her agentic activity and predicates her care work within a moral and political framework. There are ethical responsibilities around care that women believe stem from both their moral world view *and* the context within which they must care for their child. Drawing out her maternal practice in this way supports the emergence of a maternal story grounded in her socio-cultural context. Through consideration of the maternal subject as agentic, it is possible to explore how ideas about gender, class, race, culture, ability, sexuality, age and religion can be disrupted. This is the progressive potential of maternal practice. The concept of maternal practice is aimed at more than the attempt to privilege care as fundamental to the human condition. Its critical potential lies in estab-lishing maternal agency not only in terms of intent but also in potential for the effect of maternal agency. This is in contrast to patriarchal discourse about the essentialised mother who operates within a fixed construct that diminishes her agency and essentialises care as something innate. Maternal practice is instead a considered and potentially political act.

The rationale for using the concept of maternal practice in social work

Social workers are aligned with a commitment to working alongside the margin-alised and oppressed and, through promotion of human rights, actively seek social justice (AASW Code of Ethics, 2010). When working with women who mother, how are social workers to fulfil this commitment without first being willing to dismantle problematic perceptions of motherhood as an innate and essentialist extension of what it means to be a woman? Further, as women are constructed as natural caregivers with individual responsibility for the care of their child, the mother/child relationship becomes both idealised and romanticised (Tronto, 1994). The real danger here is that this de-politicises her and positions the mother outside of meaningful subjectivity. Feminist attempts to locate the mother within relations of power are going to be more successful at drawing the attention of critical social work practice to the mothering experience. In this way, critical social work practice can better realise the political act of raising awareness of the everyday lived experiences of women.

The social work commitment to socially just practice would benefit from taking into account a critical and maternal ethic of care as this enables the politicisation of maternal care work and situates caring activity outside of the innate and pre-discursive. Tronto (1994) argues that the politicisation of care is central to being able to "change its state and the status of those who do caring work in our culture" (p. 157).

Social workers are privileged by their access to women's stories about their experiences of mothering. Re-positioning women as both authoritative and agentic starts by asking women specifically about how they are experiencing mothering. This is separate to asking her about feeding, the child's weight, parenting skills and more. Rather it is about what mothering means for her. How is she making sense of herself? Does she feel like herself? The work is about supporting women to reclaim herself within the mothering experience.

The social work practice context and women

The social work practice context often entails working with women who are positioned within social locations that are at the axis of oppression (Hankivsky, 2014). This means that many of the women social workers work with are enacting caring practices that are a result of, and a response to, the context of power inequality. Understanding women's care taking in relation to these interlocking experiences of disadvantage can more fully attend to social injustice.

Women are systematically constructed as unfit mothers in case meetings, through casework and in case notes (Hughes, Chau and Vokrri, 2016). Social workers struggle with sitting on either side of the good/bad mother binary moving inconsistently between the two positions (Hughes et al., 2016). There is a chasm between "the ways in which mothers view the circumstances of their lives and how these same situations are understood differently by their child welfare workers" (Hughes et al., 2016). Attending to women's maternal practice is more likely to reveal the power relations at play in the mother and child circumstance. Valuing the lived experiences of the women social workers work with can be more likely achieved through drawing on the concept of maternal practice as an ethical activity that women engage in response to the demands they believe the context in which they mother presents to them.

The mothers who cross the social work threshold are viewed through a patriarchal motherhood lens that likely operates on the premise of mothers' failure to fulfil their maternal responsibilities. This is a regulatory discourse that "reinscribes mothers in the traditional ideological matrix of responsibility and blame" (O'Reilly, 2016, p. 23). The feminist problem is not only the surveillance of women's mothering but also the implication that the "responsibility assignment" (O'Reilly, 2016) should be hers. Society benefits from the care work of the marginalised mother (Tronto, 1994) and at the same time makes her care work vulnerable to judgement and critique.

Most of the knowledge that is circulated through public discourse about mothers is not produced from the standpoint of the mother. And most social work narratives and practices with mothers marginalise the mother while privileging the child through the promotion of best interest policy. It is important that critical social work practice, in line with broader feminist politics, aims to produce knowledge that reflects the lives of women. Working with the concept of maternal practice can support social workers to gain a more accurate picture of mothers' lives.

What do mothers care about?

Tronto (1994) posits that the primary act of engaging in an ethic of care requires a decision regarding what to care about. Respectful social work practice with women, in their mothering positions, must start with finding out what the mother cares about. In line with the concept of maternal practice, this means that the social worker is seeking to understand how and what the mother has assessed is a demand that raising her child or children presents. This means attending to the socio-cultural, political, economic context within which she is raising her child/ children. This is also about learning from her how this context presents specific risks for both her child and for the mother and child relationship.

In some instances, this may mean identifying how far the mother and child are located away from equitable and meaningful access to the resources necessary to raise her child and successfully meet the demands the mother has assessed are present. It may also mean learning how the mother's cultural or religious or ethnic position informs and constitutes specific demands. Women enact maternal practice in response to and as part of multiple contexts. Her gender takes on meaning in relation to other categories of identity, and we must be alert to how and in what ways this is happening. Learning what mothers care about can get us closer to revealing the multiple and intersecting oppressive locations as well as opportunities for privilege that create unique and contextually specific mothering conditions.

This iteration of social work practice recognises the intersecting positions where women are situated and seeks to understand how this impacts and constitutes women's lives. It follows from this that we need to think about how we might support women to be presented in ways that centralise their knowledge. Importantly, social workers are implicated (Gustafson, Swan, Gillingham and Parsons, 2016) in the way that women's maternal subjectivities are made visible.

Exploration of women's maternal practice offers a way of both moving social work practice with women outside of the good/bad mother binary and recognising the contextual conditions impacting on her maternal care work. Revealing intent and an understanding that this is grounded in a legitimate maternal assessment of need and demand is an important strategy for achieving this. Further, it has the potential to identify the relations of power that women recognise their mothering operates in and at the same time justifies their concerns about oppression.

Importantly, for social workers in the field today, the radical implications of positioning the mother as central should not be underestimated. In most Western countries where social work intersects with the welfare of the child, "best interests of the child" (Hughes et al., 2016) is the dominant organising discourse around which social workers are expected to ground their assessment and intervention practice. The "best interest of the child" discourse maintains a focus on the child and can have the effect of marginalising the mother and obscuring interlocking oppressions (Hughes et al., 2016) that impede the mother's ability to successfully meet the demands of care work. Tronto (1994) asserts that the single greatest risk to meeting care needs is lack of and impeded access to resources. Understanding how and in what way the mother is making sense of and experiencing this injustice is key to valuing the lived experiences of women. Without recognising injustice regarding access to resources the mother is vulnerable again to being held culpable, stigmatised and mis-recognised.

Conclusion

Critical social work practice with mothers requires a review of the approach to assessing women's mothering. This involves considering what it might mean when social workers sit down with new mothers, sole mothers, or incarcerated mothers and ask them how they are experiencing their relationship with their children. What if they were to ask them what it is they value the most highly? Social work practice focus may also turn to ascertaining the threats that *they* have assessed their mothering responds to. In the context of these broader cultural, economic and political forces, what hopes do they entertain for their relationship with their child and for their child's growth? What wider forces do they believe are impacting on the mother and child? Working with the concept of maternal practice can invite mothers to position their caretaking activity alongside a social justice paradigm. This is a milieu where women's care work identifies and responds to structural inequality and discursive relations of power that threaten to subjugate her maternal authority.

References

Butler, J. (1992) Contingent foundations: feminism and the question of "postmodernism". In: Butler, J. and Wallach Scott, J. (eds.) *Feminists theorize the political*. New York, Routledge, pp. 3–21.

Epstein, S. (2014) Mothers and sons: Transforming gendered subjectivities. In: Pallotta-Chiarolli, M. and Pease, B. (eds.) *The politics of recognition and social justice: Transforming subjectivities and new forms of resistance*. London: Routledge, pp. 59–76.

Epstein, S. (2015) Making women visible in boys' lives. In: Flood, M. and Howson, R. (eds.) *Engaging men in building gender equality*. London: Cambridge, pp. 234–243.

Everingham, C. (1994) *Motherhood and modernity: An investigation into the rational dimension of mothering*. St Leonards, NSW: Allen & Unwin.

Ferdinand, R. (2016) Letters to my son. In: Muhonja, B. B. and Bernard, W. T. (eds.) *Mothers and sons: Centering mother knowledge*. Toronto: Demeter Press, pp. 93–106.

Forcey, L. R. (1987) *Mothers of sons: Towards an understanding of responsibility*. New York: Praeger.

Friedan, B. (2001) *The feminine mystique*. Reprint edition. New York: W. W. Norton.

Gustafson, D. L., Swan, T., Gillingham, B. and Parsons, J. E. (2016) Complexities of negotiating power when re-constructing stories about lone mothers. *Affilia: Journal of Women and Social Work*, 31(3), pp. 303–316.

Hankivsky, O. (2014) Rethinking care ethics: On the promise and potential of an intersectional analysis. *American Political Science Review*, 108(2), pp. 252–264.

Hughes, J., Chau, S. and Vokrri, L. (2016) Mothers narratives of their involvement with child welfare services. *Affilia: Journal of Women and Social Work*, 31(3), pp. 344–356.

Jeremiah, E. (2006) Mothering to motherhood and beyond: Maternity in recent feminist thought. *Journal of the Association for Research on Mothering*, 8(1–2), pp. 21–33.

Kinser, A. E. (2010) *Motherhood and feminism*. Berkeley, CA: Seal Press.

Mattsson, T. (2014) Intersectionality as a useful tool: Anti-oppressive social work and critical reflection. *Affilia: Journal of Women and Social Work*, 29(1), pp. 8–17.

Muhonja, B. B. (2016) Introduction mothering at intersections: Towards centering mother knowledge. In: Muhonja, B. B. and Bernard, W. T. (eds.) *Mothers and sons: Centering mother knowledge*. Toronto: Demeter Press, pp. 1–13.

Muhonja, B. B. and Bernard, W. T. (2016) (eds.) *Mothers and sons: Centering mother knowledge*. Toronto: Demeter Press.

O'Reilly, A. (2004) Introduction. In: O'Reilly, A. (ed.) *Mother outlaws: Theories and practices of empowered mothering*. Toronto: Women's Press, pp. 1–30.

O'Reilly, A. (2008) Introduction. In: O'Reilly, A. (ed.) *Feminist mothering*. New York: State University of New York Press, pp. 1–24.

O'Reilly, A. (2016) In black and white: African American and Anglo American feminist perspectives on mothers and sons. In: Muhonja, B. B. and Bernard, W. T. (eds.) *Mothers and sons: Centering mother knowledge*. Toronto: Demeter Press, pp. 14–44.

Rich, A. (1976) *Of woman born: Motherhood as experience and institution*. Toronto: W. W. Norton.

Ruddick, S. (1995) *Maternal thinking: Toward a politics of peace*. Boston: Beacon Press.

Samuels, G. M. and Ross-Sheriff, F. (2008) Identity, oppression and power: Feminisms and intersectionality theory. *Affilia: Journal of Women and Social Work*, 23(1), pp. 5–9.

Tronto, J. (1994) *Moral boundaries: A political argument for an ethic of care*. New York: Routledge.

Tucker, J. S. (2008) Rocking the boat: Feminism and the ideological grounding of the twenty-first century mothers' movement. In: O'Reilly, A. (ed.) *Feminist mothering*. New York: State University of New York Press, pp. 205–218.

17 Do men care?

From uncaring masculinities to men's caring practices in social work

Bob Pease

Introduction

Caring work, both in the home and in the public world of paid work, is predominantly undertaken by women. The identity and activities of women are often defined by their caring roles in both their public and private lives (Phillips, 2007). This over-representation of women in caring roles often reflects the assumption that this form of work is naturally suited to women, as it is seen to be a reflection of their perceived natural nurturing capacities (Hanlon, 2009).

I argue against the premise that caring is a natural expression of women's nature. These views have been used to reinforce women's subordination (Robinson, 2015). The notion of feminine and masculine modes of being to describe the practices of women and men are problematic because of their essentialist connotations. There is no natural feminine approach to caring for others. It is thus important to differentiate between feminine and feminist ethics of care in this regard (Robinson, 2015). Even the association of caring with mothering does not necessarily exclude men, as Ruddick (1989) has argued, men can provide mothering as well.

These inequalities in relation to care in the home and in occupations such as social work constitute what Lynch and Baker (2009) refer to as 'the gendered order of caring', which is both a reflection of and perpetuation of gender inequalities in society. While inequality in the gendered division of caring has been the focus of much feminist work, critical masculinity studies, as a discipline, has been slow to engage with care and affective relations (Hanlon, 2009). When care is considered in relation to men, it is predominantly in relation to men's care of children, with the focus being on 'involved fatherhood' (Bjork, 2015). In this chapter, I interrogate men's relationship to the broader concept of care.

In emphasising the gendered dimension of caring in this chapter, it is important to remember that other social divisions and cultural formations such as class, race, ethnicity, sexuality, ability/disability and age are also factors in shaping care. It should also be noted that the role of care in men's lives will differ between cultures (Phillips, 2007; Tronto, 2013). Consequently, it is important to keep in mind the intersectionality of gender with other social divisions even when it is foregrounded, as it is in this chapter.

Do men care?

There has been an ongoing debate about men's capacities for caring and whether such capacities are innate or learned. What is clear from the empirical research on men who care is the anxiety that most men experience in relation to their care-giving activities (Hanlon, 2009). Many men equate caring with femininity. Consequently, when men do caring they are either seen as not being real men if they care in the same way as women or alternatively, their caring is judged as poor because they are judged against the norm enacted by women (Bjork, 2015).

It has been noted that there is a distinction between 'caring about' and 'caring for' someone (Camilleri and Jones, 2001). Whereas caring about does not require personal involvement, caring for entails the intimate practices of doing care. Some of the early feminist theorists of care (Chodorow, 1978; Gilligan, 1982) argue that there were biological differences between women and men that arose out of women's experience of mothering. Chodorow (1978), for example, argues that because most men as boys are separated from their mothers, their capacity for nurturing and caring is diminished. Such differences are seen to create different moralities and ethics and different views about rationality. In this context, it is maintained that while women have an ethic of care which is based on their connection to others, men promote a more abstract ethic of justice that does not involve direct caring relations with others (Phillips, 2007).

To what extent are the modes of caring performed by men different from the caring practises of women and do such differences, if they exist, reflect culturally scripted forms of masculinity and femininity? I am concerned with how gender is performed through the practices of caring. How are gender norms reproduced or transformed through caring practices? To what extent do men's caring practices create new forms of masculinities or reproduce traditional forms?

The gendered framing of care in social work

In social work and human services, male workers are seen as doing 'women's work' (Camilleri and Jones, 2001), as the gender division of care is played out here as well. The very notion of social work as a 'caring profession' reinforces the gendered framing of women's roles and performances. Just as in caring roles in the home, the caring dimensions of social work require workers to understand and respond to the emotions of others (Camilleri and Jones, 2001). Such practices require high levels of emotional labour which are demanding for those who are doing it.

Many men will seek to avoid having to deal with people's difficult feelings. The gendered framing of care as being natural for women allows men to absent themselves from the giving of care both in the home and in caring professions. Just as men avoid care in the home, in social work, many men tend to give priority to indirect forms of practice that take them away from direct caring roles, which are seen to challenge traditional forms of masculinity (Camilleri and Jones, 2001). Some men in social work and other caring occupations emphasise the bureaucratic and technical aspects of their work over and above what are seen as more 'feminine' caring practices (Cree, 1996).

These gendered framings about care shape the aspirations of men and women in relation to preferred roles within social work. For men to embrace the caring practices of social work, they often need to define themselves as being different from most other men. They need to see themselves as embracing characteristics and qualities that are societally deemed to be feminine (Cree, 1996).

Baines, Charlesworth and Cunningham (2015) identify three different forms of care practices by men in the non-profit human services: masculinist care practices, managerial masculinities and caring masculinities. Men in the first group, who do traditional forms of masculinity, emphasise the administrative aspects of their work, including the routinised and standardised assessment and in-take processes. They do not raise concerns about work-family balance and generally, their female partners take most of the responsibility for child care and domestic work (Baines et al., 2015). Men in the second group, who adopt what Baines et al. (2015) refer to as managerialist masculinities, exhibit gender privilege in shaping their jobs to reflect their concerns for autonomy and managerial control over their work. Men in the third group, who embrace the caring practices of their profession, are more likely to enact empathic styles of working similar to women and exhibit what Baines et al. (2015) refer to as 'caring masculinities'. Such men work in direct practice roles and emphasise the importance of client-centred care. They also struggle with trying to balance family responsibilities with work, as they are more likely to also be involved in caring roles at home. The men who adopt more caring masculine styles are supportive of gender equality in the human services and the wider community (Baines et al., 2015).

Shifting the gendered burden of caring

Various writers have noted an increase in men's care-giving in recent years (Phillips, 2007; Hanlon, 2009; Morell and Jewkes, 2011; Elliott, 2015). Such a shift has involved a relocation of care from women to men in terms of caring for partners, children and other family members.

The main focus of recent discussions in relation to men and care has been on fatherhood and increasing men's involvement in the lives of their children. 'Sonke Gender Justice', for example, has been actively involved in promoting the greater involvement of men as care-giving fathers as a strategy to improve family well-being and gender equality. They argue that the greater involvement of fathers in child care contributes to children's wellbeing, increased opportunities for women to achieve their potential, and healthier and happier men (Levtov, van der Gaard, Green, Kaufman and Barker, 2015).

While some commentators are optimistic about the shifts that are occurring in men's level of care-giving, other writers are pessimistic about the likelihood of substantial change in the gendered division of labour in the home (Hanlon, 2009). In this latter view, it is argued that men will only provide care when women are not available to do it (McMahon, 1999).

As men become more involved in caregiving, the issue of how men care and the quality of their care is opened up for discussion. Men's care is often compared with the quality of care provided by women. To the extent that men's care differs from women's care, they are judged as being deviant, whereas, if they care in ways similar to women, they are judged as departing from traditional masculinity (Campbell and Carroll, 2007).

Many claimed differences between the ways that men and women care seem premised upon essentialist gender discourses that posit biological differences in men's and women's caring capacities. In this view, as noted earlier, caring is seen as more natural for women and as dysfunctional for men. Men are seen as emotionally incapable of providing care and nurturance (Hanlon, 2012).

Any differences between the ways in which men and women care is not totally explained by childhood socialisation either. Rather, these differences may be more explicable in terms of the jobs and institutional positions in which men and women are located and the gendered expectations about care embedded within them. Thus gendered differences in care may be more to do with gendered social relations in adulthood than in socialisation experiences in childhood (Gerstel and Gallagher, 2001).

Men's roles in relation to care are framed by the norms and structures of masculinity (Robinson, 2010). Many men consider that they care through providing economically to their partner and children. Men are also able to maintain that their major breadwinning activities constitute their contribution to caring for their family (Hanlon, 2012). Good fatherhood practice still seems to be primarily measured through the expectation of men providing for and protecting their families (Morell and Jewkes, 2011). Such roles allow men to see themselves as caring without challenging traditional forms of masculinity.

Men's capacity to give priority to their career over caring roles is a reflection of their male privilege and power. Tronto (2013) frames men's avoidance and evasion of care as them having a 'production pass' and a 'protection pass' for getting out of housework and child care responsibilities. Because of men's protector role and their involvement in economic production, they are able to make the claim that they do not need to be involved in the daily activities of care.

The man who positions himself as head of the household sees himself as a protector who defends his family against dangers and risks. As he regards this as important work, he is able to excuse himself from the caring tasks in the family. Tronto (2013) also identifies the protection role of men in relation to women which allows men to present a more positive view of masculinity in opposition to the violent and aggressive construction of hegemonic masculinity. However, the masculinist protector role is also premised on the subordination of women and the expectation that women will provide care for men.

Young (2003) argues that the masculinist protector role of the man as head of the household positions women and children into subordination, drawing parallels between men's authority in the family and governmental surveillance of people in response to terrorist threats. The image of man as protector reflects the chivalrous expression of masculinity, which is premised upon the man protecting women from other 'bad' men who threaten the family from outside. Within this framework, women sacrifice autonomy and power for the protection that is provided by men. Thus the protector role reproduces male privilege and gender inequality.

Tronto (2013) has coined the term 'privileged irresponsibility' to describe the process by which men expect others to care for them without any acknowledgement. Such a process allows men to maintain their privileged positioning in the gender order and to be able to ignore the needs of others. Tronto (2013) links privileged irresponsibility to what she calls 'epistemological ignorance', whereby members of privileged groups do not have to know about the needs of those who are subjugated. This chapter is concerned with how privileged irresponsibility is sustained and what can be done to challenge it (Bozalek, 2014).

Masculinity as a barrier to caring

Are masculinity and care antithetical to each other? MacDougall (1997) does not see caring and masculinity as being mutually exclusive. However, Hanlon (2009) cites research that demonstrates how men avoid and resent caring responsibilities because such responsibilities challenge their masculinity. Hegemonic masculinity is, to use Hanlon's term, 'care-free'. The dominant portrayal of masculinity is rational, inexpressive and unemotional. Doing masculinity requires men to deny their weakness and vulnerability and this makes it very difficult for them to develop nurturing and intimate relationships with others (Hanlon, 2012).

When men do care, they are under normative pressures to do so in ways that do not challenge their masculinity. Because being a carer is associated with femininity and subordination, it contradicts the expectations of masculinity which requires men to be dominant. Some men experience caregiving as emasculating, because they regard nurturing as feminine and unmanly.

Hanlon (2012) argues that even if men initially seek to maintain their masculinity while providing care, the process of actually doing care will in itself develop in men the emotional and affective experiences that will transform their subjectivities. The issue is whether the equation of masculinity with dominance can be broken to encompass care and nurturance or whether men's capacity to care and nurture others will require men to break their identification with masculinity.

Men, gendered emotions and caring

Inequalities in emotional labour and caring are a source of gender inequality more generally. This understanding requires an interrogation of how emotions and caring are at odds with hegemonic masculinities. If this is so, it is important to understand more about how men define their masculinity in the context of love and care.

There is a significant tension in masculinity studies in relation to understanding men's power and privilege on the one hand and understanding men's vulnerability and emotions on the other hand. Theorists who focus on men's power and dominance (e.g. Connell, 2005) tend to neglect the emotional lives of men, while theorists of men's emotions (e.g. Seidler, 2006) tend to neglect the structural privileges associated with men's dominance.

There are understandable concerns that focusing on men's emotions and vulnerabilities may distract attention away from men's power and privileges. Certainly, many masculinity theorists have fallen prey to this neglect. However, this is not in itself a reason to ignore the emotional subjectivities of men which, as I have argued elsewhere (Pease, 2012), are important in understanding men's resistance to change. Understanding men's emotions in the context of affective equality and caring labour provides insights into how men's subjectivities might be transformed towards a critical ethics of care.

Holmes (2015) challenges the view that men are unable to engage in emotional caring. She argues that in the context of heterosexual relationships, men are able to provide emotional support to their partners within the context of heteromasculinity. While a form of emotional re-education may be necessary for men if they are to learn how to care for others, Holmes is optimistic that men have the capacity to express emotions in the context of caring. While she encourages women to prompt men to express themselves more emotionally, she discourages charges of emotional incompetence levelled at men because she believes that such criticisms reinforce gender inequalities.

It is clear that as men and women create and negotiate more equal relationships, greater emotional reflexivity will be required of men if such relationships are to be sustained. While Holmes (2015) is optimistic about men's capacity to shift their emotional expression and caring, it remains to be seen how men will respond to the challenges to their masculinity that such shifts will evoke.

Hanlon (2012) argues that masculinity and the power associated with it are not antithetical to the capacity for emotions and care. Hence his notion of fostering care-giving masculinities among men. However, while it is clearly important to understand men's emotional lives, as part of the process of interrogating their dominance and privilege, it does not necessarily follow that masculinity and vulnerability are compatible with each other as Hanlon maintains.

Fostering caring masculinities?

Does the increased involvement of men in caring for their children (Levtov et al., 2015) and current discussions about recruiting more men into caring professions (Pease, 2011) indicate the development of a more caring disposition among men? Does men's caring indicate a shift in dominant forms of masculinity?

Elliott (2015) constructs a theoretical framework of caring masculinities which involves integrating emotions, interdependence, relationality and care into men's identities. Drawing upon feminist care theory, she develops a practice-based model that focuses on the practices of care work performed by men. She argues that practices of care can transform masculinities and men's identities into caring masculinities that support gender equality. This involves men becoming traitors to patriarchal forms of masculinity and breaking with masculine domination. However, in Elliott's (2015) framework, caring masculinities are still based on masculine identities that reconstruct masculinity towards more emotional and relational qualities rather than break with masculine identification per se. Elliott (2015) argues that caring masculinities can make an important contribution to gender equality. This involves the integration of caring values and practices into men's identities.

We still know very little about what how men's involvement in hands-on caring plays out in their subjectivities and identities as men. Morell and Jewkes (2011), who investigated men's narratives about caring, discovered some men they interviewed regarded their hands-on caring activities as contributing to gender equality, in that they viewed their caring as an emotional and political commitment. However, it was interesting that none of the men regarded their caring as unmasculine in any way and that their masculine gender identities were able to be maintained. Some of the men were able to do this by framing their caring as alternative gender equitable masculinities. That is, they were able to reconcile the tension between the traditional expectations of masculinity and their caring practices. Men who were most able to give expression to the emotional dimensions of caring were more likely to support gender equality arguments. However, this applied only to a minority of men.

Morell and Jewkes (2011) identify contradictory consequences of men's greater engagement with care. The very act of men's involvement in care work challenges the unequal gendered division of care by demonstrating that care work is not the sole province of women. However, as other studies have also revealed, they too found that many men framed care work in ways that was consistent with patriarchal norms and practices. Many men involved in care did not support the goal of gender equality and were concerned to consolidate their privilege and power as men. Thus Morell and Jewkes (2011) conclude that men's engagement in care work per se was not necessarily a pathway towards gender equitable practices among men. The hope they hold out is that even if care work is not inspired by gender equality, men's greater involvement in caring practices will eventually lead to transformations in men's caring identities and values.

Robinson, Bottorff, Pesut, Oliffe and Tomlinson (2014) found that men in caregiving roles in relation to people with dementia found ways to preserve their masculinity while being engaged in what they understood to be feminine roles. Whenever possible, they emphasised the provider and protector roles previously discussed, even when they were involved in direct care activities. They talked also about the courage they demonstrated in providing care to their partners and reiterated their position as head of the household. All of these rationales for their work sought to associate their caregiving with masculinity. The men also emphasised their task-focused approach to providing care which drew upon skills they used in their previous work roles. Doucet (2004) also found that fathers at home taking primary care of their children created new forms of masculinity that incorporated elements of femininity into their subjectivities.

In the Swedish context where gender equality policies have been in place for many years, care-giving masculinities are said to have established a new hegemonic form (Bjork, 2015). While care-giving men had to renegotiate their masculinity, they were able to do so by *redoing* masculinity in an alternative form rather than *undoing* masculinity.

When men do caring work, it brings about psychic changes in them providing them with experiences that increase their compassion and nurturance. For Hanlon (2012), this involves integrating feminine characteristics into masculinity, constructing what he calls 'feminist masculinity'. He acknowledges, however, that developing a caring masculinity is contradictory for men. This seems to be most likely when men attempt to hold on to a superordinate or dominant identity, while engaging in emotional intimacy which they associate with women and subordination. The issue for Hanlon is how men allow themselves to be vulnerable while at the same time maintaining the normative masculine expectation that they should be powerful and dominant.

The strategy for change advocated in this chapter involves moving away from defining care as feminine and as somehow a spoiled identity for men. Thus what is asked of men is to break with traditional masculinity and construct subjectivities that are less reliant upon masculine gendered identities. There seems to be agreement among critical masculinity scholars and feminists that doing care changes men and assists them to develop more nurturing capacities (Doucet, 2004; Hanlon, 2012; Elliott, 2015). The issue is whether such transformations sustain some form of masculine identity or break with it.[1]

Lamont (2014) demonstrates how egalitarian identified men who believed that they had transformed themselves fundamentally were unable to see how their actual more limited changes reproduced inequalities in their relationships with women. While these men were able to recognise structural forms of gender inequality, they were less aware of their own privileged positioning in their relationships. As these men saw themselves as being respectful of women and involved in caring roles, they believed themselves to be more egalitarian than traditional men. As they understood themselves as being supportive of gender equality, they could not see how they were complicit with the reproduction of gender inequality. They were able to 'talk the talk' but not 'walk the walk'. Lamont's (2014) study alerts us to the importance of being cautious about caring masculinities that seem progressive but may perpetuate inequalities by failing to challenge male privilege and men's dominant positioning.

I argue here that rather than talking about caring masculinities, it is more appropriate to discuss caring practices by men. For men to adopt a critical ethics of care, they need to exit from masculinity rather than reconstruct it. This idea is in tension with those attempts to articulate and foster caring masculinities (Gartner, Schwerma and Beier, 2007; Hanlon, 2012; Elliott, 2015).

Towards men's caring practices for gender equality in social work

The unequal division of caring labour in the home and in the public world is a source of other forms of gender inequality. It has long been argued that women's capacity to increase their status and income in the paid labour force is dependent on the greater involvement of men in unpaid care in the home (Sevenhuijsen, 2003). When men avoid caring responsibilities they reproduce gender inequalities.

The exclusion of men from caring roles has also been linked to rising levels of men's violence both within the family and within the wider international arena of warfare between nation states. Tronto (2013) regards men's violence against women as the dark side of men's protection, whereby such protection is used to legitimate abusive behaviour towards women. Creating a less violent and more egalitarian world thus requires a shift from the valorisation of hegemonic masculinity to a more caring ethos that is more traditionally associated with women. This means that we need to encourage men not just to undertake more child care at home but also to adopt a more caring disposition that challenges the norms of hegemonic masculinity which legitimates violence and gender inequality. Social work is one site for this rethinking of care by men.

Structural gender inequalities in social work and the wider society will not be transformed unless men take greater responsibility for care work in their paid working lives and in their families. If men were as equally engaged in caring activities as women, we would create a less violent and a more equal society.

I have written elsewhere about the contradictory effects of men's gendered practices in social work, and I have argued that male social workers need to adopt and promote a profeminist practice to challenge the unequal gender regime in the profession and in the gendered society in which it is embedded (Pease, 2011). Given the presence of men in social work, we need to open up a debate within the profession and within social work education about the gendered nature of caring work. The aim of this chapter has been to make a contribution to that debate.

Note

1   There is an extensive debate within critical masculinity studies about the potential to transform masculinity towards a more democratic and egalitarian form that is in opposition to hegemonic and dominant practices. There is insufficient space to do justice to this discussion here. However, see Pease (2014) for an outline of the theoretical debates.

References

Baines, D., Charlesworth, S. and Cunningham, I. (2015) Changing care? Men and managerialism in the non-profit sector. *Journal of Social Work*, 15(5), pp. 459–478.

Bjork, S. (2015) Doing, re-doing or undoing masculinity? Swedish men in filial care of aging parents. *NORA: Nordic Journal of Feminist and Gender Research*, 23(1), pp. 20–35.

Bozalek, V. (2014) Privileged irresponsibility. *Ethics of Care*, 3, pp. 51–72.

Camilleri, P. and Jones, P. (2001) Doing 'women's work'? Men, masculinity and caring. In: Pease, B. and Camilleri, P. (eds.) *Working with men in the human services*. Sydney: Allen & Unwin, pp. 25–33.

Campbell, L. and Carroll, M. (2007) The incomplete revolution: Theorizing gender when studying men who provide care to ageing parents. *Men and Masculinities*, 9(4), pp. 491–508.

Chodorow, N. (1978) *The reproduction of mothering*. Berkeley: University of California Press.

Connell, R. (2005) *Masculinities*. Sydney: Allen and Unwin.

Cree, V. (1996) Why do men care? In: Cavanagh, K. and Cree, V. (eds.) *Working with men: Feminism and social work*. London: Routledge, pp. 65–86.

Doucet, A. (2004) 'It's almost like I have a job, but I don't get paid': Fathers at home reconfiguring work, care and masculinity. *Fathering*, 2(3), pp. 277–303.

Elliott, K. (2015) Caring masculinities: Theorising an emerging concept. *Men and Masculinities*, 19(3), pp. 1–24.

Gartner, M., Schwerma, K. and Beier, S. (2007) *Fostering caring masculinities*. Berlin: Documentation of the German Gender Expert Study.

Gerstel, N. and Gallagher, S. (2001) Men's caregiving: Gender and the contingent character of care. *Gender and Society*, 15(2), pp. 197–217.

Gilligan, C. (1982) *In a different voice: Psychological theory and women's development*. London: Harvard University Press.

Hanlon, N. (2009) Masculinities and affective equality: Love labour and care labour in men's lives. In: Biricik, A. and Hearn, J. (eds.) *Proceedings of deconstructing the hegemony of men and masculinities conference*. GEXcel Work in Progress Report Vol. VI. Linkoping: Linkoping University, pp. 191–200.

Hanlon, N. (2012) *Masculinities, care and equality*. Houndmills: Palgrave.

Holmes, M. (2015) Men's emotions: Heteromasculinity, emotional reflexivity, and intimate relationships. *Men and Masculinities*, 18(2), pp. 176–192.

Lamont, E. (2014) The limited construction of an egalitarian masculinity: College educated men's dating and relationship narratives. *Men and Masculinities*, 18(3), pp. 271–292.

Levtov, R., van der Gaard, N., Green, M., Kaufman, M. and Barker, G. (2015) *Men care: A global fatherhood campaign*. Washington, Rutgers, Save the Children, Sonke Gender Justice and the MenEngage Alliance. Available from: www.men-care.org [Accessed 13 August 2016].

Lynch, K. and Baker, J. (2009) Conclusion. In: Lynch, K., Baker, J. and Lyons, M. (eds.) *Affective equality: Love, care and injustice*. New York: Palgrave Macmillan, pp. 216–236.

MacDougall, G. (1997) Caring: A masculine perspective. *Journal of Advanced Nursing*, 25, pp. 809–813.

McMahon, A. (1999) *Taking care of men: Sexual politics and the public mind*. Cambridge: Cambridge University Press.

Morell, R. and Jewkes, R. (2011) Carework and caring: A path to gender equitable practices among men in South Africa. *International Journal for Equity in Health*, 10(17), pp. 1–10.

Pease, B. (2011) Men in social work: Reproducing or challenging an unequal gender regime? *Affilia: Women and Social Work*, pp. 1–13. Advanced access, doi:10.1177/088 6109911428109911428207.

Pease, B. (2012) The politics of gendered emotions: Disrupting men's emotional investments in privilege. *Australian Journal of Social Issues*, 47(1), pp. 125–140.

Pease, B. (2014) Reconstructing masculinity or ending manhood? The potential and limitations of transforming masculine subjectivities for gender equality. In: Carabi, A. and Armengol, J. (eds.) *Alternative masculinities for a changing world*. New York: Palgrave, pp. 17–34.

Phillips, J. (2007) *Care*. Cambridge: Policy Press.

Robinson, C., Bottorff, J., Pesut, B., Oliffe, J. and Tomlinson, J. (2014) The male face of caregiving: A scoping review of men caring for a person with dementia. *American Journal of Men's Health*, 8(5), pp. 409–426.

Robinson, F. (2010) After liberalism in world politics? Towards an international political theory of care. *Ethics and Social Welfare*, 4(2), pp. 130–144.

Robinson, F. (2015) Care, gender and global social justice: Rethinking ethical globalisation. *Journal of Global Ethics*, 2(1), pp. 5–25.

Ruddick, S. (1989) *Maternal thinking: Towards a politics of peace*. London: Women's Press.

Seidler, V. (2006) *Young men and masculinities: Global cultures and intimate lives*. London: Zed Books.

Sevenhuijsen, S. (2003) The place of care: The relevance of the feminist ethic of care for social policy. *Feminist Theory*, 4(2), pp. 179–197.

Tronto, J. (2013) *Caring democracy: Markets, equality and justice*. New York: New York University Press.

Young, I. (2003) The logic of masculinist protection: Reflections on the current security state. *Signs: Journal of Women in Culture and Society*, 29(1), pp. 1–25.

18 Where is the love?

Meditations on a critical ethics of care and love in social work

Margaret E. Hughes

Introduction

In recent times, the application and experience of care in human services has been the subject of enquiry by practitioners, researchers, clients, the media and the judicial system. It is clearly evident that the vicissitudes of caring need to be changed. Those with a deep desire for progressive and compassionate change have engaged with critical debate and proposed an ethic of care to address both the pragmatic and moral responsibilities of caring. But I ask is this enough, and why do we not acknowledge critical care ethics and aim higher by engaging with the universal notion of love? Love is regarded by some of the wisest and most influential humanitarians as the most powerful and transformative change agent. Its capacity to generate peace, equality, kindness and justice traverses all cultures, all creatures and all environments. Love has no boundaries, and in a world beset by terror, fear, intolerance and suffering offers a personal and global spirit of universal responsibility and transformation. My chapter asks: "Where is the love?" specifically in the context of social work. It explains why love's presence is faint in comparison to the discourse of care, and draws attention to some of the main protagonists who are engaging with the conceptualisation and enactment of love. Finally, I propose an argument for the relevance of love in social work, and I argue that by asking where is the love, we move beyond the limitations of care.

Love is a many-splendored thing

The notion and sentiment of love has been expressed in myriad ways, including but not limited to poetry, songs, tattoos, plays, emails, text messages and reality television shows. Love is mentioned in association with earthly pleasures, inanimate objects and particular situations. It is a word often used in people's vernacular, typically qualified by an additional term to convey its specific meaning, such as *love bite, true love, lost love, love child* and *lovesick*. In the context of the contemporary Western world, love is predominantly individualised, romanticised, emotional and sexualised in nature (Evans, 2002, p. 1). The feminist scholar Mary Evans (2002, p. 22) cautions

> the extent to which the same word is used to cover a multitude of possibilities should also warn us of the conceptual confusion around the idea . . . we love

too much and too widely . . . we have reached a situation where it is difficult to distinguish between different kinds of love.

Centuries ago, the ancient Greeks used the four words *storge, agape, eros* and *philia* to distinguish between different types of love (Lewis, 1960). *Storge* is a type of love aligned with a natural affection, commonly felt by parents for their children or by people towards their pets. *Agape* is a selfless type of love, altruistic and unconditional in nature personified by someone helping a stranger and expecting nothing in return. *Eros* is an exclusive type of love involving passion, often embodied in a physical sexual desire towards another. And *philia* refers to the type of love bestowed on friends in which affection, loyalty and goodwill are enacted for a person's wellbeing. New taxonomies of love have since emerged (Fromm, 1956; Lee, 1977; Berscheid, 2006), with social scientists developing no fewer than 33 scales to measure different dimensions of passionate love (Hatfield, Bensman and Rapson, 2012). Love is now understood to be "a multifaceted phenomenon" (Hatfield et al., 2012, p. 159) with more than one type of love being experienced within the same relationship at any one time (Berscheid, 2006).

Love is also a concept conspicuous in professional discourse. In the nursing literature, love in practice has been identified as love in nursing (Fitzgerald and van Hooft, 2000); tender loving care (Kendrick, 2002); the art of loving (Stickley and Freshwater, 2002); professional love (Rollings, 2008); professional loving care (van Heijst, 2009); and loving-kindness (Seppala, Hutcherson, Nguyen, Doty and Gross, 2014). In nursing contexts, love is valorised: it is an expression of ethics having beneficent intent, and operationalised both as an exceptional quality and as an occupational burden (Rollings, 2008) that extends beyond the role definition of the duty of care (Fitzgerald and van Hooft, 2000). Love is also evident in the social work literature, referred to as listening love (Tillich, 1962); a love of humanity (Morley and Ife, 2002); tough love (Limebury and Shea, 2015); emancipatory praxis (Butot, 2004); and professional loving care (Hermsen and Embregts, 2015). Loving practice is deemed transformative (Westoby and Dowling, 2013, p. 37), emancipatory (Butot, 2004) and the prerequisite for justice (Rimor, 2003, p. 167). Yet the concept of love in the discipline of social work is a notion neither popular nor fashionable (Morley and Ife, 2002, p. 69; Westoby and Dowling, 2013, p. 32). In comparison to the concept of care, love in practice has yet to achieve similar recognition and acceptance despite a growing awareness of negligence and abuse occurring in the care sector of human service organisations (Australian Broadcasting Commission, 2016a; Australian Broadcasting Commission, 2016b; Auerbach, 2016). My chapter illuminates the reasons why love remains on the fringe of social work discourse and examines whether caring in the current age is realistically enough to restore justice, autonomy and rights to the most vulnerable in the world. Building upon the work of previous scholars, my chapter aims to contribute to the small yet authoritative body of critical theory addressing this topic, ultimately claiming love's practical relevance in the contemporary world of social work practice.

Love in a cold climate

Neither love nor loving practice is mentioned in the Australian Association of Social Workers Code of Ethics (Australian Association of Social Workers [AASW], 2010), nor is it found in the Practice Standards (AASW, 2013). Love applied in practice is an idea not new or absent in social work literature, yet the language of love remains faint in comparison to the discourse of care. A reluctance to integrate love into Australian mainstream social work discourse is explained by the following reasons.

Love resides in people's affective domain and is "a language that appeals to our hearts" (Morley and Ife, 2002, p. 69). It is perceived by many to be an ephemeral construct, mysterious in nature and difficult to quantify, implying an inability to think with reason or logic. Because the sciences value objectivity over and above subjectivity, love has yet to find a robust identity in the realm of evidence-based research (Ricketts and Gochros, 1987, p. 1; Morley and Ife, 2002, p. 70). Should love ultimately find a place in this popular interdisciplinary approach to clinical practice, love would be measured and quantified, and risk losing its very essence.

Love may be a theory that some social workers have yet to consider relevant to their profession. Given that the attention given to love is faint in comparison to other theories such as anti-oppressive practice, feminism and an ethics of care, social work education, professional supervision and continuing professional development may have inadvertently neglected to integrate love into its lexicon. Conversely, the term may be consciously resisted because it implies getting too close to a client, and social work training has traditionally encouraged a neutral, safe distance between the client and the worker (Ricketts and Gochros, 1987, p. 11; Bodenheimer, 2011, p. 39).

In the Western world, love is commonly associated with passion, intimacy and sex. Any association with social work may suggest a transgression of boundaries (Morley and Ife, 2002, p. 70) whereby power differentials between workers and clients "raises the spectre of professional impropriety and implies the abuse (typically sexual) of the vulnerable" (Racine, 2014, p. 113). Bodenheimer (2011) highlights the taboo nature of any language of love regarding therapist-client relationships, adding weight to the argument that some practitioners may never incorporate the word love into their practice (other than when referring to clients' lives) because they do not want to risk being considered by others to be unprofessional.

Love requires a commitment to an authentic human relationship arising from a deep compassionate concern (Bilson, 2007, p. 1372). In the current landscape of economic rationalism, neoliberalism and managerialism, social workers – particularly those employed in large organisations – frequently find themselves occupied with doing assessments and managing risks and are "locked into a style of practice that is legalistic, formal, procedural and arm's length" (Jordan, 2001, p. 537). Love is thwarted in "systems that make little use of interpersonal skills" (Jordan, 2001, p. 537) and it is not a language commonly used at a meso level: it is rarely (if ever) explicitly mentioned in policies, evaluations or social reforms. With restructuring, ongoing pressures to reduce costs and increasing workloads

(Ferguson, 2008), social workers may view their aspirations of applying loving practice in certain organisations and political structures doomed to fail and contrary to the mission of the organisation in which they work.

Some social workers may prefer to reserve the term *love* exclusively for their private life, distinguishing between their professional and personal lives. Their individual culture and gender may also shape their attitudes and behaviours, such that masculinist and neoliberal assumptions hinder a person's acceptance of applying loving practice in the workplace. Finally, some social workers will claim not to love everyone. While purposely applying unconditional positive regard (Rogers, 1961, p. 47) as a "positive affective attitude" towards their clients (individuals, families, groups, communities and societies) in compliance with their code of ethics, love is not an action and attitude they want to bestow upon every human being, arguing that caring is enough to do their job professionally.

Is caring enough?

Caring is a popular concept in contemporary society. A range of terms is used to distinguish between the many different types, such as palliative care, foster care, child care and community care. Care is also incorporated into the branding of human service organisations to promote a particular philosophy, such as Anglicare, Baptcare, My Aged Care and Catholic Care. In the text simply titled *Care*, Judith Phillips (2007, p. 1) states: "In many ways it is a nebulous and ambiguous concept and a part of everyday life which is taken for granted." A deeper investigation reveals care's complex and multifaceted nature, showing how it affects people across their lifespan, from childhood, adolescence, midlife and old age (Phillips, 2007).

Much has been written about care. Max van Manen (2002, p. 264) argues that limiting our knowledge to the main literature and theorising about care serves to erode the lived experience, which he calls a "complex moral emotional relation of responsibility". In the experiential context, care is understood by van Manen (2002, p. 266) to be a worry rather than a duty or obligation. He maintains that the more a person cares, the more a person worries, and the stronger the desire is to care for the other. Care may not always be perceived as pleasant and it can be a burden of responsibility, but it is considered to be good. I argue that this type of care cannot operate within certain workplaces because care-as-worry embedded in lived relations of caring are subjugated for other priorities, such as the commercialisation of care (Hermsen, Embregts, Hendriks and Frielink, 2014), reducing costs, concealing malpractice and sometimes violations of human rights. For some disability activists, the term 'care' invites resistance because the concept implies subordination through means of repressing self-determination and autonomy (Hughes, McKie, Hopkins and Watson, 2005, p. 260) for the purpose of advancing others' self-interests.

Care is political and "infused with power" (Keigher, 2000, p. 84). In circumstances where others care for people, the relationship is inherently unequal. In some instances, care is done to promote self-interest. Social work has had a long conflicted and oppressive history, with the provision of care used to regulate, manage, govern and dominate individuals, groups, families and communities. Recent examples include Australia's First Nations peoples, whose children were stolen during the nineteenth and twentieth centuries by agents of governments for the purpose of assimilating children into mainstream Australia, and unmarried, young mothers whose babies were taken and adopted out to married couples.

In a response to a critique of the dominant models of care particularly in terms of what constitutes a caring relationship, Joan Tronto (1993) developed a moral theory seen through a feminist lens known as an ethics of care. This theory conceptualised care as a process with five different stages known as attentiveness, responsibility, competence, responsiveness and integrity (Tronto, 1993, p. 127). Tronto claimed that the final stage of integrity was only possible by the first four stages of care coalescing to form an integrated whole (Tronto, 1993, p. 136). Tronto (1993, p. 126) described an ethics of care as "a practice rather than a set of rules or principles" which demands a "general habit of mind" (1993, p. 127). In relational care work, this general habit of mind must refer to the political aspect because unequal power between a social worker and a client always has the potential to result in oppression.

Despite development in knowledge, a widening gap persists between care as theory and care as practice. Providing care for the most vulnerable in society continues to be deeply problematic, highlighted in the Australian context by reports of abuse, violation and in some instances death occurring in a range of residential care facilities, foster care, aged care, mental health facilities and youth and refugee detention centres. Being a recipient of care does not guarantee a person's wellbeing and can in reality reduce a person's safety. In 2014, the director of the Centre for Child Trauma Recovery at the Australian Berry Street Childhood Institute stated that children who have been placed in substitute care because of being traumatised and abused can only learn how to love by having therapeutic carers who demonstrate love (Rose, 2014, p. 4). Care alone is not enough to promote social change.

The notion of 'compassionate care' has been promoted in response to the underperformance of care. This concept is rapidly gaining traction and is considered to be an essential ingredient for a caring, humane relationship. It combines characteristics and virtues such as respect, kindness, patience and social empathy, involving doing something for another person rather than merely observing from a distance (Limebury and Shea, 2015) and feeling sympathy. In a study I undertook with 28 people who attended to the death and final arrangements of a significant other who died at home from a life-limiting illness (Hughes, 2009), I discovered that 'compassionate love' operated as a number of interdependent practices which enabled the expression of human qualities of care. While focusing on carers rather than professionals, I recognised that compassionate love was the source that guided and sustained people's endeavours, prevailing over the many challenges confronting people at end of life. Professionals have much to learn from the wisdom and insights of clients, and I realised from studying people in the community who used compassionate love that "the rewards are rich and the journey is transformative" (Hughes, 2009, p. 283).

Compassion is a concept that has relevance to all vulnerable populations such as people with addictions, people in prison, people who are homeless, refugees, asylum seekers and people who are unemployed. Allan Kellehear, the sociologist and author of *Compassionate Cities* (2005), promotes the idea of compassion at end-of-life being a holistic and ecological idea, an ethical imperative for health and a response to the concern with the universality of loss (Kellehear, 2005, p. 43). He (2005, p. 432) maintains that a compassionate approach is essentially the foundation of social empathy which requires mutual sharing rather than caring.

Clients and workers value compassionate care in the health care sector as it improves health care and patients' care experiences (Lown, Rosen and Marttila, 2011; Seppala et al., 2014), but concurrent data highlight the erosion of social empathy over time. Some studies have reported that the more experienced clinicians in the health care sector demonstrate less empathy (Nunes, Williams, Sa and Stevenson, 2011; Williams et al., 2015), explained by workers transitioning from ideas of idealism to realism, a steadily increasing workload and a response to additional responsibilities. Not even in the company of compassion will caring always be enough to help transform lives. It is under such circumstances that I argue loving practice can advance a critical ethics of care.

Where is the love in social work?

Loving practice appeared in the social work literature more than half a century ago. In 1962, an American academic journal published a paper penned by Paul Tillich, titled "The Philosophy of Social Work", in which he illuminated the powerful and transformative role of love while listening to clients during face-to-face interactions. In the next decade, Paulo Freire's groundbreaking work titled *Pedagogy of the Oppressed* (1972) made bold declaration to the notion of love embedded in the practice of dialogue, becoming highly influential in the field of social work education. In 1987, Wendell Ricketts and Harvey Gochros edited a volume in the *Journal of Social Work and Human Sexuality* titled "Intimate Relationships: Some Social Work Perspectives on Love" in which they examined three types of love: love of self, love towards others, and love between client and therapist. At the turn of this century, an article published by the journal *Australian Social Work* and written by Louise Morley and Jim Ife titled "Social Work and a Love of Humanity" (Morley and Ife, 2002), reignited international interest in love, adding fuel to the notion that love was an essential way of working with people in their environments. Morley and Ife claimed that to adopt this way of working required a stance that was inherently radical. Since 2002, love has been used as the focus for a master's dissertation investigating practitioners' conceptualisations of love in critical social work practice (Butot, 2004), and most recently in 2016, the core concept of love was examined by final year social work students at the University of Tasmania in the dialogical community development framework proposed by Peter Westoby and Gerard Dowling (2013). Sufficient evidence exists that love is neither absent nor new in the field of social work, and a compelling body of knowledge has been developing across the decades in different countries.

Social workers promoting the concept of love argue to adopt love into social work practice requires not only purposeful action (Morley and Ife, 2002, p. 71) but also an ethical, political and radical stance (Morley and Ife, 2002; Butot, 2004; Bilson, 2007). Peter Westoby and Gerard Dowling maintain that love in community practice "develops from the very beginning of an encounter" (2013, p. 35) requiring a "reflexive journey" (2013, p. 36) in which workers must move "away from egocentricity towards other-orientedness" (2013, p. 36). Community practice applied in social work is perceived as "a dynamic of awakened love invoked through a soulful movement that takes the mutuality of I and other very seriously" (Westoby and Dowling, 2013, p. 36). It evolves through a process of "deepening participation" (2013, p. 39).

Maaike Hermsen and Petri Embregts (2015, p. 825) examined how reflective processes in social work education and practice can be implemented through professional loving care by focusing on "reciprocity in relationships and relational capacity in institutional contexts". Michele Butot (2004) concluded from her empirical study of social workers in Canada that a critical emancipatory conceptualisation of love in social work practice comprised deep presence and engagement, recognition of intrinsic value, sacredness and interconnection, open-heartedness, compassionate challenge and a willingness not to know. She found that while love was not considered to be the only context of their practice, love was essential to their ways of perceiving, being and doing (Butot, 2004, p. 14). Using an alternative theory developed by the biologist Humberto Maturana known as the biology of cognition, Andy Bilson argues that love is "central to ethical action" and is "the emotional underpinning of social coexistence" (Bilson, 2007, p. 1379). Common to all those across the ages who promote the concept of love in social work practice is the notion that love can only be realised by its expression in relation to another. Some theorists propose that this is done using an ethical lens while others claim it is a philosophy or a way of life. I argue that love is a valid and legitimate practice to care for others regardless of race, class, age, sexuality, ethnicity and gender, while also caring for oneself.

Conclusion: adopting a framework of love in social work practice

Although care and compassion are necessities for a humane society, they fall short in achieving human rights and social justice especially for the most vulnerable in our society. Compassionate care can be demonstrated without love, but love can never be practised without compassionate care. Adopting a framework of love requires a commitment to understand what loving practice means. It is crucial to be able to qualify the concept of loving practice in social work and explain how it is informed by a body of knowledge that can inform a critical ethics of care.

Love embodied in social work practice is an art and a skill. I believe at the bedrock of professional loving practice is the work of Erich Fromm. His ideas appeal to me because they can be applied theoretically and experientially, both professionally and personally, thereby making interactions with all others authentic, genuine and congruent. In his seminal text titled *The Art of Loving* (1956), Fromm argued that love is an art, an activity, an attitude and an act of faith (1956, pp. 5, 22, 46, 128) requiring discipline, concentration, patience, supreme concern and the need to be sensitive to oneself (1956, pp. 109–115). Fromm (1956, p. 32) insisted that the elements common to different forms of love are care, respect, responsibility and knowledge, all of which are mutually interdependent. He further added that love required the acquisition and development of reason, humility, faith, courage and activity (1956, pp. 120–128). Perhaps most significantly to the field of social work, he argued that love had to have a connection with the social realm by the principle of fairness (Fromm, 1956, p. 129).

Fromm's theory informs us that loving practice is hard work. It does not equate to being sentimental, gullible or being prone to making decisions that reap immediate gratification. Nor does loving practice mean avoiding challenging behaviours or attitudes that create oppression, social injustice or human violation. Being loving is being deeply mindful of oneself and others and valuing the interdependency of people and their environments, including social justice and human rights.

Tillich (1962, p. 15) advised that "this love is critical as well as accepting and it is able to transform what it loves." Limebury and Shea (2015, p. 8) compound this idea by applying the term 'tough love'. They state:

> At the heart of compassion is the element of 'action' and this may sometimes involve perhaps a 'tough love' approach in order to encourage independence. Such an approach is based on underlying care and a desire to help the individual succeed in life in the longer term.

This concept is not to be confused with presumed loving relationships in which negligence and abuse occurs – for example, a relationship of domestic violence in which a perpetrator of violence murders his partner because he states he loves her too much and cannot accept her decision to leave the relationship. Control and coercion for self-gratification or vested interests are not acts of love when Fromm's theory is applied.

Understanding love in this context means that loving practice is a challenge and a daily aspiration. Enacting love will always be difficult because it is human nature to want to walk away from discomfort, suffering or frustration. Operating from a position of love means being willing to listen, which Tillich (1962) explains is to refrain from acting mechanically. It requires an acknowledgement of difference and a respect for diversity and, above all, it demands participation sometimes when situated in a place of discomfort. To work with love as the central principle in social work requires the fusion of philosophy, attitude and action, and only then can we start moving beyond the limitations of care.

References

Auerbach, T. (2016) Almost one in 10 children in residential care homes in NSW were sexually abused in a single year, shocking new figures reveal. *Daily Telegraph* [online], March 14. Available from: www.dailytelegraph.com.au/news/nsw/almost-one-in-10-children-in-residential-care-homes-in-nsw-were-sexually-abused-in-a-single-year-shocking-new-figures-reveal/news-story/5d0699c909b60e88d84be7b969a2e90a [Accessed 21 October, 2016].

Australian Association of Social Work (AASW). (2010) *Code of ethics*. Canberra: AASW.

Australian Association of Social Work (AASW). (2013) *Practice standards*. Canberra: AASW.

Australian Broadcasting Commission. (2016a) *Secret camera catches abuse of elderly man in nursing home including attempted 'suffocation'*. [Television]. Australia: ABC, 25th July, 19.30.

Australian Broadcasting Commission. (2016b) *Broken homes: On the frontline of Australia's child protection crisis*. [Television]. Australia: ABC, 14th November, 20.30.

Berscheid, E. (2006) Searching for the meaning of love. In: Sternberg, R.J. and Weis, K. (eds.) *The new psychology of love*. New Haven, CT: Yale University Press, pp. 171–183.

Bilson, A. (2007) Promoting compassionate concern in social work: Reflections on ethics, biology and love. *British Journal of Social Work*, 37(8), pp. 1371–1386.

Bodenheimer, D. (2011) An examination of the historical and current perceptions of love in the psychotherapeutic dyad. *Clinical Social Work Journal*, 39(1), pp. 39–49.

Butot, M.C. (2004) *'Love as emancipatory praxis': An exploration of practitioners' conceptualisations of love in critical social work practice*. Masters research, University of Victoria, Canada.

Evans, M. (2002) *Love: An unromantic discussion*. Cambridge: Polity Press.

Ferguson, I. (2008) *Reclaiming social work: Challenging neoliberalism and promoting social justice*. Thousand Oaks, CA: Sage.

Fitzgerald, L. and van Hooft, S. (2000) A Socratic dialogue on the question 'What is love in nursing?' *Nursing Ethics*, 7(6), pp. 481–491.

Freire, P. (1972) *Pedagogy of the oppressed*. London: Penguin Books.

Fromm, E. (1956) *The art of loving*. New York: Harper and Row.

Hatfield, E., Bensman, L. and Rapson, R.L. (2012) A brief history of social scientists' attempts to measure passionate love. *Journal of Social and Personal Relationships*, 29(2), pp. 143–164.

Hermsen, M. and Embregts, P. (2015) An explorative study of the place of the ethics of care and reflective practice in social work education and practice. *Social Work Education*, 34(7), pp. 815–828.

Hermsen, M.A., Embregts, P.J.C.M., Hendriks, A.H.C. and Frielink, N. (2014) The human degree of care. Professional loving care for people with a mild intellectual disability: An explorative study. *Journal of Intellectual Disability Research*, 58(3), pp. 221–232.

Hughes, B., McKie, L., Hopkins, D. and Watson, N. (2005) Love's labours lost? Feminism, the disabled people's movement and an ethic of care. *Sociology*, 39(2), pp. 259–275.

Hughes, M. (2009) *The lived experience of compassionate love at end of life*. Doctor of philosophy research, University of Tasmania, Australia.

Jordan, B.J. (2001) Tough love: Social work, social exclusion and the third way. *British Journal of Social Work*, 31, pp. 527–546.

Keigher, S.M. (2000) The challenge of caring in a capitalist world. *Health and Social Work*, 25(2), pp. 83–86.

Kellehear, A. (2005) *Compassionate cities: Public health and end-of-life care*. London: Routledge.

Kendrick, K.D. (2002) 'Tender loving care' as a relational ethic in nursing practice. *Nursing Ethics*, 9(3), pp. 291–300.

Lee, J.A. (1977) A typology of styles of loving. *Personality and Social Psychology Bulletin*, 3, pp. 173–182.

Lewis, C.S. (1960) *The four loves*. London: Geffrey Bles.

Limebury, J. and Shea, S. (2015) The role of compassion and 'tough love' in caring for and supporting the homeless: Experiences from Catching Lives, Canterbury, UK. *Journal of Compassionate Health Care*, 2(7), pp. 1–9.

Lown, B.A., Rosen, J. and Marttila, J. (2011) An agenda for improving compassionate care: A survey shows about half of patients say such care is missing. *Health Affairs*, 30, pp. 1772–1778.

Morley, L. and Ife, J. (2002) Social work and a love of humanity. *Australian Social Work*, 55(1), pp. 69–77.

Nunes, P., Williams, S., Sa, B. and Stevenson, K. (2011) A study of empathy decline in students from five health disciplines during their first year of training. *International Journal of Medical Education*, 2, pp. 12–17.

Phillips, J. (2007) *Care*. Cambridge: Polity Press.

Racine, C. (2014) Loving in the context of community mental health practice: A clinical case study and reflection on mystical experience. *Mental Health, Religion & Culture*, 17(2), pp. 109–121.

Ricketts, W. and Gochros, H.L. (1987) What's love got to do with it? In: Ricketts, W. and Gochros, H.L. (eds.) *Intimate relationships: Some social work perspectives on love*. Cambridge: Haworth Press, pp. 1–14.

Rimor, M. (2003) If love then justice. *Sociological Inquiry*, 73(2), pp. 167–176.

Rogers, C.R. (1961) *On becoming a person: A therapist's view of psychotherapy*. New York: Houghton Mifflin.

Rollings, J.C. (2008) Professional love in palliative nursing: An exceptional quality or an occupational burden? *International Journal of Human Caring*, 12(3), pp. 53–56.

Rose, R. (2014) What's love got to do with it? *Developing Practice*, 40, pp. 3–5.

Seppala, E.M., Hutcherson, C.A., Nguyen, D.T.H., Doty, J.R. and Gross, J.J. (2014) Loving-kindness meditation: A tool to improve healthcare provider compassion, resilience and patient care. *Journal of Compassionate Care*, 1(5), pp. 1–9.

Stickley, T. and Freshwater, D. (2002) The art of loving and the therapeutic relationship. *Nursing Inquiry*, 9(4), pp. 250–256.

Tillich, P. (1962) The philosophy of social work. *Social Service Review*, 36(1), pp. 13–16.

Tronto, J. (1993) *Moral boundaries: A political argument for an ethic of care*. London: Routledge.

Van Heijst, A. (2009) Professional loving care and the bearable heaviness of being. In: Lindemann, H., Verkerk, M. and Urban Walker, M. (eds.) *Naturalised bioethics: Towards responsible knowing and practice*. Cambridge: Cambridge University Press, pp. 199–217.

Van Manen, M. (2002) Care-as-worry or 'Don't worry be happy'. *Qualitative Health Research: An International Interdisciplinary Journal*, 12(2), pp. 264–280.

Westoby, P. and Dowling, G. (2013) *Theory and practice of dialogical community development: International perspectives*. London: Routledge.

Williams, B., Brown, T., McKenna, L., Palermo, C., Morgan, P., Nestel, D., Brightwall, R., Gilbert-Hunt, R., Stagnitti, K., Olaussen, A. and Wright, C. (2015) Student empathy levels across 12 medical and health professions: An interventional study. *Journal of Compassionate Care*, 2(4). doi:10.1186/s40639-015-0013-4.

19 Re-working self-care

From individual to collective responsibility through a critical ethics of care

Chris Wever and Simone Zell

Introduction

Social workers respond on a daily basis to the effects of trauma and societal injustice, disadvantage and marginalisation. Workers who bring a passionate, ethical commitment to systems change and to standing in solidarity with people and communities often do so despite human service organisational contexts and broader policy directives that are unsupportive of such person- and justice-oriented practice. The impact of this work over time can be extreme and is often professionally constructed as burnout. Self-care is then promoted as an antidote to such burnout or worker fatigue. We question the constructs of both burnout and self-care that give rise to the idea that if workers look after themselves well enough, they will not be severely impacted by the injustices, clients' trauma or the workplace itself. Interventions that advocate self-care to circumvent or alleviate burnout pathologise workers and invisibilise organisational and other contexts of the work. Individual responsibility is highlighted, systems that are under-resourced and deeply flawed escape scrutiny, and collective responsibility and care for the other are not prioritised. We advocate a more relational approach to the wellbeing of workers. We suggest that practices that build cultures of collective care and acknowledgement in the workplace can contribute to a conscious, critical and sometimes transformational social work response to the divisive effects of organisational oppression and injustice.

The idea of burnout in the context of human services work

There is little denying that human services work can take its toll. With the construct of 'burnout' endemic across social work and other human services contexts, professional literature abounds stressing the myriad risks for workers who practice in contexts saturated with trauma and injustice. The nature of trauma itself is generally understood as vicariously impacting most significantly on those workers who care deeply about their clients and about enabling social justice in their work. In addition, the privileges that accompany middle-class professional social workers' private lives reflect the inequities that contribute to the lives of many of their clients. Workers commonly express the impact on them of spending the morning working with a young person caught in the desperation of drugs, home-lessness, abuse and poverty, and then over lunch arranging a family holiday. The nature of trauma itself, as well as the nature of social work as a profession, means that workers bear on a daily basis often unseen effects of the work. Unacknowl-edged, these effects can paralyse or deplete – and sometimes defeat – those who have given their heart and their soul to their work.

The residue of trauma and structural oppression operating in clients' lives is only one factor that contributes to the experience of 'burnout' for workers. Also significant are the neoliberal contexts of human services work and the often unquestioned traditional Western psychological constructs that define and give meaning to the 'burnout' experience (Mathieu, 2015).

Terms that describe workers who 'burn out' vary across disciplines and pro-fessional discourses, and include traumatic stress, vicarious trauma, secondary traumatic stress, compassion fatigue, empathic stress disorder, emotional over-load and workplace stress. These terms are invoked to describe and explain the profound physical symptoms and emotional turmoil that can prevent human ser-vices and other workers from continuing to function effectively. These terms are context-neutral and individualistic. The implication is that some people can mea-sure up to the work, and some cannot. From vicarious trauma to workplace stress, these terms imply essential internal inadequacies of the individual: workers are sent to psychiatrists, psychologists, human resource and rehabilitation special-ists for assessment, diagnosis and possible medication, counselling and focused psychological strategies to fix them. This is deficit psychology, founded in deficit discourse, where problems are typically situated as internal to individual people (Gergen, 1994, 2009a; Madigan, 2012; Strong, 2012; Wever, 2015).

While there is no denying that workers are sometimes impacted in profound and harmful ways by the myriad aspects of human services work, individualising the effects of the work – claiming that a worker has a condition called burnout or compassion fatigue – shines the light on the personal inadequacies of each individual worker, and contributes to obscuring the social conditions and the organisational restraints that can weigh so heavily in many working contexts (Reynolds, 2011).

The organisational contexts of human service work have a constitutive influ-ence on the workers they employ. Workers sometimes experience being forced to act in ways that contradict their personal and professional ethics. One worker, reflecting on his work with asylum seekers in the external supervision context, said to me (Chris): "You're not just fighting the political systems that perpetu-ate the wrongs; you're fighting the organisations too that have been colonised by them."

Power structures, management systems, bureaucratic processes and general organisational cultures impact on workers every day, with sometimes profound effects on their wellbeing, personal agency and even the will to continue. Over two decades I (Chris) have supervised many workers in a wide range of services – child protection, sexual assault and trauma services, asylum seeker and migrant support services, schools, prisons and other places of detention, remote Aboriginal communities and the Pacific Islands. Through many hundreds of conversations, I have noticed that the nature of workers' expressed concerns has changed over time. Two decades ago, workers talked more with me about their interventions with their clients, the things they had to hear, to bear, the things they couldn't change, the ways they kept trying nonetheless, the times of joy and their meaning. But in recent years workers are far more concerned in the supervision context about the impact of organisational issues on them and their work – the organisational context of their work. "It's not the clients. They keep me sane. It's what's going on at work!" is an expression I've heard over and over again. So, what might be some of the factors that have contributed to this shift over recent decades?

Political bodies are issuing increasingly limited funding as, arguably, Western culture increases its expectations of professional culture while marginalised groups are valued less and less. Underfunded programs, competitive tendering, restrictive funding guidelines, competition and uncertainty, and constant measurement and evaluation have become part of the fabric of human services work. In addition, risk practices, and "the politics of fear" (Stanford, 2010, p. 1065) have permeated social work contexts where "risk dominates work process design" (Beddoe, 2010, p. 1282). Standard organisational processes include putting workers under the microscope in the guise of 'critical analysis', 'best practice', 'effectiveness and efficiency', and 'meeting key performance indicators'. This objective measuring of workers and the work has powerful effects throughout the system – felt in very real ways by workers in management roles and those at the coal-face (Stanford, 2011; Mathieu, 2015). Expectations and pressures, performance appraisals, the constant measuring of outcomes and outputs, the evaluation of everything, the gaze, more evaluation, and time sheets to measure every moment of the day are an everyday reality for many workers. Workers regularly speak with me (Chris) in the external supervision context about the cultures of fear, silence, criticism, negativity, professional distance, surveillance and the inevitable self-surveillance that have them feeling alienated and unskilled.

These are some of many powerful contextual factors in human service organisations that contribute to workers feeling drained and burnt out, but nonetheless the culture of individual blame persists (Mathieu, 2015). In our experience, human service organisation employees, at all levels, are most often people who want to make a difference – and they do. Yet in the shadows of individualistic deficit-oriented psychology (Gergen, 2009a), workers at all organisational levels look to each other to find the source of the problems. The past 20 years have seen the emergence of a wide range of constructs such as troubled working relationships, micromanagement, workplace psychopaths, difficult workers, and stressed and burnt out workers. Individual workers are thus labelled and pathologised, invited into the policing of their own and others' lives (Foucault, 1977; White and Epston, 1990). This camouflages the impact that organisational and political systems have on the work and the workers. The root cause of the problems is located in individual people.

Self-care as an antidote for burnout

Constructs of burnout have become embedded in social work theory and practice over recent decades, and with them, the challenge to workers to undertake the self-care that promises some immunity to the effects of social work practice. Organisations investing in self-care workshops inadvertently underline the message that better work-life balance means that workers will not be so overwhelmed with the work, the conditions of the work and their clients' trauma. Proliferating professional development workshops teaching self-care have had, however, little impact on deeply affected workers (Mathieu, 2015).

We believe the idea of self-care as an antidote for burnout is an ever-present, unquestioned truth in most professional social work contexts. To counter the effects of the work, workers are cautioned to do ever better self-care, and courses are developed offering, for example, assistance with developing 'personal wellness plans'. The promise is that good-enough self-care can somehow render workers less vulnerable to the effects of the trauma and social injustice, and the associated grief, powerlessness, helplessness and pain they meet every day operating in the lives of their clients.

There is little denying that workers have a responsibility to look after themselves to be able to stay in the work and remain functional and well in the work. But critics echo the thoughts of many working professionals that self-care can also seem extremely self-indulgent and limited given the contexts of despair in which social work is often practiced. Reynolds suggests:

> Burnout constructs sound like we're toys with disposable batteries that are used up. As if we're not doing enough yoga or drinking enough water. . . . I do yoga and drink water but self-care is not enough to offset the issues of poverty, violence and basic dignity people struggle with.
>
> (Reynolds, 2011, p. 29)

Self-care constructs place the responsibility of managing the effects of social, cultural and organisational injustices squarely on the individual worker. Better self-care, workers are told, will assist them to better bear the effects of workplace injustice. Self-care is advocated to address the effects of trauma. This is despite decades of understanding that legacies of trauma have much greater impact when workers are afforded insufficient support, debriefing, reflection and meaningful supervision time (Kulkarni, 2013). Self-care is promoted as a response to exhaustion, but that exhaustion has often emanated from too high organisational expectations. Self-care is prescribed in relation to the sense of helplessness experienced by workers in the face of societally created pain and injustice, despite understandings that the formal promotion of work-time contexts for reflection can have powerful effects where workers are affirmed in their ongoing commitment and acknowledged for their work (Reynolds, 2011).

Activism and policy change in organisations and funding bodies are required if things are going to change, yet the self-care paradigm locates responsibility with individuals. Workers are told to practise better self-care while the systems that perpetuate the injustices remain unchallenged and individual workers, unable to offset the effects of their work, are left struggling with their perceived incompetence, lack of skill and professional inadequacies. 'Professional self-doubt' is a term frequently coined in my external supervision work as many, many workers attempt to name the effects of this individualising of huge, societal problems where the problem has become the worker. So often,

> we experience our work as shovelling water. We're working harder and working harder isn't working. The smell of a particularly individual incompetence begins to creep in. This is the dirty work of isolation.
>
> (Reynolds, 2011, p. 31)

Isolation in the work renders workers vulnerable to the workings and gaze of modern professionalism where 'real' knowledge is located in the unread books and 'real' feedback comes from managers and supervisors (White, 1997). When discourses of burnout and self-care are invoked, when workers are blamed and rendered individually responsible for the legacies of the work upon them, workers are pathologised in powerful ways.

Care of each other and acknowledgement in practice

The idea that human services work becomes more sustainable when workers share a collective responsibility for each other's wellbeing both in the work, and in the organisational contexts they work in, is not new (Reynolds, 2011; Kulkarni, 2013; Mathieu, 2015). Indeed, workers often talk about the camaraderie that assists them to continue to practise, and practise well, in high-stress environments and compromised systems where increasing demands and diminishing resources have particularly negative effects on workers and morale. There are many ways that a critical ethics of care can be intentionally structured into organisational and collegial practice.

Social workers are familiar with these concepts. Foundational to social work is how individuals are impacted by their opportunities and environments and how changes in systems can improve people's lives, including those of workers and managers. Alongside the self-care movement, we call for a movement of caring for and acknowledging each other in human service organisations. Social workers, informed by a critical ethics of care, are well-placed and suitably skilled to work together to transform organisations into more nurturing and sustaining environments.

Looking back over 20 years working in community and health services, policy and management I (Simone) am happy to say there were times that my workplaces were supportive and acknowledging. I could see I was part of a team making a difference and my colleagues and I felt valued and supported in the work. A combination of factors influenced my experience: positive and open leadership, the team mix, more realistic workloads and a culture where respectful treatment of each other was the norm. In other workplaces, however, I have felt overwhelmed by the sheer amount and complexity of the work, exacerbated by a lack of support from management, conflict with other workers, isolation and exhaustion. To get through these times, my colleagues and I searched for strategies to take better care of ourselves, so we could continue to turn up at work and do our jobs well. I remember making a joke that we required a 'crisis self-care intervention'! Unfortunately, no amount of extreme-radical-self-care strategies or emergency meditation seemed to help. We were dealing with the futility of applying individually focused strategies in the face of systemic issues.

Advocating that people need to be educated in how to produce relationships founded upon love, nurturing and solidarity, Lynch, Lyons and Cantillon (2007, p. 11) refer to

> the inevitability of interdependency . . . in workplaces, in public organisations, in voluntary groups . . . While it is obvious that we cannot flourish personally without support, encouragement and affirmation, even in our paid work lives we can only flourish fully if we work with others who are nurtured, fed and supported so they are willing and able to work.

To re-work the idea of self-care, we will explore what it might look like to extend responsibility from the self to the collective, and to build working environments where shared responsibility for acknowledging, caring for and supporting each other is the norm. Such environments of collective responsibility could support managers to be more accountable to their employees, enable supportive and reflective supervision practices, and encourage colleagues and teams to be active participants in creating nurturing workplaces. We suggest that these ways of being can be embedded into organisations.

Building cultures of collective care and acknowledgement

We believe workers and managers contribute to a critical ethics of care when particular practices of acknowledgement and caring for each other are intentionally structured into organisational and collegial practice. Our model is illustrated in Figure 19.1.

Acknowledgement in everyday practice

Encouragement, support, affirmation and acknowledgement assist workers to reflect on what is important to them, how they want to be as workers, why they want to make a difference, the powerful factors that get in the way of being able to make that difference, and the differences they make nonetheless. Such professional reflexivity can be most effective in contexts where workers share together and are encouraged to respect each other's knowledges and skills, believe in their professional purpose and know when there are powerful forces preventing them from their preferred practice.

Figure 19.1 Building cultures of collective care and acknowledgement

Practices of collectively sustaining each other in the work can be structured regularly and repeatedly into normal team and management processes and contribute to growing a culture of acknowledgement throughout an organisation. This kind of acknowledgement is at once uncomplicated and complex. One worker described to me (Chris), in a supervision conversation, the profound impact upon her working life when her manager regularly stopped by her desk with simple words thanking her for her work. This humble act had her feeling deeply honoured and professionally respected. Simone experienced a workplace practice where workers announced a 'standing ovation' and a statement of acknowledgement to each other whenever they wanted to celebrate the work, big or small, of a colleague or the team.

Such acknowledgement involves workers and managers letting go of practices of judgment and criticism and actively looking for what can be acknowledged and affirmed in the other. It invites an appreciation of the other that is expressed in words, out loud, or in an email, a group email, or via an announcement. It requires workers to take a position of genuine, non-patronising preparedness to honour some aspect of the other. It emanates from a willingness to appreciate and freely celebrate difference in a Western culture that is colonising and obsessed with what is right and what is truth. If truth is about eliminating difference, then acknowledgement of the other involves a letting go of truth. Objectivity is not acknowledgement. Acknowledgement of otherness involves a mindfulness of the difference between secretly trying to convert the other and the appreciation of their difference. It is not covertly manipulating the other, trying to be nice, or talking the other person round, aiming for sameness. It is a celebration of the diversity of the other.

This kind of acknowledgement, this looking after the other, can contribute to the sometimes transformative construction of the other. A social constructionist perspective where we help make each other as people draws on ideas of relational being (Gergen, 2009b) and invites workers to be mindful that each time we speak or act we have some effect on the other and assist in shaping the other. Regular workplace communications can often focus primarily on problems rather than the development of preferred ways of being (White, 2007). The ethical responsibility of those practising acknowledgement is to locate the preferred ways of being of the other and assist in bringing that into being.

A commitment to practices of acknowledgement that are founded upon a critical ethics of care can be useful also in addressing workplace issues throughout the human services. Such practices include a refusal to construct broad contextual issues as individual failings, understanding that when the worker is constructed as the problem, then the worker is assisted in becoming the problem and the problem grows. A commitment to practices that assist in building a preferred identity of the other involves the externalisation of the issues and an invitation into collective endeavour in which everyone will emerge a little different. When we honour each other we all grow together. In our experience, there is a connection between the spaces that are made for acknowledgement and how power is used to create them, and the development of hope and worker wellbeing.

Care in management and supervision

It is generally accepted that workers perform better when they are acknowledged and supported well in their work. Furthermore, managers who take time to genuinely acknowledge and enquire into workers' experience can actually contribute to worker wellbeing. These ideas appear self-evident and seemingly easy, yet there are significant factors that restrain their practice, including the operations of power that impact profoundly on whose voices are privileged, what those voices can say and how they are heard in organisational contexts (Tamasese and Waldegrave, 1993).

Traditional organisational structures hold workers accountable to the managers, team leaders and executives with higher positions in the hierarchy. In effect, those with less privilege, voice and visibility are held accountable to those with greater privilege, voice and visibility. Such accountability structures reinforce and collude with the inequities of the status quo and obscure the politics of power within organisations. Appropriate workplace practice is defined by those with greater status and measured by those with greater status. Workers' knowledges and experiential learnings are often subjugated and unheard. Traditional accountability procedures are not focused on critical appraisal of the actions of those with greater status and their effects upon those with lesser status. Workers are often left floundering, pathologised and questioning their understandings, or outraged and refusing to engage.

An alternative accountability invites those who hold greater authority and legitimated power to make themselves accountable for their use of that power to those who most feel the effects of it. This idea is founded on the idea that dominant groups cannot expect to gain total awareness of the effects of their actions without enquiring into the experience of the group rendered less visible by the very practices of power themselves (Hall, 1994; Pease, 2010). Kiwi Tamasese and others at The Family Centre in New Zealand, a family therapy and research centre, spent years and many resources establishing and researching organisational practices where these often difficult kinds of conversations can happen in careful, honest and respectful ways (Tamasese and Waldegrave, 1993). Structured into their organisation were meetings of management groups with staff groups, men with women, and Pakeha with Maori people – where groups with greater status and privilege asked for feedback about their exercise of power with groups with lesser status and privilege. Such alternative practices of power indicate a profound care of the other, structured into organisational process that can assist managers and team leaders to practise humble leadership in the acknowledgement, affirmation and encouragement of workers in ways that have real meaning and real effect.

Structured care for workers and managers also has a place in the supervision context. For over two decades of independent narrative practice I (Chris) have supported workers with external professional supervision. Intentional in this work has been built-in support, encouragement, affirmation, acknowledgement and a high regard for workers' practice with their clients and in their employing organisation. Workers frequently indicate that their organisational supervision is either non-existent, purely administrative or influenced by a critical, evaluative gaze. Their experience of narrative supervision external to the organisation is usually met with relief and enthusiasm. The following describes the kind of reflective social work supervision that could be offered in organisations or accessed externally. It is an approach to supervision that is less evaluative and more informed by an ethic of care for both the worker and the work. The challenge for organisational supervisors is to prioritise reflective supervision and its possibilities over administrative enquiries.

Such reflective supervision can be conceived as an invitation for workers to situate their work in its various personal, political, organisational and professional contexts, with a view to the co-construction of stories of preferred practice, identifying together the particular discourses, values and principles which inform those preferred ways of working and which can inform future practice. Exploration of preferred ways of working can be profoundly honouring of workers themselves, the people they work with and the organisational structures, protocols and policies which support that work.

Supervision that supports the construction of practice wisdom can involve exposing the obstacles that might prevent a worker from learning from different situations. It can be hard, for example, for a worker to appreciate her practice when she is worn out from committed effort, worn down by workplace politics, controlled by ideas and beliefs no longer useful, or in the grip of self-doubt, frustration or super-critical evaluation. Supportive supervisors can listen, try to understand and assist workers to identify these obstacles, their effects and the discourses that give them power, in order that they can reengage with the aspects of themselves and their work which are useful, productive, reliable, sometimes sacred, sometimes brilliant.

Supportive supervision can be especially transformative where a group of workers join together with or without a supervisor in a peer consultative process using an outsider witnessing structure (White, 1995, 1997, 2007). Some of the group members form a witnessing or listening group which has the task of witnessing a conversation among the others and listening for meaningful aspects, themes or expressions. The witnessing group then has its own conversation giving voice to what it has heard. This becomes a retelling of the more useful and meaningful aspects of the first conversation. Such supervision is often a very moving and beautiful experience founded upon structured acknowledgement and a collective responsibility for the process and for each other. I (Simone) am part of a group of seven social workers from a mix of agencies for whom supportive supervision has been an empowering experience. We are social workers in management roles who, critical of managerialism, aspire to lead with humility, accountability and in support of socially just and participatory practices. Aware that our current political and organisational contexts present us with challenges, frustrations and stresses (Baines and van den Broek, 2016), we have been meeting for external group supervision with Chris over the past three years. One shared frustration was the onerous and wasteful bureaucratic processes and requirements – externalised as 'stupid' – that impeded the work of our teams. Over time the group process moved from debriefing in exasperation to the sharing of various ways of responding in different contexts and an enhanced sense of power and possibility. This shared connection and meaning-making has been an empowering and useful experience, helping each of us to stand up, respond critically and adapt in our specific contexts.

Structured spaces for collective care

Workplace spaces can be intentionally structured to enable workers and managers to collectively acknowledge each other's work and enable the enrichment of a collective sense of purpose through the sharing of professional values, ethics, hopes and fears (Reynolds, 2011), including the fit and tensions between workers' professional values and the practices and requirements of employing organisations. Group forums can be structured to enquire into the values, principles, and ethics that inform each worker in their work – with the intention that workers hear each other, construct frameworks of the values and ethics that commonly inform team members, and understand and respect the differences. Such shared meaning-making can strengthen workers' appreciation of each other's work, bring to life organisational purpose, enable greater collaboration and partnerships, and support workers in safer accountability practices. These spaces need to be safe enough for open, honest organisational critiques and can happen both within and outside of organisations.

Making collective spaces for relationships can contribute to a workplace being an inclusive, productive and creative place. Workers and managers having fun and laughing together in ways that are not at the expense of clients or colleagues can build connections, provide light relief and render possible reconstructions of dominant narratives that pathologise individuals. At times, personal conversations and social events can enable an acceptance between workers that can contextualise the effects of tensions that are located in the workplace. Workers can generate and co-ordinate formal or informal, work-based or non-work-based social activities that build connections and that allow people to get to know each other, setting the scene for kinder and smoother work-relations between diverse mixes of people. This requires a management that upholds the idea that healthy workplaces are founded on healthy relationships between all sectors of the organisation. I (Simone) have experienced the power and possibilities of such activities in different workplaces. One organisation had a fortnightly 'soup and scoop' lunch where team members brought soup and a topic of discussion. Another workplace decided that at each team meeting workers would take turns to pay respects and acknowledge the traditional owners of the land, sharing different meaningful reflections each time, simultaneously enhancing awareness and a sense of shared commitment in the team.

Conclusion

The impacts of working in human services can be seen across many organisations in the sector. Concepts that relate self-care with burnout individualise and deflect the effects of broader political and organisational contexts. Alternative responses, founded upon a critical ethics of care, can offset the dividing effects of oppression and injustice and are relatively simple, though there are many challenges in putting these into practice. It is our hope that workers and managers will be inspired to re-work the construct of self-care, prioritise caring for each other, and act more collectively to embed relational ways of acknowledging workers, managers and their work. Our vision is that organisations will intentionally build cultures of collective care and acknowledgement to support these practices. Managers and workers, looking after each other, can contribute to a purposeful, critical and potentially transformative social work response in the organisational contexts of human services work.

References

Baines, D. and van den Broek, D. (2016) Coercive care: Control and coercion in the restructured care workplace. *British Journal of Social Work*. Advance online publication, doi:10.1093/bjsw/bcw013.

Beddoe, L. (2010) Surveillance or reflection: Professional supervision in 'the risk society'. *British Journal of Social Work*, 40(4), pp. 1279–1296.

Foucault, M. (1977) *Discipline and punish: The birth of the prison*. New York: Vintage Books.

Gergen, K. (1994) *Realities and relationships: Soundings in social construction*. Cambridge, MA: Harvard University Press.

Gergen, K. (2009a) *An invitation to social construction*. 2nd edition. London: Sage.

Gergen, K. (2009b) *Relational being: Beyond self and community*. New York: Oxford University Press.

Hall, R. (1994) Partnership accountability. *International Journal of Narrative Therapy and Community Work*, 2–3, pp. 6–29.

Kulkarni, S. (2013) Exploring individual and organizational factors contributing to compassion satisfaction, secondary traumatic stress, and burnout in domestic violence service providers. *Journal of the Society for Social Work and Research*, 4(2), pp. 114–130.

Lynch, K., Lyons, M. and Cantillon, S. (2007) Breaking silence: Educating citizens for love, care and solidarity. *International Studies in Sociology of Education*, 17(1–2), pp. 1–19.

Madigan, S. (2012) Anti-individualist narrative practice: Listening to the echoes of cultural histories. *International Journal of Narrative Therapy and Community Work*, 1, pp. 27–34.

Mathieu, F. (2015) *Beyond kale and pedicures: Can we beat burnout and compassion fatigue?* [online]. Available from: www.tendacademy.ca/wp-content/uploads/2016/01/BEYOND-KALE-AND-PEDICURES-Article.pdf [Accessed 4 July 2016].

Pease, B. (2010) *Undoing privilege: Unearned advantage in a divided world*. London: Zed Books.

Reynolds, V. (2011) Resisting burnout with justice-doing. *International Journal of Narrative Therapy and Community Work*, 4, pp. 27–45.

Stanford, S. (2010) 'Speaking back' to fear: Responding to the moral dilemmas of risk in social work practice. *British Journal of Social Work*, 40(4), pp. 1065–1080.

Stanford, S. (2011) Constructing moral responses to risk: A framework for hopeful social work practice. *British Journal of Social Work*, 41(8), pp. 1514–1531.

Strong, T. (2012) Talking about the DSM-V. *International Journal of Narrative Therapy & Community Work*, 2, pp. 54–64.

Tamasese, K. and Waldegrave, C. (1993) Cultural and gender accountability in the 'Just Therapy' approach. *Journal of Feminist Family Therapy*, 5(2), pp. 29–45.

Wever, C. (2015) Beyond psychological truth: Deconstructing Western deficit-oriented psychology and the co-construction of alternative psychologies in narrative practice. *International Journal of Narrative Therapy and Community Work*, 1, pp. 11–25.

White, M. (1995) *Re-authoring lives: Interviews and essays*. Adelaide: Dulwich Centre.

White, M. (1997) *Narratives of therapists' lives*. Adelaide: Dulwich Centre.

White, M. (2007) *Maps of narrative practice*. New York: Norton.

White, M. and Epston, D. (1990) *Narrative means to therapeutic ends*. New York: Norton.

20 The politics of climate change

The need for a critical ethics of care in relation to the environment

Jennifer Boddy

Introduction

There is clear evidence that the climate is changing and all life will be adversely affected. The globe is warming with average land and sea surface temperatures increasing, ice in the Arctic and Antarctic circles melting, and as a result sea levels rising (Intergovernment Panel on Climate Change, 2014). Such changes lead to increasing extreme weather events (Lubchenco and Karl, 2012; Linnenluecke, Griffiths and Winn, 2012), the natural environment becoming less hospitable to current life forms (Aiguo, 2012), and increasing food and water shortages (Hsiang, Keng and Cane, 2011). Furthermore, natural habitats that ensure the Earth's ecological system *remains* balanced are being destroyed (McManus, 2010), biodiversity is decreasing, and it is likely there will be mass extinctions (Cahill et al., 2013).

Climate change has and will continue to threaten the health and wellbeing of all people and ecosystems. The scale and scope of environmental disasters has significantly increased over the last 100 years (Leaning and Guha-Sapir, 2013). According to Leaning and Guha-Sapir (2013), since 1990, approximately 217 million people have been affected by natural disasters each year. There also appears to be a positive correlation between conflict and severe weather events, with a rise of 21 percent of civil conflicts since 1950 alongside increased prevalence and intensity of the El Niño weather pattern, with its higher temperatures and increased droughts (Hsiang et al., 2011). Furthermore, as air pollution has increased, so too have respiratory diseases (De Sario, Katsouyanni and Michelozzi, 2013). The death toll following extreme weather events is also significant. For example, the UK heatwave in 2003 saw 2,234 deaths, and in 2006 there were 2,323 deaths. While this rate was much lower following the 2013 heatwave (approximately 300 deaths), the rates of mortality are still concerning (Green, Andrews, Armstrong, Bickler and Pebody, 2016).

The effects of environmental degradation and climate change are most acutely felt by those who are marginalised and vulnerable. Inequities in mobility, access to wealth, food, water, and safe places to live mean that people living in poverty, older people, Indigenous peoples, and women will be most adversely affected (Hetherington and Boddy, 2013). Such people are affected in diverse ways, particularly when race, gender, class, and so on intersect and people experience multiple oppressions. During Hurricane Katrina in New Orleans, for example, poor people were often unable to access transport to evacuate and they lived largely in low-lying, flood-prone areas (Hawkins, 2009). This meant that compared with other victims of Hurricane Katrina, they were more likely to lose their possessions (Hawkins, 2009). This was compounded by race, with African Americans four times more likely to lose their jobs in the month following the disaster than white Americans with all else being equal. However, when income differences were taken into account, it became apparent that in reality they were seven times more likely to lose their jobs (Elliott and Pais, 2006). African Americans also had a much higher death rate than white Americans (Sharkey, 2007). Thus inequities in mobility, access to wealth, food, water, and safe places to live mean that women, older people, Indigenous peoples, and those living in poverty or in rural areas will be more adversely affected by climate change (Hetherington and Boddy, 2013), and this is compounded when people experience multiple disadvantages.

The extent of global environmental degradation and the effects of climate change compel social workers and policy makers to act. Consequently, I argue that a critical ethics of care is needed, where inequity is no longer tolerated, people are understood as being interconnected with their environments and valued equally, and care is understood as a social, moral and political practice. This is in contrast to the contemporary political approaches to climate change mitigation and adaptation that I describe in the following section.

Political approaches to climate change mitigation and adaptation

Current political approaches to tackling climate change have focused on adhering to global carbon emissions targets and the economic impacts of doing so. Approaches to this vary and include regulation and legislation, carbon pricing, subsidies or tax reductions to industries that adopt a low carbon status, and the commonly adopted emissions trading schemes. According to Randalls (2011), market-based solutions have become the norm. Governments are increasingly commodifying carbon in order to reduce carbon dioxide emissions (Randalls, 2011). This is often achieved by both capping the price of carbon dioxide emissions and allowing industry to trade carbon dioxide through carbon emissions trading schemes (Randalls, 2011). Such schemes give industry flexibility to choose how they will use and/or lower their emissions. Such an approach became common following the establishment of the Kyoto Protocol in 1997, but has continued into this century with the Doha Amendment in 2012 (an amendment to the Kyoto Protocol) and the Paris Agreement in 2015, which looked at carbon emissions targets for the period following 2020. Following each of these negotiations, carbon markets have been strengthened whereby the cost of transportation, energy production, and so on are now systematically documented (Randalls, 2011).

The success of the global agreements and protocols, coupled with emissions trading schemes, is unclear. According to the European Environment Agency (EEA), greenhouse gas emissions have fallen since 1990 (see European Environment

Agency, 2016). This scheme was launched in 2005 and is the largest global scheme, covering approximately 11,000 power stations and industrial plants in 30 countries (European Commission, 2013). While Laing, Sato, Grubb and Comberti (2013) and others (see, e.g. Egenhofer, 2007; Perdan and Azapagic, 2011) have argued there have been some reductions in total capped emissions far bigger than those resulting from other policy instruments, they also point out that over-allocation of carbon permits, the recession in the early 2000s, and the resulting reduction in the price of carbon have undermined the scheme. The mixed results from emissions trading schemes is compounded by global economic turmoil, a lack of integration between different trading systems, limited international consensus on emissions targets, and unfavourable policy signals in some countries (Perdan and Azapagic, 2011). Furthermore, many countries have been conservative in their commitments to emissions reductions, preferring instead to see greater efforts made by other countries and international consensus resolution to reduce emissions before action is taken.

The current market-based approaches neglect issues related to ethics and justice. Instead, managerial, technical approaches to environmental issues have become common and neoliberal political-economic philosophy dominates (Randalls, 2011). This approach seeks to promote adherence to economic development and further industrialisation, coupled with technical and scientific solutions to climate change (Pease, 2016). Such an approach disregards the importance of addressing social and economic inequities brought about by neoliberalism; it prioritises economies over people, and it overlooks the importance of an intersectional analysis of climate change impacts. It has also resulted in governments' failure to "grasp a wider array of alternative political possibilities, or framings, generated by and through warnings about climate change" (Randalls, 2011, p. 128). Furthermore, it has created disconnect between markets, politics, and care. According to Smith (2005), there is a "persistent divide between states which manage politics, markets which perform the economy, and caring communities whose work is anchored in the spaces of the home" (pp. 1–2). Brought together, these issues constrain political vision about what governments can and should do.

A critical ethics of care for climate change mitigation and adaptation

What is often overlooked in the contemporary political approach to tackling climate change is that humanity is not only interdependent on the natural environment but is fundamentally a part of it. A critical ethics of care is needed, where inequity is no longer tolerated and people and their environments are valued equally. Solutions to climate change and environmental degradation must not be reliant on individual change alone or market-based solutions, but instead require governments and societies to work together collectively in compassionate and caring ways that recognise humanity is a part of nature, not in binary opposition to it. Care should be central to the discussions around climate change affecting more than just policies and rules, but also practices and interventions.

While an ethic of care has primarily focused on the interdependence of humans and the importance of care among humanity, I argue that our interdependence extends to the natural environment. Humans and the natural environment are fundamentally linked. Tronto (1993, p. 126) argues that "for a society to be judged as a morally admirable society, it must, among other things, adequately provide care of its members and its territory." Environmental degradation is a form of human degradation and thus not only do humans need, give, and receive care (Tronto, 1993), but so do the ecological environments in which humans live.

According to Tronto (1993), care involves five ethical elements: (1) caring about, (2) caring for, (3) caregiving, (4) care receiving, and (5) caring with. These are underpinned by (1) an awareness of the importance of care, (2) a sense of responsibility to take care of others, (3) an ability to provide care, (4) consideration of the care-receiver's response to care, and (5) commitment to justice, equality, and freedom (Tronto, 2013). These elements are premised on the belief that care is a social, moral, and political endeavour (Tronto, 1993) essential for human survival (Bozalek and Hooyman, 2013). They are not linear activities, but instead involve initiatives that are undertaken concurrently and continuously so that it becomes habitual to care. It is more than good intentions. It requires deep and thoughtful assessment of situations, as well as considered attention to the context, needs, and competencies of others (Tronto, 1993).

Applied to climate change, the first phase, attentiveness, involves paying attention to the climate and the natural environment, becoming aware of and being attentive to its need to be cared for, as well as being attentive to our own needs (Tronto, 1993). Ignorance to climate change and its effects on marginalised people is unacceptable. It is important to recognise the needs of the natural environment, as well as the needs of those who are disproportionately affected by environmental, natural, and human-made disasters. According to Tronto (1993, pp. 127–28), "the absence of attentiveness is a moral failing . . . One needs, in a sense, to suspend one's own goals, ambitions, plans of life, and concerns, in order to recognize and to be attentive to others." We have a moral responsibility to recognise the effects of global capitalism and neoliberalism on the erosion of the natural environment, the increases in global inequality and poverty, and the resulting changes in the climate. Unfortunately, ignorance is built into social and political structures that mean that environmental degradation has flourished. Tronto (1993, pp. 129–130) points out that

> virtually all human needs can now be met through the market; if we only have enough money there is no need to depend upon others in any ongoing relationships. The result of our changing ways of meeting our caring needs is a rise of insensitivity to others.

This has fuelled environmental degradation and thus climate changes. Consequently, caring must become more socially acceptable and valued in order to create genuine and meaningful change, particularly as it relates to climate change and the natural environment.

Second, adopting an ethic of care entails assuming responsibility for climate change and being willing to respond to environmental degradation. According to Tronto (1993, p. 132), "We might assume a responsibility because we recognise that there is no other way that the need will be met except by our meeting it." This is particularly true when we look at the issue of climate change. Politicians are increasingly forced to take action on the issue as it becomes more apparent that inaction will have dire consequences for the health and wellbeing of all people. Recognising the responsibility of governments promotes discussion and public debates about how to tackle climate change. Thus it is important such questions of responsibility become political. It is also important that the focus remains on citizens' and governments' responsibility to address climate change rather than their obligations to do so. This is because a focus on obligations may result in the conclusion that we are not obligated to assist. Focusing on responsibility allows space to look beyond formal commitments and agreements to consider things like what role citizens and governments have played in contributing to climate change. Does the dire situation of the changing climate create responsibilities for citizens and governments? It is thus more proactive in creating a healthy, sustainable, and caring environment for all people.

Third, in caring for the natural environment it is important to seek the skills, knowledge, and resources necessary to provide quality care. Being attentive to the need for care and assuming responsibility for it is important. However, if good care is not provided, it means that ultimately the need for care goes unmet (Tronto, 1993) and potentially harm is done. According to Collins (2015), "It is not sufficient to simply provide care – it must also be well provided." Consequently, citizens and governments must critically appraise the work undertaken to care for the natural environment, making sure that the work is done competently, informed by considered policies, and is well-grounded in research.

Fourth, caring involves being open to the benefits that arise from caring for the natural environment and thus receiving care as a result (Tronto, 1993). It means recognising vulnerability and inequality and it refers to how the care receiver experiences the care provided (Tronto, 1993). Within this phase, caregivers must be cautious about defining the needs of those being cared for, while being mindful of the effect of the care on the care receiver. Applied to climate change, it is important to take note of the results of various interventions used to address climate change and the way in which the 'care receiver', that is the natural environment, responds to the care provided. It also involves the acknowledgement of human interdependence on the natural environment: "Caring is by its nature a challenge to the notion that individuals are entirely autonomous and self-supporting" (Tronto, 1993, p. 134). Humans, and in particular those living with inequality, are vulnerable to changes in the natural environment. Thus responsiveness involves recognising our vulnerability and our interdependence with others and our environments, while seeking to care in considered and responsive ways.

Finally, the last phase involves acceptance of the political responsibility to act and care for the future. As part of this, it is important to value freedom, equality, and justice. According to Tronto (2013, p. xii), it is "not only about oneself and one's family and friends, but also about those with whom one disagrees, as well as the natural world and one's place in it". It is important to work with others to reflect on the adverse impacts of human 'progress' on the natural environment. This process involves taking responsibility for addressing the adverse impacts, in part, through political means.

The ethic of care also recognises the role of "privileged irresponsibility" in avoiding care (Tronto, 1993). This idea is used to describe how the most advantaged people within society avoid care work (Collins, 2015) and is particularly important in examining responses to climate change. Although all people will be adversely affected by climate change (as all people are adversely affected by a lack of care), it is those who are most advantaged in society that will be the least affected by climate change often having the resources to deal with drought, flooding, food and water shortages, and bush fires (Hetherington and Boddy, 2013). According to Collins (2015, p. 439), "Privileged irresponsibility affords those with means the opportunity to ignore the hardships that they do not face as well as avoiding giving care directly." This is particularly so in relation to climate change, where conservative white men, who hold considerable economic and political power, are more likely to maintain the status quo, as doing otherwise may result in structural changes that threaten their interests. Thus, they may distance themselves from the consequences of global warming (see Pease, 2016). This is compounded by the fact that both caring work and caring about the climate is often seen as the domain of women and is generally undervalued by society. Men's power and privilege often enables them to avoid caregiving responsibilities (Hanlon, 2009), which means that care work becomes "women's work . . . It is often invisible, usually accorded little value and only sometimes recognised as skilled" (Armstrong and Armstrong, 2004, p. 4). This is problematic on many levels. However, for climate change it also means that many men tend to see initiatives which care for the environment as feminine and therefore undesirable (Brough, Wilkie, Ma, Isaac and Gal, 2016). Some men may be motivated to avoid what they see as green behaviours, such as vegetarianism, because of a desire to preserve their sense of masculinity and a 'macho image' (Ruby and Heine, 2011; Brough et al., 2016). Policies and organisations seeking solutions to climate change have also generally been grounded in a hegemonic masculine approach (Pease, 2016). Additionally, men's scientific knowledge of climate change appears, from a US study, to be on the whole less than women's knowledge (McCright, 2010). Women tend to underestimate their knowledge of climate change, while also expressing more concern about it (McCright, 2010). Gender differences in environmentally friendly behaviour, knowledge of climate change, and care for the natural environment must change.

The dire situation in which we find the natural environment and the resulting changes to the climate mean that political action is essential. According to Tronto (1995), the practice and valuing of care is politically progressive, helping citizens move beyond self-interest. Additionally, the ethic of care can be used as a tool for political analysis, helping to examine the misuse of power in relationships.

A critical ethics of care critiques the influence of neoliberal ideology on society and its emphasis on efficiency, privatisation, and competition (Lawson, 2007). It recognises that constraining care work to personal and private domains overlooks the centrality of care to all people (Lawson, 2007). Instead, a critical ethics of care moves care away from individualist understanding towards an understanding in which care should be a collective and global endeavour. Care work is thus a social responsibility of all people, needing to be equally distributed (Phillips, 2007). It values both justice and care, seeking justice by challenging oppressive status quos (Ryan, 2009).

Care, however, often involves difficult decisions whereby needs are prioritised and scarce resources allocated (Collins, 2015). According to Tronto (1993, p. 137)

> Those who engage in a care process must make judgments: judgments about needs, conflicting needs, strategies for achieving ends, the responsiveness of care-receivers, and so forth. Care rests upon judgments that extend far beyond personal awareness . . . the kinds of judgments that I have described require an assessment of needs in a social and political, as well as a personal, context.

In the context of climate change, difficult decisions must be made about the development of non-renewable resources, policies that reduce carbon emissions, funding for green initiatives, and interventions to respond to disasters. A critical ethics of care is needed to guide citizens, policy makers, and politicians.

Implications for research and policy

Responses to climate change must incorporate a critical ethics of care whereby citizens, policy makers, and government recognise that caring for the natural environment is everyone's responsibility. All people must work together collectively in compassionate and caring ways that recognise humanity is a part of nature, not in binary opposition to it. Care should be central to the discussions around climate change affecting policies, legislation, and interventions.

Political solutions to climate change and environmental degradation must move away from market-based solutions and instead be informed by a caring approach. This involves politicians and policy makers (1) being attentive to the needs of others and the environment, (2) recognising their responsibility to act, (3) exercising competence in caring, (4) being responsive to care receivers' needs, and (5) demonstrating a commitment to social and environmental justice, democracy, and freedom.

Furthermore, climate change policies must be underpinned by a critical ethics of care. They must be informed by an understanding that some people are disproportionately affected by climate change and bear the brunt of environment disasters, particularly when they are at the intersection of multiple oppressions, while some others experience environmental privilege and have a disproportionately high carbon footprint. Policies must consequently be aimed at reducing inequalities, particularly as they relate to poverty, gender, class, race, ability, and so on, and they must challenge unhelpful status quos.

It is also important that the 'good life' and masculinity are reconceptualised to incorporate pro-environmental behaviours. In particular, hegemonic masculinity must be challenged and all people need to become aware of the importance of caring for the natural environment if meaningful change is to occur and further climate changes are to be stopped. As part of this, spaces must be created where it is acceptable to discuss vulnerabilities and emotions and to identify how social and environmental justice can be realised. Furthermore, it is paramount that all citizens, and particularly those with power, become aware of the importance of care work particularly as it relates to the natural environment and the unequal impacts of climate change.

Finally, research in the area of climate change must document ways in which care is fostered, coalitions formed, barriers overcome, and climate change initiatives sustained. It must look at how we can successfully shift cultural norms to create a more healthy relationship with the natural environment and other animals, and in doing so mitigate further adverse climate changes.

Conclusion

To date, government responses to climate change have been slow and have relied largely on market-based solutions. Action to address climate change and reduce greenhouse gas emissions is urgently needed. Such action must be grounded in a commitment to care and underpinned by open and democratic discussions among citizens as well as equitable access to power. Climate change policies and actions must be free from "parochialism, paternalism, and privilege" (Tronto, 1993, p. 153). In order to stop further global warming, while also promoting safe, sustainable, and healthy communities, a critical ethics of care is paramount.

References

Aiguo, D. (2012) Increasing drought under global warming in observations and models. *Nature Climate Change*, 3, pp. 52–58.

Armstrong, P. and Armstrong, H. (2004) *Thinking it through: Women, work and caring in the new millennium*. Halifax, NS: Maritime Centre of Excellence for Women's Health and Nova Scotia Advisory Council on the Status of Women, Dalhousie University.

Bozalek, V. and Hooyman, N. R. (2013) Ageing and intergenerational care: Critical/political ethics of care and feminist gerontology perspectives. *Agenda: Empowering Women for Gender Equity*, 26, pp. 37–47.

Brough, A. R., Wilkie, J.E.B., Ma, J., Isaac, M. S. and Gal, D. (2016) Is eco-friendly unmanly? The green-feminine stereotype and its effect on sustainable consumption. *Journal of Consumer Research*, 43, pp. 567–582.

Cahill, A. E., Aiello-Lammens, M. E., Fisher-Reid, M. C., Hua, X., Karanewsky, C. J., Ryu, H. Y., Sbeglia, G. C., Spagnolo, F., Waldron, J. B., Warsi, O. and Wiens, J. J. (2013) How does climate change cause extinction? *Proceedings of the Royal Society of Biological Sciences*, 280, p. 20121890.

Collins, K. J. (2015) A critical ethic of care for the homeless applied to an organisation in Cape Town. *Social Work/Maatskaplike Werk*, 51, pp. 434–455.

De Sario, M., Katsouyanni, K. and Michelozzi, P. (2013) Climate change, extreme weather events, air pollution and respiratory health in Europe. *European Respiratory Journal*, 42, pp. 826–843.

Egenhofer, C. (2007) The making of the EU Emissions Trading Scheme: Status, prospects and implications for business. *European Management Journal*, 25, pp. 453–463.

Elliott, J. R. and Pais, J. (2006) Race, class, and Hurricane Katrina: Social differences in human responses to disaster. *Social Science Research*, 35, pp. 295–321.

European Commission. (2013) *The EU Emissions Trading System*. Available from:https://ec.europa.eu/clima/policies/ets_en#tab-0-0. [Accessed 15 September 2016].

European Environment Agency. (2016) *EEA greenhouse gas – data viewer*. Available from: www.eea.europa.eu/data-and-maps/data/data-viewers/greenhouse-gases-viewer. [Accessed 22 October 2016].

Green, H. K., Andrews, N., Armstrong, B., Bickler, G. and Pebody, R. (2016) Mortality during the 2013 heatwave in England – How did it compare to previous heatwaves? A retrospective observational study. *Environmental Research*, 147, pp. 343–349.

Hanlon, N. (2009) Caregiving masculinities: An exploratory analysis. In: Lynch, K., Baker, J. and Lyons, M. (eds.) *Affective equality: Love, care and injustice*. New York: Palgrave Macmillan.

Hawkins, R. L. (2009) Same as it ever was, only worse: Negative life events and poverty among New Orleans Katrina survivors. *Families in Society*, 90, pp. 375–381.

Hetherington, T. and Boddy, J. (2013) Ecosocial work with marginalized populations. In: Gray, M., Coates, J. and Hetherington, T. (eds.) *Environmental social work*. Oxon: Routledge, pp. 46–61.

Hsiang, S. M., Keng, K. C. and Cane, M. A. (2011) Civil conflicts are associated with the global climate. *Nature*, 476, pp. 438–441.

Intergoverment Panel on Climate Change. (2014) *Climate change 2014: Synthesis report. Contribution of Working Groups I, II and III to the fifth assessment report of the Intergovernmental Panel on Climate Change*. Geneva, Switzerland: Intergovernmental Panel on Climate Change.

Laing, T., Sato, M., Grubb, M. and Comberti, C. (2013) *Assessing the effectiveness of the EU emissions trading system*. Centre for Climate Change Economics and Policy Working Paper No. 126; Granthan Research Institute on Climate Change and the Environment Working Paper No. 106. Available from: www.lse.ac.uk/GranthamInstitute/wpcontent/uploads/2014/02/WP106-effectivenesseu-emissions-trading-system.pdf. [Accessed 25 January 2017].

Lawson, V. (2007) Geographies of care and responsibility. *Annals of the Association of American Geographer*, 97, pp. 11–11.

Leaning, J. and Guha-Sapir, D. (2013) Natural disasters, armed conflict, and public health. *New England Journal of Medicine*, 369, pp. 1836–1842.

Linnenluecke, M. K., Griffiths, A. and Winn, M. (2012) Extreme weather events and the critical importance of anticipatory adaptation and organizational resilience in responding to impacts. *Business Strategy and the Environment*, 21, pp. 17–32.

Lubchenco, J. and Karl, T. R. (2012) Predicting and managing extreme weather events. *Physics Today*, 65, pp. 31–37.

McCright, A. M. (2010) The effects of gender on climate change knowledge and concern in the American public. *Population and Environment*, 32, pp. 66–87.

McManus, B. (2010) An integral framework for permaculture. *Journal of Sustainable Development*, 3, pp. 162–174.

Pease, B. (2016) Masculinism, climate change and 'man-made' disasters: Toward an environmental profeminist response. In: Enarson, E. and Pease, B. (eds.) *Men, masculinities and disaster*. New York: Routledge.

Perdan, S. and Azapagic, A. (2011) Carbon trading: Current schemes and future developments. *Energy Policy*, 39, pp. 6040–6054.

Phillips, J. (2007) *Care*. Cambridge: Policy Press.

Randalls, S. (2011) Broadening debates on climate change ethics: Beyond carbon calculation. *Geographical Journal*, 177, pp. 127–137.

Ruby, M. B. and Heine, S. J. (2011) Meats, morals, and masculinity. *Appetite*, 56, pp. 447–450.

Ryan, M. B. (2009) *Behind caring: The contribution of feminist pedagogy in preparing women for Christian ministry in South Africa*. Pretoria: University of South Africa.

Sharkey, P. (2007) Survival and death in New Orleans: An empirical look at the human impact of Katrina. *Journal of Black Studies*, 37, pp. 482–501.

Smith, S. J. (2005) States, markets and an ethic of care. *Political Geography*, 24, pp. 1–20.

Tronto, J. C. (1993) *Moral boundaries: A political argument for an ethic of care*. New York: Routledge.

Tronto, J. C. (1995) Care as a basis for radical political judgements. *Hypatia*, 10, pp. 141–149.

Tronto, J. C. (2013) *Caring democracy: Markets, equality and justice*. New York: New York University Press.

21 Critical social work and cross-species care

An intersectional perspective on ethics, principles and practices

Heather Fraser, Nik Taylor and Christine Morley

Introduction

As this book shows, care is a concept with multiple, contradictory meanings. We can care *about* others – as in showing empathy, concern and regard, as we might care about the treatment of refugees in detention. We can care *for* others – as in caring for an elderly family member where care is often shown through everyday nurturing activities such as food preparation, cleaning and emotional support. We can undertake a task *with care* – as in doing something safely and with the intent to cause no harm. Care can be a virtuous personal attribute – as in 'she is a caring person.' It is also a gendered script expected most for women, and often noticed more when it is absent – as in 'that mother didn't care at all for her children.' Yet another version of care is associated with worry and anxiety – as in having the cares of the world on your shoulders, in opposition to being carefree. Care, however, is generally taken to be something humans do for other humans. Missing is the care that humans do for other beings[1] and vice versa. Examples of these kinds of care include caring *about* the dogs abused in the greyhound racing industry and assistance dogs who care *for* humans who experience sight impairment, epilepsy or autism.

In this chapter we concentrate primarily on caring for others as a form of work, social connectedness and method for building just communities. However, caring for other (nonhuman) beings necessitates that we care about them and the situations in which they live. From a critical social work perspective, we do this within a cross-species framework that highlights care across (and in-between) species. This means power relations are examined, rather than ignored, and understood as potentially positive and/or negative. This also means that we do not view species in isolation. Rather, our use of intersectionality references interlocking oppressions and privileges distributed along the axes of gender, class, ethnicity, age, ability and sexuality but also species. Our interest in care is as much political as it is theoretical and practical, and it crosses the divides of public/private, paid/unpaid, rich/poor, man/woman and human/animal.

We have organised the discussion by the following questions, which admittedly may not seem directly connected: What is neoliberal care and why is it unjust? What can an intersectional approach to cross-species care offer critical social workers? As we will explain, the rise of neoliberal ways of viewing the world has had negative repercussions for how care is conceptualised, valued, counted and resourced – for humans but also (other) animals. For critical social workers, recognising the interconnections between sexism, classism, racism, disablism, ageism and speciesism is not just necessary and long overdue, but also provides several benefits, which we also outline.

What is neoliberal care and why is it unjust?

Neoliberalism refers to the marketisation of public utilities and services, and welfare austerity refers to the diminishing support being given to people earmarked as public welfare beneficiaries (e.g. Fraser and Taylor, 2016; Wallace and Pease, 2011). In recent decades, neoliberal ideology has infiltrated most areas of life, including some of our most valued non-government, not-for-profit organisations, which are now expected to be businesslike and 'entrepreneurial'. Narrowly defined and measurable 'outputs', 'outcomes' and 'key performance indicators' are emphasised, especially those that aim to reduce future expectations and costs (Meagher, 2004). For those receiving public assistance, the focus is on functional support, and is emptied of emotion, unless specified in measurable targets (Baines et al., 2011). Other discourses of care that go beyond measurements and monetisation are effectively silenced.

Appropriating socially progressive language, advocates of neoliberalism speak of 'public sector reform' as they force the outsourcing of public health, welfare and education services, and deepen the integration of private sector management principles into non-government organisations. This strategy is part of a larger neoliberal project to shrink the welfare state and displace public services in the public imagination (Clarke, 2014, cited in Baines and Cunningham, 2015), resulting in the contracting out, commodification, privatisation and further devaluing of care, which is inextricably linked to a reformulation of care as the work and domain of women. Social workers are encouraged to be complicit in these processes (Wallace and Pease, 2011).

Irrespective of need, neoliberal care hinges on the idea that service users should pay market rates for the care they receive. Those who cannot afford to do so are expected to be cared for through private, unpaid arrangements. Referring to the Canadian context, Outcalt (2013, p. 88) explains:

> Government policies, in line with neoliberal concerns with cost-efficiency and profit motives, have shifted responsibilities for care from formal institutional care to informal, community care (usually with the responsibility falling on female family members who are generally employed outside the home).

She uses the example of care for the elderly to demonstrate how neoliberal restructuring of the health care system in the context of austerity shifts the burden of care away from governments and on to community and family caregivers (Outcalt, 2013). This individualisation of responsibility for care has more families providing more support within institutions and opting for privately paid companion carers when they are unable or unwilling to provide it themselves. Many private companions are paid directly by the family or service user, relegating care (back) to the private sector, 'behind closed doors'. This renders workers invisible and denies the regulation of their work and industrial protection (Armstrong, Daly and Lowndes, 2015; Baines, 2004, 2014; Meagher, 2004).

Advocates of neoliberal care have little regard for the needs and interests of those who provide care to others. Evidence from studies of Australia's human service workforce shows that those employed in frontline care-work (including social workers, human service workers, health and welfare practitioners, educators and others who deliver face-to-face services to help meet recipients' daily care needs) are experiencing a rapid reduction in industrial conditions (Cortis and Eastman, 2015; Cunningham, 2015). Managerialist technologies introduced to monitor and enhance efficiency, effectiveness and accountability are intensifying scrutiny over frontline practice; standardising and routinising complex processes; and deskilling practitioners (Cortis and Eastman, 2015; Meagher, 2014). This is significant for a number of reasons. First, it is well-established that care-workers are often poorly paid (relative to other sectors) and frequently drawn from socially disadvantaged backgrounds (Milligan and Wiles, 2010). As Glenn (2000, p. 84) explains:

> To the extent that caring is devalued, invisible, underpaid, and penalised, it is relegated to those who lack economic, political, and social power and status. And to the extent that those who engage in caring are drawn disproportionately from disadvantaged groups (women, people of color, and immigrants [and animals]), their activity that of caring is further degraded. In short, the devaluing of caring contributes to the marginalisation, exploitation, and dependency of caregivers, which reinforces the existing structural disadvantages they face.

When care is privatised and promoted as a familial obligation, rather than a societal responsibility, the burden of care usually falls to women who are positioned as objects to exploit. This extends to other species who are even more marginalised than women in that their care work remains unnamed and unseen, a feature of all other animals' work (Hamilton and Taylor, 2013). This argument is well-articulated by Plumwood (2000) who has critiqued ecofeminism for failing to draw links between the animal protection movement and other social justice movements and between the marginalised and oppressed positions of women and animals in patriarchal, capitalist societies. To be clear, our use of ecofeminism does not advocate for women to be seen as 'closer to nature' in some biologically essentialist way. Rather, our interest is in intersecting oppressions: that the systems and institutions of oppression are similar for women and for animals in that they marginalise, silence and make invisible both women's and animals' rights and experiences of exploitation (for an overview see, e.g. Adams and Donovan, 1995; Plumwood, 2000).

To summarise, neoliberalism has shaped public perceptions of who should do what kind of care work, who should pay for it and in turn, who deserves access to quality care (see Campbell, Roland and Buetow, 2000). It has deepened inequality through the transfer of care work from a government responsibility to private individuals, prompting a decline in the availability and quality of care provided by public institutions. Emphasising the growing and potentially lucrative market of private care and support services, lavish care for wealthy and other privileged groups has been legitimised. Such care would be considered indulgent if provided to or expected from public welfare beneficiaries free of charge. Those in need of care who cannot afford to pay are expected to accept whatever care comes their way, and in the process, tolerate diminishing standards. When the needs of caregivers are divorced from those receiving care, both groups (who are not mutually exclusive) are vulnerable to exploitation, in both private homes and public organisations.

Other beings, such as assistance dogs and companion animals, are caught up in this neoliberal dragnet. 'Pets' tend to be relegated a similar (but still lesser) status afforded unpaid women carers, with the care work that they do ignored and/or assumed to be natural or instinctual. In contrast, service dogs may be attributed more value, given it costs an estimated AUD 25,000–30,000 to train a guide dog and that the market for service dogs is growing. Yet, this does not mean that service dogs will be treated any better. Similar to paid human caregivers, they are often expected to be self-sacrificing, if not self-abnegating (as with the recent case of Diesel, see Gadenne, 2015). From the Vegan Feminist Network (2015), several objections are made to the assumed ethical legitimacy of service dogs, as they are currently bred and treated:

> Service animals are, for the most part, purpose bred animals who are rigorously trained since puppyhood for one purpose and for one purpose only: to serve their masters. Many dogs live rather lonely lives: they are kenneled for long periods of time and they are denied free expression. People are even discouraged from showing attention and affection to service dogs because they are 'working'.

Beyond companion animals and service dogs the principles of neoliberalism have, along with their use of technologies and aggressive development of economic markets, extended the scale and extent of animal abuse. Condoned animal abuse, such as abuse through live exports and throughout animal agricultural industries, has much in common with the forms of animal abuse we are selectively 'permitted' to care about, that is, the abuse of companion animals. Either way, animal cruelty is seen as less important than violence perpetrated against human beings (Faver and Strand, 2003). While neoliberalism did not create speciesism (or the doctrines of human supremacy), neoliberal tropes of who is acceptable to care for, and how, have exacerbated this situation.

What can an intersectional approach of cross-species care offer critical social workers?

Critical, intersectional approaches are deeply concerned about and committed to social justice (Hankivsky, 2014). Intersectional approaches offer critical social workers the opportunity to acknowledge the interconnected and "interdependent dynamics of domination, oppression, and resistance" (Hankivsky, 2014, p. 252).

Cross-species care literally refers to care provided across species, such as by humans to (other) beings or by animals (dogs, cats, birds) to each other and to human beings. For humans, animal caregivers may include formal service animals, such as guide dogs for the sight impaired, but also the many education and therapy animals, including but not limited to dogs, horses, rabbits, guinea pigs, chicks, lizards, cows, goats and cats. Family pets, of many varieties, are also well-reported to provide extensive emotional support. Many human beneficiaries of this care remark about the beyond-human levels of loyalty, physical affection and non-judgemental love extended to them. Direct health benefits can also accrue to 'owners' (guardians), such as lowered blood pressure, reduced headaches (Akiyama and Holtzman, 1986), the early detection of cancer (Ferris, 2013) and fewer and less intense bouts of depression (Garrity, Stallones, Marx and Johnson, 1989) through companion animals assuaging feelings of loneliness and isolation (Risley-Curtiss, Holley and Kodiene, 2011). Some, if not many animal caregivers teach children and adults alike, how to love in more expansive ways. 'Simple pets' can show us how to engage, play and nurture each other (see Faver and Cavazos, 2008). Just being in their presence can be soothing (Wrye, 2009; Sable, 2013).

As critical social workers, we know that relationships of care can involve acts of reciprocity; that is, both carer and cared for may derive benefits from their exchanges. Thanks to a long history of critical social work's attention to the politics of care, however, we are also aware of various problems associated with care and caring, such as the concerns regarding the role(s) caregiving may play in disguising acts of control and domination. Part of this knowledge means that we appreciate the need to resource, design and deliver care programs and services that recognise the rights and dignity of both caregivers and those being cared for, and that these principles hold true irrespective of whether (or not) the caregiving involves money. What is missing is an explicit concern for, and inclusion of other species, including animals who care for humans. This is why we are arguing for an extension: that we are concerned with both informal and formal care, *but also care provided by animals to humans*. Our justifications for this extension are fourfold and identified below.

Recognising that most people live with animal companions

Between one-half and three-quarters of households in Australia, North America and Europe include companion animals, and most consider them to be family members, not property (Hamilton and Taylor, 2013). This means that as social workers, the people we serve are very likely to keep companion animals. Of these, many derive significant benefits that critical social workers could do well to understand more about, and incorporate in thinking about and planning for future critical social work policies and practices. This needs to include ethical dilemmas associated with recruiting animals as caregivers.

Improving conceptual coherence

As earlier chapters in this collection have explained, intersectionality speaks to our interest in and willingness to examine the impact of intersecting oppressions and privileges, extended on the basis of membership to devalued (and) or over-valued social groups. This applies so clearly to non-human animals. Contrast for instance, how factory farmed animals are devalued (to say the least), and how particular pedigree pets may be adulated. Both poles of experience reflect the vagaries of human power regimes and cannot continue to escape the scrutiny of critical social workers. Because the logic and meaning of 'critical' places questions about power, politics and hegemony at the centre of our inquiries, how can we continue to exclude non-human species?

Deepening our understanding of abuse

There is a considerable body of evidence demonstrating links between human and animal abuse that has much to offer critical social work. For example, Arluke, Levin, Luke and Ascione (1999) compared 153 people (146 men) prosecuted for acts of animal cruelty with a similar sample of non-abusers. They found that those who had abused animals were more likely to be involved in other criminal activity, and that 37 percent of the 'animal abuse' group had a conviction for violent, human-directed crimes. This was in comparison to a 7 percent conviction rate for the 'non-animal-abuse' group. Similarly, in one US study (Flynn, 2012), 65 percent of those arrested for crimes against animals had also been arrested for battery against humans. In another, 1.8 percent of 43,093 people surveyed (extrapolated to equate to about 215 million Americans) admitted to animal cruelty. When compared to those who did not report animal cruelty, they were significantly more likely to have committed all 31 antisocial behaviours also measured (Flynn, 2012).

An even clearer link exists between animal abuse and other forms of family abuse. For example, in a study of 1,400 Italian children aged 9–17, Baldry (2003) found that among the 50 percent who had abused animals, almost all had greater exposure to domestic violence than their non-animal-abusing peers. Volant, Johnson, Gullone and Coleman (2008) reported very similar percentages within an Australian cohort of women. They surveyed 102 women with a history of family violence, comparing their experiences to a demographically matched sample of 102 women who did not have such a history. They found that 53 percent of the women who reported family violence also reported that their pets had been harmed and 17 percent of these reported that their pets had been killed. This contrasted with only 6 percent of the matched sample reporting (accidental) harm of animals and no pet deaths. More recently Febres et al. (2014) investigated animal abuse among 307 men arrested for domestic violence. They reported that 41 percent ($n = 125$) had indicated committing at least one act of animal abuse since the age of 18. For these men, physical abuse of an animal occurred with the highest frequency (80 percent, $n = 100$) followed by threats (71 percent, $n = 89$) followed by neglect (12 percent, $n = 15$).

Developing a more comprehensive theoretical approach

Our argument is that the inclusion of knowledge about cross-species care offers critical social workers the opportunity to re-theorise care, abuse, privilege and oppression, allowing for a more comprehensive appreciation of intersectionality in action (see also Ryan, 2011). Feminist academics and practitioners have historically offered, and continue to offer, critical social workers deep insights about privileges and oppressions associated with gender and sexuality. Ecofeminists, in particular, urge us to think about the interconnections of abuse of women and the environment. Critical animal studies scholars have begun to think about intersectional analyses of links between animal oppression and that of marginalised others. Such an intersectional approach means (feminist) critical animal studies (CAS) scholars and activists have an obvious contribution to make to how we incorporate animals into critical social work (Taylor and Twine, 2014). To quote Adams (2007, p. 22), "Violence against people and against animals is interdependent. Caring about both is required."

So embedded is humanism in society and social work that arguing for other species to be included in critical social work theorising may seem fanciful and (overly) sentimental. Rather than collude with the domination of humans over (other) animals, we are advocating for critical social work(ers) to take up the challenge and step into this space (see also Ryan, 2011). We recommend following the lead of feminist scholar Donovan (2006, p. 307), who argues for us all to

> learn[] to see what human ideological constructions elide; to understand and comprehend what is not identified and recognized in these constructions; to, in short, attempt to reach out emotionally as well as intellectually to what is different from oneself rather than reshaping (in the case of animals) that difference to conform to one's own human-based preconceptions.

Donovan (2006, p. 306) draws on intersectionality to argue the case for care to go beyond humans and gender, to include animals. She explains:

> Implicit in feminist animal care theory – though perhaps not sufficiently theorized as such – is a dialogical mode of ethical reasoning, not unlike the dialectical method proposed in standpoint theory, wherein humans pay attention to – listen to – animal communications and construct a human ethic in conversation with the animals rather than imposing on them a rationalistic, calculative grid of humans' own monological construction.

Taking speciesism seriously

Donovan (2006) is arguing for humans to try to interact with other animals on their own terms, not just human terms. The incentive to do so comes from human attempts made to (1) acknowledge and face (rather than deny, minimise, trivialise or ignore) human domination and brutality over other animals, both of which

illustrate an utter lack of care; and (2) work towards the transformation of species domination in whatever ways we can. Such a position parallels the work of
critical theorists and philosophers produced several decades ago by people such
as Marx, Heidegger and Marcuse, who critically examined the human domination
and exploitation of nature, and by extension, animals (see Zimmerman, 1979a,
1979b, 1992). A clever way this occurs is through the promotion of rationality
and technology to gain mastery over the world (Klein, 2014). This is a way of
'knowing' tied closely to, and increased by, neoliberalism, that is forceful, objectifying and calculating, where the main goal is to inspect how humans may order,
use and master others (Klein, 2014). This dominant construction does not seek to
understand nature and animals on their own terms, what Heidegger refers to in
terms of 'care' and 'letting be' to anticipate their needs and potential. 'Letting be'
is far from passive, requiring a thoughtful attentiveness to, and concern with, the
unfolding of the 'other'. This is a kind of care that appreciates diversity.

Taking speciesism seriously, and in turn respecting the rights and welfare of
animal caregivers, may require a significant shift in thinking (Catlaw and Holland, 2012; Ryan, 2011). As Plumwood (2000, p. 315) elaborates:

> most of us are still to some degree entrapped by dualistic conceptual structures
> and assumptions that are part of the legacy of the western worldview. . . . The
> dominant way of thinking about these problems in the western tradition has
> been in terms of human/nature dualism as elaborated in the narrative of the
> sanctity of human life, a narrative of personal justice and salvation, carried
> over from Christianity into humanism, in which we humans are irreplaceable
> and unique individuals, who gain our right to sacrifice other species from our
> rational superiority.

In the context of understanding care, these assumptions ignore, degrade and devalue
care work performed by animals, seeing it a natural and normal role for animals
to play. We must find ways to formally acknowledge that the wellbeing of animals matters – for all animals – not just our animal companions. As Ryan (2011)
recommends, a positive step forward would be to include them in our Codes
of Ethics (see for instance, AASW, 2010). We need to remember that not all
animals – human or otherwise – make good carers or wish to perform care work.
Even adjudicating whether other animals are willing to become caregivers runs
the risk of anthropomorphism, or the projection of human views and interests onto
other species. Recognising this is a first step. Most importantly, animals are not
tools for us to use, especially if we are claiming to extend an ethic of care to them
(Taylor, Fraser, Signal and Prentice, 2016). This position stands in stark contrast
to the contemporary international contexts of neoliberalism, which have objecti-
fied and commodified care in new and dangerously unequal ways.

We realise we will not have convinced all readers with our arguments here.
Speciesism is a force to be reckoned with. Humans are encouraged (ourselves
included) to turn away from animal suffering and its reverse, caring for other animals. One of the most common ways this manifests itself is in questions about how

we can justify caring about, advocating for and expending energy and resources on nonhuman animals when there is so much human suffering that needs addressing. A good example of this was evident in the backlash of large numbers of people across the world protesting the 'hunting' of Cecil the lion by Walter Palmer, the American dentist in Zimbabwe (Actman, 2016). From the uninspected position of human superiority, support for animal abuse campaigns can be portrayed as audacious and frivolous. Often, these debates arise without a realisation of the neoliberal and economically rational environment that gives birth to such questions. They also miss the key point of intersectional theory: that the structures and systems that create and maintain a given form of discrimination and oppression occur across categories. Misogyny, racism, speciesism, disablism, homophobia and so on are interconnected and mutually reinforcing, as are the dynamics of global corporate capitalism that rely on the exploitation of subordinated classes, human and animal.

We need to avoid creating categories of worthy/unworthy or of deserving/undeserving. Otherwise we risk what Carol Adams (2007, pp. 22–23) calls a "politics of the dismissive", which ignores the interconnected nature of *all* oppressions:

> When the first response to animal advocacy is, How can we care about animals when humans are suffering? we encounter an argument that is self-enclosing: it re-erects the species barrier and places a boundary on compassion while enforcing a conservative economy of compassion; it splits caring at the human-animal border, presuming that there is not enough to go around. Ironically, it plays into the construction of the world that enables genocide by perpetuating the idea that what happens to human animals is unrelated to what happens to nonhuman animals. It also fosters a fallacy: that caring actually works this way.

Conclusion

In this chapter we have argued against neoliberal versions of care and instead offered a way to view care based on a critical, intersectional, cross-species orientation. We explained that narrowly defined social status and economically based use-value are central to neoliberal determinations of who should receive quality care. We described neoliberal publicly provided care as mean-spirited and unjust, begrudgingly given to, and performed by, the oppressed. Most importantly, we have argued for critical social work(ers) to recognise and resist speciesism, which in the case of care usually means failing to see the work that many (other) animals perform for humans, and ignoring their rights as caregivers.

Note

1 We acknowledge that the terminology here is fraught precisely because much of our language is humanist and creates/maintains binary differences, such as human/nonhuman animal, that are part of the knowledge/power nexus we are contesting. However, without

alternatives available to us, and with a view to ensuring readability, we have chosen to use beings where possible and animal and/or animal companion when we need to make a distinction between (human and other) beings.

References

Australian Association of Social Workers (AASW). (2010) *Code of ethics*. Canberra: AASW.

Actman, J. (2016) Cecil the lion died one year ago – Here's what's happened since. *National Geographic, Wildlife Watch*, June 30th. Available from: http://news.nationalgeographic.com/2016/06/cecil-african-lion-anniversary-death-trophy-hunting-zimbabwe/ [Accessed 18 November 2016].

Adams, C. (2007) The war on compassion. In: Donovan, J. and Adams, C. (eds.) *The feminist care tradition in animal ethics: A reader*. New York: Columbia University Press, pp. 21–36.

Adams, C. and Donovan, J. (eds.) (1995) *Animals and women*. Durham, NC: Duke University Press.

Akiyama, H. and Holtzman, J. (1986) Pet ownership and health status during bereavement. *Omega*, 17, 187–193.

Arluke, A., Levin, J., Luke, C. and Ascione, F. (1999) The relationship of animal abuse to violence and other forms of antisocial behaviour. *Journal of Interpersonal Violence*, 14(9), pp. 963–975.

Armstrong, P., Daly, T. and Lowndes, R. (2015) Liminality in Ontario's long-term care facilities: Private companions' care work in the space 'betwixt and between'. *Competition & Change*, 19(3), pp. 246–263.

Baines, D. (2004) Caring for nothing: Work organization and unwaged labour in social services. *Work, Employment and Society*, 18(2), pp. 267–295.

Baines, D. (2014) Care work in the nonprofits. In: Baines, D. and McBride, S. (eds.) *Orchestrating austerity: Impacts and resistance*. Halifax, NS: Fernwood, pp. 186–197.

Baines, D. and Cunningham, I. (2015) Care work in the context of austerity. *Competition & Change*, 19(3), pp. 183–193.

Baines, D., Cunningham, I. and Fraser, H. (2011) Constrained by managerialism: Caring as participation in the voluntary social services. *Economic and Industrial Democracy*, 32(2), 329–352.

Baldry, A. (2003) Animal abuse and exposure to interparental violence in Italian youth. *Journal of Interpersonal Violence*, 18(3), pp. 258–281.

Campbell, S. M., Roland, M. O. and Buetow, S. A. (2000) Defining quality of care. *Social Science & Medicine*, 51(11), pp. 1611–1625.

Catlaw, T. and Holland, M. (2012) Regarding the animal. *Administrative Theory & Praxis*, 34(1), pp. 85–112.

Clarke, J. (2014) *Austerity workshop* [unpublished paper]. McMaster University, Hamilton, Canada.

Cortis, N. and Eastman, C. (2015) Is job control under threat in the human services? Evidence from frontline practitioners in Australia, 2003–2012. *Competition & Change*, 19(3), pp. 210–227.

Cunningham, I. (2015) Austerity, personalization and the degradation of voluntary sector employment conditions. *Competition & Change*, 19(3), 228–245.

Donovan, J. (2006) Feminism and the treatment of animals: From care to dialogue. *Signs*, 31(2), pp. 305–329.

Faver, C.A. and Cavazos, A.M. (2008) Love, safety and companionship: The human animal bond and Latino families. *Journal of Family Social Work*, 11(3), pp. 254–271.

Faver, C.A. and Strand, E.B. (2003) Domestic violence and animal cruelty: Untangling the web of abuse. *Journal of Social Work Education*, 39, pp. 237–253.

Febres, J., Brasfield, H., Shorey, R., Elmquist, J., Ninnemann, A., Schonbrun, Y., Temple, J., Recupero, P. and Strart, G. (2014) Adulthood animal abuse among men arrested for domestic violence. *Violence Against Women*, 20(9), pp. 1059–1077.

Ferris, D. (2013) These amazing dogs can smell cancer. *Business Insider Australia*, August 16, 2013.

Flynn, C. (2012) *Understanding animal abuse: A sociological analysis*. New York: Lantern Books.

Fraser, H. and Taylor, N. (2016) *Neoliberalization, universities and the public intellectual: Species, gender and class and the production of knowledge*. London: Palgrave Macmillan.

Gadenne, D. (2015) '*Je suis Diesel' and the horses who need a hug: Reflecting on the role of 'service' animals* [online]. Available from: https://animalsinsocietygroup.wordpress.com/2015/11/27/je-suis-diesel-and-the-horses-who-needed-a-hug-reflecting-on-the-role-of-service-animals/ [Accessed 25 October 2016].

Garrity, T.F., Stallones, L.F., Marx, M.B. and Johnson, T.P. (1989) Pet ownership and attachment as supportive factors in the health of the elderly. *Anthrozoös*, 3(1), pp. 35–44.

Glenn, E.N. (2000) Creating a caring society. *Contemporary Sociology*, 29(1), pp. 84–94.

Hamilton, L. and Taylor, N. (2013) *Animals at work: Identity, politics and culture in work with animals*. Leiden, Netherlands: Brill.

Hankivsky, O. (2014) Rethinking care ethics: On the promise and potential of an intersectional analysis. *American Political Science Review*, 108(2), pp. 252–263.

Klein, N. (2014) *This changes everything: Capitalism vs the climate*. New York: Simon & Schuster.

Meagher, G. (2004) Modernising social work and the ethics of care. *Social Work & Society*, 2(1), pp. 10–27.

Milligan, C. and Wiles, J. (2010) Landscapes of care. *Progress in Human Geography*, 34(6), pp. 736–754.

Outcalt, L. (2013) Paid companions: A private care option for older adults. *Canadian Journal on Aging/La Revue canadienne du vieillissement*, 32(1), pp. 87–102.

Plumwood, V. (2000) Integrating ethical frameworks for animals, humans, and nature: A critical feminist eco-socialist analysis. *Ethics and the Environment*, 5(2), pp. 285–322.

Risley-Curtiss, C., Holley, L.C. and Kodiene, S. (2011) 'They're there for you': Men's relationships with companion animals. *Families in Society: The Journal of Contemporary Social Services*, 92(4), pp. 412–418.

Ryan, T. (2011) *Animals and social work: A moral introduction*. Basingstoke: Palgrave Macmillan.

Sable, P. (2013) The pet connection: An attachment perspective. *Clinical Social Work Journal*, 41, pp. 93–99.

Taylor, N., Fraser, H., Signal, T. and Prentice, K. (2016) Social work, animal-assisted therapies and ethical considerations: A programme example from central Queensland, Australia. *British Journal of Social Work*, 46(1), pp. 135–152.

Taylor, N. and Twine, R. eds. (2014) *The Rise of Critical Animal Studies: From the Margin to the Centre*, Routledge, Abington.

Vegan Feminist Network. (2015) *A feminist critique of 'service dogs'* [online]. Available from: http://veganfeministnetwork.com/a-feminist-critique-of-service-dogs/ [Accessed 24 October 2016].

Volant, A.M., Johnson, J.A., Gullone, E. and Coleman, G.J. (2008) The relationship between domestic violence and animal abuse: An Australian study. *Journal of Interpersonal Violence*, 23(9), pp. 1277–1295.

Wallace, J. and Pease, B. (2011) Neoliberalism and Australian social work: Accommodation or resistance? *Journal of Social Work*, 11(2), pp. 132–142.

Wrye, J. (2009) Beyond pets: Exploring relational perspectives of petness. *Canadian Journal of Sociology*, 34(4), pp. 1033–1061.

Zimmerman, M. (1979a) Marx and Heidegger on the technological domination of nature. *Philosophy Today*, 23(Summer), pp. 99–112.

Zimmerman, M. (1979b) Heidegger and Marcuse: Technology as ideology. *Research in Philosophy and Technology*, 2, pp. 245–261.

Zimmerman, M. (1992) The blessing of otherness: Wilderness and the human condition. In: Oelschlaeger, M. (ed.) *The wilderness condition: Essays on environment and civilization*. Washington, DC: Island Press.

Afterword

Introduction

This edited volume is an important contribution to thinking about caring practices in the field of social work, because, as noted by a number of authors of the chapters in this collection, care has not received sufficient attention in social work as a discipline. In this afterword, I would like to flesh out some of the ideas that have been touched upon in the various chapters in order to think further about them – and more particularly, I will concentrate on three main aspects regarding feminist care ethics. The first aspect that I consider is the importance of actually defining what is meant by care – specifying it, so that the readers can be cognisant of how different definitions of care might influence the ways in which it is put to work for social work.

The second important aspect I would like to pick up on is the difference between principle and care ethics and the implications that this has for social work education and practice.

The third and final issue I wish to consider in this afterword is how the moral elements of the political and critical ethics of care are currently being taken forward in posthumanist and feminist new materialisms and how theorists within these orientations might create new and creative provocations for care ethics and social work practice.

I consider these three broad issues as a way of intra-acting with the ideas put forward in the chapters of this book.

Definition of care and care ethics

As has been discussed in previous publications, the manner in which care is defined provides different ways of configuring practices and sensibilities in social work and social work practices. If care is seen as a human-centred activity which exists exclusively in a one-to-one relationship – for example, between mother and child, or social worker and client (Noddings, 1984, 2002; Ruddick, 1989) – then more than human and collective relationships in situated contexts will be elided. The political ethics of care proposed by Joan Tronto provides an alternative perspective to this. A couple of chapters in this volume, such as that of Richard Hugman, explicitly use Fisher and Tronto's (1990) definition of care, which is the following:

> At the most general level, care consists of everything we do to continue, maintain, and repair our world so that we may live in it as well as possible.

That world includes our bodies, our selves, and our environment, all of which we seek to interweave in a complex, life-sustaining web.

(Fisher and Tronto, 1990, in Tronto, 1993, p. 103)

This definition, while critiqued by some for being broad (Groenhout, 2004; Held, 2006), can be regarded as a particularly useful one for a number of reasons. First, it locates care beyond the human to include the world, things and the environment, thus disrupting human exceptionalism often implicit both in care definitions and in social work practices. Second, it foregrounds the importance of caring for the self, often a neglected aspect of social work practice, particularly in these current neoliberal times where social workers are required to take on more administrative and other responsibilities which happen with intensified bureaucratisation. Third, this definition is not trapped in one-to-one relationships, but incorporates multidirectional or broadly collective relationships. Finally, the definition gestures towards an ethic of care as contributing to flourishing – and the recognition that it is important to recognise that this could only be done 'as well as possible'. This definition of care is firmly located within a relational ontology, which has far reaching implications for how ethical decisions are made. From a political and critical care ethics perspective, deliberations are dialogic rather than based on individual or expert decisions which leads me to my next concern: principle and care ethics.

Principle and care ethics

Many of the authors in this edited collection refer both to codes of ethics in social work and to human rights or social justice perspectives and how these relate to care. Principle ethics were developed as a liberal response to human rights abuses in the Second World War where there was a concerted effort to protect the rights of individuals (Beauchamp, 2010). I am not suggesting that a universalist focus on individual human rights has not made important contributions towards alerting social workers to the need for basic socio-economic and cultural conditions which states and social policies should make possible for their citizens. On the other hand, however, rights discourses are codified in legalistic engineering models and predicated on the autonomy of the social work client. Besides the assumption of a rational, autonomous economic man underlying human rights, there is also concern about whether Eurocentric approaches to human rights ever do in fact correct dominant power structures responsible for human suffering (Zembylas and Bozalek, 2014).

The ethics of care, on the other hand, as a relational ontology departs from a different premise: the emergence of ethics from ontology (theory of being) and epistemology (theory of knowledge). Here it is impossible to separate ontology, ethics and epistemology – an onto-ethico-epistemology.

The next and final section will consider the moral elements emanating from this relational onto-ethico-epistemology and how these moral elements have been taken forward by feminist critical posthumanists and new materialists.

The ethics of care as a relational ontology

In this final section, I would like to consider how feminist thinkers such as Karen Barad (2007), Deborah Bird Rose (2004), Vincianne Despret (2004, 2016), and Donna Haraway (2016), among others, have recently started thinking in productive and detailed ways about care ethics and their associated moral elements. These authors think outside of disciplinary boundaries, using concepts such as nature/culture, body/mind and material/discursive to undo Cartesian dualisms of either/or to propose an 'and/and' approach.

These feminist new materialists also take as their point of departure a relational ontology. Recognising care as a *relational ontology* means that discrete forms of identity or entities do not pre-exist relationships, but rather, identities and entities emerge from their relationships. Furthermore, agency is not regarded as something which an individual possesses or not, but flows through relationships. Agency in social work would be seen as an enactment rather than a disposition existing with clients or social workers themselves and would also be extended to the more than human – clients' files, policies, natural and built environments all have vitality which intra-act with other entities and individuals.

What is interesting about these feminist new materialist authors is how they have engaged with notions identified by Joan Tronto (1993, 2013) and Selma Sevenhuijsen (1998) as moral elements of the care ethic; these are attentiveness, responsibility, competence and responsiveness. In an attempt to keep this afterword brief, I will confine my discussion of the contribution of feminist new materialists to two of these moral elements – that of attentiveness and responsibility. Attentiveness is regarded as a political, public and collective relational practice which also includes interdependent companion species (Haraway, 2007). Importantly, attentiveness is a reciprocal process of becoming-with each other, using all our sensibilities. Thus both social workers and clients would be seen as enabling each other, rendering each other capable (Despret, 2004, 2016), rather than it being a one-way relationship from social worker to client. Responsibility/response-ability is equated with accountability by Barad (2007), Bird Rose (2004) and Haraway (2016), and our entanglements with human and more than human others in social work means that we can never extricate ourselves from responsibility in our multidirectional relationships. We are all part of the world and there are no innocent positions. Barad aptly elaborates on this non-innocent relationship, which is pertinent for all social workers:

> What would it mean to acknowledge that the 'able-bodied' depend on the 'disabled' for their very existence? What would it mean to take on that responsibility? What would it mean to deny one's responsibility to the other once there is a recognition that one's very embodiment is integrally entangled with the other?
>
> (Barad, 2007, p. 158)

This profound observation is perhaps a good place to end this afterword, and to leave the reader to contemplate what this may mean for us as social workers to apprehend this position of non-innocence and how this may provoke us to re-imagine our relationships with those with whom we work.

Vivienne Bozalek
University of the Western Cape, South Africa

References

Barad, K. (2007) *Meeting the universe halfway: Quantum physics and the entanglement of matter and meaning*. Durham, NC: Duke University Press.

Beauchamp, T. (2010) *Standing on principles: Collected essays*. Oxford: Oxford University Press.

Bird Rose, D. (2004) *Reports from a wild country: Ethics for decolonisation*. Sydney: UNSW Press.

Despret, V. (2004) The body we care for: Figures of anthropo-zoo-genesis. *Body and Society*, 10, pp. 111–134.

Despret, V. (2016) *What would animals say if we asked the right questions?* Minneapolis: University of Minnesota Press.

Fisher, B. and Tronto, J. (1990) Toward a feminist theory of caring. In: Abel, E. and Nelson, M. (eds.) *Circles of care: Work and identity in women's lives*. Albany: State University of New York Press, pp. 40–62.

Groenhout, R.E. (2004) *Connected lives: Human nature and an ethics of care*. Lanham, MD: Rowman & Littlefield.

Haraway, D. (2007) *Where species meet*. Minneapolis: University of Minnesota Press.

Haraway, D. (2016) *Staying with the trouble: Making kin in the Chthulucene*. Durham, NC: Duke University Press.

Held, V. 2006. *The ethics of care: Personal, political, and global*. New York: Oxford University Press.

Noddings, N. (1984) *Caring: A feminine approach to ethics and moral education*. Berkeley: University of California Press.

Noddings, N. (2002) *Educating moral people: A caring alternative to character education*. New York: Teachers College Press.

Ruddick, S. (1989) *Maternal thinking: Towards a politics of peace*. New York: Ballantine.

Sevenhuijsen, S. (1998) *Citizenship and the ethics of care: Feminist considerations on justice, morality and politics*. London: Routledge.

Tronto, J. (1993) *Moral boundaries: A political argument for an ethic of care*. New York: Routledge.

Tronto, J. (2013) *Caring democracy: Markets, equality, and justice*. New York: New York University Press.

Zembylas, M. and Bozalek, V. (2014) A critical engagement with the social and political consequences of human rights. *Acta Academia*, 46(4), pp. 30–48.

Index